MASSACRE
IN THE
CLOUDS

An American Atrocity

and the

Erasure of History

MASSACRE
IN THE
CLOUDS

Kim A. Wagner

PublicAffairs

New York

PublicAffairs

Hachette Book Group

1290 Avenue of the Americas, New York, NY 10104

www.publicaffairsbooks.com

@Public_Affairs

Printed in the United States of America

First Edition: May 2024

Published by PublicAffairs, an imprint of Hachette Book Group, Inc. The PublicAffairs name and logo is a trademark of the Hachette Book Group.

The Hachette Speakers Bureau provides a wide range of authors for speaking events. To find out more, go to hachettespeakersbureau.com or email HachetteSpeakers@hbgusa.com.

PublicAffairs books may be purchased in bulk for business, educational, or promotional use. For more information, please contact your local bookseller or the Hachette Book Group Special Markets Department at special.markets@hbgusa.com.

The publisher is not responsible for websites (or their content) that are not owned by the publisher.

Print book interior design by Amy Quinn.

Library of Congress Control Number: 2024932379

ISBNs: 9781541701496 (hardcover), 9781541701519 (ebook)

LSC-C

Printing 1, 2024

I have a suspicion that we're not great at telling the truth about certain kinds of national behavior.

—Michael Herr (1989)

Contents

Photo section appears between pages 160 and 161

Prologue

A Negative Made on the Spot

I think that picture is the most illuminating thing I have ever
seen. I want especially to have it framed and put upon the walls
of my recitation room to impress upon the students what wars
and especially Wars of Conquest really mean.

W. E. B. Du Bois, October 21, 1907[1]

IN OCTOBER 1907, THE AFRICAN AMERICAN SOCIOLOGIST AND CIVIL
rights activist W. E. B. Du Bois received a pamphlet from Moorfield Storey, president of the Anti-Imperialist League, setting out the case against
US rule in the Philippines.[2] It had been almost a decade since the United
States assumed control over the islands, following the Spanish-American
War, but it remained a deeply contested issue. An outspoken critic of US
imperialism, Du Bois would have found much to agree with, yet as he was
sitting in his office at Atlanta University, it was not the pamphlet that
caught Du Bois's attention, but another item enclosed in the letter from
Storey: a black-and-white photograph printed on a single sheet of paper.

Underneath the photo, a caption in bold letters read "After the Battle of
Mt. Dajo, March 9, 1906."[3] A few additional lines provided Du Bois with
a cursory explanation to make sense of the image: "From a negative made

on the spot the day of the 'brave feat of arms' when six hundred Moros, men, women and children, were killed by the Army under General Wood; a logical incident in the sequence of events which will include the whole history of the Philippine possessions."[4] At the top of the page, a telegram from President Theodore Roosevelt to General Leonard Wood, the commanding officer of the US forces in the Philippines, was quoted in full:

> I congratulate you and the officers and men of your command upon the brilliant feat of arms wherein you and they so well upheld the honor of the American flag.[5]

The contradiction between the sentiment of the president's telegram and the content of the image itself could not have been more striking.

———

At first glance, the monochrome image shows just a grim battle-scape (see figure 13). Soldiers wearing slouch hats stand and sit around what appears to be a ditch bridged by a heavy tree trunk. The ground is littered with debris, and a collapsed hut is visible on the right. In the background, rising smoke half-obscures the outline of the jungle. Halfway out of the ditch, however, the unmistakable form of a woman's body, head thrown back as in agony, can be made out. Her right breast is exposed. A swaddled infant is lying by her side, the small head resting in her lap. Both are clearly dead. Arms and legs and faces emerge from the shapeless piles in the foreground of the image, yet it still takes a few moments to realize that the trench is overflowing with dead bodies and that corpses are in fact scattered like rag dolls all over the ground among the soldiers.

What makes the photograph so disturbing is not just what it depicts as much as the very fact that it was taken in the first place: this is no fleeting snapshot, but a carefully composed tableau taken using a heavy camera on a tripod, which produced negatives on a glass plate. Photography was still influenced by the conventions of traditional artwork, and it is indeed possible to recognize faint echoes of classic paintings such as Géricault's *Raft of the Medusa* or West's *Death of General Wolfe* in the formal composition.

The photographer had decided to set up his apparatus in the middle of the carnage and ask the battle-worn soldiers to face the camera and remain still while he captured the scene. The long exposure time required for a clear image meant that any movement would result in a blur—as can be seen in the figures in the upper left background of the photograph. The image has a strict symmetrical arrangement, with the woman's body slightly off-center in the middle. Indeed, it appears as if she was dragged from the piles of bodies in the trench and her body deliberately posed to reveal her breast. There is a clear line between the upper and lower half of the image, indicated by the horizontal tree trunk, with the soldiers standing, quite literally, on top of the dead. Sunlight falls evenly from behind the soldiers at a high angle, suggesting that it is late morning.

There is something deeply incongruous and disconcerting about the apparent ease of the exhausted soldiers resting among the torn and twisted bodies of the dead. Most of the men are looking directly at the camera, yet they betray no emotions—the proximity of death does not seem to concern them. With their sweat-grimed faces and sodden uniforms, the soldiers could easily be mistaken for a crew of navvies taking a hard-earned break along a ditch they have just excavated. But the scene shows the aftermath of a massacre, and, like hunters after a successful shoot, the soldiers are posing with the bodies of the people they have killed as if they were so many trophies. By 1906, the American West had been tamed, and the imagery of the rugged frontiersman was already becoming a thing of the past. But the Philippines offered a new frontier, and, consciously or not, the soldiers in the photo invoke a distinct vision of American masculinity, in which the pioneer, trapper, and Indian killer merge into one.[6]

The soldiers are leaning on their modern rifles, but the dead are unarmed. An officer standing on the left is also holding a long spear, and the collecting of souvenirs from the dead has already begun. The photograph itself is in fact just one more memento of the "Battle of Mt. Dajo." Such imagery was far from rare, and this was not the first time that US troops posed for the camera with the corpses of people they had killed.

The earliest battlefield photography in the US, which showed the corpses of soldiers killed during the Civil War, was sentimental in style, with the bodies often posed in a respectful and picturesque manner as the tragic embodiment of national sacrifice.[7] However, none of the empathy elicited by these images was to be found in the photographs of indigenous people who got in the way of America's relentless territorial expansion and the pursuit of its so-called manifest destiny. On December 29, 1890, US cavalry tried to disarm a small band of half-frozen Lakota Indians who had fled their reservation in South Dakota. When a gun went off, the soldiers started shooting indiscriminately at the Lakota, who were crowded together among their tents. Some fought back, and in the confusion, the artillery on the surrounding high ground opened up fire on the camp. In the ensuing slaughter of what became known as the Wounded Knee Massacre, more than 250 men, women, and children were killed, many of them hunted down by mounted troops who pursued the survivors for miles across the snow-covered prairie. Of the 25 soldiers who died, several were killed by friendly fire.[8]

The arrival of dozens of journalists and photographers soon turned Wounded Knee into a major media event, and the stark photographs of half-naked corpses frozen stiff in grotesque poses were widely reproduced and distributed in the form of postcards and newspaper illustrations.[9] Because the photographic evidence showed only the sordid aftermath of the massacre, it was left to illustrators like Frederic Remington to reimagine Wounded Knee as a pitched battle in which the only casualties were implausibly shown to be US cavalry troopers.[10] The label of "battle" was furthermore used to mask the one-sided butchery of this massacre, which is usually considered as marking the end of the "Indian Wars."[11]

Almost a decade later, when US military forces first occupied the Philippines after the brief war with Spain in 1898, the camera was again deployed to document the new colonial subjects and to sell the imperialist project to the American public.[12] Photography was in fact as much a tool of imperialism as was the telegraph, railway, or machine gun.[13] Although many of the images were ethnographic in style, the battles with poorly armed Filipino *insurrectos* (insurgents) proved particularly popular and were printed as stereographs that could be viewed with a stereoscope to produce a three-dimensional effect. None of the imagery to emerge from the Philippines showed American casualties. Instead, US soldiers were included in battle scenes exclusively as victors, often showing troops standing alongside trenches full of dead *insurrectos*, much as they do in the photo from "Mt. Dajo."[14]

It was nevertheless in the United States itself that the visual juxtaposition of living white bodies and lifeless black bodies found its most horrific expression, in the genre of lynching photography. The brutal torture and murder of countless black men by white vigilantes in the American South were public spectacles and usually drew large crowds of spectators. But they also attracted entrepreneurial photographers, whose grim images of dehumanized bodies were subsequently sold as souvenir postcards.[15] At the turn of the century, photography played a crucial role in disseminating the message of violence that underwrote American assertions of white supremacy at home and celebrated imperialism abroad.

Having personally curated the African American photographic exhibition at the World's Fair in Paris a few years earlier, Du Bois understood only too well the power of the image.[16] On October 21, 1907, he wrote back to Moorfield, thanking him not only for the pamphlet but also for sending the photograph: "the most illuminating thing I have ever seen." The image had stirred something in Du Bois, who saw its political potential as an effective message: "It has occurred to me, however, that this picture is little too small for framing. Would it not be possible to have a reproduction made considerably larger than this? And would it not be a splendid thing to distribute them throughout the United States? If there is any possibility of getting a larger print, I wish you would kindly let me know."[17]

The response that Du Bois received a few days later from Moorfield's secretary, Erving Winslow, however, was disappointing.[18] The original photograph from which the print had been made was too small to be enlarged. But Winslow did have one interesting piece of information bearing on the origins of the image: when General Wood learned of the existence of the photo, he had allegedly visited the photographer's studio and "accidentally" broken the glass negative. The image that had been sent to Du Bois was based on an earlier print, which, unbeknownst to Wood, had already been made.[19]

Du Bois's belief in the efficacy of the photograph as a means of raising awareness and mobilizing public outrage was commonplace at the time. The camera was thought to provide an incorruptible representation of reality, and it was, as such, well-suited to expose the true state of the world—whether that be the brutality of slavery and lynching, the squalid living conditions of the poor, or the horrors of imperialism in Africa.[20] For instance, photographs of the mutilated victims of Belgian king Leopold's brutal regime in Congo were widely distributed by his critics in pamphlets and other publications, and were even shown at public meetings using magic lantern projectors.[21] Just a few years earlier, the famous author Mark Twain had written a searing satire, *King Leopold's Soliloquy*, in which he imagined Leopold describing the camera—"that trivial little kodak, that a child can carry in its pocket"—as "the only witness ... I couldn't bribe."[22] The Anti-Imperialist League had in fact sought to achieve something similar with the photo from "Mt. Dajo," and hundreds of copies were printed and mailed directly to members of the US Senate.[23] It was one of these copies that Moorfield had sent Du Bois. However, their faith in the power of the image turned out to be misplaced, and the campaign failed to elicit any response whatsoever.

In the end, Du Bois never got a copy of the photograph to hang in his office, and he never found out what the circumstances surrounding the "Battle of Mt. Dajo" were. The identity of the photographer likewise remained a mystery, as did the claim that General Wood had deliberately tried to destroy the evidence. Regardless of what Du Bois saw in the grim scene depicted in the photograph, it did not speak for itself after all.

Figures and Maps

Maps

The Philippine Islands.

Jolo, 1903–1906.

The beginning of the operation against Bud Dajo, March 5, 1906.

The assault on Bud Dajo, March 6, 1906.

The assault on Bud Dajo, March 7, 1906.

The assault on Bud Dajo, March 8, 1906.

Sources: All maps are by Matilde Grimaldi. Maps 3–6 are based on the three military maps and two sketches made during the Bud Dajo expedition; see file 1108562, RG 94, entry 25, AGO Document File, 1890–1917, NARA (College Park, MD). See also a fourth map reproduced in Joseph W. Duncan, "The Fight at Bud Dajo," in *Year Book: Eighth Annual Reunion Army of the Philippines* (Kansas City: Camp Louis A. Craig, August 1907), 59.

Glossary

amok: frenzied outburst that Europeans perceived as a distinctly Malay
pathology

barong: large knife with leaf-shaped blade

bolo: machete-like knife

cotta: fortification

datu: chief or leader

juramentado: from Spanish, literally meaning "an oathtaker"; the term
used by the Americans to describe *parang sabil* (see below)

kissa: a song epic, often recounting tales of *parang sabil* (see below)

kris: knife with wavy flame-shaped blade

lantaka: small cannon or swivel gun

maharajah: local ruler

pandita: religious leader or priest

panglima: war chief or military leader

parang sabil: "to die in the path of god"; a commitment to die defending
your faith and way of life

sultan: the ruler of the Sulu region

umma: the Muslim community

Note on Terminology and Colonial Sources

In this book I refer to the Tausūg people of Jolo and the Sulu Archipelago
as Moros—a name given them by the Spanish and subsequently adopted
by the Americans, which is to say that it is inherently colonial. Today, the
people of the region have nevertheless reclaimed the name, as reflected in
the notion of Bangsamoro, or nation of Moros, and accordingly I use it

as synonymous with Tausūg. The American spelling of Moro names and words was inconsistent, and although I recognize the historical origins of English transliteration, I have retained the original spelling for the sake of consistency. Very little is known about the Moros who died on Bud Dajo, and in the following I have included every name and scrap of information I could find. Ultimately, however, the archival silences cannot be denied, and often not even the names remain.

Dramatis Personae

Jolo 1903–1906

Americans and Europeans

Captain B. M. Atkinson, 6th Infantry, Colonel Duncan's adjutant during the Bud Dajo expedition.

Brigadier General Tasker H. Bliss, Wood's successor as governor of Moro Province, was present only as an observer during the assault on Bud Dajo.

Major Omar Bundy, 6th Infantry, commanded the column on the south side of Bud Dajo at Position 2.

Ensign H. D. Cooke, *Pampanga*, commanded the naval contingent at Bud Dajo.

S. E. DeRackin, editor of the *Mindanao Herald*, based in Zamboanga.

Colonel Joseph W. Duncan, 6th Infantry, commander of the Bud Dajo expedition.

First Lieutenant Gordon Johnston, Signal Corps, commanded Signal Corps personnel at Bud Dajo.

Réginald Kann, officer in the French Army and war correspondent, was present during the assault on Bud Dajo.

Captain L. M. Koehler, 4th Cavalry, commanded the column on the west side of Bud Dajo at Position 1, after Captain T. R. Rivers, 4th Cavalry, was wounded on March 5.

Captain G. T. Langhorne, Moro Province secretary and aide to Major General Leonard Wood.

Captain Edward P. Lawton, 19th Infantry, commanded the column on the east side of Bud Dajo at Position 3.

Second Lieutenant J. A. Mack, Field Artillery, operated cannon on a small hill near Position 3 on the east side of Bud Dajo.

Captain F. R. McCoy, 3rd Cavalry, was aide-de-camp to Major General Leonard Wood.

Captain E. F. McGlachlin, Field Artillery, commanded the 28th Battery during the assault.

Captain J. H. Reeves, 14th Cavalry, acting district governor of Jolo in the absence of **Hugh L. Scott**, played a central role in building the case for the Bud Dajo expedition.

Charles Schuck, civilian of German descent who had settled in Jolo, served as translator and mediator for the US Army and was present during the assault on Bud Dajo.

Major Hugh L. Scott, 14th Cavalry, district governor of Jolo, worked closely with loyal Moros to bring the people down from Bud Dajo during 1905 but was on leave in the United States at the time of the attack in March 1906.

Lieutenant F. W. Sowers, second in command of the Constabulary company at Bud Dajo.

J. L. Travis, a writer and correspondent for the *Manila American* and the *Far Eastern Review*.

Captain John R. White, English-born, commanded a company of the Philippine Constabulary at Bud Dajo and was wounded on the southern summit on March 7.

Major E. F. Wilcox, 4th Cavalry, commander of the garrison in Jolo, was considered incompetent and consequently played no role in the assault on Bud Dajo.

Major General Leonard Wood, governor of Moro Province and in March 1906 also commander of the Philippine Division. A close friend of President Theodore Roosevelt, Wood had overall control of both the army and the Constabulary forces in Sulu, and made the final decisions concerning the Bud Dajo expedition.

Hamilton M. Wright, a writer and correspondent, present during the assault on Bud Dajo.

Moros

Datu Acku, a minor Moro chief who initially was one of the occupants of the eastern summit of Bud Dajo. Acku was convinced by Major Scott to leave the stronghold along with his family before the attack.

Hadji Butu, the sultan's chief minister and worked closely with the Americans as an adviser.

Panglima Hassan of Luuk, one of the most powerful chiefs in Jolo and the first to challenge the imposition of US rule in 1903. He was hunted down and killed in 1904.

Maharajah Indanan, the ruler of Parang in the western part of Jolo and one of the most powerful chiefs. Some of the Moros on Bud Dajo were his former followers.

Datu Jokanain and his brother **Kalbi** controlled Patikul, east of Jolo, and were two of the biggest chiefs in Jolo and close allies of the Americans. They played a key role during the negotiations with the Moros on Bud Dajo, many of whom were their followers.

Jamalul Kiram II, the sultan of Sulu, the nominal head of Moros in the Sulu Archipelago, but by 1906 was largely a puppet leader.

Pala was a shadowy character whom the sultan initially ordered to kill Panglima Hassan for a reward. He later fled to northern Borneo, but in 1905 he returned to Jolo, where he became an unlikely symbol of Moro resistance.

Sawajaan, a minor chief from Pansul just south of Bud Dajo, served as a go-between and informant during the negotiations between the Americans and the people on Bud Dajo in 1905.

Laksamana Usap, an ally of Panglima Hassan, resisted the Americans from his *cotta* known as Pang Pang in Luuk, which was attacked twice in 1904 and 1905. He was killed during the last attack.

Peruka Utig, a minor chief based in Talipao, just south of Bud Dajo. He became the target of the US forces that were hunting Pala in 1905 and was eventually killed in his stronghold.

Moros Defending Bud Dajo

Datu Adam, the Moro chief in command of the *cotta* on the southern summit of Bud Dajo.

Panglima Imlam and **Imam Harib** controlled the eastern summit.

Abu Kahal and **Sahiron** were "outlaws" supposed to be in hiding on Bud Dajo.

Imam Sanuddin and one **Agil** occupied the *cotta* on the western summit.

Acknowledgments

Massacre, *n*.: The indiscriminate and brutal slaughter of people or (less commonly) animals; carnage, butchery, slaughter in numbers; an instance of this.

Oxford English Dictionary (2022)

THIS BOOK HAS SEVERAL ORIGINS, AND I HAVE TO ADMIT THAT DONald Trump is one of them. During a rally in 2016, Trump launched into what seemed like an impromptu history lesson about the famous general John J. Pershing, who had served as military governor in the southern Philippines between 1909 and 1913:

Early in the century, last century, General Pershing, did you ever hear, rough guy, rough guy, and they had a terrorism problem, and there's a whole thing with swine and animals and pigs, and you know the story, OK, and they don't like that. And they were having a tremendous problem with terrorism—and by the way this is something you can read in the history books, not a lot of history books because they don't like teaching this—and General Pershing was a rough guy and he sits on his horse and he's very astute like a ramrod, right, and the year was . . . early nineteen hundreds, and this was a terrible problem, they were having terrorism problems just like we do, and he caught fifty terrorists who did tremendous damage and killed many people, and he took the fifty terrorists and he took fifty men and he dipped fifty bullets in pig's blood—you heard that, right?—he took FIFTY BULLETS and he dipped them in pig's blood and he had his men load his rifles, and he lined up the fifty people, and they shot forty-nine of those people, and the fiftieth person he said you go back to your people and you tell them what happened. And for twenty-five years there wasn't a problem, OK? Twenty-five years, there wasn't a problem! Alright?[1]

The story proved popular among Trump's fan base and soon became a staple in his idiosyncratic repertoire, and was even later repurposed as a tweet after he became president. Trump was adeptly playing on the widespread Islamophobia that flourished in the US following the attacks of 9/11, but he crucially offered the Pershing story as a remedy that could supposedly be emulated in the present. This was a grim story, even by Trump's standards, and a number of news outlets and online sites quickly dismissed it as apocryphal and the historical equivalent of an urban myth.

I was living in the United States at the time and immediately saw that the real significance of Trump's story was not that it was factually inaccurate but that it was so much closer to the truth than even his critics were willing to admit. Although Trump, or rather his advisers, got the details wrong, including Pershing's involvement, there is incontrovertible evidence that American military forces *did* use pigs' blood as a form of spiritual warfare against the Muslim population of the southern Philippines in the early 1900s. Notably, the Americans were copying tactics that were allegedly used by the British in India—which just so happened to be my area of expertise. I watched with disbelief as the worst Orientalist tropes about Islamic "fanaticism" were resurrected and dusted off for redeployment in the twenty-first century—even as historians and other so-called experts insisted that it never happened.[2] As I was busying myself by studying the past, the present had unexpectedly encroached upon my work.

Another point of origin for this book is more innocuous. At some point in the 1980s, when I was a still-impressionable kid, my dad gave me an Italian comic book called *The Man from the Philippines* (originally *L'uomo delle Filippine*), written by Giancarlo Berardi and illustrated by the brilliant Ivo Milazzo. Although it was part of a series about "men of action," this was no gung-ho adventure story but very much a critical narrative and a product of

Italian left-wing politics of the time. The main character, loosely based on Mark Twain, was secretly investigating war crimes, and the story combined elements from the Philippine-American War with the campaigns against the Moros, including graphic depictions of the American use of both water torture and dum-dum bullets. Parts of the story were also inspired by the 1939 film *The Real Glory*, starring Gary Cooper, although the comic presented a far grittier take on US imperialism. Crucially, Berardi's narrative concluded with the trial of Lieutenant William L. Calley, following the My Lai Massacre, and although I was too young to fully comprehend the connection being made between the Philippines in the early 1900s and the Vietnam War, that has since changed. When I started working on Bud Dajo a few years ago, I still had this historical framing, and Milazzo's striking imagery, at the back of my mind. In some ways, I already had this book in me.

Framed by the trophy photograph taken in its aftermath, this book presents a forensic study of the massacre at Bud Dajo in March 1906. It is unapologetically focused on this one image and this one atrocity, and I make no claim to being exhaustive in my account of either US imperialism or the history of the southern Philippines. For those who seek a broader history of the Philippines and its struggle against American rule, there is an extensive body of scholarship by Cesar Majul, Samuel Tan, Patricio N. Abinales, Patricia Irene Dacudao, and Vicente L. Rafael, among others, which provides just that.

The title of this book is in part inspired by a talk about My Lai that author and Vietnam veteran Tim O'Brien gave in 2012, in which he said: "Let us take a moment to consider the death of innocents, the suspension of conscience, the denial of atrocity, the erasure of history." In the following pages, I try to answer what can essentially be boiled down to one simple question: how can a nation perpetrate atrocities yet retain the conceit that it is acting as a force for good in the world? An atrocity is not simply constituted by physical acts of violence but also by the way it is subsequently legitimized, covered up, or deliberately forgotten. When people think of themselves as the "good guys" regardless of the violence they inflict, there is ultimately no atrocity they are not willing to justify. Contrary to what some people might think, this book is not "anti-American." It is, instead, what Francis Ford Coppola refers to as "anti-lie" in his description of the politics of *Apocalypse Now*: "The fact that a culture can lie about what's really going on in warfare, that people are being brutalized, tortured, maimed and killed, and somehow present this as moral is what horrifies me. . . ."[3]

In writing this book, I have amassed many debts of gratitude. Three people in particular have shaped this project in profound ways.

Oli Charbonneau, whom I first met in 2017, has been my trusted guide to the field of US empire in the southern Philippines, and his friendship, help, and advice have been absolutely indispensable. Oli introduced me to many of the key sources and archives, as well as colleagues, and anyone interested in the broader context of the Bud Dajo Massacre could do no better than consult his book: *Civilizational Imperatives: Americans, Moros, and the Colonial World* (2020).

Mike G. Price was incredibly generous in not only welcoming me to his house and offering me access to his amazing collection of historical photographs and postcards but also in sharing his deep knowledge of Jolo and its history. Many of the photographs in this book are reproduced with Mike's permission—I cannot thank him and Aires enough for their kindness and hospitality.

Finally, Jainab Abdulmajid understood intuitively why it was important for me to visit Bud Dajo and went out of her way to make it possible. Jainab is one of the kindest people I have had the pleasure to meet, and without her support, this book would have been incomplete. (For anyone interested in carrying out research in Jolo, Jainab can be contacted at jainabalfad2014@gmail.com.)

My fellow scholars of empire, violence, and photography have been vital interlocutors and have kept me going these past few years—heartfelt thanks to Hardeep Dhillon, Daniel Foliard, Susie Protschky, Mike Vann, Eric Jones, Mark Condos, Gavin Rand, Jeremiah Garsha, Alex Kay, Roel Frakking, and Tom Menger. Thanks also to Patricio N. Abinales, Karine Walther, Joshua Gedacht, and Suzanne Schneider for their help with the manuscript.

Numerous friends and colleagues have also contributed to this book by answering questions, offering feedback, or simply by letting me ramble on about Bud Dajo—in no particular order: Wendy Lower, Brian Drohan, Hana Qugana, Christopher Capozzola, Pierre Schill, Matthew Ford, Daniel Lee, Leslie James, Noam Maggor, Saul Dubow, Dan Hicks, Michael Pritchard, Karl Jacoby, Jeff Ostler, Michael Hawkins, Amy Kohout, Ricardo Roque, Jacqueline Hazelton, Nick Turse, Lyle Jeremy Rubin, Ashley Gilbertson, Huw Bennett, Temi Odumosu, Wayne E. Lee, Kendrick Oliver, Manuel Barcia, Silvan Niedermeier, Martin Thomas, John Pincince, Samee Siddiqui, Madeleine Foote, Jonas Kreienbaum, Chris Levesque, Tim Hannigan, Matthew Thompson, Alyssa Paredes, Winston Smith, Oona Paredes, Helen Kinsella, Mary Elizabeth Walters, Paul Clammer, Matt Fitzpatrick, Dirk Moses, Vicente L. Rafael, Lindsay Gibson, Tony Pollard, Emma Davies, Justin F. Jackson, Mary Dudziak, and Susan Pennybacker—and everyone else who has engaged in seminars, at conferences, or online. My apologies to anyone I may have forgotten!

It was with great sadness that I learned of Cesar Andres-Miguel Suva's death in 2022, and I hope that this book goes some way toward acknowledging his academic legacy.

In Jolo, Mc Danrey Pingay Sajili and Khalid Husain Abbuh of the Philippine National Police looked after me and were excellent company, and I am very grateful to Lieutenant Colonel E. Abolencia and the men and women of the 21st Infantry (Invincible) Battalion, who hosted me at the Bud Dajo forward position. Thanks also to Hon. Abdusakur M. Tan, provincial governor of Sulu, and to Brigadier General E. Boquio and Colonel C. C. Tampus for their help and support during my visit. Edmond Gumbahali and Professor Hanbal Bara were kind enough to share their stories with me, and I hope this book does justice to the memory of Bud Dajo. I also enjoyed spending time with Na Jib, Cathreena, Zhea, and everyone else I met in Sulu. In Manila, Sari Dalena told me the incredible story behind the filming of her documentary, *Memories of a Forgotten War*, and it was really cool to meet her husband, Keith Sicat.

Thanks to Joshua Black for help with research in the National Archives of Australia, to Michael E. Carter for suggestions for my bibliography, and to Eric Michael Burke for getting me images from a rare book in the Kansas

City Library. Patricia Irene Dacudao and Mico Aquino assisted in getting access to material in the collections of the Ateneo de Manila University. Thanks also to Noelle Rodrieguez for her support and to Michael Canilao and Jayvee Borja for help with maps of Jolo, as well as to Calbi Asian, who provided translations of some of the Moro traditional song epics (*kissas*).

I really appreciate the many hours spent talking about violence in all its ugly manifestations with Taylor Waldron, and I would also like to thank the amazing students in my history master-class seminars at QMUL in the spring of 2023—a much-needed reminder of how genuinely inspiring teaching can be!

Thanks to my agent, Sarah Chalfant at the Wylie Agency, and to Clive Priddle at PublicAffairs, both of whom understood what I was trying to do with this book. It has also been a pleasure working with Anupama Roy-Chaudhury, Kiyo Saso, Michelle Welsh-Horst, and everyone else at PublicAffairs. Finally, Donald Pharr did a tremendous job copy-editing the manuscript.

Much of the research for this book was undertaken during the COVID epidemic and would not have been possible without the help of librarians and archivists in the United States: Justine Melone and Lisa Newman (USAHEC); John P. Deeben, Todd Crumley, and Kaitlyn Crain Enriquez (NARA); Kathy Hale (State Library of Pennsylvania); Lauren Goss, Randy Sullivan, and the staff at the Knight Library, University of Oregon; as well as the staff of the Manuscript Reading Room (LOC). Also thanks to Brooke Morgan and DeeAnn Watt (Illinois State Museum); Jim Moss (University of Michigan Museum of Anthropological Archaeology); Hector Acosta (Huntington Library); and Kathy Klump (Sulphur Springs Valley Historical Society, Chiricahua Regional Museum and Research Center, Willcox, Arizona). Finally, the research for this book would quite literally not have been possible without newspapers.com, hathitrust.com, and archive.org.

A number of funding bodies did not find this project worthwhile to support, but my own department, the School of History, QMUL, stepped in and offered vital financial support that allowed me to complete my research in the United States and the Philippines. The maps were made by the brilliant Matilde Grimaldi (www.matildegrimaldi.com), with generous support from the Isobel Thornley Fund, and the photograph of the trench at Bud Dajo was digitally restored by Paul Bourke.

Last but not least, thanks to Elaine and Pop Pop for having me and the family stay during numerous visits to Maryland, which also doubled as research trips. Yet again, I find myself apologizing to my Danish-American crew for burying myself in a book project, and I only hope that I can, in time, make it up to Ada "Future Sailor" Mae, Max, Sigrid, and Gustav. Julie already knows how much I owe her—though not how much I love her.

Introduction

"Slaughter" Is a Good Word

The official report stated that the battle was fought with prodigious energy on both sides during a day and a half, and that it ended with a complete victory for the American arms. The completeness of the victory is established by this fact: that of the six hundred Moros not one was left alive. The brilliancy of the victory is established by this other fact, to wit: that of our six hundred heroes only fifteen lost their lives.

General Wood was present and looking on. His order had been "Kill *or* capture those savages." Apparently our little army considered that the "or" left them authorized to kill *or* capture according to taste, and that their taste had remained what it has been for eight years, in our army out there—the taste of Christian butchers.

Mark Twain, March 1906[1]

O N MARCH 9, 1906, MARK TWAIN WAS BUSY DICTATING HIS AUTOBI-
ography to his secretary in Manhattan when his reminiscences about
old schoolmates were interrupted by a news story that soon came to domi-
nate the newspaper headlines across the country. Over the following days,
Twain digressed from his memoirs to provide a running and bitterly sar-
castic commentary on the newspaper coverage of what became known as
the "Mt. Dajo Fight." Twain, the pen name of Samuel L. Clemens, was one
of America's most celebrated writers, but he was also a deeply committed
member of the Anti-Imperialist League.[2]

The league had been formed in 1898 in opposition to the American war
with Spain and subsequent invasion of Cuba, which ultimately resulted
in the annexation of Puerto Rico, Guam, and the Philippines, along with
Hawaii.[3] For many Americans, overseas expansion looked uncomfortably
like imperialism, which was perceived to be incompatible with the founding principles of the republic.[4] For those in favor of expansion, however,
there was a strong moral case to be made for the annexation of new territory, along with the promised financial gains, as Senator Albert J. Beveridge
put it in 1900:

> The Philippines are ours forever, "territory belonging to the United States," as
> the Constitution calls them. And just beyond the Philippines are China's illim-
> itable markets. We will not retreat from either. We will not repudiate our duty
> in the archipelago. We will not abandon our opportunity in the Orient. We
> will not renounce our part in the mission of our race, trustee, under God, of the
> civilization of the world.[5]

Initially, Twain had been convinced by the rhetoric of "benevolent assimilation" and considered himself "a red-hot imperialist," as he later explained:
"I wanted the American eagle to go screaming into the Pacific."[6] Following the US occupation of the Philippines, however, he changed his mind:
"We do not intend to free, but to subjugate the people of the Philippines.
We have gone there to conquer, not to redeem."[7] In his striking critique of
the hypocrisy of US imperialism, "To the Person Sitting in Darkness," written at the height of the Philippine War in 1901, Twain suggested that a different version of the Stars and Stripes should be flown in the Philippines—a

version that better represented the reality of colonial occupation: "We can have just our usual flag, with the white stripes painted black and the stars replaced by the skull and cross-bones."[8]

By March 1906, however, the war was long over, and it was only in the southern Philippines, in Mindanao and the Sulu Archipelago, which were populated by Muslims, where US authority had yet to be fully established. The local population was known as Moros, after the Spanish word for "Moors," or Muslims, and were infamous as slave raiders, pirates, and polygamists who once dominated the Sulu and Celebes seas and controlled the major trade networks of Southeast Asia.[9] However, most Americans would have known of the Moros only through George Ade's popular musical comedy *The Sultan of Sulu*, which had been running on Broadway since 1903.[10] Or they might have seen "living specimens" in the Philippine Reservation at the Louisiana Purchase Exposition in St. Louis in 1904, where Moros were exhibited under conditions not too dissimilar from a human zoo.[11] Even so, the news that six hundred Moros had been killed by US forces on the island of Jolo and that eighteen Americans had died during the fighting came as a shock to many, including Mark Twain.

The initial reports were short on details but described the crushing defeat by heroic American soldiers of people who were variously referred to as "Moro outlaws," "hostiles," or "insurgents." The disparity in casualties was seen as a tribute to the US Army and proof of the soldiers' skill and bravery. "No one can read of that valorous fight," the editorial of one newspaper proclaimed, "without a thrill of pride in the boys of the United States Army, who scaled the almost perpendicular crags and wiped out the incensed heathen from the face of Christendom."[12] The publication of the telegram sent by President Roosevelt to General Wood, in which he congratulated the general and his troops for having "upheld the honor of the American flag," seemed merely to confirm that this had indeed been a remarkable feat. Yet for readers like Twain, it simply revealed the rank hypocrisy of the affair:

> He knew perfectly well that to pen six hundred helpless and weaponless savages in a hole like rats in a trap and massacre them in detail during a stretch of a day and a half, from a safe position on the heights above, was no brilliant feat of

arms—and would not have been a brilliant feat of arms even if Christian America, represented by its salaried soldiers, had shot them down with bibles and the Golden Rule instead of bullets. He knew perfectly well that our uniformed assassins had not upheld the honor of the American flag, but had done as they have been doing continuously for eight years in the Philippines—that is to say, they had dishonored it.[13]

The tone of the public debate soon changed, as a contemporary account described: "A list of the papers that express their horror and disgust at this thoroughgoing victory would include practically every Democratic and 'antiimperialist' paper in the United States."[14] The coverage of Bud Dajo divided along party lines, with Democrat-leaning newspapers criticizing the Roosevelt administration while the Republican or "expansionist" press rallied to the defense of Wood and the US military.[15] As more news made its way across the Pacific over the course of the following days, the story of Bud Dajo kept changing, and Twain acerbically commented on the headlines as the latest developments were reported:

> The first display head shouts this information at us in stentorian capitals: "WOMEN SLAIN IN MORO SLAUGHTER."
>
> "Slaughter" is a good word. Certainly there is not a better one in the Unabridged Dictionary for this occasion.
>
> . . .
>
> The next heading blazes with American and Christian glory like to the sun in the zenith:
> "*Death List is Now 900.*"
> I was never so enthusiastically proud of the flag till now![16]

Mark Twain was not alone in his outrage, and the *Boston Daily Advertiser* published a letter by Moorfield Storey, president of the Anti-Imperialist League and a well-known public figure, in which he decried the massacre that exposed America, and American imperialism, in a grim light: "Suppose we had heard that the British had dealt thus with a Boer force, that the Turks had so attacked and slaughtered Armenians, that coloured men had so massacred white men, or even that 600 song birds had been slaughtered for their plumage, would not our papers have been filled with protests and expressions of horror?"[17]

Storey saw US rule in the Philippines in a global context, comparing American colonial policy to that of other contemporary imperialist powers. But he also situated Bud Dajo within a distinctly American tradition of racialized violence, arguing that "the spirit which slaughters brown men in Jolo is the spirit which lynches black men in the South." Similar to lynching, the extermination of "Filipinos," as Storey put it, had the unhappy effect of tarnishing America itself: "When we honor brutality in our army we brutalize ourselves." For Storey, Bud Dajo was thus revelatory of the moral cost of American imperialism in the Philippines: "Why must we persist in a policy which is repugnant to all our beliefs, which has lowered all our standards, which brings us no material profit, which has reduced the Filipinos to misery and which has placed upon our flag so many indelible stains of which the bloodshed in the massacre of Jolo is the latest!"[18]

Heated debates took place in both the Senate and the House, yet despite repeated calls for an official explanation and for the release of all official correspondence related to the assault on Bud Dajo, the government released only a handful of telegrams that were already in the public domain. Like everyone else in the United States, Mark Twain had been able to formulate an impression of events in the southern Philippines based only on what was being reported in the press. Yet even with the very limited, and often contradictory, information available, it was quite clear to him what had happened:

The dispatches call this battue a "battle." In what way was it a battle? It has no resemblance to a battle. In a battle there are always as many as five wounded men to one killed outright. When this so-called battle was over, there were certainly not fewer than two hundred wounded savages lying on the field. What became of them? Since not one savage was left alive!

The inference seems plain. We cleaned up our four days' work and made it complete by butchering those helpless people.[19]

The criticism and moral outrage mobilized by anti-imperialists such as Twain and Storey, however, could not in the long run be sustained, and the Roosevelt administration successfully managed to bury the story. Having completely dominated the headlines in the US for two weeks in March 1906, Bud Dajo simply disappeared from the public eye. When Congressman William A. Jones questioned the official version of the so-called Battle of Mt. Dajo in the House of Representatives on March 15, he explicitly appealed to the moral decency of his fellow countrymen: "In my deliberate judgement the killing of 600 men, women, and children in the crater of Mount Dajo by the troops under the command of General Wood was a wanton and cruel act of butchery, and one which cannot be justified and which the American people will never excuse and never forget."[20]

As we now know, Jones could not have been more wrong. Despite the headlines and the controversy, and regardless of the existence of the photograph, the massacre at Bud Dajo was almost entirely forgotten. This was no accident.

———

Some six decades after Bud Dajo, harrowing images of Southeast Asian civilians slaughtered by US troops once again emerged, this time from the Cold War mire of the Vietnam War. In March 1968, "a search-and-destroy" mission in the Quảng Ngãi Province was initially reported as having been a resounding success, with 128 enemy killed and only one US casualty from a self-inflicted wound. As conflicting accounts began to appear, the army eventually had to concede that there had been civilian casualties, but these were described as "collateral damage" and the result of long-distance shelling. It was more than a year later when the full story finally emerged: on March 16, around a hundred troops from Charlie Company had entered two small hamlets, collectively referred to as My Lai, which were supposed to be full of armed Viet Cong. Encountering no resistance, and finding only unarmed villagers, the soldiers embarked on a five-hour long orgy of violence, which included rape, torture, and the mutilation of bodies. The soldiers killed 504 Vietnamese civilians, mostly women, children, and old men.[21]

Despite official attempts to cover up the massacre, an investigation was underway by the time that photographs taken by army photographer Ronald L. Haeberle were first published. The images of bullet-riddled corpses and burning huts revealed the grim truth of what had happened at My

Lai, and one particularly graphic photo showed the bodies of women and half-naked infants scattered along a dusty road between two fields, where they had, in Haeberle's words, been "indiscriminately and wantonly mowed down."[22] Unlike the grainy black-and-white images of earlier historical massacres, Haeberle's photographs were in color, and the visceral red of the victims' blood was splashed across the glossy pages of *Life* magazine.[23]

In the end, a military court found just one officer, Lieutenant William Calley, to be guilty of the killing of villagers. He was originally sentenced to life imprisonment with hard labor, but his sentence was commuted to house arrest, of which he served just three years before being paroled in 1974. The photos from My Lai, however, were mobilized by the growing antiwar movement, and posters of Haeberle's image of the "clump of bodies" were distributed throughout the United States by the activist group Art Workers Coalition and carried during demonstrations.[24] Along with photographs of Vietnamese children burned by American napalm, and summary executions in Saigon, the images from My Lai thus came to visually define public memory of the war.[25]

———————

Whereas My Lai and Wounded Knee have become emblematic of American atrocities during the Vietnam War and the "Indian Wars," respectively, Bud Dajo has instead faded into complete obscurity.[26] More people were killed at Bud Dajo than at My Lai and Wounded Knee combined, yet outside Jolo and the Philippines, few people would today recognize, let alone be able to pronounce the name (Boo-<u>Dah</u>-Ho).

In today's public memory, the US military occupation of the Philippines has long been overshadowed by the more recent experience of Vietnam—a point obliquely made in Francis Ford Coppola's classic 1979 movie *Apocalypse Now*. The dossier of Colonel Walter E. Kurtz, Marlon Brando's character, reveals that the rogue officer had a master's degree in history from Harvard and that his thesis was titled "The Philippines Insurrection: American Foreign Policy in Southeast Asia, 1898–1905."[27] America's campaigns in the Philippines are remembered today mostly as a supposedly useful historical model for later wars. The much-debated Army and Marine Corps *Counterinsurgency Field Manual* (FM 3-24) from 2007 thus recommends

Brian McAllister Linn's book *The Philippine War, 1899–1902* as "the definitive treatment of successful U.S. counterinsurgency operations in the Philippines."[28] Yet even with the renewed interest in Muslim militants in Southeast Asia in the wake of September 11, 2001, the history of US rule in the southern Philippines has received little attention and is largely absent from the American historical consciousness.

A small number of academic studies—by Joshua Gedacht, Michael C. Hawkins, Karine Walther, and Oli Charbonneau—have in recent years touched on the subject of Bud Dajo as part of a more general reappraisal of the history of US colonialism in the southern Philippines.[29] Deeply researched and significant in their own right, these are nevertheless fairly brief treatments, and there has to date been no major study focusing on the events of March 1906.[30] Robert A. Fulton's self-published book *Honor for the Flag* (2011) provides a good overview, but it is based only on a very narrow range of sources, which are furthermore inadequately referenced.[31] In most standard histories, Bud Dajo is just a footnote—if it is mentioned at all—and the massacre is certainly never discussed as a significant historical event in its own right. In Paul Kramer's study of US imperialism in the Philippines, *The Blood of Government* (2006), the image is reproduced, but the massacre itself is mentioned only in passing.[32] The photograph is accordingly used simply as an illustration of US imperialism, and it is no coincidence that it is also included in Howard Zinn's graphic adaptation *A People's History of American Empire* from 2008.[33] In two more recent books, however, a very different approach is taken. In Daniel Immerwahr's *How to Hide an Empire*, Leonard Wood and the Bud Dajo Massacre, including the photograph, are introduced merely as foils to John J. Pershing's allegedly heroic and humane approach to colonial governance.[34] The same line is taken by Ronald Edgerton in his 2020 book, *American Datu*, in which Pershing is credited with "the most successful example of American counterinsurgency warfare in history," while Wood is written off as a crude strategist whose approach to colonial warfare culminated in the massacre at Bud Dajo.[35] The Bud Dajo Massacre is thus invoked as a brutal exception to an allegedly enlightened rule embodied in the figure of Pershing.

Beyond academia, the situation is hardly any different. When Andrew J. Bacevich wrote about Bud Dajo in the *Boston Globe* during the centenary year of 2006, it was framed mainly as a cautionary tale in the context of the ongoing US occupation of Iraq and Afghanistan.[36] Ten years later, then-president of the Philippines Rodrigo Duterte famously waved a print-out of the photo from Bud Dajo during a press conference in which he called for the withdrawal of US military personnel from the country. President Obama had previously criticized the violation of human rights in the Philippines, and Duterte angrily asserted his country's sovereignty and invoked Bud Dajo as evidence of American hypocrisy. What few commentators at the time noticed was that Duterte was also showing a second photo. It may superficially have looked like the burial of the Moro victims at Bud Dajo but was in fact a photograph taken in 1895 at a mass grave in Erzerum during the Hamidian massacres. In other words, Duterte did not mention Bud Dajo to raise awareness of the historical massacre as much as to simply score political points against America—and for that purpose any photo was as good as the other.[37]

Today Bud Dajo exists only in the image of the trench. Had it not been for this one photograph, it is unlikely that the massacre would have been remembered at all. The image itself can easily be found online in different versions, but most of them with little or no context, so the photo no longer tells the story of what happened at Bud Dajo; instead, it is invoked simply as a visual metaphor for "atrocity." On the website of the *Journal of Perpetrator Research*, for instance, it is one of three photos on the banner, the other two being Eddie Adams's iconic photo of the execution of a Viet Cong prisoner in 1968 and Coleman Doyle's equally famous shot of a female IRA volunteer in Belfast in 1973.[38] Whereas the two images from Vietnam and Ireland are immediately recognizable, and historically placeable, the photo from Bud Dajo lacks a meaningful context.[39] Without prior knowledge, we do not know what we are looking at.

In this book I seek to rectify this situation and do what Du Bois suggested more than a century ago: use the photo of the trench at Bud Dajo to show what wars of conquest mean. First and foremost, this requires us to recognize the humanity of the Moros, whom we see only as silenced corpses. Despite the popular notion that photos somehow "speak for themselves" or are "worth a thousand words," images of violence are never self-explanatory and the stories they tell never uncontested. The meaning of an image is determined not only by *what* we see but also by *how* we see and, crucially, by *who* "we" are. What lies beyond the frame is as important as that which lies within, and this book may accordingly be considered as a 100,000-word caption. As a work of historical recovery, the book thus seeks to expose what came before and what came after the moment of the shutter's release.

In attempting to reconstruct the events of March 1906, I have been faced by the fundamental challenge of most studies of colonial violence—I have, as Karl Jacoby so eloquently describes it, had "to confront the inequities of the historical archive."[40] In the case of Bud Dajo, the imbalance of evidence is particularly striking: the Moros did not have a strong written tradition, but the Americans produced detailed reports of the operation, which have been preserved in archives and libraries along with hundreds of pages of official correspondence, published eyewitness accounts, private letters, memoirs, and diary entries—in addition to almost thirty photographs, of which the image of the trench is just one. Though virtually unknown today, Bud Dajo is probably the best-documented massacre of its time, at least from the perpetrators' perspective. While there are countless sources documenting every aspect of the American experience, the voices of the Moros have not been preserved; in many cases they have been deliberately erased.[41] At both My Lai and Wounded Knee there were survivors who were able to tell their own stories, and thus help shape a critical narrative, but the same cannot be said for Bud Dajo. As one critic put it in 1906, "The lips of every Moro are sealed in death," and for more than a century there has been no one to speak out for the victims.[42]

It is nevertheless possible to recover traces of Moro voices in transcripts of interviews and petition letters that can be found scattered throughout the official reports and documents produced by the Americans. This fragmentary evidence, it goes without saying, has to be used with great care, and the usual caveats concerning issues of translation and the power dynamics inherent to the colonial archive must be kept in mind.[43] I have tried to be as sensitive as possible in representing Moro voices and not to merely replicate colonial stereotypes, yet it should be obvious that we are always constrained by the nature of our sources. Finally, I have drawn on interviews with the descendants of those who were killed at Bud Dajo as well as local Moro narratives, including songs and poems, that still circulate in Jolo today.

However, there is no hiding the fact that a study of Bud Dajo can never fully recover the experience of the victims and will as such always be incomplete.[44] As I do not consider silence to be an option, I have written the story of the massacre relying largely on American accounts, which is to say almost exclusively from the perspective of the perpetrators.[45] This approach, taken by necessity rather than by choice, brings its own challenges, and—just like showing and reproducing the trophy image—it does not come without responsibility.[46] Yet if the colonial gaze can be turned onto itself—and made to reveal the deadly double standards of Western imperialism—the act of bearing witness can perhaps be more than just a cliché.[47] When historical violence is whitewashed and justified through narratives of exceptionalism, reading the colonial archive against the grain becomes a moral imperative.

Ultimately, there can be no justice for the dead, but I can at least make sure that the photographer who captured the soldiers proudly posing with their victims does not get to define what we see in the image. During the intense debates in the House of Representatives in March 1906, Congressman John Sharp Williams openly questioned the truth of the official narrative provided by General Leonard Wood: "I do not know but that future history may show that the battle of Mount Dajo was not as first reported."[48] This book is that future history.

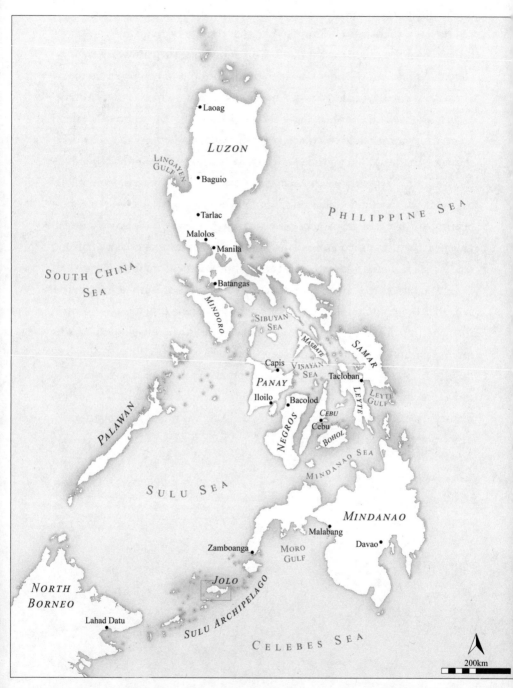

The Philippine Islands

ONE

In the Path of God

The most ultimately righteous of all wars is a war with savages,
though it is apt to be also the most terrible and inhuman.

Theodore Roosevelt, *The Winning of the West* (1894)[1]

IN THE THIRD VOLUME OF HIS ACCOUNT OF THE FOUNDING OF THE
United States, future president Theodore Roosevelt argued for the necessity and justness of violence in the establishment of the white man's rule.
Although his book told the story of the frontier campaigns of the newly
independent American nation during the final years of the eighteenth century, Roosevelt drew explicit parallels to the conquest by white settlers elsewhere in the world:

> The rude, fierce settler who drives the savage from the land lays all civilized man-
> kind under a debt to him. American and Indian, Boer and Zulu, Cossack and
> Tartar, New Zealander and Maori,—in each case the victor, horrible though
> many of his deeds are, has laid deep the foundations for the future greatness of
> a mighty people. The consequences of struggles for territory between civilized
> nations seem small by comparison. Looked at from the standpoint of the ages, it

is of little moment whether Lorraine is part of Germany or of France, whether
the northern Adriatic cities pay homage to Austrian Kaiser or Italian King; but
it is of incalculable importance that America, Australia, and Siberia should pass
out of the hands of their red, black, and yellow aboriginal owners, and become
the heritage of the dominant world races.[2]

This was more than just a historical narrative of a bygone era; Roosevelt
was comparing criticism of the treatment of Native Americans in the
US—just four years after the Wounded Knee Massacre—with contemporary British liberals who were speaking out against Cecil Rhodes's brutal conquest of present-day Zimbabwe: "The home-staying Englishman
of Britain grudges to the Africander [sic] his conquest of Matabele-land;
and so the home-staying American of the Atlantic States dislikes to see
the western miners and cattlemen win for the use of their people the Sioux
hunting-grounds. Nevertheless, it is the men actually on the borders of the
longed-for ground, the men actually in contact with the savages, who in the
end shape their own destinies."[3]

Readers were given to understand that the real American, and by extension the real white man, was not the softhearted East Coast liberal but the
sturdy figure of the Indian-fighting pioneer, a role that Roosevelt had himself performed so effectively earlier in his career. Violence and masculinity,
race and empire, were all intimately connected in this vision of manifest
destiny.[4]

Just a few years later, in 1898, Roosevelt had become one of the strongest proponents of an American intervention in Cuba, ostensibly aimed at
putting an end to Spanish oppression of the local population. The resulting war with Spain, however, led to a significant expansion of US overseas
territories, including the prospect of the annexation of the Philippines. It
was at this point that the British author Rudyard Kipling wrote the famous
poem "The White Man's Burden," exhorting the United States to accept
its moral responsibility and, as Britain had done throughout its colonies,
civilize the Philippines.[5] Kipling knew Roosevelt personally and had sent
the future president a copy of the poem in late 1898, before its formal publication. Although Roosevelt was unimpressed by the poetry, he recognized
that the message made "good sense from the expansion standpoint."[6] On

February 4, 1899, the same day that US soldiers opened fire on Filipino troops in Manila—thus kicking off the Philippine-American War—people back home could for the first time read Kipling's poem, which had just been published in *McClure's*.[7] By that point, Spain had officially ceded the Philippines to the United States, which launched its imperialist project under the guise of "benevolent assimilation."[8] There was, however, nothing benevolent about the brutal war fought over the next few years against Filipino nationalists who had been promised liberation from Spanish rule but instead found one colonial ruler simply replaced by another. Despite the deeply entrenched sense of exceptionalism underpinning American identity, it turned out that manifest destiny and the white man's burden were merely variations on the same theme.[9] Kipling's incongruous concept of "the savage wars of peace" echoed the exact sentiment expressed by Roosevelt and perfectly captured the deadly logic of Western imperialism at the turn of the twentieth century, which both prescribed and justified unrestrained violence in the name of progress.

———————

Although the Americans proclaimed themselves to be the liberators of the Philippines, the US Army soon became bogged down in a brutal and bitter guerrilla war with the forces of the Philippine Republic under Emilio Aguinaldo in Luzon and the Visayas.[10] With the prospect of having to fight simultaneously in the North and in the South, in 1899 the US administration signed a separate treaty with the sultan of Sulu, Jamalul Kiram II, one of the most significant Moro rulers.[11] Unlike in the North, the Spanish had never been able to fully establish their rule in Mindanao and the Sulu Archipelago, and the Americans were as a result faced with a very different situation there. The notion of an alliance between Aguinaldo and the sultan was in truth entirely implausible, since there was more that divided the Catholic Filipinos and the Muslim Moros than might have united them. However, the very idea of such a coalition was enough to prompt the Americans to settle for indirect rule and pursue a noninterference strategy in the South, at least for the time being. According to what became known as the Bates Treaty, the United States maintained a military presence in the Sulu region, but no sustained efforts were made to assert US authority, nor to implement any major colonial policies. The sultan recognized US authority in return for a promise that Moro religion and customs would be respected, and that he would retain the authority to manage internal affairs. The US government also agreed to pay the sultan and the main *datus*, or Moro chiefs, an annual pension, just as the Spanish had done.[12]

When the war in the North officially ended in 1902, the Americans remained bound by the treaty, though reluctantly so. The fact that the Moros practiced both slavery and polygamy, and lived according to Islamic tradition, remained a sticky point for the American military authorities—it was one thing to break with the Monroe Doctrine, but much harder to justify the occupation of the Philippines when such practices were tolerated under US rule.[13] In parts of Mindanao, where no treaty had been signed, military campaigns were soon launched to bring the Moros under US authority like the rest of the Philippines. In May 1902, US forces thus for the first time confronted the Moros during a punitive expedition to Bayang, on the southern shore of Lake Lanao in Mindanao. As a grim indication of things to come, American forces attacked two *cottas*, or fortifications, suffering just eleven dead and forty-two wounded, while between four hundred and five hundred Moros were killed. President Roosevelt sent a message to the commanding officer, expressing his "congratulations and thanks for the splendid courage and fidelity which has again carried our flag to victory."[14] It was also in the Lanao region that a young Captain Pershing was to win his first laurels. Over the course of the following decade, US forces, assisted by members of the locally recruited Philippine Constabulary, engaged in countless expeditions against different groups of Moros throughout the South.

———

On March 11, 1903, the British traveler and writer Arnold Henry Savage Landor arrived in Jolo onboard the US Coast Guard steamer *Tablas* as part of a trip that had taken him all over the islands newly occupied by the United States.[15] Jolo formed a part of the string of volcanic islands that stretched from Zamboanga, on the westernmost tip of Mindanao, all the way to Borneo, dividing the Sulu Sea from the Celebes Sea. The island was thirty-seven miles long, east to west, and fourteen miles north to south at its widest. *Jolo* was the Spanish rendition of "Sulu," which was derived from the local word *sūg*, meaning "sea current."[16] The Moros in fact referred to themselves as *Tausūg*, which translated as "people of the current." Jolo was both the name of the island and of the main port town on the northeastern coast, behind which rose the ragged outline of more than a dozen mountains covered in thick jungle. Landor liked the look of what he saw:

> We went round the Diangappik Point, a spit of white sand with lots of trees upon it, and we now had, disclosing itself gradually before our eyes, the neat, quite ideal little walled town. . . .
>
> Jolo is undoubtedly the prettiest and cleanest little settlement in the archipelago. The houses within the walls are handsome, of whitewashed masonry and wood, with corrugated iron roofs. Steamers of small draught can go alongside a masonry pier, which has a lighthouse upon it.
>
> Sulu settlements occupy the coast line on each side of the town, the houses being built on piles upon the water. There is also an extensive Chinese settlement pile-built on a rambling jetty, which stretches a long distance over the water. Cocoanut groves are numerous, as usual, along the beach, and a broad valley on an inclined plane stretches beyond the city to the east.[17]

Landor and his fellow passengers, who included David P. Barrows, chief of the Bureau of Non-Christian Tribes of the Philippines, and Najeeb M. Saleeby, a Lebanese Christian physician who also worked for the American administration, disembarked on the T-shaped pier with the old Spanish lighthouse and two diminutive guardhouses, which were the most recognizable landmarks of Jolo. The walled town had been built by the Spanish after they first established a garrison in 1876, and it was from this little enclave that they retained a tenuous hold over the rest of the island, rarely venturing outside its walls. The American forces who now occupied this small outpost of progress had so far maintained only a nominal presence on the island, and a semblance of peace prevailed.

The religious and cultural identity of the Moros encountered by the Americans in Jolo had been forged through centuries of incessant fighting with the Spanish, yet the power of the once-proud rulers of the Sulu Sea had been much diminished by the beginning of the twentieth century.

European steam-powered gunboats had effectively put an end to Moro piracy and dominance of the sea, including their involvement in the lucrative
trade networks that connected Brunei with Singapore and Batavia. Jolo remained a thriving entrepot, but the Moros themselves no longer engaged in
the long-distance trade of products such as *trepang* (sea cucumber), bird's
nest, or dried fish, which was instead left to Chinese merchants, and much
of the harvesting of pearls and mother-of-pearl had been taken over by Japanese boats. The upheaval caused by the Spanish occupation of Jolo in the
1870s had furthermore been exacerbated by more than a decade of bitter
succession struggles over the sultanate, and internecine warfare among
rival factions of Moro chiefs continued right up until the arrival of the
Americans.[18]

By 1903, Sultan Jamalul Kiram II had a small council consisting of his
brother, Attik, known as the *Rajah Muda*, as well as Hadji Butu, who
served as the chief minister, or *Datu Bendahara*. Butu was the key interme-
diary between the sultan and the American administration and occupied
what was in practice the single most important position in Jolo because he
was able to directly influence colonial policies through his advice. Although
the sultan represented the highest religious and political authority in the
region, he did not actually possess the means or manpower to enforce his
policies, and instead he had to act through the Moro chiefs. These *datus* each
commanded groups of followers and were organized in a complex system
of alliances and kinship networks associated with particular parts of the island. Although the town of Jolo had formerly been the seat of the sultanate,
Kiram now occupied the new capital in Maimbun, some ten miles away on
the southern coast of the island. On the westernmost part of Jolo, the district
of Parang was under the powerful *Maharajah* Indanan, and east of Jolo,
the district of Patikul belonged to two brothers, Kalbi and Jokanain. Farther to the east, the districts of Luuk and Tandu were divided up between a
number of smaller chiefs, including *Panglima* Hassan, who had once been
a contender for the sultanate. The sultan's power was constantly contested
and negotiated by the different chiefs, and Kiram was only as strong as the
loyalty that he could command at any given point of time. Both collaboration with, and resistance against, the Americans was ultimately shaped by
the dynamics of preexisting rivalries between the sultan and various Moro

elites in Jolo. Colonial officials thus pursued a US policy against a back-drop of local power struggles, the nature of which the Americans were often unaware.[19]

Despite the official policy of noninterference, American colonial proj-ects, including a naval survey and official census, caused widespread fears and suspicion among the Moros. Similar to the rest of the Philippine is-lands, the Sulu Archipelago was plagued by a severe cholera epidemic, and the American garrison in Jolo had set up armed guards to keep locals from entering military quarters in and around the town. In January, shots were fired at the quarantine guards near the barracks in Asturias, and the fol-lowing month, US survey parties that were mapping the island and sur-rounding waters were also fired upon on several occasions.[20] Around the same time, a turf war broke out among Moros who owned stalls in the markets on the Chinese pier in Jolo harbor, and one *datu* set fire to several shops owned by his rivals. Because the Chinese traders whose goods were destroyed were technically foreigners, the case fell under US jurisdiction. The military governor of Jolo, Colonel W. M. Wallace, had several *datus* arrested and subsequently sent to a prison near Manila, which caused much resentment. American rule was tolerated only as long as it did not interfere in local politics, and the arrest of Moro *datus* was perceived as a grievous abuse of authority.[21] By the time that Landor and his companions disem-barked in March of 1903, the situation had worsened:

> The American military colony was in a commotion when we arrived. A soldier had been terribly gashed and killed by a *juramentado*. These *juramentados*, as the Spanish word expresses, are religious maniacs, who, after having undergone certain exorcisms in the mosque, proceed to kill any non-Mahommedan and then commit suicide, in order to obtain a happy existence in paradise. This makes it rather unpleasant for those who do not believe in the Koran, for one never knows when one of these devils may be about and treacherously hack one to pieces.[22]

There had actually been three separate attacks in the course of a single week. On Sunday, March 8, a Moro man entered the local marketplace and started attacking people at random with a knife. Having killed a Filipino man and wounded several other locals, the attacker was killed by another Moro. Just two days later, US Army engineers were working near a rock quarry at Tando Point, on the beach north of Jolo, when they were approached by a Moro carrying a musket:

> He spoke in a friendly manner, saying "holloy-bugay" (friend). Immediately then he aimed his musket at the group and snapped it. When it did not explode he rushed upon them with a barong [sword-like knife] and killed one of the men of the Engineer corps. The first blow severed the clavicle and nine ribs along the back. Two more blows completely lopped off an arm and a limb, although the man was shot twice with .30 calibre revolvers, before he could strike another blow.[23]

Finally, on Saturday, March 14, three Moros again entered the market at Tullai and started slashing at people indiscriminately with their *barongs*. An Indian merchant and two Moros were killed, and several others wounded, including a Moro woman and a Filipino man.[24] At that point a troop of the US 15th Cavalry Regiment arrived on the scene, as Wallace described: "Upon the approach of the soldiers the crazed fanatics came rushing at them and struck them with their barongs. In the melee that followed, the soldiers, to protect themselves, killed all three of the juramentados."[25]

The term that both Wallace and Landor used to describe the attackers, *juramentado*, literally meant an "oath taker" in Spanish. Like so much else in the Philippines, it had been inherited by the Americans from their Spanish predecessors.[26] Spanish records in particular were regarded as authoritative manuals for successful colonial governance and were mined for useful information about the Moros.[27] When officers of the 15th Cavalry regiment who had been stationed in Jolo in March 1903 returned to the US later that year, they were said to have "secured a very interesting translation of a Spanish account of the Moros."[28] The same account was formally added to the annual report of 1902–1903 for the Mindanao Division, which included Jolo, and copies were later also published in the American press.[29] According to this account, the *juramentado* were frenzied fanatics who sought martyrdom and entry into paradise by attacking and killing as many Christians as possible.[30] Although the Spanish described the religious fanaticism of the *juramentado*, they did not, as a rule, portray these attacks as caused by insanity or as a psychological condition.[31] However, the Americans also drew inspiration from British colonial narratives of what was referred to as *amok*, or temporary fits of violent madness, usually associated with Malays in Singapore or Borneo.[32] Whereas *juramentado* was explicitly linked to Islam, *amok* had a longer history as both a racial stereotype and a colonial pathology, as described in a British account from 1874:

> The nature of the Malays of our islands is not unlike their clime. Beneath their civil and apparently gentle surface fierce passions smoulder, which require but a spark to kindle into a devastating flame. Maddened by jealousy, or some real or fancied wrong, the ordinary mild Malay becomes a demon. Then his eyes glare like those of a wild beast, out leaps his kris (ceremonial knife) or parang, and he rushes on the amok, smiting everyone he meets.[33]

In the southern Philippines, the Americans used both terms—*amok* and *juramentado*—as more or less interchangeable, without apparently recognizing the fact that a sudden and uncontrollable outburst was logically incompatible with the notion of first taking an oath before launching an attack. In fact, it was the very ambiguity of the concept that made it so useful for the colonial administration in places such as Jolo: by defining *juramentado* both as a form of involuntary madness and as an expression of Islamic fanaticism, the Americans effectively pathologized the entire Muslim population, with the result that Moro resistance against US rule could simply be dismissed as irrational.[34] This had obvious parallels in the British construction of Muslims within their colonies and especially in India, where suicidal attacks by so-called *ghazis* were also known.[35] The young Winston Churchill, who saw active service along the North-West Frontier in what is today Pakistan, provided a particularly grim and demeaning example of this kind of colonial "knowledge":

> The Mahommedan religion increases, instead of lessening, the fury of intolerance.... All rational considerations are forgotten. Seizing their weapons, they become *Ghazis*—as dangerous and as sensible as mad dogs: fit only to be treated as such. While the more generous spirits among the tribesmen become

convulsed in an ecstasy of religious bloodthirstiness, poorer and more material souls derive additional impulses from the influence of others, the hopes of plunder and the joy of fighting. Thus whole nations are roused to arms.... In each case civilisation is confronted with militant Mahommedanism. The forces of progress clash with those of reaction. The religion of blood and war is face to face with that of peace. Luckily the religion of peace is usually the better armed.[36]

Accounts of the Moros were often little different, and one popular book actually described the *juramentado* in the exact same terms: "This is the most dangerous sect of Mahometans, for no exhibition of force can suffice to stay their ravages, and they can only be treated like mad dogs, or like a Malay who has run ámok."[37] Affirming the racial hierarchies that justified colonial rule, such accounts also served to further dehumanize the Moros and pave the way for a particularly heavy-handed approach to American rule in the southern Philippines.

Before 1903, there had been no open attacks on the American forces in Jolo, and Major Wallace feared that no ordinary measures could stop *juramentado*, whose death granted the attackers "an exalted position as martyrs."[38] Wallace subsequently had the bodies of the three attackers who had been killed on March 14 placed on display in the hospital, and he called on the Moros living in the vicinity to come and, if possible, identify them. While the bodies were in the hospital, Landor was allowed to examine them; like many explorers of the time, he was also an avid amateur craniometrist, and he took every opportunity to measure the heads and bodies of the different peoples he encountered during his travels:

As a type they all three bore marked characteristics of criminal lunacy, and I firmly believe that the *sherifs* or priests select these weak-minded fellows who are murderously inclined, and play upon their credulity until they reduce them to a condition of wild frenzy and incite them to commit murder.

These men had square faces, very flattened skulls, and low foreheads, cheek bones low down in the face, and so prominent that when in profile they nearly hid the excessively flat noses; weak and small receding chins, and the square-fingered, stumpy, repulsive-looking hands typical of criminals—as cruel

hands and heads as I have ever examined, the animal qualities being extraor-
dinarily developed. Their repulsive appearance was also somewhat enhanced
by the hair of the head being shaved clean, and the moustache and eyelashes
removed so as to leave a mere horizontal tiny strip of black hair. The teeth had
been freshly filed and stained black; the hair of the arm-pits pulled out, and the
nails of the fingers and toes trimmed very short.[39]

Landor's examination of the three corpses reflected a heady combination of
racial science, craniometry, and criminology, which, just like the stereotype
of *juramentado* itself, relied on a number of different and not necessarily
compatible discourses. The shaved heads and other features of the corpses
that he noted were actually the traditional burial rituals of the Moros,
which in this case had been done while they were still alive in preparation
for their imminent death.[40] Anthropologist David Barrows, who had arrived at the same time as Landor, wrote a lengthy report to the government
in Manila describing the situation in Jolo, praising Wallace for "acting with
great forbearance": "The temptation of course is strong to stop this outra-
geous fanaticism by impressive acts of retribution upon the communities
where those juramentados make their preparations and where it is fair to
presume the people knew of the intentions of the juramentados if they do
not sympathise with them."[41]

Evidently, neither Barrows nor Landor was aware of what subsequently
happened to the corpses of the three *juramentado*. Colonel Wallace later
recounted that he had "decided that perhaps the best way to impress the
lesson of lawfulness upon the natives was to administer the worst form of
punishment to them by burying their bodies with a hog."[42] Wild hogs were
common throughout Jolo and were often hunted for sport by the Moros but
never eaten: they were considered *haram* (forbidden) and ritually polluting.
Wallace had the corpses taken to a spot outside the walls, and, as he put it,
the proceedings were given "the greatest publicity":

A great crowd gathered about the grave where the internment was to take place,
and it was there that a dead hog in plain view of the multitude was lifted and
placed in the grave in the midst of the three bodies, the Moro grave diggers
themselves being required to do this, much to their horror. News of the form

of punishment which had been adopted to put an end to the juramentados soon spread.[43]

When later asked how he conceived of such a horrific spectacle, Wallace replied: "I am informed that the same form of punishment was put to effect by the English at Singapore and had effective results."[44]

———•———

The source of Wallace's inspiration was actually a letter published in a newspaper in Singapore in 1901, which recommended the use of pigs against Muslim "fanatics," described as either "*amok*" or "*ghazis*":

> One quite convincing suggestion is that all persons who run amok should be buried with the carcass of a pig tied to their bodies. In the similar cases of amok, perpetrated by Indian frontier ghazis against Europeans, the criminal is burnt after execution and the ashes scattered. An amok runner does not fear death, but rather courts it. Well, we deal with his ideas of a post-mortem future as the next and only argument. It is there we have him on the hip. With Oriental phases of crime we must apply Oriental remedies. The pig is our ace of trumps in this case.[45]

The British did not actually use this practice in Singapore, but the story evidently circulated among European settlers and military personnel in Southeast Asia as a sort of colonial rumor.[46] Moreover, the story originated in real events, and within the British Empire, and especially in India, there was a long tradition of such kinds of spectacular punishment.[47] In 1857 *sepoys* (Indian soldiers in the service of the East India Company) rebelled over fears that Christianity was being duplicitously forced upon them and that their social and professional status was being undermined. These fears revolved around the introduction of a new cartridge for the Enfield 1853 rifle that, rumor had it, was covered in the grease of pigs and cows—highly offensive to both Hindus and Muslims.[48] The uprising was eventually suppressed, and the British set to the task of punishing the rebels and reasserting their authority. Following what had originally been a Mughal practice, Indian prisoners were strapped to the mouth of cannon and literally blown to pieces in front of local spectators forced to watch the execution. A contemporary British newspaper report elaborated on the cultural specificity of the spectacle enacted during one such execution:

> You must know that this is nearly the only form in which death has any terrors for a native ... if sentenced to death in this form, he knows that his body will be blown into a thousand pieces, and that it will be altogether impossible for his relatives, however devoted to him, to be sure of picking up all the fragments of his own particular body; and the thought that perhaps a limb of some one of a different religion to himself might possibly be burned or buried with the remainder of his own body, is agony to him.[49]

British retributions during 1857 targeted the very issues that had precipitated the mutiny of the *sepoys*: their religious and ritual purity. Colonial knowledge was thus turned against colonial subjects in a form of spiritual warfare that transcended mere physical punishment. The formal executions were not the only such instance, and the British went to extraordinary lengths to ensure that the punishment was made as culturally offensive as possible, as the wartime correspondent William Howard Russell described:

> All these kinds of vindictive, unchristian, Indian torture, such as sewing Mahomedans in pig-skins, smearing them with pork-fat before execution, and burning their bodies, and forcing Hindus to defile themselves, are disgraceful, and ultimately recoil on ourselves. They are spiritual and mental tortures to which we have no right to resort, and which we dare not perpetrate in the face of Europe.[50]

Whereas such retribution would indeed have been unthinkable in conflicts against white people, the perceived need to reassert racial hierarchies during a time of colonial crisis made this violence both permissible and seemingly indispensable. During the second part of the nineteenth century, the British even incorporated similar types of punishment within the legal regimes implemented on the North-West Frontier. Special legislation not only allowed for the summary execution of "fanatics" but also made it part of the punishment to have the bodies be burned in order to prevent Islamic burial. In 1896, one officer described the rationale behind this measure:

> People may say what they like: but burning has a most terrible significance to these uneducated tribes, and it is the only thing they seem to fear. . . . When I said they would be hanged, they answered they were quite prepared for that. But when I added that they would be subsequently burnt, their colour changed, and thenceforward they were different men. The "kick" was entirely taken out of them.[51]

It was this very logic that Colonel Wallace sought to apply in Jolo, based on the erroneous assumption that Muslims all over the world were identical in their beliefs and practices, and that lessons from the British Empire could simply be applied in the southern Philippines. Invoked as a force multiplier, colonial knowledge was accordingly not just descriptive, in terms of identifying the putative danger of "fanatics"; it was also prescriptive in that it provided what was supposed to be an efficacious remedy against an extraordinary threat.[52] Wallace had in fact resorted to the exact kind of "impressive acts of retribution upon the communities" that Barrows had applauded him for avoiding—because all Moros were considered to be complicit, the spectacle of the burial with a pig was intended as a warning to the entire community and the punishment thus inherently collective.[53] Similarly to public executions and lynchings, Wallace's improvised "lesson for the natives" was an act of performative violence that also sent a reassuring message to the Americans in Jolo that the attacks were being duly punished.[54] Wallace, of course, had no way of knowing what the Moros who witnessed the ritual desecration of three corpses actually thought, and the fact was that the pig-burial was more likely to provoke than intimidate the Muslim population of Jolo. As a deliberate attempt to use religious beliefs to terrorize colonial subjects, it was as far from a noninterference policy as could be imagined.

———◆———

"The Moro name for *juramentado* is *macsabil*," an American officer explained, "which means 'to die for the faith.'"[55] The practice described as *juramentado* by both the Spanish and the Americans was indeed understood very differently by the Moros, who used the term *parang sabil*, which can be translated as "war in the way of Allah," and sometimes rendered as *magsabil*.[56] As opposed to the colonial definition of *juramentado*, however, *parang sabil* could also apply to women and children, for instance, who were unjustly killed and thus martyred. Despite its obvious origins in a distinctly Islamic tradition of martyrdom, *parang sabil* or *juramentado* was not reducible to a simplistic notion of *jihad*—nor was it some kind of mental condition. Instead, it was a complex and historically contingent phenomenon that was social and political as much as it was religious.[57]

Islam was first introduced in the Sulu region in the fourteenth century through trade and pilgrimage networks across the Indian Ocean, and the first Muslim sultan established his rule in Jolo at some time around 1450. A century later, however, the Spanish arrived, and with the occupation of the northern islands of the Philippines came also a policy of forced conversion to Roman Catholicism. In 1578 the Spanish launched the first of many military expeditions against Jolo to establish their authority in the South but crucially also to convert the Moros of the Sulu Archipelago. For the next three hundred years, the Moros fought off the Spanish in a near-constant series of brutal conflicts, and in the absence of an overarching national identity, religion provided a powerful means of mobilizing resistance. Just as conquest and proselytizing were intrinsic parts of the Iberian imperialist project, so, too, did the anticolonial resistance of the Moros become indistinguishable from their defense of the Islamic religion. Foreign occupation was synonymous with an attack on the faith, and the inevitable result was a religious ethos that placed particular emphasis on a willingness to sacrifice one's life fighting the *infidels*—as was also the case in other Muslim regions, including Malabar and Aceh.[58]

A traditional song epic from Jolo called "The Parang Sabil of Abdulla and Putli' Isara" reveals how the practice of *parang sabil* was conceived and commemorated locally.[59] Two young Moro lovers, Abdulla and Isara, were engaged to be married during the period of Spanish occupation. When the beautiful Isara went to bathe in a river, a Spanish lieutenant passing by saw her and raped the girl despite her protestations. When Abdulla learned of this, he swore to undertake *parang sabil* and kill the lieutenant, who had

not only violated Isara but also dishonored him as her husband-to-be. Notions of honor and shame were central to a Moro's status and played a significant role in social interaction; as a Moro man, it was inconceivable not
to respond to an insult or threat, and the maxim of "death before dishonor"
was thus taken literally.[60] As Abdulla prepared to single-handedly attack
the Spanish headquarters, Isara pleaded with him to let her join in this
undertaking:

> *Sir if you do sabil,*
> *Let us do it together.*
> *We will not surrender*
> *In the fight against the infidels.*
> *Should we be slain,*
> *I will regard you as my husband.*
> *Though we are not married on Earth,*
> *In death it shall be done.*[61]

Abdulla picked up a *kris* while Isara seized a *barong*, and together they
went to the military camp, where they cut down the Spanish lieutenant
with multiple blows, uttering *bismilla* or "in the name of God."[62] Having
fulfilled their task, the young lovers rushed the Spanish soldiers who had
surrounded them. Abdulla and Isara fought furiously but were eventually
killed, surrounded by the bodies of their enemies:

> *When the firing ceased,*
> *The two had already died*
> *They had fallen side by side;*
> *The horse nuzzled them.*[63]

The last line refers to the winged horse, or Burāq, which according to Islamic belief carried dead martyrs to heaven, indicating the final stage of
the *parang sabil*, and Abdulla and Isara were finally united in death.[64] The
performance of this form of song epic was considered meritorious in its own
right and was referred to as *langkit parang sabil*, glorifying the heroic deeds
of people who had died while resisting foreign invaders.[65] Despite the fact

that the story provided a highly formalized narrative, it does reveal how Islamic martyrdom, anticolonial resistance, and the defense of personal honor merged and were in effect inseparable aspects of the same practice. For the individual as much as the *umma*, or wider Moro community, *juramentado* offered redemption and spiritual merit in the face of defeat.

The story of Abdulla and Isara furthermore reveals that the attacks of *juramentado* were not simply random outbursts but took place in response to colonial occupation, often under very particular circumstances. This was also apparent from earlier European accounts. The Spanish description of *juramentado*, on which the Americans placed so much emphasis, was actually written by a Frenchman, Dr. Joseph Montano, who had visited Jolo around 1880, when he personally witnessed an attack and even photographed its aftermath.[66] Parts of his narrative were later translated into Spanish, and the version on which the Americans relied was incomplete and in many ways missing the most important parts: according to Montano, it was only after the sultan accepted Spanish control of Jolo in 1876 that leading *datus* continued to fight the colonial rulers and resorted to suicidal attacks by small groups of warriors. A *juramentado*, he explained, was essentially a bondage slave who bought the freedom of his family by sacrificing his own life fighting the Spanish. Although Montano did describe *juramentado* as a frenzied and suicidal attack, in which the Moro expected to die and gain entry to heaven, he thus provided an important political as well as socioeconomic context for the practice—one that was never really acknowledged by the Americans. Following Montano's account, it would appear that the practice of *juramentado* in the 1870s was part of an open struggle against the Spanish occupation of Jolo, framed in religious terms as a defense of the faith.[67] By 1903, however, *juramentado* had become a largely symbolic act of desperation: the continuation of armed resistance, expressed through a religious idiom, at a time when open warfare was no longer possible. According to Dr. Saleeby, Landor's travel companion, the situation in Jolo was furthermore highly critical, as he noted just after the last *juramentado* attacks on March 14:

> I found out that afternoon that the whole island was in a state of fear and disturbance and very hostile at heart. The naval survey of the shores of the islands and

the census of the people seemed to them to be evident signs of some ulterior mo-
tive the Americans have. They thought that the Americans intend to fight them
and tax the people and raise the customs. The chiefs that were hostile to the Sultan accused him of treachery and thought he was going to sell the country to the
Americans. The people and the secondary chiefs distrusted the Americans and
were afraid and very suspicious of every move, action or word. The country has
been in a state of anarchy ever since the war between the Sultan and Datu Kalbi
began. The people are in a distressing condition. Cholera caused many deaths. The
ignorance of the people is extreme and their patience was taxed to the last limit.
Then they resorted to juramentado acts to give vent to an accumulating and exas-
perating angry sentiment.[68]

According to another report, the Moros believed that the Americans
were responsible for the spread of cholera and "maintained that it was better
to die in the path of God fighting the Americans, than die of cholera."[69]
Colonel Wallace was later able to gather some information about the *juramentado* attacks: Datu Kalbi explained that the man who was responsible
for the killing of a US soldier at Tando Point was likely a Moro named Katibun who was one of his brother Jokanain's followers and was said to be "mad
with grief" after the death of his son.[70] Katibun's personal circumstances
thus appear to have played a key role in this attack, which was very much
an individual undertaking and did not involve the wider community. The
attack by the three *juramentado* on March 14, on the other hand, seemed
to follow a very different pattern. The three men, whose bodies Landor later
inspected, were named Seiril, Ahmad, and Omag, and they were part of
the retinue of a minor Moro chief from Luuk, the easternmost district of
Jolo.[71] The three men had personally informed Maharajah Indanan of their
intention to become *juramentado*, and he warned them that the sultan had
prohibited the practice on the island and that accordingly they ought to go
to Zamboanga instead. They nevertheless went to Jolo town accompanied
by two other men, and it was reported that they were "behaving strangely
and singing religious songs."[72] In the end, only the three of them participated in the attack and were subsequently killed, but this was, in part at
least, a demonstration by Moro chiefs from Luuk, traditionally opposed
to the sultan, that they were able to launch such attacks in defiance of his

orders—which is to say that this was as much a part of a local feud as it was about resistance against the Americans. To the Americans, the *juramentado* attacks appeared simply as mindless outbursts of crazed fanaticism, although they were in fact shaped by a range of idiosyncratic factors. Widespread fears over the spread of cholera, high food prices, and political turmoil also coincided with the festivities associated with Muslims who had returned from pilgrimage to Mecca, which suggests that the timing of these attacks was anything but accidental.[73] Unique among the Americans for his understanding of the Moros' way of life, Saleeby actually recognized the political significance of the attacks:

> "Juramentados" are not religious fanatics. . . . There has been no greater misunderstanding by Spaniards and Americans on any one Moro subject than on this—the juramentado question. The juramentado is not actuated by a religious feeling. It is fierce patriotism that excites his rashness. . . . A man who runs amuck in a manner avenges himself and his personal grievances, but the juramentado avenges his people and his chief. His chief's call for vengeance rings in his ears and he immediately comes forward as the hero and avenger of the datuship.[74]

However, Saleeby had little influence on US policies, and few of his colleagues accepted that their presence in Jolo might be the root cause of the violence. Instead, they preferred to view Moro resistance as nothing more than innate expressions of fanatic savagery. In the immediate aftermath of the *juramentado* attacks in March 1903, the division commander, Brigadier General S. S. Sumner, arrived in Jolo with military reinforcements to prevent the situation from escalating further.[75] As part of the stipulations of the Bates Treaty, the sultan had issued an edict prohibiting *juramentado* attacks against the Americans, and the US authorities intended to hold him accountable. On March 23, Sumner held a meeting with the sultan and several of the main Moro chiefs, warning them that in case of any further attacks on US forces, the retaliation would be indiscriminate. The sultan responded:

> **Sultan:** Please do not punish the innocent for the wrongs of the bad people.

General Sumner: The innocent must get out of the way. The Sulus must learn to obey American customs, or somebody is going to get hurt. When people fight they cannot tell who is innocent. Again, I warn them to stop this juramentado business. We cannot stand having soldiers and other peaceful people killed. The Sultan and Dattos must be held responsible if permission is given to these fellows to go juramentado.

Sultan: But the Sultan and Dattos do not know any more than you when these people go mad. When people lose their fathers and mothers, and will even kill their own near relatives—a woman lately killed her mother—how can you hold me responsible for the actions of these people?

General Sumner: Because you are the Sultan.

Sultan: I am not God, though. . . .[76]

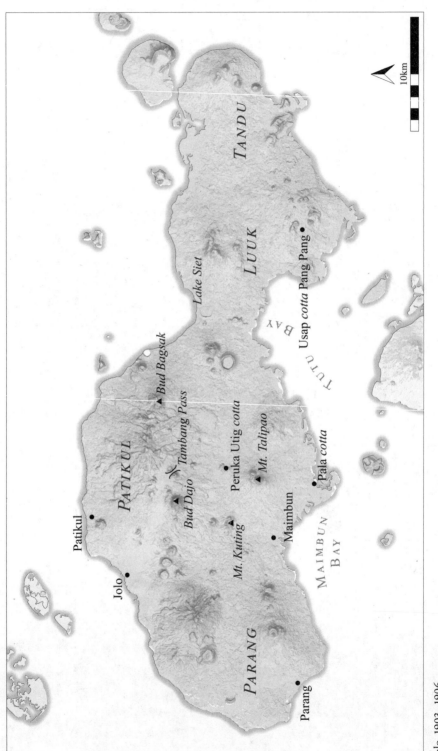

Jolo, 1903–1906

TWO

One Clean-Cut Lesson

If a policy of war is to be followed, war must be made in a way
that the Moros can understand.... It is to look at your enemy as
untameable, to seize any trifling opportunity for the end in view,
to have an overwhelming force, and to strike without conscience;
literally killing every living thing when the battle occurs, and de-
stroying everything that cannot be carried away after the victory
is won. The expense of such a policy will be great, the bloodshed
terrible; but a few successful encounters conducted on this principle will secure abject submission and peace for a generation.

Henry Otis Dwight, "Our Mohammedan Wards" (1900)[1]

IN 1903 THE AMERICANS ESTABLISHED THE MORO PROVINCE AS A DIS-
tinct administrative region that would be under the control of a military governor rather than the civil administration being introduced in the
North. The Moros, it was believed, first had to be "pacified" before the project of so-called benevolent assimilation could be extended to Mindanao
and the Sulu Archipelago. One of the key figures to undertake this "civilizational" project was a close friend of President Theodore Roosevelt—the

ambitious but controversial officer Dr. Leonard Wood (1860–1927).[2] He
was a graduate of Harvard Medical School, and his first assignment was as
a contract surgeon with the US Army in Arizona, where he participated in
the 1886 expedition to capture the famous Apache chief Goyaałé, better
known as Geronimo. Wood later served as the personal physician to President Grover Cleveland as well as McKinley, and in 1898 he was awarded the
Medal of Honor for his services back in 1886, despite the fact that he never
saw any action. When Roosevelt raised the First Volunteer Cavalry Regiment, the so-called Rough Riders, ahead of the Cuba expedition, he made
Wood the commanding officer, and it was then that the ambitious doctor
first came to the attention of the public. After the war, Wood served as military governor in Cuba, a position that he occupied until 1902, and the following year Roosevelt assigned him to a senior position in the Philippines
and eventually ensured that he was promoted to major general. In the military and among Roosevelt's political adversaries, however, there were many
who thought that Wood had been promoted beyond his capabilities, and his
close connection to the president made him an easy target for accusations of
favoritism. Mark Twain, for instance, referred to Wood as Roosevelt's "fra-
grant pet" and blamed the president for having "foisted this discredited doctor upon the army and the nation."[3] As a result, Wood was highly conscious
of his own reputation, as one of his junior officers noted: "He spoke much of
himself and how he was regarded by the Army and the public."[4]

Although Wood coveted the position of commander of the Philippine
Division, he initially had to contend with the more modest governorship of
the Moro Province, with headquarters in Zamboanga on the westernmost
tip of Mindanao. When he left for his new assignment, he was accompanied
by two officers—his aide, Captain Frank McCoy, and Major Hugh Lenox
Scott—who had extensive experience in the American West and had also
served with Wood in Cuba.[5] While US troops would usually leave from the
West Coast, taking the shortest route to the Philippines across the Pacific,
Wood received instructions from Roosevelt to travel eastward and stop
over in both British and Dutch colonies along the way. Cultural and ethnographic knowledge was considered a vital tool for colonial governance, and
because US experience had up until then been limited mainly to its own

continental frontiers, American officers and officials looked to European imperial powers for lessons in colonial administration.[6]

Wood had in fact been touring Europe during the latter half of 1902 and attended the German army maneuvers before visiting London. Here he met Lord Roberts and Lord Kitchener—two officers who more than anyone else embodied the British experience of colonial warfare.[7] From Europe, Wood and his companions continued their journey, first stopping over in Constantinople, which made a deep impression on McCoy: "I believe in the crusades, and feel like joining one myself against the Turks and his dogs."[8] Subsequently meeting with Lord Cromer in Cairo, Wood and the British colonial administrator discussed at length the challenges of governing "fanatical Mohammedan tribes."[9] The purpose of this tour of the European imperial metropoles was clearly more than just a tourist outing, as McCoy wrote: "Everything has taken interest; and much . . . may be of use to us in time and occupations to come."[10] Traveling through the Suez Canal, they then went on to British India and finally stopped over in Java, to study what could be learned from Dutch colonial methods. Wood was not impressed, and he openly voiced his disgust at what he perceived as the servile attitude of "the natives" toward white people—in fact, the future governor of the Moro Province expressed his hope that *his* colonial subjects would "take the to the woods occasionally and kill a few of us, for their rights and manliness [rather] than squat and cringe."[11] As it turned out, it was Wood himself who brought about the violent confrontation that he so wished for.

———

Wood arrived in the Moro Province in early August of 1903, having already decided on a suitable strategy to deal with the local population, as he informed Roosevelt:

> Governor Taft, General Davis, General Wade and others feel that we shall have one sharp brush with the Jolo Moros, and this I think, you can expect with reasonable promptness, unless the Moro attitude changes. . . . If they still insist, as they may, upon a row, it won't amount to much. I think one clean-cut lesson

will be quite sufficient for them, but it should be of such a character as not to need a dozen frittering repetitions.[12]

The idea of "one clean-cut lesson" had a specifically colonial origin.[13] As British officer C. E. Callwell argued in his manual on colonial warfare, *Small Wars*, first published in 1896, "The lower races are impressionable. They are greatly influenced by a resolute bearing and by a determined course of action."[14] Callwell's text drew from the shared experience of all the major European powers, as well as the US, and it proved to have a lasting impact on how wars with "savages" were fought throughout Africa and Asia at the turn of the century.[15] One of the key tenets of colonial warfare, in Callwell's definition, was in fact the great principle of "overawing the enemy by bold initiative and resolute action."[16] Indigenous people who opposed colonial conquest were not, as a rule, considered to be rational political actors and accordingly could not be negotiated with. The only language that "savages" understood was brute force.

Wood's first action in Jolo was to take a military column of more than five hundred troops and artillery on a week-long tour of the island as a show of force, demanding that the *datus* and Moro chiefs of the different districts appear before him. The sultan was in Singapore at the time, allegedly gambling away what remained of his wealth, and when Wood arrived at Maimbun, he met with the chief minister, Hadji Butu, instead. In no uncertain terms, Wood informed Butu that things were about to change: "A new order of things has come about. A new and very strong country now owns all these islands; that is the United States."[17] The Americans would introduce new laws, Wood explained, and the Moros would simply have to change their ways—even if it might be a slow and difficult process. The new governor also reminded the minister of the ever-present threat of brute force: "We want to do as much as possible through the *dattos* themselves, as we want them to help us in every way they can. But if they do not help us, and things go wrong, we will bring soldiers here and settle the matter in a very short time."[18]

Butu, who was an experienced and crafty statesman, responded mostly in monosyllables. Wood's parting words were in the form of yet another warning: "We shall always be here with sufficient power so that the laws will be obeyed; and shall be very quick to punish any wrongdoing."[19] A few days later, Wood publicly humiliated the sultan's brother, *Rajah* Muda, by having him dragged out of his house and forced to witness a display of American technological superiority—one of the oldest techniques of the colonial tool kit: "We gave him a little artillery practice and sent him home wiser and much meeker. . . ."[20] Marching across the island with his force, officially known as the "First Sulu Expedition," Wood also sought to intimidate *Panglima* Hassan with a demonstration of both machine guns and artillery.[21] This was the Moro chiefs' first experience of Leonard Wood's new style of colonial rule.

Immediately after Wood's tour of the island, he replaced Wallace with his close friend Hugh L. Scott as governor in Jolo in order to ensure both a more assertive style of governance and a ready compliance with his own policies. Although Wood had told Butu that establishing a new colonial order was "going to take time and patience," the new governor had little of either. In September the Legislative Council of the Moro Province, on which Wood had two votes and could effectively dictate policy, introduced a series of acts that had widespread ramifications for the Moros and their society: these included the introduction of a cedula, or poll tax, which would be collected from all adult males; the establishment of a public school system where Moro children would be taught in English; and, most dramatically, a ban on slavery throughout the Sulu Archipelago. Slavery in particular was a sore point of contention between the Americans and the Moros in the region, although the local practice was very different from chattel slavery and more like indenture or debt servitude. In Jolo, slaves constituted a source of political capital as much as a source of labor, and the abolition of slavery directly challenged the status and power of Moro chiefs.[22] Although the American administration was technically bound by the principles of the Bates Treaty, Wood nevertheless insisted—in true Orientalist fashion—that he was working within the framework of Islamic jurisprudence to abolish one of the most central features of Moro society.[23] "It may cause fighting," Captain McCoy noted, "but better [to] fight and [fight] often than permit it longer."[24]

Even before the new legislation was officially announced, a *juramentado* attack in Jolo revealed just how volatile the situation was. On September 25, a single Moro charged a detachment of the 15th Cavalry and managed to

wound a trooper before being shot down, although a stray bullet accidentally killed the regimental bugler.[25] Lieutenant Colonel Rodgers, in command of the 15th Cavalry, recalled the example set by Wallace the previous
March and ordered that the Moro be buried along with a pig: "A deep grave
was dug just outside the walls of the city of Jolo. Stark naked, the juramentado was thrown into it. Above the grave was placed a derrick, from which
was hung a large dead pig. The animal's throat was cut and the blood allowed to fall upon the Moro's body."[26]

The Moros witnessing the spectacle were deeply angered, and various rumors circulated about new policies being implemented. As one newspaper
recounted, "Their anti-American feeling was increased by the receipt of the
news that Gen. Wood intended to disarm every Moro on the island."[27]

In his new role as governor of the island, Scott was at the very same time
trying to maintain some semblance of law and order while also navigating
the different political factions among the Moro chiefs. A minor case involving a Moro named Biroa, who had murdered his former slave, caused much
tension as the Americans tried to get the sultan to apprehend the fugitive.
The sultan in turn reluctantly appealed to the different chiefs, including
Panglima Hassan, who resented outside interference in what he considered a private issue. Hassan had reportedly expressed his frustration with
both the sultan and the Americans: "We Moro Chiefs are attending to this.
Biroa has only killed a slave. If a Moro chief cannot kill a slave, what can he
do? Can he drink water—can he breathe air—hasn't he any rights at all?"[28]

Despite a later meeting between Scott and Hassan, the relationship between the American administration and the Moro chiefs quickly deterio-
rated. Eventually, Scott himself had to take a detachment of soldiers and
negotiate the surrender of Biroa, but the fallout with Hassan remained, and
the headstrong chief soon came to be regarded as the main obstacle to the
establishment of US authority in Jolo.[29]

In early November, a military surveying expedition came under fire while
mapping the foothills east of the town of Jolo. Scott immediately reported
the incident, adding that intractable *datus* were now mobilizing under Hassan and that "an attacking force should be organized to reduce them."[30]
What Scott did not mention, or perhaps failed to realize, was the fact that
November was the month of Ramadan, one of the most important Muslim

festivals, and that the appearance of US troops planting flags on Moro land would inevitably be perceived as a major provocation. A contemporary Moro account described Hassan's response to the attack on the surveying party as he rallied the Moro chiefs: "'Let us all fight. If we don't be quick our religion will be taken away from us.' He called the people from the hills and the coast to go to Andung and help him to fight. 'Let us fight well and not hesitate to protect our religion.'"[31]

At the time, Wood was bogged down with a military force in the swamps near Lake Lanao in Mindanao, yet when he learned of the incident, he immediately abandoned the expedition and instead launched a punitive campaign in Jolo. Outside of Cuba, Wood had so far seen little action, and as a result, he eagerly seized the opportunity to teach the Moros a lesson and to prove his mettle as an officer in the field.

Scott had been in the process of negotiating with the local chiefs, trying to apprehend Hassan without bloodshed, when Wood arrived at the head of a large force. Despite the fact that Scott had a better knowledge of the local situation, Wood simply assumed command.[32] What followed was a brutal punitive expedition, similar to the countless scorched-earth campaigns against Native Americans or the colonial wars fought by European powers throughout Africa and Asia.[33] The first Moro casualties occurred as soon as the troops disembarked near Lake Siet, between Jolo and Luuk, and there was intensive fighting as several large contingents swept the island. Hassan was actually captured shortly after, but the detachment escorting him was subsequently ambushed. Scott was severely injured while Hassan made his escape and went into hiding with his followers. Following this setback, Wood stepped up the operation, as McCoy described: "The infantry swept over every part of [Jolo] and in two days' fighting killed about 300 Moros without the loss of a man. Then Mr. Andung's turn came and his cotta was taken by a pretty bit of work, with the loss of one man killed and three wounded. The lesson will do for all time."[34]

McCoy's description of the expedition made it sound like little more than a game—and considering the negligible losses incurred by the American forces, it probably felt like one. However, the whimsical language obscured the actual extent of the violence suffered by the local population. Another US officer conceded that the killing had been entirely indiscriminate:

"There was considerable destruction of the country necessary to impress the natives. Many cottas were destroyed and many houses burned. Some women and children were unavoidably killed in battle as they mixed with the men."[35]

Wood himself stated that 1,000–1,200 Moros were killed during the expedition, but this was almost certainly an underestimate.[36] Among the Moros of Jolo, the expedition was especially remembered in relation to a massacre of a wedding party, which took place when Wood's force first landed:

> *The first place the Americans came to was Apute's house,*
> *where a wedding party was.*
> *The soldiers fired, nobody could stand against,*
> *People were killed like a flock of birds.*
> *The wedding took place in Saidu's house,*
> *The bridegroom was there, he was the guest of honor.*
> *The soldiers at once went up to them,*
> *The people were killed and smashed up like dough.*[37]

A US officer, who was present, later confirmed the story.[38]

Meanwhile, Wood eventually lost interest in the operation and simply abandoned it, as Scott explained: "General Wood came in from the field in a few days, leaving Hassan still at large. He took his troops back to Mindanao, without any decisive result in Look [Luuk]. . . ."[39] This was characteristic of the impatient general, who had a preference for what the British referred to as "butcher and bolt"—launching a quick and brutal campaign and then quickly withdrawing from the field. But Wood had achieved what he set out to do, and apart from acquiring some much-needed combat experience, he had also "proven" that the Moros were incapable of responsible government. Ever since his arrival in the Moro Province, Wood had effectively been working to create the conditions that would make it possible for the Americans to argue that the sultan and the Moro chiefs had failed to comply with the stipulations of the Bates Treaty.[40] Upon his return to Zamboanga, he submitted a report to Taft, formally recommending that the treaty be abrogated:

[The Moros] are nothing more nor less than an unimportant collection of pirates and highwaymen, living under laws which are intolerable, and there is no reason, in view of the numerous acts of bad faith on their part, why the so-called Bates Agreement should be longer continued, involving as it does the payment of salaries to a number of people who have never been loyal to the United States, and who in their ignorance and conceit interpret this Agreement as indicating that they are a people of great importance and that we are willing to pay them to be good.[41]

One of the key points raised by Wood was the allegedly collective nature of *juramentado* attacks, which allowed him to tar all Moros with the same brush: "It is safe to say that every juramentado who has come into Jolo in recent years has come with the knowledge of the majority of the people of the section in which he lived, and the dato and principal priests of his district, all of whom have directly or indirectly taken part in preparing him for his mission."[42]

The idea that the Moros were irredeemable fanatics was accordingly used not only to justify indiscriminate violence but also to argue for the annulment of what remained of their independence. The report was duly forwarded to Washington, where the official decision would be taken, but Wood had provided the necessary ammunition that allowed the US government to abrogate the Bates Treaty—as it had done so many times before during its long and sordid interaction with Native American nations.

While the American government was preparing to fundamentally change its political standing in the southern Philippines, the hunt for Hassan continued throughout the spring of 1904. Apart from US military forces, Scott was also aided by a number of Moro chiefs, including Indanan and the two brothers, Kalbi and Jokanain, who were only too happy to see one of their rivals defeated and on the run. Hassan kept slipping away from his pursuers, but on February 14, Scott attacked the *cotta* of one of his closest allies, Laksamana Usap, along with a substantial force that included artillery. Usap's *cotta*, known as Pang Pang, was located in the Luuk district and was known to be one of the strongest fortifications in Jolo. Usap refused to surrender, and after a day-long bombardment, the American forces successfully assaulted the *cotta* and killed everyone inside. US casualties amounted to just 7 wounded, but the corpses of some 226 Moros were counted—including women and children.[43] Usap himself had managed to escape.

In early March, Scott and his forces, along with Moro allies, finally tracked down and cornered Hassan in the crater of the extinct volcano known as Bud Bagsak near the coast east of Jolo. Finding himself surrounded, Hassan fought desperately but was hit multiple times and fell heavily wounded into a ravine. Scott described Hassan's final moments as a sergeant carefully approached the Moro chief: "Hassan drew his barong and charged the sergeant, who put a bullet from a Colt .45 through both the chief's ears, and the fight ended then and there, a great joy rising from every side."[44] A military surgeon who inspected Hassan's body told Scott that "he had thirty-two Krag balls through him and was only stopped by the Colt .45—the thirty-third bullet."[45] Hassan soon became part of Moro folklore, celebrated as a brave freedom fighter who embraced martyrdom in defense of the faith, but the circumstances of his death also came to form a crucial part of American mythology in the southern Philippines.[46]

———◆———

Countless stories were told about Moro warriors who seemed impervious to ordinary bullets and who were stopped only when shot by a large-caliber gun through the head. These accounts were largely anecdotal, yet the idea of the unstoppable Moro was one of the most persistent tropes among American troops and came to assume the force of fact. One of Wood's officers, Robert Lee Bullard, even wrote an article, "The Caliber of the Revolver," to lobby for the necessity of replacing the army issue Colt .38 revolver with a heavier and presumably more effective sidearm in the Philippines.[47] Bullard recounted one incident during an expedition near Lake Lanao when he was confronted by a knife-wielding Moro who had entered his boat and cut down several soldiers:

> Too fast to tell I poured four shots into the mad Moro, but to my consternation they seemed wholly, wholly without effect; and in desperation and bitterness of heart, cursing such an arm and the fate that had given it to the soldier to fail him in his hour of need, I spared the last two shots, springing forward in the

last hope of shoving the muzzle against him, and so to *blow* out his brains or heart. . . . I thrust my muzzle against the top of his close-cropped head and fired. Then at last he felt the .38 and sank forward. . . .[48]

As a result, many officers preferred to use the slightly outdated single-action Colt .45 revolver, which fired a larger bullet and was believed to be more effective against Moros. Another weapon that became popular in the Moro Province, for much the same reasons, was the pump-action shotgun, which was highly destructive at close range. In his annual report for 1904, Wood thus recommended that troops stationed in the South be formally equipped with both .45-caliber revolvers and 12-gauge shotguns.[49] Additionally, some troops preferred to simply modify the ammunition with which they had been issued, as one visitor to Jolo described: "The officers claim that the Mauser and Krag bullets have no effect on the Moros when worked up to action, and although against the regulations, most of the soldiers, as well as civilians who carry revolvers, dum-dum their bullets by filing them across the top. This is the only way, they say, of killing at first shot."[50]

When the tip of a bullet was filed down, it would more easily expand upon impact, and a bullet with a diameter of .357 inches could thus cause a much larger and much more destructive exit wound.[51] The term *dum-dum* was derived from the name of a munitions factory in India, where less than a decade before the British had developed similar bullets for the explicit purpose of using them in colonial warfare. The special ammunition, known as the Mark III or Dum-Dum, was based on the same principles as hunting ammunition used against large game such as tigers and rhinos. The perceived need for a special type of bullet thus relied on the implicit dehumanization of nonwhite enemies within the British Empire. Although there were some objections against the use of such bullets, which were explicitly designed to cause horrific wounds, the criticism was quickly dismissed with reference to the "uncivilized" character of the people against whom they were likely to be used. A British medical officer at the time argued the following:

> The employment of a bullet of this destructive character in European warfare might be against the spirit, if not the letter, of the Congress of St. Petersburg; but the fanatical Asiatic knows nothing of congresses, and would only laugh

at the suggestion of waging war on such principles. All his efforts are directed towards causing the greatest possible injury to his enemy, and he fully expects his enemy to do likewise by him. No purely humanitarian sentiments, therefore, need interfere with the use of bullets of a destructive nature by civilized nations when at war with people of this class.[52]

The very same argument was later made by an American officer who had served in the Philippines: "Our soldiers found this practice, which added greatly to the shocking power of the bullet, was about the only thing that assured the stopping in his tracks of a Moro running amuck. The soldiers knew that the Moros had never heard of this convention banning dum-dums and would not be bound by it themselves anyhow."[53]

When expanding bullets were officially prohibited at the Hague Convention in 1899, only two countries refrained from signing the ban: Britain and the United States.[54]

———————

Following the death of Hassan, Wood triumphantly wrote a friend, claiming that the "Moro question" had now been settled: "The Sultan and the Jolo Moros have been completely smashed, and I do not think we shall have any more trouble with them."[55] Despite the protestations of the sultan and the Moro chiefs of Jolo, the American government unilaterally abrogated the Bates Treaty on March 4, 1904—effectively assuming complete control of the region in disregard of preexisting arrangements. The sultan would continue to receive a nominal pension, yet his status was reduced to that of a puppet figure whose position depended entirely on the goodwill of the Americans. The abrogation of the Bates Treaty marked the final abandonment of an American noninterference policy and opened the way for unfettered development of the Moro Province in order to turn it into a "white man's country."[56] A eulogy to the pioneering spirit that had supposedly made the subjugation of the Moros possible was later published by the American-owned newspaper *Manila Times*:

The same spirit which crossed the Rockies, blazed trails through the pathless forests, transformed the vast prairies into fields of waving grain, and won a continent for progress and civilization. And, whether in the frozen fastnesses of Alaska 'neath the weird lights of the aurora borealis, or in the dark and steaming forests 'neath the Southern Cross, where grows the stalwart oak or where rises the graceful palm, that spirit will not be denied. Artificial barriers may be raised against it, and it may be hindered and temporarily checked, but so long as Anglo-Saxon is Anglo-Saxon and natural law holds true it must prevail. And, as has been more than once said in these columns, "to him that hath shall be given and from him that hath not shall be taken away even that which he hath" and, "the fit will enter upon the unimproved heritage of the unfit."[57]

THREE

A State of Unrest, 1904–1905

It seems a shame to have to kill any more Moros, but I suppose civilization has to be shot into them. One would think the severe lesson just administered would be lasting but these people are savages and treacherous and won't stay civilized after a good beating.

Captain Oscar J. Charles, 17th Infantry, Jolo, 1905[1]

FOLLOWING HASSAN'S DEATH, JOLO HAD BEEN RELATIVELY QUIET, although American control remained tenuous in the easternmost district of Luuk. By the mid-summer of 1904, reports reached Scott that one of Hassan's former allies, Laksamana Usap, was reinforcing his *cotta* at Pang Pang, that he was in possession of a number of firearms, and that he had gathered several hundred followers.[2] Scott did not appear to notice that he was deliberately being plied with information that made Usap seem suspicious by Moro chiefs who were trying to oust him. One of Usap's main rivals was Bandahalla, who had recently been promoted by the

Americans. Usap had publicly humiliated him, declaring that "the reason Bandahalla was made Panglima by the Governor and the Sultan, is that he should ask people to pay poll tax."[3] The rivalry was evidently part of a local power struggle, and Usap's enemies had already divided up his land between them.[4] In his official report, Scott noted that Usap had "made his cotta a rendezvous for thieves; refused to come to Jolo when sent for; became a center of rebellion for the whole island. . . ."[5] In reality, Usap hardly posed a serious threat, but the continued existence of the stronghold and the chief's public rejection of American rule exposed the limits of colonial power and undermined Scott's position.

There were several reasons for Usap's defiance, as one Moro explained to Scott: "He wants to come in but he doesn't want to be brought in by force."[6] Being compelled to appear before the Americans was humiliating, as was the demand that Usap demolish his *cotta*, the very symbol of his status in Luuk. Like so many of the other *datus*, Usap furthermore feared that he would be punished if he went to Jolo town. The deep-seated distrust of the Americans was based on prior experience and also a profound uncertainty about the motivation and aims of the new rulers.[7]

Meanwhile, Scott became increasingly concerned that the US administration risked losing face if the intractable chief was allowed to ignore the summons. He informed the Moro chiefs that he wanted Usap "dead or alive" and reminded them that no one could escape his reach—the Americans were able to apprehend anyone anywhere if their authority was challenged.[8] Before a group of loyal *datus*, Scott explained how he controlled them like a horse on a leash—he might let them have more rope, but he could also tighten the reins whenever he wanted.[9] It goes without saying that such language did nothing to allay the fears of any Moros who might be concerned about the shame of submitting to the Americans. Nevertheless, just a few days later, several of the sultan's men brought Usap to Jolo to appear before Scott, who gave the errant Moro chief a stern warning:

> You came in here in good time to save yourself. I had heard that you were digging out a big cotta and a pit [defensive trench]. I went over to Zamboanga and got a gun, a bigger one than I had before to knock down your wall and bamboo fence and throw the stones right on top of you, like a grave.[10]

Usap promised to behave well in the future, and Scott let him go after ordering him to either dismantle his *cotta* or hand it over to Bandahalla. The governor's parting words to Usap were ominous: "Building that cotta was the same as pointing a gun at me. I don't allow anybody to point a gun at me."[11] Although Usap had exhibited signs of genuine contrition, Scott's order to demolish Pang Pang or hand it over to his worst rival was a step too far. Usap had sworn an oath not to give in to the Americans, while publicly berating those Moro chiefs who had, and now he was to suffer the shame of seeing Bandahalla take control of his *cotta*. Once back in Luuk, Usap as a result doubled down on his original stance and began preparing his stronghold for a siege. "If I am fought, I will defend myself," Usap was reported as saying. "I have done nothing wrong."[12] Once Usap went into his *cotta* and prepared to resist the Americans, several of the other chiefs of Luuk felt compelled to stand by him: "Opao said: If the Americans fight Usap and I do not assist him, people could call me a coward. And then all of them stood up and said the same. . . . They have an agreement that all chiefs should help Usap. Whoever would not help him would be cursed by God."[13]

Support for Usap was a matter of religious honor: the disgrace and potential stigma of not staying true to one's word was a vital mobilizing force in Moro resistance to US colonial rule. One of the minor Luuk chiefs, Bairulla, was a particularly vocal supporter of Usap, as a Moro informant later described: "The reason of Bairulla's attitude is the rumours about the poll-tax. Bairulla says he prefers to die; he will not pay one cent. If he goes to Bud Lumping [where Usap's *cotta* was], he will put up 4 pieces of red cloth as flags on 4 banyan trees."[14] Red flags were often flown by the Moros during battle as a symbol of defiance, and the Americans in fact referred to them as "war flags."[15]

As time dragged on and Usap still refused to either dismantle or abandon his *cotta*, Scott decided by January 1905 that the time for action had come. Usap's *cotta* had already been assaulted once during the Hassan campaign the previous year, as Scott noted: "The lesson conveyed at Pang Pang was a very severe one and it was believed that Laksamana Usap would never give any more trouble. . . ."[16] Now it appeared that the effects of the "lesson" had worn off and that new punishment would have to be inflicted. It was furthermore rumored that Usap had buried magic charms in the four corners of the fortification, thereby rendering it unimpregnable.[17] "Cotta Usap was considered by the Moros to be invincible," Scott reported, and it was thus of vital importance that he proved them wrong.[18] As a colonial power that ruled through coercion rather than consent, the Americans could not afford to appear weak: every confrontation between them and the Moros effectively became a test of strength that almost invariably led to bloodshed.

The military and cartographical assertion of US control was closely linked, and the expeditionary force that Scott assembled was concerned not only with the destruction of Usap's *cotta* but also with the completion of the American map of Jolo.[19] Slowly making its way eastward from Jolo town, along the northern coastline of the island, Scott's force passed the heart-shaped Lake Siet and eventually made camp within the district of Luuk. Then a lengthy process of negotiations began as Scott tried to reassure the other chiefs of Luuk that they would be safe while at the same time trying to establish contact with Usap. A number of local *datus* were used as middlemen to negotiate with Usap at Pang Pang and, if possible, to get some of the hundreds of people, including women and children, to leave. That some of these chiefs were, unbeknownst to Scott, pursuing their own feuds against Usap meant that these attempts were doomed to fail: Usap was never going to surrender before his rivals. Having meanwhile ascertained the strength of the *cotta*, Scott sent an officer to Zamboanga to request a six-pound gun from one of the warships in order to be able to breach the heavily fortified walls if negotiations failed.

Scott had previously sent a warning directly to Usap: "I want to make sure that this message gets there, because if I have to go there, I want the women and children away from there. Bullets don't make any difference between men and women. Americans don't make war on women and children."[20] Such a message, however, was unlikely to impress Usap, whose daughter had been killed during the attack on his *cotta* the year before, when he himself had also been wounded and survived only by hiding among the dead.[21] Usap had in fact been heard saying that "if I see the Governor's hands and think of the death of my daughter who was killed in Pang Pang, I may do things that may bring others in trouble."[22] What Scott regarded as blind stubbornness was more likely a matter of anger and grief; the experiences of the previous years' fighting certainly gave the Moros no reason to believe that the Americans would be merciful.

After several days passed with no further progress, Scott finally decided to launch the attack. On January 8, Usap was given one final chance to surrender, but when the only answer received was several shots from the *cotta*, the American troops moved into position. Fire was opened up at close range with no fewer than four artillery pieces, including the large naval gun, in addition to M95 Colt machine guns. By the afternoon, a breach had been effected after nearly four hundred artillery shells had been spent, and ammunition was running low. Throughout the operation, the American troops had received sporadic fire from the jungle behind them, and Scott was far from confident about the situation:

> The position was three miles from water, night was coming on and we had received many warnings from different Moros saying that if the cotta was not taken before night it would be considered an evidence of weakness on our part and all Luuk would rise and assist Usap by reinforcing his cotta and rushing in among us in the darkness with bolos. . . . The talk among the Moros was that, if we did not gain a decided victory in Luuk, Parang would attack the post. Taking into consideration all these facts, I believed that it was necessary to take the cotta by assault.[23]

Although Scott did not have to seriously fear military defeat, he could not risk losing face by failing to take Usap's stronghold there and then. A combined force of US infantry and dismounted cavalry broke through the defenses and charged the *cotta*, which was quickly taken.[24] Just nine Moros remained alive; after they surrendered, they were allowed to leave because Scott wanted to demonstrate that the Americans were merciful and "so induce surrenders in the future."[25] Usap was found dead among the corpses of his followers, and although no body count was made, between 175 and 200 were estimated to have been killed, most from the artillery and machine-gun fire.[26] "The Cotta was a terrible sight," one officer noted, "and should serve as a lesson for some time to come, but this remains to be seen."[27] Scott's force suffered just one dead and three wounded. Before the small expeditionary force left, what remained of Usap's *cotta* was blown up with dynamite to prevent the stronghold from being used again by recalcitrant Moros. The final step was to complete the map of Luuk—the other goal of the expedition—and then the force returned to Jolo, "having accomplished the objects of its mission," as Scott put it.[28]

Scott later arrested an Arab who had been selling magic charms to Usap.[29] The use of talismans and other forms of magic to protect oneself against the enemy's weapons had a long history among the Moros, and sometimes knives and swords would be inscribed with Koranic verses to impart similar protective powers as well.[30] It was hardly coincidental that Usap would have recourse to so-called war magic at a time when the Americans were deploying new and increasingly deadly firearms. Rather than a "superstitious" practice based on "primitive" beliefs, attempts to acquire spiritual protection from the white man's bullets might better be understood as an empowering narrative by people on the receiving end of colonial violence, outgunned by modern weaponry.[31]

In his post-expedition analysis, Scott linked Usap's refusal to comply with the Americans to the broader concerns affecting the entire population of Jolo:

> The whole island was in a state of unrest over the change in the currency and the payment of the cedula tax which was very unpopular. Usap was particularly bitter saying, rather than pay it, he would die in his cotta and declaring that it was a "poll tax," a word which has been used for several generations by the Moros to inflame the people. That this was not a "poll tax" has been many times explained, but it has been continually revived by professional agitators who announce that Americans are going to tax the Moros so they cannot exist, and, in addition are going to make them wear hats.[32]

Although Scott dismissed Moro grievances as the work of "agitators," it was evident that the introduction of the tax was regarded as deeply detrimental to the lives of ordinary Moros. The seemingly silly mention of hats nevertheless reflected an even bigger concern. Historically, the wearing of European hats had been associated not only with Westernization but also with attempts to proselytize colonial subjects; after all, many Christian Filipinos wore hats in the same fashion as did the Americans. Rumors that the Americans were trying to "make them wear hats" was accordingly a clear indication of widespread anxiety that the religious identity of the Moros was under threat. American colonial rule in Jolo was perceived as both a material and a spiritual assault on the Muslim faith and way of life. The conclusion drawn by Scott, however, was not that American policy might need to be changed but rather that future confrontation was inevitable:

> The Moros . . . are a proud and fierce people, unused to foreign domination. Peace has been maintained with them for nearly a year only by the exercise of patience, firmness and diplomacy and these conditions must be expected, notwithstanding the severe lesson received in the past, every time a law is put into effect which they do not like or the arrest of any man for crime is attempted who has a cotta and sufficient influence to induce others to go into the Cotta and die with him.[33]

When Wood informed his superiors in Manila of the successful expedition against Usap, he insisted that there was no longer any "organized resistance on a large scale" in Jolo and that any future disturbances would be "minor" and "matters of military police."[34]

————

After the death of Usap, the issue of the cedula could no longer be postponed. Although Scott had spent much time negotiating with the various *datus* and Moro chiefs to use their authority over their followers and collect the cedula for the US government, little progress had been made by January 1905, when the poll tax became due. During a meeting on January 23, Scott prevailed in getting the sultan to publicly state that the cedula did not interfere with the Moros' religion and that he had taken out the very first one for himself.[35] The plan now was for the main *datus* to pay cedulas for their followers in bulk and then later reclaim the one peso per head on behalf of the government. This was a classic technique of colonial indirect rule, but it put pressure on the relationship between the Moro chiefs and their people. At least one *datu* had been shot and wounded by some of his own followers when he first attempted to collect the cedula. "This tax was still unpopular among the Moros," Scott noted, "many of whom declared that they would die before they would pay it. That it was not the custom of their ancestors, and they would prefer to throw ten pesos in the mud than to pay one to the American Government."[36]

Some progress was made, and the money began coming in, with Kalbi accounting for more than 2,000 and Indanan some 3,000, when an incident in nearby Borneo threw Scott's plans into disarray.[37] In 1903, when the hunt for Hassan had been ongoing, the sultan had offered a reward of 500 pesos to a Moro named Pala if he would assassinate the recalcitrant chief for him. Pala took the money but ended up joining Hassan, and when Hassan was killed, Pala and his men left Jolo and settled on an island near British Borneo.[38] When one of his slaves ran away in January 1905 and sought refuge within British territory, Pala, along with eighteen followers, set off in pursuit in three *prahus* (small boats) to the town of Lahad Datu.[39] Instead of lodging their bladed weapons with the port authorities as formally required, Pala and his men made their way to the house of the British magistrate to inquire about the fugitive slave. When challenged about their weapons, the entire group went on a rampage through the town, indiscriminately attacking anyone they came across. By the time the police arrived, Pala and his men had run into the nearby mangrove swamps to make their escape by sea. Four people were left dead, with four more dying of their wounds soon after and some seventeen others wounded. The attack, it was noted, had been launched by Pala to "relieve his 'sakit hati'"—to wipe away the shame caused to him by the loss of a slave—and it was reported in the British colonial press as a clear case of mass *amok*.[40]

The Americans were also quick to label the attack as a case of *juramentado*, yet the fact that Pala and all his men fled instead of standing their ground and fighting to the end would seem to indicate otherwise. Rather than a case of frenzied insanity, Pala's horrific attack on innocent villagers was a sort of warped retaliation for allegedly providing his former slave with sanctuary. The shame he had suffered was, according to the Moro code of honor, erased by this act of violence. Ultimately, Pala and his men got away despite the efforts of the British authorities, and the fugitives returned to Jolo, where they went into hiding. By early March, Pala was still on the loose, and Wood was becoming nervous that a British request for extradition would embarrass the US government. More importantly, as Wood reminded Scott, the continued failure to capture Pala risked undermining respect for the Americans in Jolo:

> It seems that a failure to arrest men of this kind will be taken as an indication of weakness and do much to oppose the extension of our authority. This man and his people have murdered a number of residents of a friendly country, and undoubtedly a formal request for their extraction will soon be made. If the Moros in the districts referred to are in any way our friends, I cannot see why the arrest of a man of this sort should cause a serious disturbance in the island. If it does it simply indicates that our authority there is still seriously open to question.[41]

As was his wont, Wood believed that quick and decisive action would easily resolve the situation:

> I should think that a squadron of cavalry moving out from Jolo by night and moving rapidly, could reach this place, surround it and take in Pala and his gang without any widespread notice being given. I think the matter is one in which action should be taken, when decided on, with great promptness.[42]

Pala had by this point been traced to an area south of Mount Talipao, but Scott had deliberately refrained from pursuing the fugitive and instead focused on collecting the cedula, "as a failure to carry it out will cause the Moros to think they have made the government to weaken."[43] The situation in Jolo was highly volatile, Scott wrote to Wood, and trying to apprehend Pala at that moment risked upsetting the tenuous progress being made:

> Pala has many relatives and connections in Talipau—the whole island has been uneasy about the change of currency and now about the cedula, many see great evils in both of these [and] some are saying they are against the Koran. You will say "of course that this is absurd—no one thinks of interfering with their religion"—but if they think so it is just the same to them as if it were really so. . . . They are a proud fierce stubborn ignorant fanatic superstitious unstable

people who have the courage of their convictions and are willing to die when
they think the time comes.[44]

Scott knew how easily the Moros might be provoked, and he pleaded
with Wood to let him proceed with caution to try and avoid confrontation:
"If I adopt any other course it would mean the constant attack of cottas[,]
the loss of Americans and the killing off of numerous Moro people & I cannot believe that these results are such as you would wish."[45]

Wood nevertheless insisted that Scott actively pursue Pala, and when the
fugitive was reported to be hiding in a *cotta* on the coast south of Mount
Talipao on March 22, a cavalry force was quickly dispatched.[46] Approaching the stronghold from both the sea and land during the early hours of
dawn, the American troops were nevertheless spotted, and Pala and his
followers managed to slip away into the surrounding jungle. During the
subsequent search, the US troops were fired on from unseen Moros hidden in the dense foliage. The failed expedition was soon recalled to Jolo,
having achieved nothing more than stirring up anti-American sentiments.
Although Pala was on the run because of the killings in British Borneo, he
had, as Scott noted, become "a rallying point for all the discontented, and
particularly those who were most opposed to payment of the cedula tax.
He was constantly drawing supporters; terrorizing the section in which he
was located; was in open and avowed opposition to the sovereignty of the
United States."[47]

The situation continued to deteriorate, and in April a cavalry detachment
was fired on during an expedition to destroy foodstuffs that were allegedly
being stockpiled near Mt. Talipao in preparation for conflict.[48] Followers
of two minor chiefs—Panglima Imlam and Peruka Utig, who were both
based near Bud Dajo—were subsequently blamed for this attack on US
troops and therefore considered to be in league with Pala.[49] For Scott, it
mattered little that to actively resist the destruction of food stores during
a time of political turmoil and widespread hunger was largely a matter of
survival for the Moros.[50]

The very kind of unrest that Scott feared had in fact happened as a result
of Wood's insistence that Pala be apprehended, and now the governor felt

that the situation was getting out of control. Scott went to Zamboanga to talk to Wood personally, but Wood refused to redirect any more troops to Jolo: he had just reported to Manila that the island had finally been pacified after the death of Usap.[51] In the past, Wood had proven himself to be more than happy to deploy his forces on a quick expedition, yet he was evidently worried about the optics of having to undertake a punitive expedition so shortly after he had declared the situation in Jolo to have been settled. An operation at this point in time would be a sign of failure and likely seized upon by his political enemies.

Scott, who had previously favored a less confrontational approach, now found himself in the peculiar position of having to ask Wood for reinforcements so that the Moros of Jolo could be fully subdued:

> The results of a small force operating... among the hills and jungle are very unsatisfactory. You cannot get at the enemy to do him damage and put an end to the trouble and its continuance will bring all the other districts of the island into it for they have grown bolder already and when the others believe they can fight us without damage they will all go, the burning of a few bamboo houses is in reality no punishment to them and they care but little for it.[52]

In this strategy, Scott was invoking the key tenets of colonial warfare, in which the necessity to inflict a "moral lesson" was key. One of the main challenges of colonial warfare, according to Callwell's manual, was the difficulty in striking a decisive blow against an enemy who refused to give battle: "Hill-men and savages . . . dwelling in the bush are very difficult to meet in open ground, they stick to their cover obstinately and never give the [colonial] troops a chance. . . ."[53] Scott's proposed strategy was accordingly to bring about a decisive victory:

> A small column can undoubtedly go about, defend itself and burn a few houses, but it cannot accomplish the results that circumstances call for and every time it fails to make a big impression on the Moros the circle of disturbance widens. It seems to me much better to recognize the facts at once and put the trouble down immediately with a strong hand than to let it grow and spread over the

island and be obliged to call for troops in the end and have a much worse condition settle.[54]

As had been the case at Usap's *cotta*, the prospect of not following through on an armed challenge and inflicting a decisive victory on the Moros was perceived as damaging to American prestige, and Scott repeated his assessment that he did not have sufficient forces to "give them any kind of body blow that will keep the others out of a fight."[55] A defeat of Pala and others openly resisting US rule was accordingly only part of the strategic aim of a punitive expedition, the other—and equally vital—part being to set an example and deter all the Moros of the island from similar resistance.

On April 29, 1905, Wood finally relented and launched what was to become known as the Third Sulu Expedition.[56] Pala was the main target, but local Moro chiefs in the vicinity of Bud Dajo were also included in the field orders as being part of the "opposition." Arriving in Jolo the following morning, General Wood had mobilized a force of 726 US troops, which combined with Scott's force brought the total amount to almost 1,000—including engineers, mountain artillery, and detachments of local troops from the Philippine Scouts as well as the Constabulary for support. This was the biggest force mobilized in Jolo since the Hassan campaign two years before. The troops were provided with ten days' field rations and 150 rounds of ammunition each, and Wood had evidently planned the expedition as a quick and final sweep of the island.[57] Scott also received explicit orders to wait until Wood arrived and personally took charge of the operation.

While Wood and the main force, including infantry and the mountain battery, were to move south from Jolo toward Talipao, Scott and the 3rd Squadron of the 14th Cavalry were to move ahead and assume a position at Mount Kuting, south of Bud Dajo, to cut off any Moros fleeing the main column. The advance guard of the main column first came under fire at Tambang Pass in the morning of May 1 and suffered one dead and one wounded, but the attackers were quickly dispersed. In his diary, Wood noted simply that "the Moros were driven out of their positions and fled across the plain below.

Many of them killed in the action. . . . Moved on, cleaning up the country of hostiles and camped under Mount Suliman."[58]

Early next morning, Wood's forces resumed their sweep of the countryside, setting fire to villages, food supplies, and fields as they advanced. One officer, H. P. Hobbs, remembered how "we did some firing at hostile Moros at long range and burned many of their houses."[59] Watching from his position on Mount Kuting, a few miles away, Scott noticed that "the approach of the main column could be traced by various lines of smoke left in its rear."[60] As the morning progressed, however, it soon became clear that the route taken by Wood ran in an easterly direction and was not driving the enemy south toward the cavalry, as Scott described:

> It was at once seen that this column was coming into the hostile country from the east and that the people instead of running south were making for Mt. Dajo, intending to hide thereon. This suited them better than going towards the coast and also they were more inaccessible than if they had reached the jungle in which Pala was located. The squadron Commander [Scott] at once [pushed] the Squadron forward [to] cut off any further retreat to Dajo, Panglima Imlam had however gotten upon this mountain.[61]

Wood's scorched-earth strategy made no distinction between armed warriors and women and children, and the entire Moro population trapped between the two columns became caught up in the violence and destruction of the punitive expedition. The very first Moros to seek refuge on Bud Dajo were desperately fleeing for their lives, and the American pincer movement left them no other way out.

Frustrated by the attempt to trap the fleeing Moros, Scott and the cavalry column turned its attention to Peruka Utig's *cotta*: "the strong hold of this section and one that had been fortified with the intention of resisting to the death."[62] The *cotta*, which was located about three miles due east of Mount Kuting, was almost surrounded by dense jungle and completely hidden by foliage and bamboo: it could be approached only on foot. Scott's troopers suffered several casualties without being able to locate the defenders, and eventually it was decided to wait for the arrival of the main column. Once Wood and reinforcements arrived, the mountain artillery began shelling the stronghold, but a final attack had to be postponed as the encroaching darkness made it impossible to maneuver. Early the next morning, Wood ordered the final preparations for an attack: "The artillery has been placed in such a position that it is hoped we can drive the Moros out of the cota or at least thoroughly demoralize them that they cannot make much resistance to the infantry attack."[63]

Following a brief bombardment, US infantry and dismounted cavalry assaulted the *cotta*, which was captured after a hard struggle. The American forces suffered six dead and eighteen wounded, which was unusually high, whereas some fifty-four Moros were killed. There were no survivors inside the stronghold, as Wood noted: "Peruka Utig was found dead in his cota also most of his following. It is much to be regretted that there were a number of women killed, but very few children. The women were armed and fighting among the men. Among the women was one known as one of the beautiful women in Jolo. She had been a leading spirit in the uprising and in the resistance."[64]

The main column subsequently proceeded to the jungle south of Mount Talipao in pursuit of Pala, while Scott's squadron "completely overran the country from Dajo through Talipao and on to the town of Maibun."[65] The entire island south of Bud Dajo was scoured by substantive US forces hunting for Pala and the "opposition to Government." On May 5, Pala was cornered in an old *cotta* in the swamp near the southern coastline, and after a brief fight he and his remaining followers were killed, twenty-three in total.[66] One of Pala's allies was shortly afterward surrounded in his stronghold, and because of the intervention of Scott and the memory of what had happened to Utig and Pala, the Moros ultimately surrendered.[67] A few days later, a US detachment killed sixty-eight Moros during a standoff on the small island of Pata, just south of Jolo.[68]

On May 13 the third Sulu Expedition officially ended, and Wood and the reinforcements returned to Zamboanga. The expedition had cost eleven US dead and twenty-five wounded, and although there was no detailed count of enemy casualties, it was later reported in the American press that some six hundred Moros had been killed.[69] A regimental musician wrote a song titled "General Wood's Third Sulu Expedition," which included the following verse:

We started out from Jolo, with a column brave and bold,
To fight those murdering Datos, and their warriors, young and old.
We met stout opposition and the hiking it was bad,
But the loss of our brave comrades, it nearly drove us mad.
We had scarcely reached the outskirts, when we were fired upon,
But we filled the woods with shot and shell, and made the Moros run,
We started in to devastate their "cotas" and their rice
And if Jim Moro tells the truth, he'll say "we did it nice."[70]

This was indeed the shared sentiment among the Americans, and, once again, Wood could report that Jolo had been pacified. He nevertheless cautioned that "periodical trouble must be expected until [the Moros] have thoroughly learned the lesson of obedience to the government, and the hopelessness of resisting it."[71] Immediately after his return from the expedition, Wood decided to leave for the United States in order to undergo surgery on a suspected brain tumor, which was the result of an old head injury.[72] Just ten days later, Wood sailed from Manila, and Scott was accordingly left more or less in control of affairs in Jolo for the next five months. Before leaving, Wood had noted in his diary: "Everything quiet in the province."[73]

The fact of the matter was that Pala and the minor chiefs who had been targeted during the expedition were not particularly important in the context of Moro politics and had not been able to put up any serious resistance against the overwhelming US force during the Third Sulu Expedition. The destruction of the entire countryside around Bud Dajo, however, was far more consequential. At the end of May 1905, Scott was informed that Panglima Imlam, along with one hundred followers, still remained on Bud Dajo.[74] "As to those on Mt. Daho and vicinity," Scott wrote on May 28, 1905, in the very first official report referring to a stronghold on the mountain, "notice has been sent them that if they will turn in their guns and ammunition they will be allowed to surrender."[75]

FOUR

The People on
the Hill, 1905

Panglima Imlam still on Mt. Daho, a volcanic mountain close
to the post, about two thousand feet in height. It has a crater on top with water in it. The sides are so steep that in many
places the Moros climb by vines. It is fortified wherever practicable and is a powerful stronghold.

Major Hugh Lenox Scott, July 1905[1]

T HE VERY FIRST MOROS TO TAKE REFUGE ON BUD DAJO WERE FOL-
lowers of Maharajah Indanan from Parang who went up on the
mountain in early 1905, when Indanan ordered them to pay the cedula.[2]
The stronghold on Bud Dajo was thus established initially as a safe haven
for Moros who refused to accept the much-hated tax and sought to escape
their own chiefs. The Moros on Bud Dajo had in fact endeavored to put
as much distance between themselves and the colonial state and its local
allies as possible, using a strategy of evasion rather than confrontation.
When Indanan later warned his erstwhile followers that their position

was not as impregnable as they thought and that it would be easy for the Americans to take the hill, their reply was plain: "Just leave us to ourselves."[3] When the Third Sulu Expedition took place, Panglima Imlam and his people fled up there, and more soon followed as a result of floods that destroyed what was left of the crops in the plains surrounding Bud Dajo. According to Indanan, the people on the mountain were desperate: "At the time Peruka Utig was fought their houses and homes were destroyed; then they told me that they did not have any houses down below, so where were they going to live?"[4]

On May 31, the deadline for all adult Moro males to have paid the cedula passed, which caused yet another exodus from the lowlands to Bud Dajo; two weeks later, Scott learned that the community on Bud Dajo had grown to more than five hundred men, women, and children. Sawajaan, a Moro chief from Pansul, just south of Bud Dajo, had visited the stronghold and was able to describe how Imlam's group had been joined by two more, with each occupying a position at the top of one of the three trails leading to the summit.[5] The three different factions settled on Bud Dajo reflected the political map of western Jolo, where the territories of the three major Moro power holders of the time converged: the sultan in Maimbun, to the south; Datus Jokanain and Kalbi in Patikul, just east of Jolo; and finally Maharajah Indanan, who controlled Parang on the western coast. Decade-old rivalries between the island's major Moro leaders, including the sultan, were replicated on Bud Dajo, and the three runaway factions were internally divided. The Maimbun faction, under Datu Adam, occupied the southern summit; the Patikul faction, led by Panglima Imlam and Imam Harib, was on the eastern summit; and finally the Parang faction, under Imam Sanuddin and one Agil, occupied the western side. Sawajaan, who was closely aligned with the sultan and who had access to the Maimbun faction leader Datu Adam on the south side, admitted to Scott that he was likely to be killed if he tried to approach the group on the eastern side, for Jokanain and Kalbi were traditionally opposed to the sultan.[6]

According to Sawajaan, there were altogether some 610 Moros, about half of whom were men. He estimated that the three groups had 136 rifles among them and also had stores of *palay* (unhusked rice). At that point, trenches had been dug on the paths, but apart from that there were no defensive positions on the top. Sawajaan also described a fourth group consisting of twenty men who lived in a small structure halfway up the mountain, between the south and east trail; this group was apparently destitute, having sold their buffalos and barely having any food: "Many have nothing, and they have to live on others."[7] There was plenty of water inside the crater, where some sweet potato and tapioca had been planted, but every day the men would have to go down to the foothills to get mangos. When prompted by Scott, Sawajaan said what the people on Bud Dajo had told him: "They say they have gone up there because of the flood, not to fight. . . . They are afraid to go down, as they would have to take out cedulas, and you would take their guns away from them."[8]

With Jolo being relatively quiet, and the collection of cedula finally underway, Scott did not consider it wise to provoke a confrontation:

> Bud Daho was a difficult nut to crack, and I did not want to be obliged to assault it. The Moros had discovered that I could take any of their forts, and if I should fail here it would be a perpetual stronghold for insurgents within five miles of Jolo, and I did not want them to learn how difficult it really was, and have to contend with it more than once. . . . It was plain that many good Americans would have to die before it could be taken, and, after all, what would they be dying for? In order to collect a tax of less than a thousand dollars from savages! Obviously the thing to do was to get the rebels down off that mountain peacefully before it became necessary to make an assault.[9]

A long and drawn-out process of negotiation began during the summer of 1905, with Scott relying on the Moro chiefs, especially Kalbi, Jokanain, and Indanan, to act on his behalf. Another important figure was Charles Schuck, the son of a German traveler who had settled in Jolo and married a Moro woman. Along with his brother, Schuck owned a large plantation northwest of Bud Dajo. The Schuck family enjoyed the trust and respect of many of the Moros, and Charles in particular worked closely with the Americans, both as a translator and as a cultural mediator.[10] By July, some progress was made as Imlam yielded to the pressure asserted by Kalbi and Jokanain, giving up nine guns as a token of good faith, and some of the families went down from Bud Dajo.[11] Most of the Moros nevertheless refused to leave, as Schuck described it: "[They] begged that they be allowed to remain on the hill, as they had already planted their crops for the coming season; that if they left the hill now they would be destitute and they would starve because all their homes and property had been destroyed in the last fight."[12]

Scott replied that he was afraid that the Moros on Bud Dajo would cultivate "bad ideas instead of crops" and that eventually the mountain holdout would become a refuge for thieves and robbers—much as Usap's *cotta* was supposed to have been earlier that year:

> The people, however, were persistent in their prayers, promising to be law abiding and not harbor thieves or criminals, declaring that they themselves were law abiding citizens, that they had not gone upon the hill because they were criminals, but because of fear on account of the late fight; that in view of the labor they had undergone in cultivating in their fields and sowing their crops (their only means of livelihood) it would be a great hardship on them if they left the hill just now, that all they wanted was to stay there until they reaped their crops, which were growing exceedingly well, and that they would come down after the harvest.[13]

After having consulted with the *datus*, as well as Hadji Butu, Scott eventually agreed to allow the people to remain on Bud Dajo until after the harvest, although he enjoined the chiefs to keep trying to get them down.[14] Scott appeared to be only too happy not to have to deal with the Bud Dajo issue for the time being.[15]

———————

On Bud Dajo, the harvest was collected in September, and although a couple of the leaders came down, Imlam and the other groups remained where they were—all the while strengthening their defenses on top of the mountain. Moro resistance to the cedula was never simply an economic matter; it was also a religious one. Similarly to Muslims elsewhere in the world, the Moros perceived the poll tax to be a form of tribute, and thus a symbol of submission to a foreign government of unbelievers. "The attempt to collect the tax," Scott recalled, "was regarded by the Moros as an attack upon Islam."[16] Years before, the Spanish had tried to collect a similar tax but were forced to abandon the project when the Moros rose up in revolt. When a *datu* offered to collect the cedula if he would be recognized as sultan, his own subjects, including Jokanain and Kalbi, turned against him.[17] The Moros had never submitted to the collection of tax by a foreign ruler until the Americans made them do so at the point of the bayonet.

Although American officials such as Scott perceived the standoff at Bud Dajo as merely an upshot of the recent unrest, the fact was that it came at the end of years of devastating military campaigns and all-out assaults on Moro customs and religious practices. Jolo had been the scene of almost constant fighting since Wood's arrival in the summer of 1903, with at least four major punitive expeditions as well as countless military sweeps. The accumulative effect of the establishment of US rule could be measured not only by the number of Moros killed, which was in the thousands, but also by the destruction of villages, crops, and livestock. Following the defeat of Pala, one Moro chief who lived just south of Bud Dajo informed the Americans that his people were simply too poor to pay the cedula: "If the people can get the cedula on credit, to pay when they have the money, they will gladly take them. Or if the Governor will wait till they have the money. The people are now so poor they have to eat roots. There has been so much trouble in their country they have had to leave their homes."[18]

To make matters worse, US economic policies, and especially the change from silver to gold, had severe repercussions for the Moros, as Scott himself acknowledged: "The currency situation is a serious block and an important crisis, there is little money yet among the Moros other than Spanish silver."[19] Oral histories (*kissas*) that to this day circulate among the Moros of Jolo further reveal how the imposition of taxes, the mapping of the land, and numerous other bureaucratic features of the civilizing project were perceived as existential threats.

The establishment of schools for Moro children was regarded with particular suspicion because it was feared that this was part of a wider proselytizing agenda—a fear that was not entirely unfounded. The *kissas* thus warned how the children's minds would be corrupted and how they would no longer respect their elders and would ultimately be turned against their parents. One Moro, hailed for his piety, was known for saying that "even if my body is pulverized, I will not allow my children to go to school."[20]

Despite extensive efforts by the American administration, the schools established in the Sulu Archipelago were thus able to enroll very few Moro
students.[21]

Another grievance concerned the registration of land and the branding
of cattle, which threatened informal claims of hereditary ownership and
was seen as causing divisions among the Moros and making family members fight one another.[22] At the heart of these grievances was a basic fear
that rights to land and livestock would be taken from them and that the
Moros would be displaced, as had so often happened during the many punitive expeditions that had taken place since 1903. Whether it was Western
education or government measures aimed at making the Moros and their
land legible to the colonial state, the *kissas* present a grim narrative of the
Moros' entire world being turned upside down, if not outright destroyed, by
the Americans.

The implementation of American rule in Jolo did indeed have a severely
disruptive effect on social cohesion and local hierarchies of power, and ultimately alienated many Moros from their own leaders. The moral authority
of chiefs like Jokanain and Kalbi traditionally depended on their ability to
mobilize followers, mediate conflicts, and administer justice: the very attri-
butes of power that the Americans had taken away and claimed for themselves as part of a distinctly colonial vision of state sovereignty. This was a
source of great frustration to the Moro elites, as Indanan explained: "If a
chief or headman punishes one of his men, and this man goes to the governor, and appeals to the governor, and the governor tries the case over again,
and it turns out that the governor gives the man the right, then the man
will have no more respect or fear for his chief."[23]

The legitimacy of the sultan and other Moro chiefs had also been com-
promised by their collaboration with the Americans, whom many Moros
regarded simply as infidels. Panglima Hassan had openly rejected the authority of the sultan for this very reason back in 1903, as had Laksamana
Usap a year later. Some of the Moro chiefs closely aligned with the Americans, including Scott's close confidante, Hadji Abdullah, actually had to
live in a blockhouse near Jolo for their own protection, as Scott explained,
"in order to prevent their assassination by other Moros, for being *Ameri-
canistas*."[24] The holdouts on Bud Dajo did not just represent a rejection of

colonial rule but were also a challenge to traditional chiefs; the real danger, Indanan argued, was that the people on the mountain "considered themselves as a government of their own": "Before the Americans came, the Sultan and the Datus were the rulers of the country, the people used to follow them, but after the Americans came the people had the governor. But these people would not follow the governor, they would not follow the Sultan, they would not follow anybody...."[25]

The policies pursued by the Americans in Jolo had systematically undermined the traditional authority of the sultan and the *datus*, even as they relied on these local elites as vital interlocutors between the colonial state and the local population. The expansion of the colonial state furthermore had a very direct impact on the standing of many chiefs for whom the abolition of slavery in particular represented a significant loss, financially and politically. Datu Kalbi, one of the Americans' closest allies, even wrote a letter to the US president in which he complained that the *datus* had never been reimbursed for the loss of their slaves.[26] A second point raised by Kalbi was the "deprivation of the pearl fisheries" by the US government, which in 1904 assumed control of the extremely lucrative pearl beds in the Sulu Archipelago; these had traditionally been in Moro hands.[27] Not only did the government confiscate the pearl beds without compensating the original owners, but the Moros now had to pay the Americans for the right to fish for pearls in their own waters.[28] Some of the Moros evidently benefited from the colonial system, yet many more were left poorer.

By 1905, all opposition to American rule had been brutally crushed, and the only form of resistance that remained was largely symbolic. The refusal to pay the cedula was at this stage one of the few options left for Moros who refused to submit to the Americans—and as such became a matter of both honor and shame.

During one of the many meetings Schuck had with Moros living in the foothills of Bud Dajo, he tried to acquire the help of a local chief, whose brother Sanuddin was one of the leaders on the mountain:

> I said further ask your brother to come and see the governor, and have a talk with him. You may guarantee his safety or the safety of anyone else who goes down to see him. I pledge my word for it. He said, I have tried my best. They

won't listen to me. My brother looks upon me now as an unbeliever, he won't pray in the same mosque with me. I asked why is this. He said, well, on account of the cedula. They believe the governor is going to fight them if they don't pay.[29]

The following day, Schuck managed to talk in person to Agil, another of the leaders on Bud Dajo, who had come down to attend a local wedding along with twenty of his heavily armed followers. Schuck tried to convince Agil and the gathered Moros that the Americans had their best interests in mind and that living conditions were much better in Jolo than they had been under Spanish rule. He then directly addressed the matter of the holdout on Bud Dajo:

Agil said that he had an agreement with the other leaders to remain on the hill, and he would be disgraced if he broke his word. I said there is no disgrace if a person does something that benefits the country. Set the example and they will follow suit. He said that the reason we live upon the hill is because we are afraid to stay down below. I assured him that he would be perfectly safe, as long as he did nothing wrong. He said that he was a law abiding citizen, but could not go back on his agreement. On taking leave, I said, now that I have paid you a visit I hope you will pay me a visit in return. He said, perhaps, I will try.[30]

When another of Scott's Moro allies talked to Agil a week later, he was still adamant that he would not come down and he would certainly not go to Jolo to see the governor.[31] By late fall of 1905, however, living conditions at the top of Bud Dajo appeared to be deteriorating, as Sawajaan informed Scott:

The pallay [rice] at first grew splendidly, but it yielded very little pallay, almost nothing. They have to come down the hill to work their hemp in order to get a living. A great many come down and remain there a few nights, working the hemp, then returning to the top of the hill after having sold their hemp. Nothing grows well up there. And they do not enjoy the comfort of a man on that hill.[32]

There were also reports that a thief, Abu Kahal, had stolen some horses and arms from a local Moro chief and sought refuge on Bud Dajo, where

Imlam and Harib were said to be protecting him on the eastern summit.[33] The theft of cattle and horses was endemic in Jolo, yet what the Americans perceived as a reflection of lawlessness was in fact an intrinsic part of local politics. When arrested by the Americans for stealing carabao (water buffalo) from his longtime rival, one Moro defended himself by explaining that "I am no thief, we were enemies. . . ."[34] Within the moral economy of the Moros, cattle raids were considered a legitimate and even honorable way to pursue feuds.[35]

The presence of different factions on Bud Dajo, all of whom were part of different kinship networks and alliances, further complicated the matter.[36] Old feuds also lingered, and Jokanain would later accuse one of Sawajaan's men, on the south side of Bud Dajo, of stealing his cattle.[37] Although Scott claimed that the people on Bud Dajo were now engaging in cattle theft and were preying on peaceful Moros, his informants and the *datus* most loyal to the Americans were far less confident. When asked about the matter, Jokanain simply said that "I do not know whether they committed these depredations or not, it was reported that they did."[38] The fact remained that the stronghold on Bud Dajo provided a convenient foil for Moros elsewhere on the island, as Hadji Butu explained: "People from Look [Luuk] and other parts of the country would commit depredations, and steal, and it would be laid to the Dajo people, and that is what they said when they were told to come down from the mountain."[39]

Divided by different loyalties, the Moros on Bud Dajo nevertheless remained united in their opposition to US rule. While Sanuddin and Agil, on the western crest, declared that they would not help Harib, on the eastern side, to protect thieves, they insisted that they would help him if he was attacked by the Americans on account of the cedula.[40]

———

"The situation continued very tranquil all autumn," Scott later recalled, "until I went up to Zamboanga for three days at Thanksgiving." November was the month of Ramadan, when Muslims would traditionally fast and pray during the day, and the Moros would be particularly sensitive about any perceived inflictions of religious practices. On Bud Dajo, the breaking of fast on November 29 was celebrated with a feast at which a buffalo and two cows, which had been stolen from Schuck, were slaughtered as was custom for the Hari Raya (Eid) festival.[41] Hundreds of people had gathered for this important occasion when some of the Moros on the east side returned from the valley below and started beating their gongs.[42] Rumors soon spread to all the people on the mountain, as Jokanain described, "to the effect that the Americans were going to attack the hill and that the people were very much excited over it."[43] "They got ready for a fight," Scott was later informed, and "many of their relatives from below went up on the mountain, beat their gongs all night expecting an attack at daylight. They considered that a state of war was on. . . ."[44] The panic, however unfounded, had the effect of strengthening the resolve of the Moros on Bud Dajo, as well as in the surrounding lowland areas, and reinforcing their commitment to taking a firm stand against the Americans. When Scott returned to Jolo in early December, he found the situation regarding Bud Dajo had dramatically changed, and he lamented that "the work of getting them down had to be started all over again."[45] According to Schuck, the Moros on the mountain began openly challenging the Americans:

> Then rumours here and there sprang up that they were beginning to be rather defiant, going to their markets only in large numbers and armed with rifles, spears etc. Friendly Moros, who acted as secret service men, reported that fortifications had been built along the trails leading up the hill, and that the place generally was considered impregnable. On several occasions when troops passed near the mountain on their practice marches through the island, gongs were beaten on the hill to warn those who had come down in search of food or on some other business in order that they could get back to the hill.[46]

Bud Dajo was first identified as a potentially serious problem for the US administration on December 5, 1905, when Scott sent a brief notice to Captain G. T. Langhorne, Wood's secretary in Zamboanga:

> There is some unrest among the Moros of Mount Dajo which may turn serious. Negotiations are now going on thro' Joaxanain who hopes to allay it. If he does not it will be bad for that mountain is a hard proposition to take. Am doing the

most we can do and hope to pull through and get our ends without proceeding to extremities.[47]

Given the weakness of the military force available in Jolo, the news worried Wood, who at once prepared reinforcements to get ready for deployment to Jolo. When Scott next saw Wood in Zamboanga, he nevertheless reassured the colonel that everything was under control: "[I] told him the two companies of the 19th would not be needed for the present, as the Moros were being kept down by Jokanain and the order sending them to Jolo was revoked."[48]

Soon after, Jokanain actually made some progress and came to Jolo along with Datu Acku, who was occupying the eastern crest of Bud Dajo along with Imlam and Harib. Acku had not set foot in Jolo since the Spanish occupied the town in 1876, and Schuck, who acted as translator, later described the chief's meeting with Scott:

> The Governor had a long talk with Acku, saying that he had nothing but the kindest feelings for him and all the Moro people, that it was the aim of the Government to make them rich and happy. He advised them to plant cocoanuts and hemp and not live on a hill where they did not have the same facilities as down below. He advised Acku to go back to the hill and advise the others to follow his example, and to show them that the Governor did not hurt him; that it was not for the Governor's good, but for their own and their families if they went back to their homes, now that the harvest was over, and get ready to prepare new fields for the coming season.[49]

Before Acku left, Scott gifted him a black dog, a much-prized status symbol in Jolo, and the Moro was so pleased with his present that he carried the dog home in his arms. The result was that Acku subsequently came down from Bud Dajo and brought his family with him. In the hope of keeping up the momentum, Jokanain convinced Acku to negotiate on behalf of the authorities, as Schuck recounted:

> Then Acku made a visit to Dajo hill, and related his experiences to his former comrades. He told them all that the governor had said and urged them to follow

his example. They jeered at him, complimented him because he was still alive, and called him an American, and a coward. Very much disheartened, Acku descended, and when Jokanein asked him again to go up he refused to do so, saying that he preferred to be killed on the instant, than to expose himself again to such insults.[50]

At one point, Datu Kalbi sent two men up to negotiate with the people on Bud Dajo, but they received a reception similar to that of Acku, with the "Dajo people jeering them and calling them Americans."[51] By openly shaming those who left Bud Dajo, the remaining Moros effectively committed themselves to staying, come what may. Fear of losing face was further combined with peer pressure, as Sawajaan also explained to Scott:

> I have tried to convince people on Bud Dajo to come down. I went to see Adam on Bud Dajo. I tried to persuade him to follow me to Jolo to see the Governor [Scott], but he said that he was afraid of the people on the other side of the hill. If he come down the hill, they will take away his property and his wife and children, and besides he is closely watched. He has all his property on the hill.[52]

"The people on the other side of the hill" were Imam Harib and Imam Sanuddin, who as religious figures were able to exert spiritual authority over the other Moros on Bud Dajo. One US officer claimed that "twice the Colonel had persuaded the poor fanatics to come down off their perch and go home, and just so often the priests and easily influenced wives shamed the men back to defiance."[53] This was obviously a biased assessment, yet it would appear that appeals to religion and honor were crucial in maintaining the cohesion of the different factions on the mountain.

———◆———

As the end of the year drew nearer, Scott was preparing to leave for the United States, a much-needed trip home that had been postponed several times already. In his absence, Scott's position as Jolo district governor was to be taken over by Captain James H. Reeves of the 14th Cavalry, a relatively young West Pointer from Alabama who had served both in Cuba and during the Boxer Rebellion in China. Before he left Jolo, Scott had a final meeting with the sultan, Maharajah Indanan, and several other Moro chiefs and reminded them "to keep the peace and look out for the Dajo people."[54] On New Year's Day of 1905, Scott stopped over briefly in Zamboanga to see Wood and reassure him that all was well:

> Only eight men remained on top of Bud Dajo with their families by Christmas-time, and these were very peaceable and could be brought down one or two at a time if gently handled; once their tax was paid they would have no incentive to run away again. This was the condition when I left for a four month's leave in the United States in January 1906, with peace everywhere in the archipelago.[55]

This was a dangerously naive prognosis. The number of Moros who remained on the mountain was far greater than Scott admitted, and it was hardly reasonable to expect that the local chiefs would be able to assert any authority over their estranged followers. Jokanain himself admitted as much, as one American noted: "He freely says that he has not much control of the people."[56] Worst of all, Scott underestimated the depth of the Moros' despair and defiance. Following Scott's departure, Reeves nevertheless continued the strategy of sending up loyal Moros to try to convince the people on Bud Dajo to come down. One of these mediators later recounted that "I told them to come off the hill, that there was nothing against them, that if they stayed up on the hill the troops would come to them, and that they were already protecting thieves; that it would be best for them to come off the hill and keep out of trouble."[57]

The man went up Bud Dajo at least three times: "My knees got very sore from going up and down the hill from talking to them; I did my best."[58] However, his efforts were wasted and might even have made matters worse; the warning that troops would attack Bud Dajo unless the Moros came down was more likely to confirm their fears and strengthen their resolve to remain. The Americans also believed that the precedent set by other Moros who had in the past surrendered to US forces—including a chief named Hati who had abandoned his *cotta* and given himself over to Wood during the Third Sulu Expedition—would help convince the people on Bud Dajo to come down. As Jokanain explained, such examples actually had the opposite effect: "The people on the hill would not come down, they would not surrender, because they were very proud, they did not want to be treated the way Hati's people were treated, have their guns taken away, and this is why they did not behave like Hati did."[59]

In their refusal to submit to American authority, the Moros on Bud Dajo were not simply defending their own honor but that of the entire Muslim community in Sulu—the *umma*. Their defiance was in truth a response to decades of incessant conflict and the slow but seemingly inevitable destruction of their way of life. Reeves was explicitly informed by Jokanain and Kalbi that the Moros on the mountain were

> making a daily boast that they have established a strong point, in fact, an impregnable position, and that they are in open defiance of the American authority, and that we can not take their position, that we cannot force them off the hill and cannot make them obey the laws. They further boast that but for this the American government would have run rough-shod over all the Moro people. They claim, in fact, to be a set of patriots and semi-liberators of the Moro people.[60]

To the Americans, Moro resistance to the colonial order was perceived as irrational and morally illegitimate; in regards to the holdout on Bud Dajo, General Wood later claimed that "back of it all it is not the cedula, it is not anything in particular, it is the general desire to be rid of the white man's control."[61] One of the defining features of the imperialist project during the turn of the century was the inability of colonizers themselves to recognize their primary role in creating the conditions for mass violence in the first instance. It never seemed to occur to the likes of Wood and other American officials that conquest by a foreign government, taxation without representation, the abolition of slavery, or the threat of disarmament might cause resentment among a proud people with a long history of fighting for their independence.

A traditional Moro *kissa* titled "The Fight at Bud Dajo" describes the defiance of the group of *datus* who gathered their followers on the mountain, including the historical figures of Adam and Agil:

The seven Datus
Climbed up Bud Dajo
To fight the Americans
For they refused to give in

Even if all of them are killed
They have already agreed
Whatever happens to them
They will not get the cedula

They refused to register their land
Seven of them agreed to support one another
Even if their bodies would be broken
They refused to let their cattle be marked

Adam answered the call
Brandishing his barong
If their land was to be registered
He would rather burn it

The people of Dajo
Refused to send their children to school
Agil said:
He was prepared to die fighting

Bud Dajo will not surrender.[62]

FIVE

They Will Probably Have to Be Exterminated

[T]he art of war is a natural art of acquisition, for the art of acquisition includes hunting, an art which we ought to practice against wild beasts, and against men who, though intended by nature to be governed, will not submit; for war of such a kind is naturally just.

Aristotle, *Politics*, Book 1, Part 8

L EONARD WOOD'S SURGERY IN BOSTON IN JUNE 1905 HAD BEEN SUCcessful, and after a few months' rest he left for the Philippines, once again traveling eastward through the Suez Canal. As had been the case during his first trip, he made the acquaintance of various British officers destined for service in colonial India. Among these officers was General Sir Archibald Hunter, who had personally commanded the Egyptian Army Division at the Battle of Omdurman in 1898 during the Soudan expedition.[1] During this battle, the Anglo-Egyptian force under the command of Major-General Kitchener, as well as Hunter, deployed and tested the very latest military technology against the numerically superior Mahdist forces under Abdullah al-Khalifa.[2] As thousands of Mahdists launched a mass assault over open ground against the Anglo-Egyptian lines, they were met by a deadly hail of Lyddite shells launched from rapid-firing artillery and by expanding bullets fired from Maxim machine guns at a rate of 600 per minute. Altogether, Kitchener and Hunter's troops expended more than 200,000 rifle rounds, and the Mahdists never made it closer than a thousand yards; an estimated 11,000 were killed and 16,000 wounded. The combined British and Egyptian forces suffered just 48 killed and 148 wounded. "It was not a battle," a British journalist noted, "but an execution."[3] With little else to do on the slow journey through the Red Sea, Wood noted how he "enjoyed many long pleasant talks with General Hunter."[4]

Wood arrived in Manila in late October of 1905, but it was not until the following January that he found the time for an inspection tour of the different US posts in the Sulu Archipelago, including a one-day stopover in Jolo on January 9. The officer commanding the military station at Jolo, Major E. F. Wilcox, 4th Cavalry, did not make a positive impression on Wood, who dismissed him simply as a "drunkard."[5] Wood had full confidence in Scott's replacement, though, as he noted in his diary: "Reeves is an excellent officer, fully alive to the situation. Told him in case of an emergency to communicate directly with me and to state exactly what the conditions were."[6] Although the situation in Jolo appeared to have been settled, Wood was evidently keen to ensure that it remained that way.

By early 1906, Wood learned that he was to take over the Philippine Division from General H. C. Corbin, which would make him the senior commander of US forces in all the Philippines. This was a big position that Wood had coveted, and it would serve well as a stepping-stone for his career. Wood's successor as governor of the Moro Province, and hence taking over responsibility for Jolo, was General Tasker H. Bliss, who was supposed to assume that role on February 1. However, Wood was not yet ready to relinquish control over the Moro Province because, as he noted in his diary, "there are a number of things I want to complete before turning things over to [Bliss]."[7] The result of this irregular move was that from February onward, Wood occupied two senior military positions simultaneously. As governor of the Moro Province, he would answer only to himself in the double role as commander of the Philippine Division. This effectively dispensed with any pretense of administrational checks and balances, and allowed Wood to operate with absolute discretionary power in the South. The unfinished business that Wood referred to was indeed the situation in Jolo, as he noted in his diary: "The only serious situation remaining there is the presence of a considerable number of disconcerted people in the crater and on the slopes of Bud Dajo. These people represent the remnants of all the hostile bands which have been broken up."[8]

Wood had effectively staked his career on his success as the subjugator of the Moros, and having already declared mission accomplished several times over the course of the previous three years, he could hardly leave the province with any unresolved trouble. As Wood was later to admit to Roosevelt, this was a matter of pride: "I felt that I should clean up this place before I left the department and turned over the Governorship to General Bliss."[9] In his new role as commander of the Philippine Division, Wood nevertheless had more urgent issues to deal with.

In early February, Wood had unexpectedly received orders to draw up plans for a military expedition to China to protect US interests in Canton and other port cities.[10] Relations between China and the US had been tense for a while, not least because of US discriminatory immigration policies that had led to a widespread boycott of American goods in China. Troops were also being mobilized in the US itself, and officers on their way to San Francisco to board transport ships told journalists that "while they are ostensibly going to the Philippines, it is not because they are really needed for duty there, but to be held in reserve in case there is a Boxer uprising in China against the several thousand Americans who are in the confines of the oriental land."[11] In 1900 an international relief expedition that included US troops had been sent to Peking to relieve the foreign legations and defeat what was known as the Boxer Rebellion. The popular movement known as the Boxers was completely crushed, and the Chinese government had to settle for a humiliating peace and give in to the demands of the Western powers. With a possible resurgence of antiforeign unrest in China and the Russo-Japanese War having been so recently brought to an end, it was now deemed necessary to make the American presence in the region felt.

Wood immediately sprang into action, gathering provisions, mobilizing an expeditionary force more than twice as large as the one that had been launched in 1900, and putting troops on the alert across the Philippine islands, including Jolo and nearby Malabang.[12] After several weeks of hectic activity, Wood informed Roosevelt that the preparations for the expedition were almost complete:

> I have got everything ready here to move 5,000 troops on the shortest notice. By this I mean that we have figured out everything pertaining to an expedition, so that troops can be landed ready to fight and to live, and supplies from the store-ships can be reached for any department without interference with those of any other. I of course want to go in command of this expedition.[13]

Wood evidently regarded the prospect of leading a major military expedition as a god-sent opportunity to earn fame and glory—just as he and Roosevelt had done in Cuba. The political crisis soon passed, however, and nothing ultimately came of the China expedition; it was indeed unlikely that it had ever been more than a contingency plan, as Roosevelt later informed Wood: "I wanted to be sure that if it was needed, we would not be unprepared."[14]

———

While Wood was busy in Manila, events continued to unfold in Jolo. Initially, things had gone well for Reeves, and in his weekly updates to Scott, he noted simply that all remained quiet in Jolo: "Have heard nothing from the Daho crowd since you left."[15] Yet Reeves did not have nearly as much experience dealing with the Moros as his predecessor did, and he also lacked the personal connections that had allowed Scott to navigate the intricacies of local politics in Jolo. On January 31 the military target range near the barracks in Asturias was set on fire, and a storage building with targets, flags, and other inventory was completely destroyed.[16] Considering how much effort the Americans took to demonstrate their technological superiority to intimidate the Moros—firing cannon and machine guns for display—the shooting range was perhaps not such an odd target for locals to express their defiance of the authorities. The fact that the streamer pole on the range had been riddled by bullets strongly suggested that this seemingly random destruction of government property was primarily symbolic.[17] Despite the lack of evidence, Reeves was quick to identify who the attackers were:

> On the night of January 31st, the house on the target range was burned, and the target butts partially destroyed. At once every effort was made to find and punish the perpetrators, but nothing definitely could be obtained, other than that all the people said it was done by Moros from Daho. The target range was again visited on February 7th, and further depredations committed. In the meantime it was definitely known that the thief who stole the property near Mr. Schuck's house about December 1st, was on Bud Daho.[18]

Reeves was in fact responding to the alarmist information provided by Jokanain, Kalbi, and other Moro chiefs who were by this stage openly encouraging the Americans to attack Bud Dajo. Not only did the presence of the holdout on the mountain challenge US authority; it was also a source of embarrassment for the Moro chiefs, who had so evidently lost control over their own followers.[19] It would thus appear that all sorts of crimes were being blamed on the people on Bud Dajo, who provided a convenient scapegoat. At the same time, it was in the interest of the colonial administration to portray the runaways on the mountain as the only troublemakers in Jolo, isolated from the majority of loyal and law-abiding Moros. When a band of suspected thieves was apprehended in Luuk, on the easternmost side of the island, Reeves was informed that some of them had run away to join the people on Bud Dajo. "About this time," the acting governor reported, "several strange people were picked up in Lati District, who could give no good account of themselves, but it was believed they were part of this band making their way to Bud Daho."[20] The fact that these stories were based on nothing more than rumors did not trouble Reeves, who seemed to be prepared to believe the worst; his reports at the time indeed had all the hallmarks of a colonial panic.[21] Afraid that any inaction would ultimately be held against him, Reeves decided to alert Langhorne in Zamboanga and inform him that things had come to a head regarding Bud Dajo.[22] Crucially, Reeves also included a plan for how the Americans might be able to seize the stronghold when he wrote Langhorne around February 8—accompanied by a simple line drawing.

Rather than simply assaulting the stronghold, Reeves suggested that the internal divisions among the Moros could be exploited and that one of them could be bribed to allow the Americans to gain the summit unopposed:

> To the top of the mountain there are only three steep trails, each fortified, and each protected by a gang of Moros. Those at "A" guard the trail towards Maymbun [and] are of the Sultan's people who were determined to assist the two other parties in their resistance against the payment of cedulas, but they are not willing to assist the others at present in the protection of cattle thieves and outlaws. The other two parties are said to have received cattle thieves and offenders lately, and are harbouring and intending to protect them. They are becoming a menace to the people in the lowlands, as they go down in bunches and rob them of their cattle and other things.[23]

The faction most amenable to such a proposition was thus believed to be Datu Adam's on the southern crest: the Maimbun faction. Langhorne immediately forwarded the report to Wood in Manila, along with his own assessment:

> The Moros on Daho mountain, back of Jolo, are violating their alleged agreement in that there are two parties of them now harbouring cattle thieves and other outlaws and giving trouble. They will probably have to be exterminated. . . . Reeves may be able to win over the party at "A," that is, the Maymbun outfit, so that they will receive and guide the party of infantry which might go

over the trail in the night and at daylight fall upon the other two and exterminate them, the other trails being guarded below. In case of treachery, of course
this assaulting party would have to take the consequences, which they would
probably easily do.[24]

Langhorne finished his message to Wood by emphasizing the urgency of
the matter: "If you approve of this plan, please wire your consent to it as it
might become over-ripe, and negotiations that would once work up to the
right point might afterwards fail."[25] Occupied with the plans for the China
expedition in Manila, Wood did not respond until February 17, when he
sent a terse telegram to Langhorne: "Arrangements concerning cleaning up
of Daho can be made. Hold actual execution unless absolutely necessary to
do otherwise until my arrival."[26] With everything prepared for a major expedition, and thousands of troops ready to go, the last thing Wood needed
was an outbreak in Jolo that might require his attention and perhaps keep
him occupied while others reaped the glory on the battlefield in China. The
ambitious general had in fact told Langhorne that he regarded Bud Dajo as
a minor inconvenience and a distraction: "This is a ridiculous little affair,
from every standpoint, and should be brought to an end. . . . A couple of columns should take the place some night and clean it up."[27] That was exactly
what he had told Scott about Pala a year before.

By early February 1906, the US military administration was accordingly
pursuing a strategy that involved the "extermination" of the Moros on Bud
Dajo. The language of "extermination" had a long history in the US, where
it was routinely invoked as a key feature of settler violence and military operations against Native Americans, in what amounted to a centuries-long,
drawn-out genocide.[28] In 1866, for instance, Union general William
T. Sherman stated that "we must act with vindictive earnestness against
the Sioux, even to their extermination, men, women and children."[29] To
be sure, "extermination" had different connotations in the US than in the
southern Philippines, and Langhorne was not advocating a genocide against
the Moros—but he was recommending the unrestrained use of indiscriminate violence against those entrenched on Bud Dajo. This approach was of
course characteristic of the kind of warfare conducted by European imperialist powers at the time, and the British tactician Callwell insisted that

when fighting "savages," "success in action shall mean not merely the defeat of the hostile forces but their destruction."[30] At the situational level, it hardly mattered whether an attack on a village or stronghold was part of a project of genocidal settler violence or a colonial punitive expedition—the result was the same.[31] Wood's phrasing in his response to Langhorne, giving the green light to "clean up" Bud Dajo, simply added a euphemistic gloss that sanitized the logic of colonial violence: literally and figuratively.

On February 25, having finalized all the preparations for the China expedition, Wood informed Henry Clay Ide, governor-general of the Philippines, that he was leaving for Zamboanga, expecting to be away for about a week, "to make the preliminary arrangements for the transfer of the Moro Province to my successor, which I recommend be made on or about April 1, 1906."[32] Wood was eager to tie up any loose ends as quickly as possible before handing over; no mention whatsoever was made of Bud Dajo. That same evening, Wood left Manila on the small steamer *Sabah* along with General Bliss, their aides, and a few other civilians, including "a Mr Wright and his stenographer."[33] Originally from Connecticut, Hamilton M. Wright had relocated to California for health reasons; after receiving a law degree in 1899, he began working as a journalist for various newspapers in Los Angeles.[34] By 1905, he was doing publicity work for the California Promotion Committee, which had been set up to advertise the state's resources for investors and migrants.[35] That same year, Wright was sponsored by the Pacific Commercial Museum to undertake a trip to the Philippines in order to promote the islands.[36]

The first article Wright wrote from the Philippines set the tone for much of his subsequent journalism: "Opportunities in the Orient" described Luzon as a fertile *terra nullius* just waiting for white settlers and investors. "There is lots of money to be made by American capital in hemp, tobacco, copra, cocoanut, sugar and rice growing," he advised.[37] This was followed by a spate of articles, sold through the Newspaper Enterprise Association to a range of papers and magazines, that varied between shameless advertisements for settler colonialism and more ethnographic accounts.[38] Wright simply happened to be in Manila at the time of Wood's departure and went to Zamboanga to collect more material for his articles.

Wood and his entourage arrived in Zamboanga on February 28 and was informed by Langhorne "that affairs at Jolo are in such shape as to require action immediately."[39] Rather than proceeding to Jolo himself, however, Wood simply let General Bliss and his aides, along with Wright, continue onboard the *Sabah*. Wood did not inform Bliss that any operations were underway in Jolo and instead just gave his successor a written dispatch to Reeves with instructions to furnish Bliss with a cavalry escort for an inspection tour of the island.[40] Despite his earlier concerns about leaving unfinished business behind, Wood had apparently convinced himself that the situation on Bud Dajo did not require his personal attention. His perfunctory diary entry for March 1 indeed gave little indication of the events that he had set in motion: "Busy at headquarters all morning. Afternoon, out shooting on the *mesa*; had fair luck."[41]

In Jolo, Reeves had received notification from Langhorne that Wood had given the green light to go ahead with his proposed plan. The acting governor's first move was to provide a legal pretext for military intervention, as he himself later explained to Wood:

> I then went forward with the civil side of the case so far as to make it a clear case wherein the civil authorities have failed and we can legally call upon the Military to step in and take charge. Acting upon this idea I have issued a warrant of arrest for a certain thief who stole property from Mr. Schuck's, took his property up on the mountain and has been protected there.[42]

On February 21, Reeves thus issued a warrant for Abu Kahal, who was suspected of having stolen items from Schuck almost three months before and who was now said to be hiding on Bud Dajo. Another Moro fugitive, Sahiron, was likewise said to be in hiding on the mountain: "It became definitely known that Sahiron, a follower of Jokanain, something of an outlaw, was on the hill. Sahiron had been tried and fined by the Datu in accordance

with the Moro law, but refused to pay his fine or conform to the decision of
the trial, and went to Bud Dajo, where he found a ready shelter."[43]

The entire community on the mountain consisted of Moros who defied
their chiefs, however, and this was hardly the damning evidence that Reeves
thought it to be. Yet Sahiron enjoyed something of a legendary status
among the Moros of the island, and it was his name that later became most
closely associated with Bud Dajo in local folklore. Reeves called on Indanan
to make the arrest but to no avail, just as the acting governor had expected:
"The leaders on Daho refused to give up the thief or property or allow the
warrant to be executed."[44] The fact was that the decision for a military operation to get the Moros off Bud Dajo had already been made; Reeves was at
this point merely going through the motions of due process. He also summoned Jokanain and Kalbi, and instructed them to use whatever authority
they possessed to convince the Moros on Bud Dajo to surrender:

> I sent them out to make one more effort to persuade these people to come down,
> giving the order as the chiefs and headmen of these people. Failing in that, to
> give it to them as the Governor's order. I told the Dattos to be as expeditious
> about this matter as possible. To let me know at once the results after they had
> made all efforts.[45]

Meanwhile, military preparations got underway, and since Bud Dajo
had not previously been the scene of fighting, US cavalry and artillery detachments from the Jolo garrison made a reconnaissance around the mountain.[46] Captain E. F. McGlachlin, commanding the 28th Battery, stationed
in Jolo, along with Major Wilcox, went out with seventy troops and found
a suitable position for the artillery southeast of Bud Dajo, from where the
cotta on the southern summit could be targeted. "Although we were in plain
view we were not seen for ten or fifteen minutes," McGlachlin later recalled:

> But then their gongs commenced to beat and many gathered at the cotta and
> yelled most defiantly at us. Whatever they said would not bear repeating, I
> imagine. When we had determined the range and made some sketches we came
> back by the base, found two of the trails, determined where there was water and
> good camping ground and came home. We were followed by a crowd on the

edge of the crater still yelling who finally put up a red flag which we interpreted to be a final act of defiance, but did not shoot.[47]

Considering the panic caused by rumors of an imminent American attack in late November, the actual appearance of a large military force in the vicinity of the stronghold was bound to provoke the defiant Moros. If the negotiations had previously stood little chance of success, they were now destined to fail. When Jokanain and Kalbi left to make a final attempt at negotiating a surrender in late February, Reeves noted their parting words:

> [The two chiefs] told me they would let me know by Sunday, March 4th, but that if in the meantime I saw General Wood, simply tell him that their efforts had failed, that they could do nothing. They said they believed these people had gone up there to die, and that they would fight, and further that they would force our hand by committing depredations[, and] that they could see no peaceful solution.[48]

In the early hours of March 2, the small gunboat *Busuanga*—one of the many little vessels that constantly cruised back and forth between the dispersed islands of the Sulu Archipelago that had no other contact to the outside world—arrived in Zamboanga. It carried three urgent messages from Jolo: from Reeves, Wilcox, and Bliss, respectively. Reeves's letter, addressed to Langhorne, described the confusion caused when Bliss arrived in Jolo without any knowledge of what was going on.[49] Reeves and Wilcox had expected General Wood at the head of reinforcements for the expedition against Bud Dajo. The acting governor nevertheless described all the preparations he had made, including the issuance of a warrant and Jokanain and Kalbi's latest attempt at negotiation. On the night of February 28, Abu Kahal was moreover said to have attacked the house of a Moro in his hometown and driven away the occupants with shots before setting fire to rice stores. Although this was almost certainly a personal feud, it was reported as merely the latest act of defiance by the Bud Dajo Moros.[50] The conclusion to Reeves's letter was an unequivocal call for the immediate attack on Bud Dajo:

I have refrained from definitely saying that these people would be attacked at
any time whatever, but undoubtedly their minds are made up to have a fight and
they are going to pursue the same tactics that were followed here last April and
May. Last night they came down near Mr Schuck's place, burned up a house, de-
stroying a quantity of "palay" and firing some thirty or forty shots at the people.
I am convinced that this will continue nightly until we finish the job and these
people are whipped.[51]

In a society where personal feuds and raids were endemic, the unrest
caused by one or two Moros in hiding on Bud Dajo at the beginning of
March 1906 was hardly extraordinary, and it was certainly not a sign of a
crisis that demanded a large-scale punitive expedition. The American response to the holdouts on Bud Dajo, however, was never really a matter of
law and order but rather the assertion of US colonial authority in Jolo once
and for all. In his later report on the lead-up to the attack on Bud Dajo,
Reeves indeed admitted as much:

The greatest danger to be apprehended was not so much from the depredations
or raids that the people on Dajo would make, but from the attitude of the entire
Moro people. They had been generally refraining from taking part or special
interest in the Dajo situation, but it was a grave question as to how much longer
they would refrain from participating.... It was therefore a time to strike and
finish the matter, as further delay would have brought on a conflict with all the
Moro people.[52]

As had been the case on so many occasions before, the Americans were
concerned that they did not appear sufficiently strong in the face of Moro
opposition. Just a year before, Scott had requested that a large cannon be
positioned in Jolo for that very same reason: "The first cotta attacked and
not captured will give immense encouragement to the disaffected."[53] In his
situation report of February 28, Wilcox similarly cautioned about potential
setbacks during an attack on Bud Dajo: "In my opinion, this matter will
have to be very delicately approached, in as much as the slightest repulse
of our troops would cause a large augmentation of hostiles in the Island."[54]
Given the tenuous nature of their rule in the Moro Province, the Americans

had to back up their authority with brute force, and fear of failure created an escalatory dynamic that made their response to any resistance inherently excessive.[55]

Wilcox's letter to Langhorne, which also arrived in Zamboanga early on March 2, was based on the reconnaissance previously undertaken around Bud Dajo. The assessment of the strength of the fortification on the volcano was not encouraging:

> From all I can learn, there are only three possible trails leading to the top of this mountain. All of these trails are well fortified with parapets, bamboo, and earth obstructions (about seven feet through) and ditches, also brass cannon (Lantaka). These trails are only passable in single file, and to attempt to take the place by assault would involve great loss of life and would probably be unsuccessful.[56]

Instead of a full-on assault, Wilcox proposed a radically different approach to get the Moros off Bud Dajo: the whole mountain should be set on fire, as Wilcox put it, to "burn the people out."[57] Strongly defended camps should furthermore be established at the foot of the three main trails, and the crater subjected to constant shelling by artillery. The people on Bud Dajo were said to have gathered provisions for six weeks, yet the arrival of an expeditionary force, Wilcox reasoned, would drive more refugees to the mountain, with the result that their provisions would not last so long. Wilcox's plan was intended to minimize US casualties, but it was by the same token deliberately intended to trap the Moros and maximize their casualties. Using fire and smoke against "savages" was not an unknown tactic in colonial warfare and had been used to horrific effect by the French in Algeria during the 1840s and also by British forces and settlers in southern Africa during the 1890s.[58] This was a method of violence predicated on the dehumanization of nonwhite enemies, and it was certainly no coincidence that the Moros were referred to as "human hornets," just as the Apache in the US were described as "the wolf of the human race."[59] Wilcox was completely serious about this proposal and in fact requested military reinforcements to carry it out and to strengthen the defense of Jolo town: the operation against Bud Dajo, he feared, would likely cause more widespread unrest.[60]

Alongside the two letters to Langhorne, General Bliss had addressed a brief message to Wood in which he simply reiterated what Reeves had told him in Jolo: "From what I learned from him, a situation has been created since the receipt of your telegram from Manila [of February 17] from which it is impossible to recede."[61] In the early hours of March 2, Wood quickly gleaned the content of the three messages and in his diary noted briefly: "Letter received from General Bliss, describing conditions on Mount Dajo; he is of the opinion that something will have to be done. Also letter from Major Wilcox, 4th Cavalry, commanding officer at Jolo, containing a good many impracticable suggestions."[62] The mobilization of US forces ahead of the planned China expedition meant that on March 2, 1906, Wood already had a large number of troops fully equipped and "ready for immediate field service" within reach of Jolo.[63] The time had come, Wood decided, to do something about Bud Dajo.

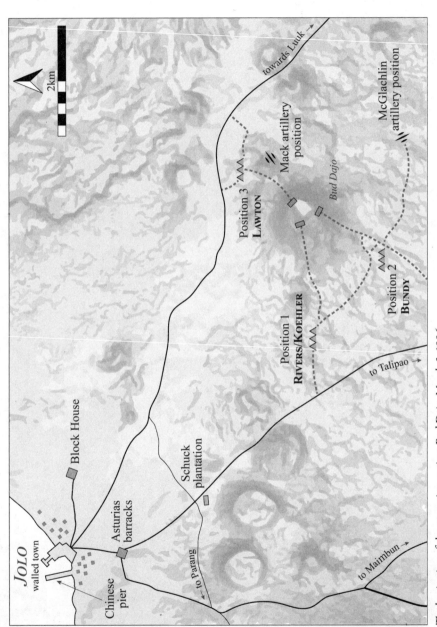

The beginning of the operation against Bud Dajo, March 5, 1906

Map labels:

Jolo walled town
Chinese pier
Block House
Asturias barracks
Schuck plantation
to Parang
to Talipao
to Maimbun
2km
towards Lutuk
Position 3 **LAWTON**
Mack artillery position
Bud Dajo
Position 1 **RIVERS/KOEHLER**
Position 2 **BUNDY**
McGlachlin artillery position

SIX

March 2–5, 1906

Dear Colonel: I wish you would get two of your companies together and go to Jolo at once, nothing but blanket rolls, field
mess outfit, 200 rounds per man, 7 days field rations. In haste,

Yours truly, Leonard Wood
PS: Regular orders will reach you later.[1]

A T 7 A.M. ON MARCH 2, 1906, COLONEL JOSEPH W. DUNCAN OF THE
6th Infantry Regiment received a brief note from General Wood.
Duncan and his troops had only just been moved from Leyte to Zamboanga
as part of the relocation of US military forces ahead of the China expedition. Orders were immediately given for Companies K and M, 6th Infantry, to prepare for deployment, and Duncan was shortly after summoned to
Wood's headquarters. Duncan had no prior experience of dealing with the
Moros, yet Wood ordered him to take charge of the expedition and "proceed without delay" to Jolo that very afternoon aboard the US Army transport *Wright*.[2] The troops being deployed wore tan, wide-brimmed slouch
hats with a center crease, and they were dressed in the tropical service uniform, which consisted of a khaki tunic and trousers, with canvas leggings

and leather boots. Because of the heat, soldiers would often discard their tunics in favor of the iconic dark-blue flannel shirt or white linen sack shirt, which was worn tucked into the trousers. The infantry carried the standard firearm of the US Army, the .30–40 Krag-Jorgensen rifle, with a double-row Mills cartridge belt, as well as a bayonet, haversack, and canteen.[3]

On March 2, Wood also dispatched a company of Philippine Constabulary to assist the military forces going to Jolo. The Philippine Constabulary had been established in 1901 with mostly American officers and locally recruited soldiers who served as a sort of gendarmerie under the American civilian administration of the islands.[4] As with the French Foreign Legion or the Force Publique in King Leopold's Congo, the Philippine Constabulary attracted a number of European adventurers, including an Englishman, John R. White. In 1897 White had volunteered to fight on the Greek side in the brief Greco-Turkish War, and he subsequently went to Alaska during the gold rush. In 1899 he joined the American forces that were sent to the Philippines, and when they were disbanded, he signed up for the Constabulary. On the morning of March 2, 1906, White was working with Colonel W. S. Scott, assistant chief of the Constabulary, in the Zamboanga headquarters:

> I was in my office at Zamboanga when a telephone message came from General Wood, asking whether a company of constabulary was immediately available to accompany the army in an attack on Bud Dajo. As a matter of fact, there was no company ready. But Colonel Scott wanted the Constabulary to get into the fight and we patched up a detachment from the First Zamboanga Company and the First Sulu Company, the latter having just arrived from Bongao for a change of station which might benefit its discipline and instruction. No experienced officer was available to command the provisional company thus formed of twenty Filipino and thirty Moro soldiers, so I begged Colonel Scott to let me take charge of the expedition.[5]

White's request was granted, and his quickly assembled force included Lieutenant F. W. Sowers as second in command, as well as two Constabulary NCOs who had previously served under him.[6] The headdress of the

Constabulary was the signatory red fez, but their uniforms were otherwise similar to those of the US troops, and their arms and equipment were discarded army issue; in the field, they wore dark-blue flannel shirts with khaki trousers and matching puttees, and often discarded their shoes to go barefoot. They were equipped with the old breech-loading .45–70 Springfield Cavalry carbine, and some additionally carried a machete-like *bolo* knife. In addition to revolvers, both White and Sowers carried a Winchester Model M1897 12-gauge pump-action shotgun. Sowers had sawed off the long barrel to make the weapon less cumbersome in a jungle environment and to achieve a greater scattering effect of the buckshot at close range.

Apart from the fifty constabularies, the force that Colonel Duncan assembled consisted of Major Omar Bundy as second in command of the 6th Infantry and the two companies, K and M, each comprising fifty-five men.[7] Additionally, four men of the Signal Corps were under First Lieutenant Gordon Johnston with their day-and-night signaling equipment. Signaling in daytime involved the use of so-called wigwag flags, which required a direct line of sight for communication, whereas acetylene lamps were used in a similar fashion at night.[8]

By 6 p.m. on March 2, *Wright* left, on course for Jolo, just under a hundred miles away. It was less than ten hours from the moment Duncan first received his orders to the time the expeditionary force set off. Before his departure, Duncan received formal mobilization orders, although Wood's instructions for the objective of the expedition were perfunctory:

> In view of the fact that the organizations have been sent from three different regiments, Colonel Duncan has been placed in command of the field forces, the Acting Governor of Jolo having called for, and the Provincial Governor having approved the detail of a military force to capture or destroy the band of lawless characters on or in the vicinity of Bud-Dajo Mountain.[9]

Duncan was struck by the brevity and vagueness of his instructions: "to capture or destroy," as he later noted. "That was all; the ways and means were left to [me]."[10] Wood's orders were accordingly understood as a carte blanche.

In addition to the forces dispatched from Zamboanga, Wood also mobilized troops from the garrison in Malabang, 146 miles to the northeast, across the Moro Gulf.[11] *Busuanga* was sent from Zamboanga to collect this force.

At Malabang, the French army officer and war correspondent Réginald Kann was preparing to leave for Manila after an uneventful and ultimately disappointing visit to Mindanao.[12] A veteran war correspondent, Kann had already covered the Spanish-American War in Cuba, the South African war, the Moroccan revolt, and the Russo-Japanese War, publishing his reportage in several books and journal articles.[13] In the southern Philippines, Kann was both a correspondent and a military observer, and he benefited from unlimited access to the US military.[14] After several weeks, however, he had yet to see any fighting, and his time in the country was running out.[15] Following lunch on March 2, the American officers of the garrison met at the military club to see off their French guest in proper style and were all seated when an officer came running, brandishing a piece of paper. After the officer had caught his breath, aided by a glass of whiskey, he read out the message just received from Zamboanga, ordering the immediate deployment of the troops as part of the expedition to Jolo. At this news, a storm of cheers erupted in the club. The married officers hurried home to take leave of their families as Kann and the other bachelors emptied the club's cellar in anticipation of their future exploits.[16]

The Malabang contingent consisted of 110 dismounted troopers of the 6th Cavalry: Troop F, under Captain T. R. Rivers, and Troop G, under Captain L. M. Koehler. The same number of infantry was also dispatched, namely Companies B and D of the 19th Infantry, under the command of Captain E. P. Lawton and Captain A. M. Wetherill, in addition to Assistant Surgeon Brown of the Medical Department and two Hospital Corps men.[17] These were all troops who had already been prepared for the China expedition. Night had fallen by the time that *Busuanga* arrived from Zamboanga, and Kann and the troops boarded in darkness. Provisions and ammunition had been prepared earlier in the day, and the Malabang contingent was able to set off for Jolo within a few hours. Kann and the troops from Malabang were a day's sailing behind *Wright*, heading on a parallel course for Jolo. *Busuanga* was a small steamer with cabin room for just 11 passengers, but for the overnight journey to Jolo, 260 men had been crammed on board. There was, Kann noted, literally no space to move on the deck, so tightly were the men packed. The officers, on the other hand, had to sit all night in the small cabin that served as a lounge. During the night the weather changed as the small steamer hit choppy waters off the island of Basilan and large waves washed over the deck, drenching the tightly packed troops. According to Kann, however, this did not ruin the general excitement among the men, who joked that they were being baptized to protect them against Moro bullets.[18]

Wood had not seen the troops off as they left for Jolo, but instead spent the afternoon pursuing his favorite pastime of shooting ducks on the *mesa* near Zamboanga, accompanied by captains Langhorne and McCoy.[19] Before *Wright* and the expeditionary force left, however, Wood had given Colonel Duncan a letter for General Bliss:

> I think the time has come for cleaning up the place, and I am sending down about three hundred men, so there will be enough for two or three columns of one hundred men each. . . . I do not think the affair will be serious, if properly handled; there will be no great difficulty in active men going up other than by trail when they reach a point near the fortification.[20]

Evidently, Wood did not expect the matter to be any different than the countless little expeditions he had himself undertaken in Jolo during the preceding years. His final words indeed conveyed a degree of indifference:

> I do not think I shall come down myself, unless there is something more serious than the present outlook. If you desire to stay, don't hesitate to do so; it may be worth watching, although I doubt if there is anything seen, or much heard.[21]

The Zamboanga contingent arrived in Jolo in the morning of March 3, and the troops disembarked and marched to the Asturia barracks, where they were quartered with the other companies of the 6th Infantry already there.[22] Duncan was met at the pier by Reeves, who offered his own residence as quarters for the expedition commander. Shortly after, they held a strategy meeting attended by all the senior officers and their aides.[23] Scott's friend Hadji Abdullah and another Moro informant were present during the meeting and provided crucial information concerning the strength of the stronghold:

> [Th]e force on Bud Dajo was about six hundred, armed with about two hundred guns, six or seven *lantacas* (a muzzle-loading cannon, firing a ball about an inch and a half in diameter), also innumerable spears, barongs, krisses and kampilans, huge knives more effective in a hand-to-hand fight than any gun. It was further stated that there were three or four springs in the crater and that the outlaws had rice and other supplies stored up sufficient to feed six hundred or more persons for about four and a half months.[24]

In planning their operations, the officers were also aided by two sketch maps that showed the different trails and structures visible from the valley and had recently been prepared by one of Bliss's aides.[25] However, more important was "a crude clay model of Bud-Dajo which Captain Reeves had had constructed by natives who were thoroughly familiar with the mountain."[26] Duncan carefully recorded the intelligence concerning the layout of the fortifications and the strengths of the defenses along the different trails provided by Hadji Abdullah:

> The east trail, it was said, invitingly offered the easiest means of approach to an attacking force, but the defenses were said to be really stronger than those on the other trails. Reports indicated that the outlaws thought this trail would be the objective of the main attack. The west and south trails, as indicated by the clay model and information, were more difficult of ascent than the other trail, the south trail being the most difficult of all. The natural disadvantages to an attacking party on the west and south trails were so great, that these trails did

not require as strong a defending party as the east trail. It was said that from the cotta at the head of the south trail could be seen the whole interior of the crest and the defenses on the lip of the crater commanding the other trails. At the summit of the west trail stood the largest cotta or citadel which was constructed as a final rallying place.[27]

This was the sum total of information available to Duncan and his officers as they drew up their plan. In the evening, the troops from Malabang arrived after what Kann referred to as grueling "24-hour confinement" onboard the gunboat.[28] The officers and men disembarked, and White noted how the usually quiet town of Jolo had suddenly been transformed into a busy military camp:

> Squads and companies of armed men tramped under the acacias planted by some thoughtful Spanish commandant; wagons and ambulances were being loaded, mule trains assembled, and packs selected; everywhere was that bustle and suppressed excitement, that rattling and snapping of weapons, that hot smell of sweaty men, horses, and leather accoutrements, that accompanies a campaign.[29]

Duncan had been eager to personally undertake a reconnaissance around Bud Dajo earlier that day, but Reeves persuaded him to wait, for General Bliss was still out on an inspection tour of the island with all four troops of the 14th Cavalry as his escort. There was also another reason: Reeves had made contact with Datu Adam, who commanded the south trail on Bud Dajo, and was trying to convince him "to sell out so as to give the troops the use of the trail."[30] This was the plan that Reeves had initially suggested a month before, and if successful it would significantly reduce American casualties during an attack on the mountain. The negotiations, however, were in the hands of Sawajaan, and for the time being there was nothing to do but wait. In the afternoon, Bliss and the cavalry returned from an uneventful tour of Jolo.[31]

As the hours went by, it became apparent that Reeves's plan had failed. Finally, late that night, a Moro arrived with a message, as Duncan later recalled:

Adam had promised to meet Acting Governor Reeves at a certain point, after dark, but a messenger arrived from Adam about 8.45PM and informed Acting Governor Reeves that Adam had started in from the mountain but on part of the way in had met a Moro who induced him to return to his forces, stating that the Americans were there and would attack him the day after tomorrow and cut his head off anyhow, so that he might as well go back.[32]

Once Duncan learned of the failure of the negotiations on the night of March 3, he prepared to go ahead with the plans for the assault on Bud Dajo:

> All means of peacefully and bloodlessly capturing the malcontents were exhausted and forcible means became a necessity. In the event that the outlaws preferred to fight to a finish rather than surrender as everything seemed to indicate, the blood would be upon their own heads.[33]

Adam's near-betrayal of the Moros on Bud Dajo later became a central theme of the local narratives that are still told in Jolo. According to Moro tradition, the mountain was impossible to climb and the stronghold impregnable unless one knew the secret paths that led to the top. However, Adam was "seduced by money" to betray his people for a reward and thereby ruined the name of his family:

> *He was persuaded by a reward*
> *Adam himself wanted to become a leader*
> *That is the reason he broke the oath*
> *And gave in to the unbelievers.*[34]

The stories, interestingly, do not include the fact that Adam changed his mind and returned to Bud Dajo at the eleventh hour. The arrival of the US forces ahead of the assault had caused widespread panic on the island, and hundreds of Moros fled to the top of Bud Dajo, swelling the size of the stronghold.[35] That the Americans were believed to have tried to deceive Adam was moreover likely to provoke in him and his followers an even greater commitment to fighting. Whereas the *juramentado* actively sought out a glorious death at the hand of the enemy, the people on the mountain had done the opposite and entrenched themselves in the most inaccessible part of the island in order to escape the Americans. Outnumbered and out-gunned, the Moros on Bud Dajo prepared to make a final stand, invoking the empowering narrative of martyrdom (*parang sabil*), which allowed them to accept defeat without dishonor. When the Moros on Bud Dajo communicated with Indanan for the last time, their desperation was palpable, as he later told the Americans: "If they went below they would die, and if they stayed up on the hill they would die, so they might as well stay on the hill."[36]

———————

In the morning of March 4, Colonel Duncan and the senior officers of the expeditionary force set out on a reconnaissance of Bud Dajo with a mounted escort of two troops of the 14th Cavalry, Kann tagging along as an observer.[37] Two miles from Jolo town, the column split up, and Reeves and Lawton went northeast to go clockwise around Bud Dajo, while Duncan, Bundy, and Rivers continued in a southeasterly direction to inspect the foothills and western and southern parts of the mountain. Even though Wilcox and McGlachlin had undertaken a reconnaissance a few weeks earlier, this was the first time that Duncan and the officers of the expeditionary force saw the mountain up close. With its distinct sloping summit, the cinder cone was clearly visible as it rose sharply from the surrounding jungle just six miles from Jolo town. It was only as one approached the foot of Bud Dajo, however, that its imposing size and the sheer steepness of its slopes, the top of which were often lost in the clouds, became really apparent. The undulating foothills, thick jungle, and lack of elevated vantage points further made it difficult to get a clear sense of the surrounding landscape; there was, for instance, rumored to be a fourth trail, somewhere on the southeastern slopes, that was not located until several days later and never fully explored.[38]

Two hours after they had left Jolo, Duncan's column reached the site of what was to become Position 1, near the approach to the western trail, which was assigned to Captain Rivers. Moving on in a southeasterly direction, the column continued for about forty minutes until it reached a spot just below the foothills that guarded the southern trail. This was one and a half miles from Position 1 and was selected as Position 2, which would be under Major Bundy's command. Finally, an artillery position was established little more than a mile southeast of Position 2, which Captain McGlachlin had identified two weeks earlier. From this point, the *cottas* on both the southern and western crest could be enfiladed by the mountain guns of the 28th Battery, which fired 12.5-pound shells and had a maximum range of more than four thousand yards. As the column turned back, Duncan noted, they got a distant glimpse of the Moros: "At the crest of Bud-Dajo south and west trails natives could be plainly seen beating tom-toms, and a number of defenses could be plainly seen."[39]

Duncan was back in Jolo by four in the afternoon, where he found Lawton and Reeves, who had returned to report that an excellent location on the eastern side of Bud Dajo had been found for Position 3.[40]

During the reconnaissance on March 4, Kann had taken his first photograph in Jolo with the Kodak that he had also used during the other conflicts he covered (see figure 7).[41] A large group of officers and aides are standing in the tall grass of a jungle clearing, with palm trees and clumps of bamboo behind them. Their horses are grassing in the background. On the right, McGlachlin and several others are looking at Bud Dajo towering before them out of frame, while Duncan is talking with Colonel Scott of the Constabulary and Major Bundy wearing a pith helmet. The scene gives little indication of the gravity of the plans being prepared in that very moment, but right after his return to Jolo, Duncan wrote up the plan for the attack on Bud Dajo that was to commence the following day:

> Headquarters Mt. Dajo Expedition, Near Jolo
> Jolo [town], Jolo [island], P.I., March 4, 1906
>
> Field Orders No. 1
>
> The object of this expedition is to capture, or destroy, the malcontents on or in the vicinity of Bud-Dajo, Jolo, Jolo, P.I. These malcontents under the following leaders: Agil, Imam Sanudin, Imam Harip, Panglima Imlam and Adam, are reported to be strongly intrenched on the top of Bud-Dajo, having

(estimated) about 600 persons in the crater of the volcano. This crater is approached by three trails, which will be known as the west trail, the south trail, and the east trail.

The sides of the mountain being very precipitous, the summit is approachable by these trails only. All these trails have been prepared for stubborn resistance and defense by parapets, pits and other obstructions, parapets loop-holed to command trail. At the summit of the west trail is a large cotta or citadel, constructed as understood for the final rally. The trails are each defended by from two to three *lantakas*. After going into positions the first duty will be a careful reconnaissance of the trail at which stationed, with the object in view of ascent by flanking trails. Assault to an extent necessary to take a trail from base to summit will not be made unless ordered by the Expedition Commander.[42]

The expedition was to take the field the following day, March 5, with the forces organized in three columns in the following manner:

Position 1 under command of Captain T. R. Rivers: Troop F and G, 4th Cavalry, Company F, 6th Infantry (total: 152 men)

Position 2 under command of Major Omar Bundy: Company E, K, and M, 6th Infantry, and one company Moro Constabulary (total: 216 men)

Position 3 under command of Captain E. P. Lawton: Company G, 6th Infantry, Company B and D, 19th Infantry (total: 165 men)[43]

Additionally, a moving column was to operate under Duncan's personal command "around the base of the mountain." It was composed of Troop I and K, 4th Cavalry, and 28th Battery, Field Artillery (total: 178 men, 3 guns). The Signal Corps (4 men) and medical personnel (10 men) were to be divided among the different columns, which would also be assigned local guides and interpreters, including Charles Schuck, who was to assist Duncan.[44] The total force was more than 700 strong and could if necessary be reinforced by troops from the Jolo garrison.

Although the expedition had ostensibly been launched to secure the arrest of outlaws hiding on Bud Dajo, neither Abu Kahal nor Sahiron was mentioned in the field orders; in fact, they were never referred to again in any of the official reports and dispatches. The outstanding warrant issued by Reeves had only ever been a pretext, and once the military operation was underway, the presence of suspected cattle thieves became entirely irrelevant. Instead, it was the five Moro chiefs who had originally refused to pay the cedula who were now identified and targeted as the "leaders" of "malcontents." Notably, no mention whatsoever was made of the presence of women and children.

Beyond instructions for reconnaissance and ascent along the three trails, the military strategy outlined by Duncan was rather vague, yet years of bloody campaigns against Moro chiefs like Usap and Pala had already established a deadly precedent. The order to "capture or destroy" the Moros on top of Bud Dajo was clearly interpreted by the officers and men of the expedition as referring to the latter option alone. Speaking of the Moros on the mountain, one officer explicitly described how "our regiment was sent to subjugate and disperse them which meant an order to kill them for they know not fear and are taught by their Mohammedan priests and fanatics that there is celestial reward eternal if they but kill one Christian dog before death."[45] Ideas about Moro fanaticism were evidently used by the Americans to define the mission and frame the methods of violence even before the assault itself had begun.[46] Instructions given by the commanding officers are similarly damning: according to one soldier, he and his comrades "went under orders to fire on sight and take no prisoners," and White was informed that "all except the children in arms might be considered as fighting units."[47]

These orders were eerily similar to those infamously given by General Jacob "Howling Wilderness" Smith on the island of Samar during the Philippine-American War four years earlier: "I want no prisoners. . . . I want all persons killed who are capable of bearing arms. . . ."[48] The indiscriminate killing of men, women, and children was moreover a recurrent feature of warfare in North America and had been so since the first European settlers arrived; Wounded Knee was only the last major example of this kind of violence. During the Sand Creek Massacre of 1864, in which hundreds of Cheyenne and Arapahos were brutally slaughtered, Colonel John M. Chivington had reportedly ordered: "Kill and scalp all, big and little; nits make lice."[49]

Most of the senior officers at Bud Dajo were veterans of the "Indian Wars" and steeped in the bloody tradition of settler violence.[50] Born in 1853, Colonel Duncan, for instance, had grown up on the Texan frontier, and was later taught scouting by William F. Cody, better known as "Buffalo Bill," while his army father was stationed in Wyoming.[51] As a young officer in the 1870s, Duncan fought in the Nez Perce War and the Bannock War and later on participated in the Ghost Dance War in 1890–1891, during which the Wounded Knee Massacre took place. Major Bundy had also participated in the military operations in 1890, and the chief medical officer, Major Charles Beverley Ewing, had personally attended to the casualties after the massacre on Pine Ridge. All the officers, and many of the rank and file, had furthermore fought in Cuba in 1898 and subsequently in the Philippine-American War.

Additionally, the Americans were influenced by lessons derived from European colonial warfare in Africa and Asia, which provided countless precedents of punitive campaigns in which villages had been burned, crops and livestock destroyed, and men, women, and children killed indiscriminately. During the hunt for one particularly troublesome Moro chief in Mindanao the year before, Langhorne had thus advised against accepting a surrender with the following argument: "From our own experience with Indians and the English and Dutch in their various colonies it would seem better to get entirely rid of a disturbing element. . . . Every concession to an Asiatic is a mistake. It is only when they beg for mercy that they should get, not more than they beg for, if anything less."[52] The strategic considerations that shaped the operation against the Moros on Bud Dajo were as a result informed by diverse strands of experience and expertise, and the expedition might in fact be considered as a moment when an older tradition of settler violence coalesced with the formal doctrine of colonial warfare.

Ultimately, the order to "destroy" the Moros on Bud Dajo, and to treat them all as legitimate targets, did not arise out of the frustration of fighting an elusive enemy in an inhospitable environment, nor was it the product of a process of gradual brutalization during a drawn-out campaign. Rather, it was the explicit strategy right from the outset and the inevitable outcome of Wood's original plan to teach the Moros "one clean-cut lesson." As White later described, the Bud Dajo expedition was furthermore unusual in that it took place under rather comfortable circumstances and within easy reach of "civilization":

> For a Constabulary officer accustomed to lonely bushwhacking there were plea-
> surable thrills about a nice sociable engagement such as Bud Dajo was to afford:
> Jolo town was only five miles astern; surgeons, hospital, and, ye Gods, cool-clad
> American nurses within cannon shot of the fight; fellow countrymen as soldiers
> on either side and behind—it was for me a fight de luxe.[53]

White and the constabularies were in the advance as the three columns left Jolo in the morning of March 5:

> Before daylight on the next day we moved out from Jolo, under the acacias,
> through the postern gate where the officer of the guard flung a greeting
> and a "wish I were going with you"; out under the stars, past waiting mule
> trains and cursing packers, past long lines of American soldiers resting on
> their rifles and joking with one another somewhat nervously; up dew-wet
> grassy slopes between groves of bamboo and breadfruit that were now but
> darker blotches in the night; on through the heavy tropic darkness, until we
> reached our place near the head of the column that moved out to attack the
> mountain.[54]

With most of the troops on foot, traveling in the gloom along the rough jungle paths, it took several hours for the different contingents to reach their preassigned positions. Bundy's column had the farthest to go, and by the time that it arrived at Position 2, the light was sufficient for White to make out their surroundings:

When the brief dawn glared into full day we were almost within rifle shot of Mount Dajo and could see along the crest, clear-cut against the sky, many flags and banners waving defiance over the Moro forts. The Moros themselves lined the parapets. Their cries and taunts floated faintly to us down the steep sides of the mountain, and over the rolling grassy upland that billowed to the forests of the steeper slopes.[55]

Camp was set up in a clearing at the foot of Bud Dajo (see figure 8), and a section of the Constabulary under Lieutenant Sowers secured the perimeter at the edge of the jungle, where the ground began to rise. "As the last of his blue-shirted, red-fezzed detachment disappeared in the timber, shots rang out," White noted. "We had disturbed the nest of hornets."[56]

The other two columns also came under fire from the Moros as they arrived at their positions on the eastern and western side of the mountain, and soon the first US casualties were reported. At Position 1, Captain Rivers was hit in the leg by a stray bullet as he inspected the western trail through his binoculars.[57] With Rivers out of action, Captain L. M. Koehler, 4th Cavalry, assumed command of Position 1. On the eastern side, Captain Lawton's column was fired upon with rifles and what was assumed to be a *lantaka*, and one soldier was wounded. A Moro outpost on the east trail was soon driven back and a small hut set on fire. Lawton left a company on a small foothill to snipe at the Moros on the crest while the rest of the column went into camp just outside the range of fire.[58]

A few hours later, Duncan and the mobile column arrived at Position 3 with Captain McGlachlin and the three 2.95 Vickers-Maxim guns of the field artillery. A single gun was set up on the foothill, and fire was opened directly on the *cotta* at the top of the eastern crest at a range of 780 yards. The intention at this point was simply to get the range right and to test different types of artillery shells, including common exploding shells; shrapnel, which exploded over the enemy's position, scattering hundreds of steel balls; and finally star shells, which were used to illuminate and looked almost like fireworks.[59] McGlachlin and the artillery officers took careful notes on the effects of the various types of ammunition, yet this initial probing fire also served another purpose, as Duncan later explained: "One object of this fire at this time was if possible to convince the outlaw Moros of the futility of their expectations to hold out."[60]

After about an hour, the gun was packed up, and Duncan proceeded due south toward Position 2, at the base of the south trail. This path had not previously been reconnoitered, and the column had to advance slowly, with the Moro guides and Schuck, the interpreter, leading the way ahead of the advance guard. The column had to change direction several times as the trail led through overgrown ravines, which were impassable for the horses and the mules carrying the dismantled mountain guns. An hour and a half after they had set off, all signs of the trail disappeared, and Duncan had to admit that the column was lost.[61] The only option was to return to Lawton's camp and abandon the plan to link Position 2 and Position 3. Passing through Position 3, McGlachlin left Lieutenant J. A. Mack with one gun and eighteen men there, while Duncan and the column returned to Jolo. A troop of the 4th Cavalry was dispatched to Position 1 and Position 2 to explain to Koehler and Bundy why the expedition commander had failed to turn up as planned. Despite the fact that Bud Dajo was no more than six miles from the military garrison in Jolo, Duncan's unsuccessful attempt to circumvent the volcano had taken him and the column on an eighteen-mile march. At Position 3, Lieutenant Mack subsequently had the mountain gun pulled up on a small hill right in front of the east trail, from where he would be able to target the *cotta* on the crest from a distance of just 880 yards. The Moros had apparently expected the Americans to occupy the hill, and one artillery man was wounded by sharpened bamboo sticks hidden in the grass.[62]

———◆———

At Position 2, Bundy decided to begin the ascent up the south trail around noon, and Captain White was ordered to take the lead with the constabularies, followed by Captain S. J. Bayard Schindel and two companies of the 6th Infantry. White and his men picked up Lieutenant Sowers and the picket, which had been exchanging fire with Moros hidden in the jungle farther up the mountain, and the full Constabulary company began making its slow way uphill: "Leaving the open hillside the trail ascended a gradually steepening hog-back which fell precipitously away on either side: the ridge being at no place more than ten or fifteen yards wide and frequently narrowing to a few feet, while, owing to the trees and brush, it was rarely possible to see more than a few yards ahead."[63]

White had received explicit orders not to engage the enemy but only to scout the trail and locate the trenches that the Moros were supposed to have prepared. The troops were spread out along the trail, with White in the front and two men on point 30 yards ahead of the rest in order to draw fire or spot any Moros lying in wait.[64] The temperature hovered around 90 degrees Fahrenheit, and under the thick jungle canopy it felt even hotter, as one officer noted: "The sun being very hot and the ground of the trail so dry and hot that a person sitting upon it would almost suffocate."[65] After more than an hour of climbing, White and his men were "sodden with perspiration and sore-muscled in the calves of our legs. The ascent was at an angle of forty-five degrees. It was like ascending the stairway of two or three Woolworth Buildings, piled on top of one another."[66] Suddenly, Corporal Savary, who was on point, came sliding back down and whispered to White that he had heard voices up ahead.[67] White halted the column and ordered strict silence while he, Savary, and two others crept back up to get a better look at the defensive works, which were believed to be very near. As White recalled,

> On hands and knees, on bellies and often almost on our faces, we crept up inch by inch, taking advantage of every bit of cover, hugging the jungle or worming into it when the trail was exposed, scratched by thorns and bamboo, bitten by ants and assorted bugs, but always winding upward and nearer to the trench. At last I could hear a faint murmur of voices that was less a conversation than an unaccustomed note in the chorus of the jungle birds and insects.[68]

While White and the others waited, Savary crawled even closer and could soon report that he had spotted a small trench between two trees that appeared to be occupied by four Moros. They all crawled down to the rest of the company, and White informed Major Bundy that they had reached the first obstacle. Bundy in turn sent a message to Duncan, who by that time had returned to Jolo.[69] Upon receipt of the update, Duncan's adjutant, Captain B. M. Atkinson, dispatched a messenger to Lawton at Position 3, which was received late in the afternoon:

> Expedition commander directs me to inform you that he has received positive information that Captain Schindel, 6th Infantry, with two companies and a detachment of Moro Constabulary, are two-thirds the way up the south trail on Position No. 2. This may render an assault on the stronghold on the mountain by Major Bundy's troops, Position No. 2, a necessity, consequently you will be extremely careful in the use of your artillery fire, and should the mountain be taken, allow no one to escape down the trail. The artillery leaves here tonight for Position No. 1 and 2, and will open up early tomorrow morning.[70]

This message would have given Lawton the impression that Bundy's attack on the *cotta* at the top of the south trail was imminent and that his own column, in Position 3 at the east trail, might end up playing only a supportive role. It was furthermore clear that no advance could be made by any of the columns without close coordination with the other commanders.

Close coordination, however, was already proving to be nearly impossible. In the absence of telegraph or phone lines, the military would usually rely on signal flags to communicate over vast distances. But the thick jungle and hilly landscape, combined with the fact that Positions 1, 2, and 3 were all located on opposite sides around Bud Dajo, ruled out visual communication. The only option was written messages that had to be delivered by hand, and with just four men of the Signal Corps attached to the expedition force, volunteers among the soldiers as well as local Moros had to be involved.[71] This added hours to the time it would take to carry potentially urgent orders, and without reliable lines of communication, the level of coordination that Duncan's strategy required would be next to impossible.

As darkness descended on Bud Dajo on March 5, only Bundy's column had so far made any progress. At the head of the troops on the south trail, White and the constabularies were sitting and waiting for orders when word reached them that they were to remain on the trail for the night. Food and water were brought up by Moro porters, known as *carcadores*, and White prepared to find a level spot to lie down on the steep incline:

> I made myself fairly snug between two trunks of fallen trees, with my soldiers close on either side and at my head and feet. But it was a poor night's rest, disturbed by occasional shots fired by nervous sentries, by the regular beat of brass gongs and chanted war songs in the enemy trenches not far above our roost, by the vicious attacks of warrior ants and other jungle pests, as well as the brooding thought that the morrow would bring a bloody piece of work and a "five to one against" chance of living through it.[72]

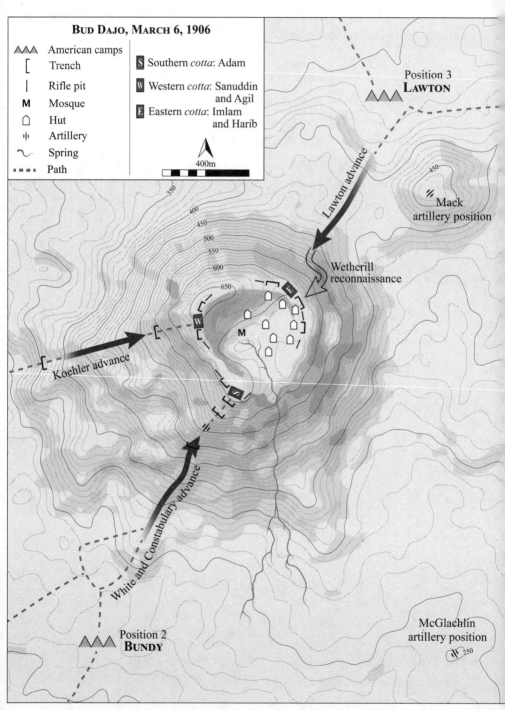

The assault on Bud Dajo, March 6, 1906

SEVEN

March 6

The Americans surrounded the mountain
The cannons started shooting
They fired day and night
Trees were uprooted
But the mountain never moved

Moro song[1]

IN THE EARLY HOURS OF MARCH 6, ALL THREE COLUMNS RESUMED their ascent up Bud Dajo, under cover fire from the three mountain guns that during the night had been put in position at the base of each trail. Duncan was with McGlachlin at the artillery position, southeast of Position 2, from where the first shot was to be fired:

At 7:15 am from the artillery position, McGlachlin's first gun was aimed to command the defenses at the head of the south trail—a jerk of the lanyard, a puff of smoke, and a roar from the belching mouth of the mountain gun warned all that a fight to the finish was on. Almost simultaneously around to the left [Position 1,] Koehler's piece re-echoed the roar, which was then answered away around on the other side of the mountain, by Mack's gun back of Lawton

[Position 3]. Then followed a furious cannonade from all sides, the mountain seemed to fairly shake, the reverberations were almost deafening; startled birds from the thick jungles flew hither and thither uttering discordant notes of fright, great pieces of earth and rock detached from the summit rolled down the mountain side. Earthworks, stone, breastworks, and bamboo stockades were in places scattered like chaff.[2]

At Position 3, Lawton dispatched Captain A. M. Wetherill with Company B and Company D, 19th Infantry, on a reconnaissance up the east trail to locate the best route for a full assault. Positioned on the small hill next to the camp, Lieutenant Mack was keeping up a steady fire with his one gun, clearing the trail ahead of the troops as they advanced.[3] Along with Wetherill, First Lieutenant J. S. Cecil was part of the probe up the slopes of the mountain: "We had to go very slowly and carefully, all the while the field gun was firing along ahead of us and onto their works, from a ridge some one thousand or twelve hundred yards away."[4] The troops met little resistance, and as they got closer to the top, they were able to inspect the *cotta* and the fortifications along the crest through their binoculars, as Cecil described:

They had the front walls of these forts loop-holed throughout; these loopholes consisted of bamboo tubes worked into the parapet at such an angle as to sweep the trail. They only had to put their rifles inside these tubes and pull the trigger. They also had traps for rolling boulders down onto us; these traps consisted of a kind of a platform, with a long lever attached, by which they raised the boulder up to the top of the parapet, then tipped it over. It was arranged so the boulder would strike in and roll down a short, sunken, roadway, this in order to give it the desired direction. The works in between these main forts consisted in lines of pits for riflemen, spearmen, bolomen, etc., worked right round the inside lip of the crater.[5]

To avoid the traps that were aimed right at the narrow trail, Wetherill and Cecil ordered their men to cut a path through the thick undergrowth to the left of the path to see if a less exposed route could be found. Soon, however, the Moros at the top discovered their presence and consequently set off the traps. Despite their precautions, several soldiers were wounded by large boulders that came rolling down the steep slope.[6] "One might find cover from rifle fire and be safe, but there was no cover from these things," Cecil noted. "They came where you were."[7] Wetherill nevertheless managed to find a path and reconnoiter just below the crest to the left of the *cotta*. At 9:40 a.m., he sent a message down to Lawton in the base camp:

[Wetherill, east trail, to Lawton, Position 3]: Captain Lawton, Sir: At 8.45am I with one man went up on the edge of the basin, about 75 yards to the east of the cotta, obtained a good view of almost all the top of the hill. There are numerous shacks in the basin apparently with Moros in them; this is a most excellent point for the assault. I killed a Moro sentinel with a shotgun before returning to my lines. The left of my line is touching the edge of the cleared grounds east of the cotta and visible from your camp. If we are not going to assault today I see no reason for remaining here. Three men have been wounded by boulders. Please send instructions.[8]

Wetherill added a note, suggesting the artillery adjust its range and "fire over edge and into basin from cotta east—150 yards." Along with his companion, Wetherill was the first American to gain a foothold on the summit of Bud Dajo—however furtively. Having pulled back a few hundred feet, out of range of the Moros' rifles, Wetherill's two companies settled down in the undergrowth along the trail, waiting for Lawton's reply. Once Lawton received the report from Wetherill's reconnaissance, he immediately sent it to Colonel Duncan, at Position 2, along with a brief message:

Two companies under Captain Wetherill are up within 50 yards of cotta and are anxious to go right in. We have shelled cotta all morning, also "sniped" it so that there is no sign of life. The walls are mostly gone and the whole thing ramshackled.

If I had authority I would direct them to go in, but must await your authority. In the meantime I have directed them to work around so as to command the position if possible and await orders. If you authorize this please notify Positions 1 and 2, that my men are at top of ridge.

E. P. Lawton, Captain, Commanding Pos. 3.[9]

Given the urgency of the message, Lawton dispatched an officer to personally deliver it to the expedition commander.

———— ✦ ————

At Position 1, Koehler, who had taken over from Rivers, moved out just after daylight. Because the slopes on either side of the west trail were less steep, and the jungle not so thick on this side of Bud Dajo, he was able to advance with one detachment in the center and one on the flank. The troops quickly moved up toward the first of four defensive works obstructing the access to the *cotta* that commanded the western crest. The first fortification was a strong palisade built across the path 150 yards from the bottom of the trail. As far as the troops could tell, the position was manned by fourteen Moros.[10]

Using visual signal flags operated by a private from the Signal Corps, Koehler was able to signal First Sergeant Taylor, in charge of a cannon back in Position 1, less than a thousand yards away. Koehler could thus direct accurate supporting fire, and fourteen shells were subsequently fired directly into the small fortification. Meanwhile, the flanking detachment was providing covering fire, allowing Koehler and the main column to advance. Before Koehler's force reached the palisade, however, the Moros abandoned the position, leaving behind three dead.[11] Slowly working its way up, the column was able to drive off the Moros from a second position a bit farther up the trail, relying only on rifle fire. A few hundred yards beyond, the advance was once more blocked by a third position, which consisted of several large trees, including a massive banyan tree, the roots of which formed an arch over the trail. "The trail at this place was so steep in places that steps had been cut by the natives," Koehler recalled, "and we found it necessary to pull ourselves up from place to place by holding on to roots and vines."[12]

Koehler nevertheless managed to take this position without major opposition, because the Moros retreated before they closed in, leaving only a trail of blood to indicate they had suffered any casualties. It was now half past twelve, and Koehler's column had so far not suffered a single casualty. Koehler signaled back to Position 1, from where Réginald Kann was dispatched to inform Duncan of the column's progress.

The column now found themselves facing the final defensive point, 250 yards below the *cotta*, yet this proved to be a very different and much stronger position, more heavily defended compared to the obstacles they had so far faced. Koehler had already had the cannon moved closer at the base of the trail, and he ascertained the range. As they had done earlier, the artillery fired 14 shells, yet at a range of 1,575 yards they did not seem to make much of an impact on the sturdy blockhouse, made from heavy timber and stamped earth.[13] Koehler's men then advanced to within 120 yards of the blockhouse but, as he later recalled, "found the position so strong and so stubbornly maintained that I halted for an hour and finally found a place off the trail to the right, 75 yards from the blockhouse, from which I could slightly enfilade the blockhouse. I made two attempts to take it but found I would have to do so at a considerable loss."[14] Koehler's advance had finally been stopped, and while he kept up sniping fire on the blockhouse, he ordered his column to halt for the day and reported to Duncan that he was near the crest and would be able to assist the other columns should they make it to the top before him.

———◆———

At Position 2, Bundy's column began its advance, with White and the constabularies in front, supported by four sharpshooters of the 6th Infantry under First Sergeant Knox.[15] As they slowly climbed the trail, the sharpshooters opened fire at the fortifications farther up, visible through an opening in the trees. Continuing, they came across several abandoned trenches, and although there was sporadic fire from the top, they were able to continue their advance. White and the constabularies were well-concealed under the trees, whereas the Moros at the top made easy targets when they exposed themselves from the walls of the *cotta* to shoot, and the sharpshooters were busy firing back.[16] It was, White recalled, "like shooting crows out of a tree."[17] It was nevertheless clear that approaching the top along the trail would eventually expose them dangerously, and, leaving the sharpshooters behind to keep up suppressing fire, he advanced with twelve men to try and locate another way. On either side of the trail, however, there were steep gorges, and the only way up was along the hogback ridge of the trail. Shortly after, White and his men hit the first obstacle:

Soon we ran into an abatis of felled trees which completely blocked the trail. Sergeant Arasid with half the detachment attempted to climb over the abatis. With the remainder I crawled around one flank, and was greeted with such a fire from above and also from the opposite side of the canyon that I withdrew my small detachment with the loss of one killed and one wounded. Private Diukson, mortally wounded, was hanging in the abatis exposed to fire from the fort. He was shot through the jugular vein. As I crawled up to haul him down his head fell over and great gouts of warm blood spouted over my face and chest, making me almost sick at the stomach.[18]

White nevertheless managed to get a good look at the defensive works on the trail ahead of them. Just below the summit, the path widened, and all the trees had been cleared, which meant that the only option was a frontal attack up a steep slope without any cover. Withdrawing his men to a sheltering ledge, White wrote a note to Bundy asking for permission to attack. As they were waiting, shrapnel from McGlachlin's artillery in the valley below began exploding uncomfortably close, and White decided to pull his men even farther down the trail.[19] The jungle on the slopes of Bud Dajo covered the trail completely and made it impossible for the artillery to see the advancing troops beneath the dense foliage. Bundy eventually came up to inspect the column's progress, and it was decided to request that a cannon be brought up to help clear the *cotta* at the top of the trail.[20] "For the rest of the day," an exhausted White noted, "we advanced no further."[21]

While the infantry columns had been gradually making their way up the trails, the three guns of the expeditionary force had kept up a steady fire throughout the day, shooting overhead of the columns. From his forward observation post on the east trail, Captain Wetherill had been able to adjust the range of the gun placed on the small hill next to Position 3, and he later confirmed the damage to the fortifications. In the artillery position southeast of Position 2, Captain McGlachlin had meanwhile set his gun at a 14-degree angle, which not only allowed him to fire directly at the *cotta* at the top of the south trail but also to enfilade the *cotta* on the western summit.[22] At around 2 p.m., the gun from Position 1 was taken to the south trail and dismantled to be hauled up, a laborious process that took more than three hours.[23] After McGlachlin had supervised the positioning of the cannon on the south trail, he returned to the artillery position and resumed the bombardment with the remaining gun: "I had the fun of shooting some more at the cotta at the top and at a barricade just below it on the [south] trail. Nothing else was doing and a lot of officers stood about and watched some very pretty and effective shooting."[24]

The US forces had by this point barely seen the enemy and had themselves suffered just a few casualties. And yet they were pouring an intense and indiscriminate artillery fire at the summit of Bud Dajo, as McGlachlin described triumphantly: "We certainly filled that crater full of iron and lead."[25] The gun at the artillery position alone fired 100 common shells, 12 double common shells, and 98 shrapnel shells during March 6.[26] One eyewitness described the spectacle:

> Hundreds and hundreds of pounds of lead were fired into that hill, and the sound of the volleys echoed from the crater-side like the roar of thunder peals. It seemed as though the sound itself must be some huge, solid body which rushed against Mount Dajo with terrific impact.[27]

By midday, March 6, Major Bundy's column had stopped halfway up the south trail as the gun was being brought up, while both Koehler and Lawton's columns were in positions just beneath the summit at the top of their respective trails, waiting for orders to launch an attack on the Moro fortifications. From where Colonel Duncan was directing the operations, however, it was difficult to get an accurate overview of the progress and relative positions of the three columns. Duncan had been receiving running updates from the west trail throughout the morning, and because Koehler was meeting little resistance and suffered no casualties, he began to think that the strength of the Moros had been exaggerated.[28] Just before noon, Duncan accordingly decided that the advance had progressed sufficiently and that the final preparations for the assault could be made. At 10:50 a.m., simultaneous orders were dispatched to Bundy, Lawton, and Koehler:

Colonel Duncan expects you today to obtain, secure and hold a position on your trail from which you can deliver an assault which will reach the crest within two hours after receipt of orders to do so.[29]

Duncan was not at this point aware that Wetherill had already occupied such a position on the east trail, nor did he seem to have realized that there were serious delays in relaying messages. Bundy, who was closest to Duncan, did not receive this order until three hours later, which was even longer than it took to reach Lawton, who was much farther away.

By 1:30 p.m., Duncan received the news from Koehler that his column had halted and was in position near the crest on the west trail, ready for the final assault. Around the same time, however, he also learned that Bundy's progress had been stopped and that a cannon had been requested to be brought up the south trail. Duncan thus decided to postpone the final attack until the following morning, March 7, at 7 a.m. However, the events of the day had not made Duncan change his strategy, and he still believed that a coordinated attack by all three columns stood the best chance of overwhelming the Moros. Issuing the orders for the following day's attack, Duncan gave Bundy and Lawton similar instructions. The message to Lawton read as follows:

You will begin the assault of Mount Dajo at daylight tomorrow morning, 7th. Attack will be simultaneous from all three positions. You will give such orders as will prevent men from your command from firing into brother soldiers of the other two commands. After reaching crest do your best to have as little mortality as possible while capturing the position, killing and routing the enemy. Duncan.[30]

Soon after, however, Duncan changed his mind about a simultaneous attack and informed Koehler that the column on the west trail would have to hold back just below the summit, to avoid being hit by friendly fire from the other two columns.

It was only after these orders had been dispatched that Lawton's message, about Wetherill's reconnaissance on the east trail, finally reached Duncan.

Without apparently noticing that this had been written several hours earlier,[31] the expedition commander sent off a brief reply:

> Your report . . . most satisfactory. Thank Captain Wetherill for me. I have just finished message to you to attack at daybreak tomorrow, 7th. Have confidence in your judgement, but advise that you hold a good position tonight in order to get a good start tomorrow morning.[32]

This message, however, was lost en route and never reached Lawton. Consequently, Lawton did not receive confirmation that his urgent request to launch an attack had been received by the expedition commander. It was now late in the afternoon, and having waited for a reply all day, Lawton finally ordered Wetherill to withdraw from his position halfway up the east trail. Wetherill and the two companies had been up there since the early morning hours, ready to commence the attack, but were now pulled back to Position 3. Around 6 p.m., Lawton finally received Duncan's original order for the three columns to attack simultaneously early the next morning—a message that had been written four and a half hours earlier and that Duncan had already revised. Without realizing that there was a significant time lag and that he was responding to obsolete instructions, Lawton immediately wrote Duncan, warning that "it would be extremely risky for three columns to meet at top of the mountain. The distance across is very short and in an assault there would be great risk of one column shooting into another. We are constantly getting projectiles even now in our camp from the column opposite us and the danger would be far greater at the crest."[33]

This message reached Duncan only late that night, and because the expedition commander simply assumed that Lawton had already been notified of the change of plans, he ignored it. As a result of the poor communication lines, none of Lawton's messages that day had received a reply.

By nightfall on March 6, the preparations for the final assault on Bud Dajo were accordingly not as far advanced as the initial progress had led Duncan to expect. Although Koehler's column on the west trail was ready and in position to take the summit, it had been ordered to hold back. Lawton, who was expected to attack the next morning, had withdrawn his forces back to the base camp at Position 3 while awaiting further orders, and only Bundy's column on the south trail had got the cannon in place and was fully prepared for the morning's advance.

On the west trail, Captain Koehler instructed his men to settle down for the night where they were along the trail:

> The bivouac was made by each man and officer either sitting or lying down in his place in column. The command did not have a single blanket or shelter tent, and as the trail was exceedingly steep and narrow the troops spent a very uncomfortable night, sleeping and resting but very little. I kept the command fairly well fed and supplied water by the aid of twenty *carcadores*, who made trips from our different positions on the trail to our camp throughout the day.[34]

Réginald Kann had initially been posted at Position 1, and besides taking photos and recording the unfolding of events, he had also assisted in firing the cannon to clear the fortifications on the west trail.[35] When Koehler's advance was eventually halted by the blockhouse in the afternoon, Kann was dispatched with a message to Duncan at Position 2. Once he learned that Koehler's column was to hold back during the final attack, Kann asked permission to join Major Bundy's column to make sure he would not miss out on any of the action. Permission was granted, and the eager Frenchman immediately started up the south trail, following a convoy of porters who were bringing provisions up to the soldiers.[36] Kann eventually joined White and the constabularies, who were exchanging sporadic fire with the Moros in the *cotta* at the top, visible through the leaves of the surrounding trees.[37] By 7 p.m., White received the latest instructions from Bundy to the effect that the assault would be made just after daybreak, at the signal given by the artillery: "the mountain gun to fire five rounds at the trenches before the rush was made."[38] Kann shared a basic meal with the troops around him:

> With the final instructions having been communicated, we began to consume the rations each of us have been provided. Such meals are seldom joyful, regard- less of the bravery and natural cheerfulness of the company, since the men can't

help but turn their thoughts to the fight the next day—from time to time—and wonder if they will all be there for the next meal they share.[39]

That night, White and Sowers set up camp next to the small mountain gun that had been assembled at the very top of the column, with a sentry on either side.[40] Like the previous evening, however, the Moros kept up harassing fire after dark had descended on the mountain, and White and the column spent "a restless night within stone's throw of the enemy who had beaten gongs, fired muskets and cannon, and yelled defiance all through the hours of darkness."[41]

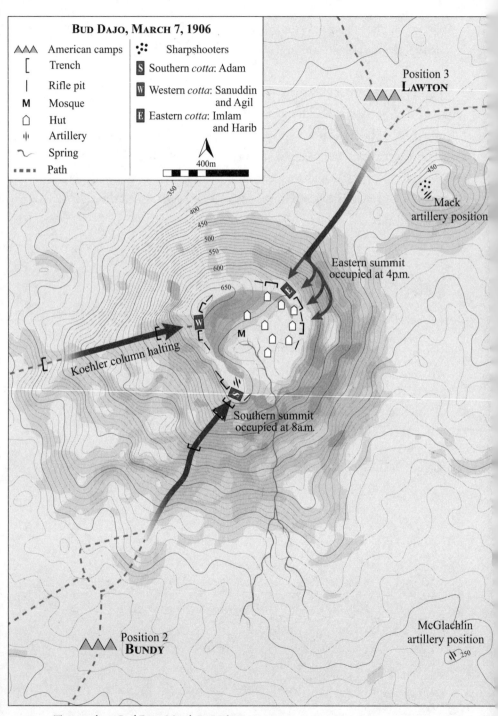

BUD DAJO, MARCH 7, 1906

▲▲▲	American camps	⋮⋮	Sharpshooters
[	Trench	S	Southern *cotta*: Adam
|	Rifle pit	W	Western *cotta*: Sanuddin
M	Mosque		and Agil
⌂	Hut	E	Eastern *cotta*: Imlam
⬦	Artillery		and Harib
∿	Spring		
▪▪▪▪	Path		

400m

Position 3
LAWTON

Mack
artillery position

Eastern summit
occupied at 4p.m.

Koehler column halting

M

Southern summit
occupied at 8a.m.

Position 2
BUNDY

McGlachlin
artillery position

The assault on Bud Dajo, March 7, 1906

EIGHT

Morning, March 7

When morning came
The Americans were still clinging to the slopes
The stench of the dead filled the air
There were no more stones to roll down
No more logs blocked their path
The path to the summit was open

Moro song[1]

IN THE PREDAWN GLOOM OF MARCH 7, WHITE AND SOWERS HAD A hurried breakfast consisting of bacon, hardtack, and boiled water. The upper slopes and crest of Bud Dajo were entirely lost in a white shroud of heavy mist that washed over the mountain every night. The men were sitting where they had slept on the slope of the trail, uniforms sodden with cold morning dew, waiting for the order to advance.

Having spent the night in the comfort of a tent in the base camp, Bundy made his way up the trail, closing up the gaps between the different companies. Captain Schindel and M Company, 6th Infantry, were right behind White and the Constabulary, followed by K Company and detachments of E Company, 6th Infantry, with I Troop, 4th Cavalry, making up the rear.[2]

Strung out along the entire length of the southern trail of Bud Dajo, Bundy's column was altogether 246 men strong.[3]

As the white pall slowly lifted, the trenches and steep climb that awaited them were revealed in the pale light of dawn. Everything was set for the attack, and Bundy joined White at the very head of the column: "I went forward to where the mountain gun was mounted and as soon as there was sufficient light to see the trench in front of us I ordered Lieut. Worcester to shell it."[4] A single shot was fired at the *cotta*, and McGlachlin responded according to the plan by firing five shells in rapid succession from the artillery position in the valley below. Whereas Worcester could actually see his target at the top of the trail, a few hundred feet away, McGlachlin was compelled to fire blindly into the clouds, going only on the coordinates of the previous day: "A mist was hanging over the top and it was difficult to lay the gun," he recalled, "but there may have been some moral effect."[5]

White now moved out with the Constabulary advance party: "I placed six of the best men in front of me, twelve more behind followed by Lieut. Sowers and the remainder of the detachment brought up the rear of the advance."[6] They slowly ascended the narrow trail in single file until they reached the second trench, which turned out to be empty, and the path widened sufficiently for the troops to deploy. A steep slope led to the top of the trench, where a palisade of spiky bamboo had been erected. While White and the rest of the constabularies provided covering fire, Sergeant Arasid and Corporal Savary climbed up to the top to force a path through the primitive chevaux-de-frise. "Every moment I expected a heavy fire to be directed against us at a range of a few feet," White recalled, "but we safely reached the outer face of the trench, the Moro fire from above being almost harmless. It took a few minutes to break through the bamboo entanglement: here the four sharpshooters of Co. 'M' 6th Infantry, joined me."[7]

Any hope that the Moros might be running low on ammunition was brutally dashed once White's men began crossing through a small opening in the bamboo and over the edge into the trench, meeting a barrage of gunfire:

It seemed they were killed or wounded almost as fast as I could push them through. For, once around the corner, we came under the direct fire of the large fort which crowned the summit. Between us and the loopholes which spouted fire, there was nothing that would shelter a rabbit.[8]

White himself went through the bamboo and into the exposed trench, with bullets throwing up clouds of dirt all around him:

> Sergeant Arasid on my left went down with a severe wound. I was giving him an order as he was hit and will never forget the look of blank astonishment which spread over his face as he spun round, dropped his carbine and looked at his right arm which was ripped open from wrist to elbow by a piece of *lantaka* junk.[9]

Seeking cover inside the dugout, White looked up at the last trench and the *cotta* at the top, from where the mist was still rolling across the crest. To reach the stronghold, the soldiers would have to cover more than fifty yards at a steep incline, and apart from a few tree stumps there was no cover for the fire from above. "There was nothing to do but rush the cotta as rapidly as possible," White reasoned:

> Several of my men had already dropped, so, yelling to the rest I rushed without stopping past the third trench which was empty until I pitched up against a bamboo fence a few feet from the wall of the fort. I tried to tear this fence down with bare hands. Looking around I saw that I was the first to reach the fort, but the three American sharpshooters came up on my left while the Constabulary were struggling slowly up and the blue shirts of "M" company were rounding the trench below. Sergeant Knox, Meacham and Wreidt of the 6th were close beside me and having scrambled through the fence we took a breathing spell with our backs against the earthen wall of the fort, the Moros firing harmlessly through the tubes on either side of us.[10]

From the base camp at Position 2, a soldier of the 6th Infantry was following the progress of the assault through his binoculars:

> The battle can well be called the "Second Battle Above the Clouds," for at times early in the morning . . . the fighting was not visible to those in the

valley below, the clouds covering the top of the mountain, and only the report of the rifle firing or the boom of the artillery or crash of the shell as it struck the top of the mountain could tell one what was going on far up the mountain side. Finally the clouds rolled away, and near the top could be seen the thin line of khaki-dressed men that had finally passed out of the narrow trail and spread out around the foot of the stockade that protected the last cotta on the summit of the hill.[11]

At the top, White and the handful of constabularies and soldiers who had made it to the dead ground at the base of the *cotta* were pinned down and unable to advance any farther. Private Hill of M Company, 6th Infantry, was among the troops following closely behind the Constabulary on the final approach to the *cotta*:

> There was a clearing there of about sixty feet down from the *cotta* and about seventy feet wide in front.... We crawled from the trail through that clearing, and boy was that scary! The Moros had guns out there levelled on that clearing. But we soon located where they had their portholes, and we got between them, and since they couldn't turn them, they had to shoot straight. So we crawled up close to the *cotta* that way.[12]

Even from the distance of the artillery position in the valley below, the furious struggle at the summit of the southern trail was now clearly visible to McGlachlin: "We could see first a man or two at a time climb this steep path, then a little bunch and then a larger one, and could see the black powder puffs of smoke from the Moros' Remingtons and hear the reports of our Krags."[13] At the *cotta*, White and the sharpshooters were meanwhile engaging the Moros, who were just a few feet away, on the other side of the earth wall:

> I was using a Winchester riot gun with buckshot shells, a very deadly weapon in hand to hand fighting. One Moro who stood up was dressed in gorgeous red trunks and vest: he held a rifle in his right hand and a revolver in his left: with the latter he fired twice at me while my shotgun jammed but at last I let him have a charge full in the chest and he tumbled back into the fort. A few inches to my right a bamboo tube projected from the wall: through it came a steady

fire. A piece of wood thrown as a missile from within fell close at hand and I jammed it into the tube, which it fitted like a cork in a bottle.[14]

By this time, Private Hill had made it to the cover of the wall, ending up right next to White. "We heard the Moros commence to chanting," Hill recalled, "and this man White knew them people and he said, 'They're singing their death song.' He said, 'This is the time to go over after 'em.' When they commenced singing their death song, he knew what they were doin'."[15] Lieutenant Sowers was on the ground a few feet below, and White ordered him to gather as many constabularies as he could and work his way around the right side of the *cotta*, where the walls appeared to be lower, to outflank the Moros.[16] Right after giving this order, White stood up to look over the earthworks:

> A spear or thrown barong passing almost through my hair made me sit quickly down and in front of the loop hole I had blocked with a piece of wood. A bullet fired from within pierced the "cork"—I saw the splinters fly and passed through my left leg just above the knee: this was about 7:00am and we had been fighting perhaps half an hour. The shock was tremendous and every nerve seemed paralyzed. I rolled a few feet downhill when Sergeant Alga got hold of me and hauled me to partial shelter behind a stump; he cut off my trousers and puttees and applied a first aid bandage.[17]

With the assault having stalled, Schindel, who was at the last trench just below the *cotta*, requested Bundy to bring up K Company and the other reserves to advance to the right and left of M Company, to execute the flanking maneuver that White had begun.[18] The Moros seemed to be running out of ammunition and were by that point throwing spears and even knives at the attackers—as well as improvised grenades made from conch shells filled with gunpowder, which proved to be more noisy than dangerous.[19]

First Lieutenant Gordon Johnston of the Signal Corps asked permission to join the assault and rushed up, grabbing White's shotgun and ammunition belt on the way. Johnston, who was a veteran of San Juan Hill and an old acquaintance of both Wood and Roosevelt, made it to the top of the trail, yelling for the troops to follow him. As he was trying to gain a foothold on the parapet, however, he was shot at close range. As one of Johnston's men recalled, "They did get our Lieutenant through the shoulder with a Remington ball. He rolled nearly 30 feet before we could get at him to fix him up with a 'first aid.'"[20] Johnston was quickly carried down to the trench, where he had just passed White on the way up (see figure 11).[21] From the safety of his position at the bottom of the trench, White watched the action around him:

> More wounded were continually arriving in the trench while fresh troops passed one by one above us, coming up from the rear. Badly as I felt I could not but notice the strained intense expressions on the faces of the new men who came under fire as they passed the corner of the trench, a few feet from where I lay. Overhead hurled a continuous stream of bullets.[22]

Meanwhile, the soldiers of the second wave had reached the top and maneuvered around the Moro defensive works, as Private Ed Hodges, Company K, 6th Infantry, described: "The flankers on our right finally got around, and the way they set those 'coons' afire made us feel good. This discouraged or excited our fanatical enemies so that many of them jumped right over the breastwork on top of us in front of the trench."[23] Surrounded on all sides, some of the Moros actually threw themselves against the American forces in a final act of desperation. From his position in the trench, White noticed the firing suddenly increase and people yelling:

> "They're coming over, bolo rush!" shouted a soldier, who jumped from above the trench and on to my wounded leg causing me further agony. I apostrophized him for a coward as he disappeared at the back of the trench. . . . About a dozen [Moros] had jumped over the wall in an attempt to get at the troops.[24]

From the valley, McGlachlin watched through his binoculars as a Moro "was caught on his bayonet by an infantryman and held there until another could kill him. Some struck the ground and bounded down the steep slope like balls until they disappeared in the jungle, undoubtedly dead."[25] One of the Moros who chose to die fighting was none other than Datu Adam, who had almost betrayed his people just a few days before. Crouched behind the *cotta* wall, Private Hill witnessed Adam's final act of defiance:

> All of a sudden Adam—that Moro chief—jumped over those breastworks with a little baby under one arm, and a bolo knife in the other. It was a long steel sword that was sharp as a razor. He had that in his hand and the baby in the other, and I'll bet you a dozen bullets hit him before he ever hit the ground.[26]

Adam and his baby were both killed instantly, as were the other Moros who launched this last-ditch counterattack.[27] The attack reached its final bloody phase when the Americans overran the *cotta* and the trenches. "We climbed to the top of the wall," Private Hodges recalled, "and gave them our magazine fire until the last one of the black fiends was dead."[28] In a letter to his mother, Private Frank Townsend, Company K, 6th Infantry, described the taking of the fort:

> Our hardest fight was after we got over the walls. . . . It was a terrible slaughter, but could not be averted. The intense heat, with the sight and scent of so much blood, crazed me and I lost all respect for human life and fought like a demon everything in reach of me, regardless of age or sex, and thought nothing of it at the time, but it shocks me to think of it now. When I lost my gun, I picked up a bolo and I sure did do some slaughter with that. My clothes were wet with blood, I was bareheaded and there was blood in my hair.[29]

Private J. F. Mahoney of the Signal Corps was with the troops who went over the southern crest and killed the last surviving Moros:

> A non-com[missioned officer] of the cavalry came near getting his[,] only for a lad from the 6th and myself. The non-com was using one of those automatics that Uncle Sam gives to the non-coms now and this man fired 10 shots in three seconds with it into a Moro and didn't stop him. This lad from the 6th cut loose at him and he sure dropped. I was firing a dum-dum and I know I hit him because half of his head was gone where the ball hit him. Say, you often hear of a steel ball not stopping anything, but it's a mistake, because every

nigger that was hit above the waist dropped, and stayed down, but a 38-calibre won't hurt much.[30]

Mahoney and Townsend were not exceptional in either action or attitude. Lieutenant Dewitt C. T. Grubbs, who commanded Company M, 6th Infantry, proudly told his father about the attack: "I had the pleasure of killing nine Moros with my revolver and a long, heavy knife that I carried."[31] The time was 7:30 a.m., and the Americans had gained their first foothold on the summit of Bud Dajo.

———————

Barely conscious, White noticed how the sounds of battle seemed to diminish:

> The firing slackened and soon dribbled down to an occasional shot. I heard that the "cotta" was taken and the troops on the summit of the hill. . . . Major Bundy and other officers passed on up: More wounded came into the trench. A hospital corps man arrived and began to give first aid. Sergeant Knox, whom I had left at the wall of the fort, came in with his right hand almost shot away: it was hanging by threads from the wrist. He said that as he put his hand on the top of the wall a Moro thrust a musket against it and the whole load of slugs went through his hand. The more slightly wounded after being dressed, made their way down the hill.[32]

Among the wounded was Private Townsend, who had not emerged unscathed from his rampage in the trenches:

> I was wounded in the right thigh, was shot with a 45 calibre Remington. 'Tis a wonder it didn't tear my leg off. I can't see how I ever came out of the fight alive. The top of my hat was shot off. My gun stock was shot in two right in my hand and my cartridge belt was almost severed with a bolo. The belt saved me from what might have been a fatal wound.[33]

From the top of the *cotta*, which was clearly visible from the base camp at Position 2, Private Mahoney now used the signal flags to report to Duncan that the south crest had been secured and what the US casualties were.[34] Of the four sharpshooters who had advanced with White, two had been severely wounded and one killed, and the Constabulary had suffered two dead and thirteen wounded.[35] Altogether, the American casualties that day had been seven killed and forty-four wounded.[36] Bundy's report on the casualties suffered by the Moros was somewhat more cursory:

> On the enemy's side I estimate the number killed in this part of the engagement at 150. The trench at the cotta was nearly filled with the dead, and there were many outside of it. I signalled to the Expedition Commander that 100 of the enemy had been killed but at that time I had had no opportunity to observe the full effect of our fire.[37]

This estimate was a gross underestimate, and to the soldiers who had fought their way to the top, the "full effect" of their fire was impossible not to notice: the mangled bodies of dead Moros were piled high in the *cotta* and surrounding trenches, and scattered across the slope on the inside of the crater.[38] As one artilleryman described, "The sight of the dead and dying as we took possession of the Moro stronghold is one that I will never forget."[39]

Réginald Kann, who had been farther down the track, made his way to the top immediately after the fighting had stopped and took a photograph of the exhausted troops as they were resting next to the *cotta* (see figure 12).[40] Half a dozen soldiers of the 6th Infantry and the Constabulary, distinguished by the red fezzes, sit along the edge of the trench where White was wounded, which is filled to the brim with the tangled bodies of dead Moros. One of the men is resting his feet on a corpse. On the opposite side, on the earthworks, the boots of more soldiers are visible, along with a local porter, the only person facing the camera. Various objects can be identified scattered around the trench, including a fabric bag tied to a wooden stake and four small metal gongs, the sound of which had kept the Americans awake during the preceding two nights. Beneath the gongs, a man's torso is sitting, with the head, still wearing a turban, hanging at a strange angle and attached to the body only by the skin. This horrific injury was likely caused by an artillery shell or the sharp blade of a bolo wielded by a constabulary or a soldier like Townsend. In the foreground of the image, a woman's face can be seen, and although the image is obscured by blood-splattered clothes and contorted body parts, it is clear that she died embracing another Moro. Because of Kann's camera, the scene that so disturbed the artilleryman was not only captured and preserved for posterity but was later also turned into a postcard.[41] Kann himself counted about 175 corpses in the trench alone, although some of the soldiers put the number much higher.[42]

As Bundy's troops took up positions along the edge of the crater on the southern side of Bud Dajo, just before 8 a.m. on March 7, it soon became clear that they were the first to reach the top. To their right, on the eastern side of the mountain, Lawton's column was nowhere to be seen.

NINE

Afternoon, March 7

When the Americans reached the summit
Men and women, children and elders
All came out to fight them
The struggle was furious
People were shooting everywhere
There were so many killed
You could wash yourself in the blood

Moro song[1]

As soon as Colonel Duncan was informed that the southern summit had been successfully occupied but that there was no sighting of an attack on the eastern side, he sent a message to Captain Lawton at Position 3. Lawton was still waiting for a reply from Duncan when a message arrived informing him that he was supposed to have launched an attack in conjunction with Bundy's column at dawn. Flustered, Lawton wrote a brief response to Duncan, which he immediately dispatched with Lieutenant Cecil and another officer:

March 7, 1906, 10 am
Col. Duncan

Please send me orders, have re[ceiv]ed none since I sent those messages
to you yesterday—Have just heard that you sent message to me to assault at daylight—No such message was re[ceiv]ed by me—I withdrew
those companies after they had been up there all day—Shall I go up
now and what about my artillery fire?

E. P. Lawton
Capt. 19 Inf
Com. 3rd Column[2]

When Cecil reached Position 1 on his way to Duncan, he was met by
the surprising sight of General Wood and his entire entourage, who had
just arrived. At Zamboanga, Wood had not given the expedition much
thought, but when he learned that the attack on Bud Dajo was well underway, on the evening of March 6 he boarded one of the small gunboats with
McCoy, Langhorne, and Wright, along with Wright's stenographer.[3] Arriving in Jolo at 9 a.m. the following morning, Wood and his party immediately set out for Bud Dajo, along with a small naval detachment consisting
of two officers and nine seamen with two Colt-Browning machine guns
from the gunboat *Pampanga*.[4]

The party reached Koehler's camp at Position 1 a few hours later, and
Wood was brought up to date regarding the ongoing attack.[5] Shortly after
that Cecil arrived, and it became evident that there had been a severe failure
of communication—Bundy had attacked according to plan and successfully
gained a foothold on the summit, but Lawton was still in the base camp at
Position 3.[6] While Wood was taking stock of the situation, the wounded
from Bundy's column passed through Position 1 on their way to Jolo, and
Wood had a brief exchange with Gordon Johnston, whom he knew from
their service with the Rough Riders in Cuba. Despite the fact that he was
not in command of the expedition, Wood sent Cecil back to Lawton with

orders to proceed with the attack immediately, along with Langhorne and the naval detachment, who were also ordered to Position 3.[7] With the prospect of witnessing a real battle, Wright decided to join the group heading to the eastern side of Bud Dajo.

It was around noon before Cecil and Langhorne arrived at Lawton's position, and preparations for the assault soon began. Lawton placed Captain Wetherill at the front of his column, which consisted of Company B and Company D of the 19th Infantry, along with Company G, 6th Infantry. That very morning, Lawton had also been sent reinforcements from Jolo, Company F of the 6th Infantry, following rumors that hostile Moros were planning to attack the Americans at the foot of the mountain.[8] The naval detachment with the machine guns and ammunition, carried by mules and *carcadores*, completed the assaulting force. Wright remained behind at Position 3, but he carefully took notes of what was happening around him. This was the first time that he found himself as part of a military expedition, and it proved very different from his usual reporting:

> At the time I did not realize the nature of this particular expedition, having just got into camp on foot from Jolo, and so took up my position with the artillery, who were shelling the fort with a 2.95 shrapnel gun, and their riflemen were clearing a path for the advance of Lawton's men to the summit.[9]

Carrying his small Kodak that he had so far used only to take picturesque images of the Philippine islands, Wright took several photographs of the mountain gun and the sharpshooters in action (see figures 9 and 10). Positioned on the small hill in front of the east trail, the five men are sitting and lying on their blankets in a small clearing surrounded by waist-high grass. Forked sticks have been driven into the ground to support their Krag rifles and carbines. One of the men is smoking a cigarette, as are two other soldiers standing casually in the background, all of them focused on the mountain rising sharply before them.

Next to the sharpshooters, Lieutenant Mack and his firing team had been shelling the *cotta* on the eastern summit throughout March 6 and 7.

Wright described with admiration how effectively the small Maxim-Vickers was operated:

> This gun did remarkable work. It was like target-shooting; every shot seemed to strike just where aimed by the veteran gunner, Corporal Ryan, of the Twenty-eighth Battery. On the summit of Dajo, just in front of the trenches, four or five Moros were running along, evidently watching Lawton's forces, who had already begun the steep ascent. "Catch them just under the coconut-tree," said Mack. Ryan sighted the gun, the string was pulled; there was a deafening explosion, a huge puff of smoke and debris rose as the shrapnel, timed to a nicety, exploded and there was one less Moro.[10]

Whereas exploding shells were used to destroy fortifications and structures, shrapnel was typically used against enemy personnel and was designed to cause maximum bodily injury. Mack's gun fired some 150 shrapnel shells on the Moros' entrenchments on the eastern side of Bud Dajo, and McGlachlin later reported on the deadly effect: "From many conversations with persons of all arms, Lieut. Mack's fire must have been extremely effective, the lip of the crater, on his side, the barricade and the entrenchments being studded and many dead being found horribly mutilated with shrapnel fragments."[11] (See figure 17.)

Over the course of the three days that the assault lasted, more than four hundred artillery shells were fired by the three mountain guns positioned around Bud Dajo. Although most of the bombardment was aimed at the fortifications on the summit of Bud Dajo, many projectiles were fired blindly into the confined space of the crater itself, where Moro men, women, and children were effectively trapped. As Lawton and his column began making their slow way up the east trail, around 1:30 p.m., Wright noted how the troops were "stepping off as gayly as though going to a pigeon shoot."[12]

Once the troops of Bundy's column gained the top on the southern crest, they came under fire from the Moros below, hidden among the jungle and scattered huts inside the crater, and from the two other *cottas* on the western and eastern rim. While the constabularies, who had sustained the heaviest casualties relative to their strength, were allowed to rest under cover just below the rim on the outer slope, the men of the 6th Infantry and the 4th Cavalry took up positions along the crest and responded to the fire.[13] Although the inside slopes were covered in deep jungle, the entire crater was fully exposed to the American line of fire, and the mountain gun on the trail was ordered to be taken all the way up.[14]

In preparation for the final assault on the south crest, a small detachment under Lieutenant Powell of the 6th Infantry had also been ordered to bring an M1895 Colt-Browning machine gun from Jolo to Position 2, along with some 3,800 rounds of ammunition.[15] By noon on March 7, both the mountain gun and the machine gun had been positioned on the southern summit, and the US forces were able to bring the entire range of their arsenal to bear on the Moros on Bud Dajo. It was considered too dangerous to target the eastern *cotta*—they might overshoot and hit Lawton's troops as they ascended from that side—so both guns opened up on the main fortification on the western side, just a few hundred yards away.

On the western trail, just below the *cotta*, Koehler's column had slowly been advancing since sunrise. A few sharpshooters had crept forward to within a hundred yards of the top, from where they kept up a continuous fire to distract the Moros in the hope that the two other columns would face less opposition.[16] It was at this point, sometime before 1 p.m., that the mountain gun and the machine gun on the southern summit began firing. Despite all precautions, one of the shells landed right in the middle of Koehler's column. One trooper, crouched close to the ground with the other men on the steep slope, just beneath the western *cotta*, later recalled the accident:

There was a shell exploded and killed two men right by me. The concussion knocked me down and threw one of the men right across my shoulders. He was blown all to pieces, his right arm and leg were both shot clear off; we never did find his arm. The other fellow was just chuck full of pieces of shell. He did not even kick after he was hit. The man next to him had his gun blown squarely in two right between his hands and did not get a scratch. The fellow next to him was an infantry man. He got the bayonet knocked off his gun. I got a chunk knocked off my right shoe, but did not get a scratch deep enough to bleed out of the whole thing.[17]

Koehler now realized how exposed his men were to friendly fire and hastily pulled the men back down the trail, leaving an advance guard at the Moro blockhouse. However, this was not enough to take them safely out of their own line of fire, and rounds from the machine gun on the eastern summit soon started hitting the ground on the trail all around the retreating troops. Koehler decided to withdraw his column even farther down the trail and set fire to the blockhouse. In the official report, one man was listed as having been "killed by bursting shell," while another was more misleadingly described as having died from a "bolo wound of abdomen."[18] Although it was widely known that they had been killed by friendly fire, this was never formally acknowledged.

Given the delay in communicating between Position 1 and Position 2, the officers and men operating the guns on the southern crest never realized that they were hitting their own forces just below the crest. Instead, they kept up the devastating fire on the western *cotta* all through the afternoon. At one point, there was suddenly some movement near the stronghold as a large group of Moro women and children came out. An officer present described how the officers in command of the machine gun

> plainly saw these women and children arrange themselves in line, and that they were unarmed and that their action meant surrender; but that after a few moments' observation they turned the guns on them and mowed them down to the very last one. Some after being shot down once, struggled to their feet and were again shot down. They were afterwards found in line with dead babes in their arms and not a weapon of any kind in their possession.[19]

Although the incident was never mentioned in any of the reports, it was noticed by several other eyewitnesses, including Réginald Kann:

> They slowly came out of their fort, neatly lined up in plain sight on the crest, then, covering their heads with their coats, they intoned the song of the dead.

The machine guns and the musketry cut down these unfortunates like card
houses: in a few minutes it was all over.[20]

Nearby, Private Hill of the 6th Infantry was also watching the machine
gunners:

They turned that machine gun on them and they'd stand there, the Moros
would, and just look like dominoes falling when they brought the machine
gun around there. And that's the first time I ever saw a machine gun in action. They were out there five hundred yards—just curious—and that's the way
they went.[21]

Lieutenant Powell's subsequent report gave no indication of the kind
of work that he and the machine-gun team had carried out on top of Bud
Dajo, stating simply that "the detachment and gun was brought up to the
top of the mountain and went into action against all parts of the crater that
were visible, remaining throughout the day of March 7th."[22] The soldier
who had actually manned the machine gun, Charles E. Burke, told his father only that "I was detached with our Colt's automatic, which shoots four
hundred rounds per minute. We trained it all over the hill until four p.m."[23]
By this time, the guns were ordered to cease fire because Lawton's column
was expected to gain the crest on the eastern side imminently.

———————————

Once Lawton's column reached the head of the east trail, where the moun-
tainside rose steeply, they abandoned the mules, and the *carcadores* were
given the task of carrying the two machine guns and ammunition.[24] Moros
on the top were firing at the troops as they began the slow ascent, but
Mack's gun and the sharpshooters on the small hill kept up a continuous
covering fire ahead of the column. Lieutenant Wetherill, who had been over
the same ground the day before, took the advance with Company D, 19th
Infantry, and, following the plan agreed with Lawton, halted the approach
just before the path opened up below the *cotta*, where the troops began
working their way to the left. The column now came under intense rifle fire
from the fort and trenches, and large boulders were rolled down onto the

troops exposed in the open on the trail. The hillside along the trail was covered in thick jungle, and the men at the front had to cut a path through the
undergrowth to allow for the flanking movement. Farther down the trail,
Lawton observed the slow progress of the assault:

> A foothold being obtained by Captain Wetherill for his command, at
> twenty-five or thirty yards from the cotta. . . . This preliminary work for the
> assault was extremely difficult and dangerous, especially to the advance party,
> which was under a galling fire from the moment of arrival in front of the cotta.
> Wetherill and Cecil did great work. In some instances the latter officer had to
> push men by force up the steep hillside and into the destructive rain of bullets
> and other missiles, besides carrying with his own hands the wounded to a place
> of safety. We had numerous casualties at this time, the enemy firing, throwing
> stones, javelins, etc., but the work went on nevertheless, the command closing in
> on the cotta.[25]

Langhorne was just behind Wetherill's company and was able to get up
under the cover of trees, along the parallel trail:

> The navy detachment was brought from the rear and they planted their guns
> most fearlessly below the rim of the crater, where the soldiers of the advance
> were already clinging, preventing by their fire the Moros from showing them-
> selves over the edge of the very strong fortifications and a couple of logs placed
> as breastworks on the rim of the crater, some trenches being just back of these,
> although we did not then know it.[26]

With the first machine gun positioned near the top of the trail, the naval
gunners were able to lay down suppressing fire at close range, sweeping the
cotta and the trenches, and more troops were moved up into position just
below the rim.[27] Lawton made his way to the front:

> Having a large part of the command well to the front, I now decided to sound
> the charge, which was done by a bugler, and the whole line responded as one
> man; yelling and cheering, they rushed up the steep slope, some on their hands

and knees, some erect, many pulling themselves up by means of the underbrush
and grass.[28]

Lieutenant Cecil of the 19th Infantry was among the first to leave the
cover of the jungle and reach the lip of the crater:

> Our line rose and charged right into their line of rifle pits. I wish I could find
> words to properly describe what followed. The Moros would not run a step but
> had to be shot down, hand-to-hand right in their trenches. We not only had
> their rifle fire to contend with, but the air was full of flying spears at the same
> time and one bolo rush followed another, the Moros shrieking like devils all the
> while.[29]

A few hundred yards away, sitting just below the summit on the south
side, Kann could hear the cheering troops as Lawton's column came into
view: "Soon we saw our comrades coming over the crest and bayoneting the
Moros whose shooting had been bothering us for hours."[30] The eastern rim
of Bud Dajo sloped downward from right to left, which meant that once
the Americans gained the top, a machine gun was set up at the extreme left,
and from there it opened up a deadly enfilading along the entire length of
the fortifications. In a letter to his father, Private Mahoney described how a
large group of Moros charged the troops:

> Well we turned a magazine fire into them and you could see them drop like
> grass, but it looked bad for us, as they were getting close and they meant biz.
> Well, by that time the sailors had got the Colt's automatics into action and run
> through a belt of two hundred and fifty without stopping. Well, when they did
> stop there was not a Moro on his feet. I can tell you old man, it was something
> fierce.[31]

The fighting, however, was far from done, and Lawton now ordered de-
tachments to clear the rim on either side of the eastern summit. On the left,
Captain Bolles of the 6th Infantry was assigned one of the machine guns, as
Lawton reported: "His work was thoroughly done, the crest to the left with

numerous shacks being riddled with bullets and then advanced by our men, who burned the latter."[32] Bolles soon reached the deep ravine that separated the eastern and southern rim, and there made contact with Bundy's troops on the other side. While clearing the rim, three more American soldiers were shot and killed by a Moro who was hiding in a rifle pit.[33] This brought the total number of casualties in Lawton's column that day to ten dead and nineteen wounded, including a Hospital Corps man who was killed while treating a wounded soldier.[34]

Wright was later to claim that the American soldiers had acted with greater restraint than their British colonial counterparts in Africa, even to their own detriment: "Our soldiers did not fire into the wounded as Kitchener's men did, and so the Americans lost their lives or were wounded."[35] Following the Battle of Omdurman in 1898, Lord Kitchener had been criticized for the slaughter of captured and wounded Dervishes, although there had also been those ready to justify this. "When the forces of a civilised power are employed against semi-barbarous enemies it is not possible to control excesses," argued the *Army and Navy Gazette*.[36] Wright's praise of the American soldiers nevertheless turned out to be misplaced; Mahoney had joined the assault with Lawton's column, and his account made it clear exactly what happened after the eastern summit was seized:

> I don't think any of the wounded Moros got away, because that is where the six-shooters came in—see a nigger moving in the pile of dead and three or four shots into him to be sure. Three of our outfit were killed by them playing dead and when we would get up to them they would make a swing with a bolo or a spear, so we took no chances.[37]

The eastern rim of the crater presented a gruesome sight as Lawton inspected Moro trenches afterward and came face-to-face with the results of the attack:

> The whole crest of the mountain was covered with corpses, the bodies filled with wounds of every description, headless and dismembered trunks scattered about as they fell, skulls crushed in and brains scattered about, disjointed hands, legs, etc., here and there. One of the worst, most pitiful features of the

fight, one to invoke the pity of the most hard hearted, was the sight of the little helpless babies, some with a number of wounds, groping amid the mass of dead for the mother's breast. Women would occasionally be found struggling to sit erect hemmed in by the mass of dead around them.[38]

"It was," Lawton noted, "almost impossible to move along the parapet, or lip of the crater, without treading on the bodies of the slain."[39]

Once the last firing had stopped on the eastern summit, Lawton received instructions from Duncan, via Bundy, that he was to clear the crest of the mountain toward the last *cotta* on the western side. Lieutenant Bond and Lieutenant Cecil were given the task, and they proceeded with a company of the 19th Infantry in a counterclockwise direction around the rim, toward the highest point of the mountain.[40] However, fire from the mountain gun at the southern rim prevented the troops from proceeding any farther.[41] While the summit on either side was being secured, Lawton also ordered Langhorne to clear the crater in front of his position:

> I had sent detachments down into the mouth of the crater to burn the shacks and destroy all Moros who might be alive there, which work was thoroughly accomplished, Captain Langhorne taking a detachment and killing many Moros there.[42]

According to local tradition, the last surviving women and children had taken refuge in the hut that served as a mosque inside the crater of Bud Dajo, and it was indeed the only place left where anyone trying to escape the fighting could possibly hide.[43] At no point during the assault on Bud Dajo was the possibility of taking prisoners even mentioned.

As it was getting late in the day, it was decided that the assault on the last *cotta* would be postponed to the following morning, and the troops began setting up camp for the night along the crest. With a Colt machine gun positioned on either side, the men of Lawton's column prepared a bivouac along the eastern crest, as far away as possible from the corpse-strewn trenches.[44] There were, however, too many dead bodies to avoid altogether, as Lawton later recalled:

In the midst of this mass of dead we had to bivouac that night, and as it was cold up there we built fires the light from which reflected the distorted countenances and horribly mangled bodies of those about us. The horror of the scene was added to by an occasional agonising groan during the night from the lips of some dying Moro on the crest, or in the dark depths of the crater.[45]

From the valley below, at Position 3, Wright watched the flames blazing in the dark at the top of Bud Dajo:

The soldiers built a great fire on the hill of Dajo that night. It lit up the ghastly trenches of the dead. It flared among the great trees of Dajo and reached toward the heavens with its glow. The Moros on hundreds of hills saw it, and they knew that at last, after centuries, they were finally to be conquered.[46]

———◆———

Late that night, Lawton went down from the eastern summit to his camp at Position 3 along with some of the wounded from his column, who were carried by their comrades because no *carcadores* were available. Since more fighting was still expected the next day, the only medical officers, Surgeon C. R. Reynolds and an assistant, had remained at the top, which left all the wounded without care in the camp below. Langhorne brought those wounded who could move into Jolo in the middle of the night, and porters and Hospital Corps men were sent out to Bud Dajo, arriving early next morning with medical supplies.[47] Throughout the night, Wright was busy at Position 3, helping out as best he could:

That night I had the honor of meeting Captain Lawton—a braver or a kinder man never lived. He had not slept for thirty-six hours, it was said. Probably he had eaten little or nothing. He was cool, mentally calm, physically nervous, active in caring for the wounded in the temporary hospital, but terribly depressed over the loss of his men and the death of the women and the children in the trenches.[48]

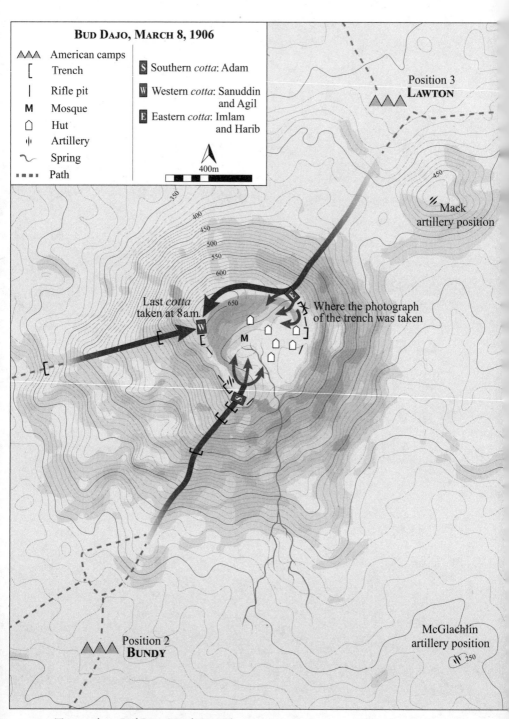

BUD DAJO, MARCH 8, 1906

ᐃᐃᐃ American camps
[Trench
| Rifle pit
M Mosque
⌂ Hut
� Artillery
∿ Spring
▪▪▪▪ Path

S Southern *cotta*: Adam
W Western *cotta*: Sanuddin and Agil
E Eastern *cotta*: Imlam and Harib

400m

Position 3
LAWTON

Mack
artillery position

450

350
400
450
500
550
600
650

Last *cotta*
taken at 8 a.m.

W

M

E

Where the photograph
of the trench was taken

Position 2
BUNDY

McGlachlin
artillery position

250

The assault on Bud Dajo, March 8, 1906

TEN

The End, March 8

As the first streaks of day pierced the fog which overhung the mountain and the dark crater beneath us, the scene about us became even more weird and awful, the mass of corpses, along the full extent of the lip of the crater cone and in the cotta, coming into full view in all their ghastliness.

Captain Edward P. Lawton, letter, 1906[1]

BEFORE DAYLIGHT IN THE MORNING OF MARCH 8, CAPTAIN LAWTON was back at the eastern summit, preparing for the assault on the last *cotta*. Wright also decided to climb up with his camera and see firsthand the scene of the fighting. Around the largest trench, which was traversed by a huge tree trunk, Wright took several images of the aftermath of the previous day's assault, with piles of corpses clearly visible amid blasted tree stumps along the rim of the crater. He also photographed a small group of Moro survivors (see figure 16) right next to the trench:

When dawn broke the soldiers were gathered around the trenches taken the night before. A half-dozen Moro children played on the blankets of the soldiers,

153

and one little hungry fellow was shivering with cold and hunger. There were two women wounded and all around were the bloody-mouthed, frightful, rigid dead. Within two feet of the children were the bodies of six American soldiers, covered with tarpaulin.[2]

When this photo was later published in the United States, the caption described how Lawton's men had "miraculously rescued" the women and children.[3] One officer later claimed that "only about twenty women and children were saved at great danger to the men. Our soldiers acted with great restraint."[4]

———————

The attack on the *cotta* at the western summit began when the mountain gun with Major Bundy's column opened fire. Meanwhile, Company B of the 19th and Company F and Company G of the 6th Infantry, along with one of the Colt machine guns, proceeded counterclockwise along the rim from Lawton's position.[5] As the troops approached the fortification, they came under fire, and the machine gun was brought up to the front by the naval detachment. Ensign H. D. Cooke was wounded by a shot from somewhere in the crater as he was placing the gun, and an officer promptly took over and opened fire on the Moro fortifications. However, the previous day's slaughter had exhausted almost all of the 4,500 rounds that had been brought from the gunboat *Pampanga*—the equivalent of ten minutes of continuous firing. Accordingly, Lawton ordered the troops to advance along the rim, driving out the last surviving Moros, who were hiding in the trenches and rifle pits, at the point of the bayonet. Lawton later recounted the final approach to the Moro stronghold:

Knowing the desperate nature of the opposing force, rendered if possible more desperate by the fact of this being the last stronghold, I approached the cotta in a very deliberate way, but slow as it was, it was sure and e'er long my men surrounded them at pistol shot distance.

The Moros not having fired for some time, and it being impossible to tell what resistance, if any, there was left without seeing into the cotta an officer volunteered to go up to the mouth and look in.

This he did, but hardly had he put his foot on the outer logs of the fort when he and his men were hurled back by rifle fire from within, and a bolo rush. Fortunately the officer escaped with a bullet through his hat, and though thrown back by the suddenness of the attack, he, nevertheless, with great coolness and presence of mind, saved the life of the soldier beside him, by shooting through the head with his revolver a Moro who was on the point of boloing the soldier.[6]

The soldier saved by the officer was the trigger-happy Mahoney, who had volunteered for the final push. In a letter to his father, Mahoney described the incident:

I had one narrow escape as a Moro made a rush at me and I made a reach for him with my carbine, but did not get him, but knocked his bolo out of his hand and then we clinched. Well he got me down, and I was trying to get my six-shooter into action, but could not, and in the meanwhile my Moro gets a small dagger and was about to case it into my gizzard when Lieut. Bissel of Company B, 19th Inf put a .45 to his head and blew Moro brains all over me. I sure was scared for a minute.[7]

That morning, General Wood, along with General Bliss and his aides, had climbed to the southern summit and, as McCoy recalled, witnessed the last desperate struggle at Bud Dajo:

It was most remarkable the fierce dying of the Moros. At every cotta efforts were made to get them to surrender, or to send out their women but for answer a rush of shrieking men and women would come a cutting the air, and dash amongst the soldiers like mad dogs.[8]

Unwilling to risk any more lives, Lawton asked for a volunteer to approach the *cotta* and ascertain how many Moros were left defending the place. A young seaman, the Austrian-born nineteen-year-old Joseph Fitz, came forward and climbed up a tall tree from where he could look directly into the fortification. "He reported very few left alive," Lawton noted, "so I pushed the line gradually forward and a sudden rush enabled us to carry the place. We found a mass of bodies piled up, some fifty in number."[9]

"The entire crest was now in our possession," Bundy noted after the last *cotta* had fallen, and his troops prepared to "clean up" what remained of the Moro stronghold:

> At about 10.00am my command was formed in a skirmish line which advanced to the opposite side of the crest covering the entire crater. No living Moro was found. We destroyed all of the houses, and burned about 450 bushels of rice. We discovered there were many springs, which supplied the Moros with all the water they needed. Our interpreters [including Charles Schuck] who were acquainted with the conditions and were best able to form a correct estimate, stated that about 1,000 Moros had been living in the crater, and that of this number nearly all were killed.[10]

Wright also ventured into the crater and inspected the ruined remains of the small community that had been built at the top of the mountain:

> Going over the basin after the fight was over and the smoke had cleared away, one could see the springs where the Moros had drawn their water, the little cultivated patches of ground, the chickens, and the abundance of palay, or rice, in sacks newly shipped, which would have supported a besieged population for months.[11]

"Every house in the crater," Wright noticed, "was shelled like a sieve by the Colt's automatic gun."[12] As the troops went over the huts and fortifications, the Moros' weapons were collected to be recorded and later lodged in the armory in Zamboanga. Many of the officers and soldiers, however, were busy collecting souvenirs for themselves. Those of Bundy's column who had scoured the crater, Réginald Kann recalled, "returned loaded with trophies: knives, spears, rifles, silk fabrics, snuff and betel boxes."[13] Captain Lawton's "rewards" after the massacre similarly "included a collection of Moro bolos, spears, barongs and knives."[14] One soldier later sent part of the red flag that had flown over the *cotta* on the south side in a letter home to his brother: "The Moro battle flag was captured by our company and divided among the boys. I enclose you a small piece of it."[15] Collecting weapons, sculptures, "ethnographic" objects, and other valuables was standard military practice at the time, and all the major imperial powers filled their museums and private collections with loot from countless punitive expeditions throughout Africa and Asia.[16] In their subsequent reports, the commanding officers at Bud Dajo more or less admitted that many of the highly sought after bladed weapons had "disappeared," and Bundy, for instance, described how:

> My command captured twenty-three (23) guns, one (1) lantaka and forty-three (43) bolos. Some bolos were not turned in and therefore were not counted. The enemy threw their spears at the men who first assaulted, and I do not know what became of them.[17]

According to Wright, a total of 135 firearms were found among the dead Moros, many of them old and obsolete, although there were also a few modern rifles, including Krags and Mausers.[18] One of the firearms collected was an old muzzle loader that upon closer inspection turned out to be stamped "Athens, GA, 1864," with the serial number 5455.[19] This was an Enfield made for the Confederate Army during the American Civil War by the Cook and Brother armory, although how it ended up in Jolo in 1906 remained a mystery.[20]

———————

Having witnessed the final charge, General Wood was evidently done with this "ridiculous little affair" and keen to return to Zamboanga—the expedition had taken far longer than expected, and he did not want to risk any new developments in regard to the China expedition while he was away. Despite the fact that Colonel Duncan was technically in command, Wood ordered Lawton and his troops to return to the garrison immediately, as Lawton later reported:

> Soon after, I received orders to proceed down the mountain, and, before I could get anything in shape in camp after the confusion following the battle, sort out the arms captured, or even attend to the sending in of the dead, I was ordered in

to Jolo at once with two companies of the 19th Infantry. . . . I regret that some
of the captured arms disappeared, but absolutely no time was given me to look
after those things.[21]

It was probably no coincidence that Lawton's column was composed of the
troops from Malabang who had been mobilized specifically for the China
expedition. The other two columns also began preparing for a hurried return to their respective camps in the foothills of the mountain.

There was another, grimmer reason for the Americans' hasty departure
from Bud Dajo: the entire crest and crater of Bud Dajo was full of decom-
posing bodies, as Wood noted: "The effects of the large number of dead
were already becoming apparent, and it was deemed essential to get the
troops off the mountain as soon as practicable."[22] On the southern summit, the trenches full of dead Moros had been hastily covered with dirt
the day before, although some of the bodies had simply been thrown over
the edge of the mountain. "Because we found ourselves just four degrees
from the equator," Kann recalled, "the bodies were already beginning to
decompose in the sun."[23] At the top of the western trail, Koehler's men
doused the bodies found in the *cotta* with petroleum and turned the fortification into a makeshift funeral pyre.[24]

The last photograph taken by Wright on the eastern summit shows a single US soldier standing on the rim in the far distance (see figure 15). The soldier and a few blasted tree trunks are silhouetted starkly against the all-white
background of mist enveloping Bud Dajo. The ground along the summit is
completely covered by corpses, fallen trees, and bits of collapsed huts, intermingled in chaotic profusion. The scene looks just like the aftermath of a
particularly devastating natural disaster. In the foreground the shadow of
a person next to the photographer falls on the contorted bodies of dead Moros.

———————

The final verses of a Moro song about Bud Dajo describe the scene of the
aftermath, once the Americans had left the mountain:

> *A strong wind started blowing*
> *There was thunder and lightning*

A heavy rain fell
As the horse descended
In the midst of the storm

Bud Dajo will not surrender
The Moros would rather face death.

That is the end.[25]

Figure 1: Jolo town with Bud Dajo in the background, circa 1903 (Mike G. Price Collection).

Mt. Daho Jolo. P.I.

Figure 2: Aerial photograph of Bud Dajo from 1936, showing the southeastern side of the mountain (VIRIN: 230124-O-D0439-037.JPG, NARA).

Figure 3: Moro village in Jolo (Mike G. Price Collection).

Figure 4: Moro chief Kalbi (far left) and his brother Jokanain next to him, wearing a traditional hat, accompanied by two followers (Leonard Wood Papers, LOC).

Figure 5: Jamalul Kiram II, sultan of Sulu, in conversation with Charles Schuck. Photograph taken by Hamilton M. Wright in March 1906 (Edgar A. Stirmyer Photograph Collection, USAHEC, Carlisle, PA).

Figure 6: Leonard Wood (fourth from left, with one foot on ladder) and American officers visiting Jokanain's house, circa 1905. Jokanain is standing next to Wood, and Charles Schuck is on the far right in a white suit (Leonard Wood Papers, LOC).

Figure 7: Photograph taken by Réginald Kann during the reconnaissance on March 4; the officers are (left to right): Captain E. F. McGlachlin, Field Artillery; Captain J. H. Reeves, 14th Cavalry (wearing a pith helmet); Captain W. D. Chitty, 4th Cavalry; 2nd Lieutenant B. W. Field, 6th Infantry; 1st Lieutenant J. E. Stedje, 4th Cavalry; Major Omar Bundy, 6th Infantry (wearing a pith helmet); Colonel Joseph W. Duncan, 6th Infantry; Colonel W. S. Scott, Philippine Constabulary (talking to Duncan, with back to camera); and Major Charles B. Ewing, Hospital Corps (wearing a pith helmet) (John R. White Papers, Knight Library, University of Oregon).

Figure 8: The camp at Position 2, under Major Omar Bundy's command, in the foothills below the trail on the south side of Bud Dajo. Photograph taken by Kann on March 6 (John R. White Papers, Knight Library, University of Oregon).

Figure 9: Second Lieutenant J. A. Mack, 28th Battery, operating one of the small Vickers-Maxim 2.95 mountain guns on the hill near Position 3. Photograph taken by Wright on the afternoon of March 7 as Lawton's column was making the final assault on the eastern summit (Edgar A. Stirmyer Photograph Collection, USAHEC, Carlisle, PA).

Figure 10: A group of sharpshooters of the 19th Infantry positioned next to Mack's gun, photographed by Wright as they clear the path ahead of Lawton's column (Edgar A. Stirmyer Photograph Collection, USAHEC, Carlisle, PA).

Figure 11: Top of the south trail just below Datu Adam's *cotta*, photographed by Kann on the morning of March 7. After he was wounded, Captain White was dragged back to the palisades visible farther down the trail. On the bottom left, three Moro survivors are visible (John R. White Papers, Knight Library, University of Oregon).

Figure 12: The trench at the southern summit, with the corpses of the Moro defenders, photographed by Kann immediately after the summit was taken on the morning of March 7 (John R. White Papers, Knight Library, University of Oregon).

Figure 13, following page: Trench on the eastern summit of Bud Dajo on the morning of March 8 (John R. White Papers, Knight Library, University of Oregon; digitally restored by Paul Bourke).

Figure 14: General Wood and his aides on the southern summit, photographed by Kann as they watch the final *cotta* being assaulted on the morning of March 8. Wood is sitting down, face toward the camera, while McCoy is standing just behind him (second from left) and Langhorne is sitting next to Wood (third from left) (John R. White Papers, Knight Library, University of Oregon).

Figure 15: Aftermath of the massacre. The last photograph taken by Wright on the morning of March 8, just before the US troops abandoned Bud Dajo (Edgar A. Stirmyer Photograph Collection, USAHEC, Carlisle, PA).

ONE OF SEVERAL GROUPS OF WOMEN AND CHILDREN, SPARED DURING THE FIGHT AT LAWTON'S TRENCH, ALTHOUGH THEY WERE MIXED UP IN THE TRENCH WITH THE FIGHTING MEN & WOMEN.

Figure 16: Photograph taken by Wright on the morning of March 8, showing a small group of women and children who survived the attack on the eastern summit. The caption: "One of several groups of women and children spared during the fight at Lawton's trench, although they were mixed up in the trench with the fighting men and women." (Edgar A. Stirmyer Photograph Collection, USAHEC, Carlisle, PA).

Figure 17: Effect of the US artillery shells near Lawton's trench, photographed by Wright on the morning of March 8. The image is taken from the ridge looking across the crater toward the last *cotta* on the western summit (Edgar A. Stirmyer Photograph Collection, US AHEC, Carlisle, PA).

Figure 18: Wounded US soldier being taken to the hospital in Jolo by the pack train (Mike G. Price Collection).

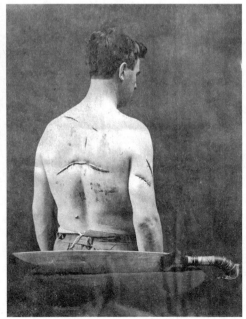

Figure 19: Photograph of the injuries sustained by Ernest J. Packard, Troop I, 4th Cavalry, along with the *barong* with which he was wounded (Sulphur Springs Valley Historical Society, Chiricahua Regional Museum and Research Center, Willcox, Arizona).

Figure 20: The trench at Bud Dajo six weeks after the massacre. This is the same tree trunk as in the photograph of the trench, although the photograph is taken from the opposite side (John R. White Papers, Knight Library, University of Oregon).

Figure 21: Photographic postcard of the twenty-one coffins of the American and Constabulary who were killed during the assault on Bud Dajo, neatly stacked and individually identified (Mike G. Price Collection).

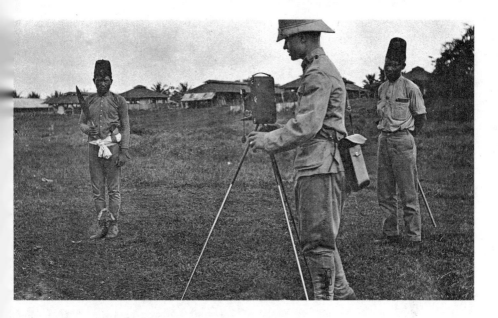

Figure 22: A US officer photographing a Moro in Jolo (Mike G. Price Collection).

Figure 23: Brigadier General Tasker H. Bliss and Maharajah Indanan of Parang photographed by Hamilton M. Wright in early March 1906. Wright's shadow is clearly visible, the only existing "image" of the photographer who documented the Bud Dajo expedition (Edgar A. Stirmyer Photograph Collection, USAHEC, Carlisle, PA).

Figure 24: Photographic postcard of the little girl known as "Miss Bud Dajo," said to be the only survivor of the massacre (Mike G. Price Collection).

ELEVEN

Telegram Blackout

The crossing took all night; luckily, we were blessed with a calm sea and cool air. Most of the wounded had been hit in the arm either by bullets or by slashes with a barong, the terrible cutlass of the natives of Jolo. The nursing staff being absolutely insufficient, passengers and soldiers who had been only lightly wounded helped look after the patients. For my part, I took care of five infantrymen who were absolutely incapable of moving; one of them, who had received three injuries, could only endure his suffering by smoking continuously and as both of his hands had been pierced, I was obliged to serve as his cigarette holder throughout the night—a thankless task to fulfill when you have just spent 36 hours without closing an eye, fighting under the equatorial sun.

Réginald Kann, Manila[1]

L EAVING BEHIND THOSE MEN WHO WERE TOO SEVERELY WOUNDED to be moved, the Bud Dajo expedition left for Zamboanga, where it arrived on the morning of March 9, as Réginald Kann described:

> All of Zamboanga was anxiously waiting for us on the pier; since no telegraph cable connects the town with Jolo, everyone had come to receive news about relatives or friends. We were soon able to reassure the families of the officers that none of them were grievously injured—the doctors having answered for the life of Captain White, whose bleeding had been stopped in time. The natives, on the other hand, burst into lamentations, hitting their faces and tearing their hair out in Muslim fashion; almost all the soldiers from the Constabulary company, who had been severely wounded, were originally from Zamboanga.[2]

Immediately after disembarking at Zamboanga, General Wood proceeded to his office to prepare a report on the operation in Jolo for Colonel George Andrews, adjutant general of the Philippine Division, in Manila.[3] Before leaving for Jolo, Wood had given instructions to the officer in charge of the telegraph office, as one soldier noted: "From the moment the fighting began until the fort was taken all communication was forbidden and a strict censorship of all telegrams established."[4] Wood had a history of trying to keep the press from reporting on his actions. One of his subordinates recounted how the general had evaded journalists in Mindanao a few years earlier:

> "Any newspaper correspondents up there?" came a message from him to me in the Moro country at a time when I knew he had received general instructions coming from political Washington to have no fighting. "No," I answered. In a few days he was there conducting a punitive expedition against rebellious, marauding Moros who could be handled no other way.[5]

Wood was equally keen to keep the expedition against Bud Dajo under wraps. On March 7, J. L. Travis, who was reporting for the *Manila American* as well as the *Far Eastern Review*, was with Wood at Position 2 at the foot of Bud Dajo. After Major Bundy's column had taken the southern crest, Travis wrote a brief account of the assault, which he sent to Jolo, from where it was taken to Zamboanga by boat. Addressed to the *Manila American*, this was the very first news to emerge from Jolo:

> Attack on Dajo Hill Monday. Fierce fighting since. Twelve cottas on hill, four strongest to take. Fourteen American soldiers killed. Many wounded. Constabulary cut to pieces. Captain White constabulary, knee shattered. Wounded, Capt. Rivers, Fourth Cavalry, Lieut. Johnston, Signal Corps, Lieut. Agnew, Sixth Infantry, Lieut. Conway, Sixth Infantry, two hundred dead Moros. Wood, Bliss and staff in field. Sabah sent to Zamboanga for Doctors and Nurses. Hard fighting expected tomorrow. Estimate wounded seventy-five.[6]

At the telegram office in Zamboanga, however, the message was refused in accordance with Wood's orders. The editor of the local newspaper, *Mindanao Herald*, S. E. DeRackin, was furious that the military was controlling the telegraph lines and compared it to the strict censorship that had been in place during the Philippine-American War. During the war, DeRackin objected, the governor-general had a "scheme of keeping back newspaper reports until his lying official reports were thoroughly digested by a gullible public, when he recently issued an order to hold back all newspaper dispatches covering engagements in these Islands until after official reports were dispatched."[7] However, DeRackin's complaints were to no avail, and no telegrams were allowed to be sent from Zamboanga until Wood finished his dispatch.

Wood's official report was 600 words long, written in the staccato shorthand of a telegram:

> Severe action took place between troops, naval detachment, Constabulary and hostile Moros at Mount Dajo, near Jolo, opening afternoon of March 6th and lasting until morning of March 8th. Action involved the capture of Mount Dajo, a lava cone 2100 feet high, with crater at summit, the cone extremely steep and rugged, the last 500 feet lying at an angle of from 50 to 60 degrees, the last 50 feet practically perpendicular, approachable only by lava ridges, covered with heavy growth of timber strongly fortified; fortifications generally invisible from a distance.[8]

Wood named the involved officers and detachments, listed the US Army and Navy casualties—which were eighteen dead and fifty-nine wounded, not including the Constabulary losses—and additionally identified the names of the officers who had been wounded.[9] The context provided for the operation was brief:

> Action was incident to destruction of band of outlaws recognizing no chief, who have been occupying the summit of Mount Dajo for the past eight months. The sultan and various datus had made unsuccessful efforts to get them out. Major Scott, Governor of Jolo, has worked unremittingly to this end. Since his departure especially they have been raiding friendly Moros and burning houses and buildings, including the target range buildings at Jolo. Through their defiance of authority they were stirring up a dangerous condition of affairs. The operations were under the direct charge of Colonel Duncan, 6th Infantry, who was placed in command of all the troops in Jolo, and directed to take the place, and capture and destroy the hostiles.[10]

The report praised the effort of the officers and men who participated in the assault on the stronghold, described as "the most difficult one we have ever had to take," and Wood even added that "it is impossible to conceive a naturally stronger position." As for the Moro casualties, the dispatch stated simply that "the defences were also very considerable and the resistance was literally to the death. All the defenders were killed, as near as could be counted from the dead about six hundred."[11]

Once Wood's report had been sent on March 9, the reporters were finally able to take their messages to the telegraph office.[12] There were at this point several journalists in Zamboanga, including Wright, who had been present at Bud Dajo, as well as others, such as DeRackin, who had talked to a number of the officers and soldiers who participated in the expedition. Wright rushed to send a message to a contact in Manila to get the story out as quickly as possible:

> Please query New York Herald under my signature how many words gallant storming Dajo Hill Sulu Islands loss 50 Americans 800 Moros. Saw fight answer.[13]

Wright also sent a second message to one of the sponsors for his trip, an American planter in Luzon:

Will remain Zamboanga. Just returned from Jolo saw big fight eight hundred Moros killed got good photos missed boat. Stenographers funds and baggage enroute to Manila. Please wire money.[14]

DeRackin, on the other hand, sent his report directly to the *Cablenews American* in Manila:

Attack Dajo Hill commenced Monday. Four days hard fighting. Eighteen Americans three Constabulary killed, sixty wounded. Estimated nine hundred Moros killed. Wounded arriving Zamboanga today. Whole trouble according consensus opinion due Major Hugh L. Scott permitting discontented Moros fortify within sight of Jolo. Telegram Thursday civil government station refused by military authorities. Wire notifying you of fact treated likewise. This telegram may be refused. Copy by mail.[15]

DeRackin's message was the only one to contain any overt criticism of the US administration, and that was focused entirely on Scott's alleged failure to prevent the Moros from fortifying Bud Dajo. Many of the American settlers in Zamboanga felt that Scott's "soft" approach was an obstacle to the development of the region, as DeRackin put it in the pages of the *Mindanao Herald*: "Give us a governor of the District of Sulu who has some qualifications other than that of being a fatherly old Indian agent. What that country needs is to be opened up."[16] One crucial piece of information provided by DeRackin was potentially more damaging, namely that 900 Moros had been killed rather than the 600 reported by Wood. It is nevertheless evident that the editor did not think of this as anything other than accurate reporting—that was the number he had been told by the officers returning from Jolo. At least two other correspondents also sent reports from Zamboanga to some of the main English-language newspapers in Manila, listing Moro casualties as being 700–800.[17] Unbeknownst to Wright, DeRackin, and the others, however, the telegraph office held their messages overnight, which meant that

Wood's report was the only account of the assault on Bud Dajo to reach the outside world on March 9.

Exactly a month after Langhorne had first informed Wood that the Moros on Bud Dajo were suspected of "harbouring cattle-thieves and outlaws," the general's report referred to everyone in the stronghold as "a band of outlaws" who had "been stirring up a dangerous condition of affairs." Considering that the pretext for the entire expedition was the arrest of two specific individuals, and there had been just one or two instances of arson, this was hardly an accurate description of the prelude to the attack. However, the most egregious claim of the report was that only "about six hundred" Moros had been killed.

Because of the rushed nature of the Americans' departure from Bud Dajo, no exact body count was made of the enemy's dead. "The number of Moro dead is variously estimated," Wright later explained. "It is impossible to give an exact number." Having personally walked over the eastern summit as well as the crater itself, it was nevertheless clear to him that far more than six hundred had been killed: "The trench captured by Captain Lawton probably held about 350 Moros, and that was my estimate at the time. The other two trenches held 150 and 450 Moro dead. The number altogether, including many who were killed in the brush and at the side trenches, was probably closer to 1,000 than 600, the original estimate."[18]

This was similar to the number given by Bundy, and it was further supported by several American officers and soldiers who independently estimated the number of Moros killed at Bud Dajo between March 6 and March 8 as somewhere between 900 and 1,200.[19] Frank Townsend of the 6th Infantry later suggested that as many as 1,200–1,500 Moros were killed, of whom 300 were supposedly women and children.[20] It is also worth noticing that every single reporter in Zamboanga who talked with the troops as they disembarked in Zamboanga gave numbers between 700 and 900. General Wood's claim that only 600 Moros had been killed was in fact a deliberate fabrication, as several of the Americans privately admitted. Burke, the machine gunner on the south summit, thus told his father: "There were at least a thousand killed; some officers say fifteen hundred. The official report says seven hundred, but this will be cut down to three or four times before it is made public."[21] A cavalry trooper, Edwin Macdonald, similarly stated that "it is estimated that we killed about 900 Moros, but, of course, official report will be suppressed and the report will likely be about 300 or 400 killed."[22] The reason behind the tampering with the figures was also obvious to the soldiers: "Altogether the number killed was about 900. But you will never see that in the paper for the American people would never understand how the women and children were killed, but under the circumstances it was unavoidable."[23]

The truth was that the number of six hundred was derived from the original estimate of the Moros' strength as stated in Duncan's Field Order No. 1—and because all but a handful had been killed, it followed that this was also the total number of dead. Wood had subsequently been informed by Langhorne that there were far more Moros on the mountain than originally estimated, yet six hundred was the number he settled for; incidentally, this was also the number of Moros killed after the Third Sulu expedition, as reported in the press.[24] Moreover, Wood's report studiously avoided mentioning the fact that there had been women and children among the "hostile Moros." Just twenty-four hours had passed since the last Moros had been killed on Bud Dajo, and Wood was already working to establish a highly selective narrative that turned the massacre into a battle and presented himself and the officers and men of the expedition in the best light possible.

———◆———

In 1906 the United States was connected to the rest of the world through an elaborate network of telegraph lines and submarine cables. A message sent by Morse code from the Philippines could cross the Pacific—with relays through Guam and Hawaii—and reach the US mainland in a matter of minutes. When Wood's telegram reached the US Army headquarters in Manila, Colonel Andrews immediately forwarded a condensed version to the War Department in Washington, DC.[25] The report was also released to the English-language press in Manila, and the local Associated Press office had cabled this version to the United States as well. Thus, by the time the report was publicized by the War Department on the afternoon of Friday, March 9, it had accordingly already reached the American press by other channels.[26] Because of the fifteen-hour time difference between Manila and the West Coast, evening newspapers in the United States could print the news on March 9, whereas the papers in the Philippines had to wait until the following morning. The headlines all presented slight variations of the same basic facts gleaned from Wood's report: the *Los Angeles Record*, for instance, ran with "18 Americans and 600 Moros Slain in Battle," and in Manila, the headline of the *Cablenews* read "600 Mad Moros Killed—Not One Escaped from Fort."[27]

Although the cross-Pacific cable allowed for the near-instantaneous communication of news from the Philippines, it also severely limited the range of information available in the United States. The American press was in fact entirely dependent on the information released by the US authorities, padded out with whatever news could be gleaned from newspapers in Manila as communicated by local correspondents. As a result, the initial coverage of Bud Dajo consisted mostly of the uncritical dissemination of the content of official telegrams, no matter how trivial the information. In New York, Mark Twain noted with his usual sarcasm:

> The official report quite properly extolled and magnified the "heroism" and "gallantry" of our troops; lamented the loss of the fifteen who perished, and elaborated the wounds of thirty-two of our men who suffered injury, and even minutely and faithfully described the nature of the wounds, in the interest of future historians of the United States. It mentioned that a private had one of his elbows scraped by a missile, and the private's name was mentioned. Another private had the end of his nose scraped by a missile. His name was also mentioned—by cable, at one dollar and fifty cents a word.[28]

The fact that Twain got the numbers of the US casualties wrong reflects the confusion that characterized much of the early reporting, which was full of errors and guesswork, a situation that was further amplified when newspapers simply copied each other. Despite the scarcity of information available, some of the newspapers still managed to capture a sense of what had happened at Bud Dajo; in the *Los Angeles Record*, for instance, it was described how, once the Americans gained the summit, "followed a veritable massacre, as the Moros refused to surrender and fought to the death." In the same news story, a caption underneath a portrait of Wood stated: "He

Gave Col. Duncan and His Men a Free Hand and the Moros Were Annihilated."[29] Similarly, the *Hawaiian Star* reported that "the force of Moros was exterminated."[30]

Wood's control of the telegraph lines had bought him a day's head start but could not in the end prevent independent accounts from reaching the US. By Saturday afternoon, March 10, reports based on telegrams sent directly from Zamboanga, including DeRackin's delayed messages, began appearing in the American press. The public now learned that troops just returned from the expedition estimated that nine hundred had been killed, and an Associated Press telegram from Manila late that night provided another shocking piece of information:

> An unofficial report says that the families of the Moros remained in the village located at the apex of the mountain, and the women and children mingled with the warriors during the battle to such an extent that it was impossible to discriminate and all were killed in the fierce onslaught.[31]

As these latest stories emerged over the course of the day, the tone of the press coverage changed dramatically, as a British correspondent in New York described:

> This news has somewhat modified the jubilation with which the first report of the suppression of Moro outlaws, containing no reference to the women and children, was received. Some newspapers, indeed, do not hesitate to describe the affair as a "massacre"—a necessary massacre, perhaps, but a massacre all the same.[32]

President Roosevelt's telegram congratulating Wood and his men was released at the same time by the War Department, yet it ultimately did not distract from the impact of the latest news, which seemed to put the "brilliant feat of arms" in a very different light. Reports of the massacre in Jolo elicited no sympathy for the Moro men, who had for several years been portrayed as dangerous fanatics. But the women were another matter. It did not help that in George Ade's popular comedic opera *The Sultan of Sulu*, the women of the sultan's harem were presented as deserving of American protection—as one American officer reassured them, "Young ladies, don't be alarmed. We may slaughter all the others, but *you* will be spared."[33] In early March 1906, Ade's opera was still being played in several theaters across the US, which means that American audiences could see the show and read the news about Bud Dajo on the very same day.[34] Despite the ubiquity of indiscriminate violence in the "Indian Wars," the killing of women and children was still controversial and held a particular significance in American culture—it was, after all, inscribed as a defining characteristic of Native Americans in the Declaration of Independence itself, which referred to "the merciless Indian Savages, whose known rule of warfare, is an undistinguished destruction of all ages, sexes and conditions." Although it was generally accepted as a military necessity in wars against "savages," in the United States and within the European empires the killing of women and children was still transgressive and thus more difficult to justify to the wider public. An editorial in the *Time's Tribune* actually compared Bud Dajo with previous Indian massacres:

> The sentiment in Washington is that the war department or congress should investigate the circumstances of the Moro slaughter. Not since the battle of Wounded Knee, nearly twenty years ago, have soldiers of the United States army been called upon to slay women and children.[35]

The *Washington Post* opted for a simple yet striking headline:

No Moro Survived
Battle of Mount Dajo Was One of Extermination[36]

General Wood had left Zamboanga on March 10, along with his staff, General Bliss, and Réginald Kann, and he was out of reach for the entire duration of the journey to Manila.[37] On the morning of Tuesday, March 13, Wood landed in the capital, where the president's congratulatory message awaited him, which was promptly communicated to the troops of the Bud Dajo expedition.[38] The joy was short-lived, however, and the message from the president was soon overshadowed by the arrival of an urgent cablegram from the secretary of war, William Howard Taft. Taft himself appeared to have been blindsided by the reports that a battle had taken place in Jolo. When asked by journalists in Washington, Taft issued a statement on March 10 in which he "denied that the action was a punitive expedition." He further claimed that Wood's presence at Bud Dajo was a mere coincidence and that Wood had gone to Jolo "without any idea of what was going to happen."[39] The damning headlines that appeared over the weekend had nevertheless put Taft in a difficult position and forced him to demand an explanation from Wood:

> It is charged there was wanton slaughter of Moros, men, women, and children, in the fight at Mount Dajo. Wish you would send me at once all the particulars with respect to this matter, stating exact facts.[40]

"Wanton slaughter" was not a direct quotation from any of the news reports; it was Taft's summary of the subsequent press coverage.[41] Yet this precise wording came to assume a life of its own, and the subsequent debates fixated on this phrase. Wood immediately wrote a reply to Taft, here reproduced in full:

> In answer to the Secretary of War's request for information March 12, I was present throughout practically the entire action and inspected top of crater after action was finished. Am convinced no man, woman, or child was wantonly killed. A considerable number of women and children were killed in the fight— number unknown, for the reason that they were actually in the works when assaulted, and were unavoidably killed in the fierce hand to hand fighting which took place in the narrow enclosed space. Moro women wore trousers and were dressed, armed much like the men, and charged with them. The children were in many cases used by the men as shields while charging troops. These incidents are much to be regretted, but it must be understood that the Moros, one and all, were fighting not only as enemies, but religious fanatics, believing Paradise to be their immediate reward if killed in action with Christians. They apparently desired that none be saved. Some of our men, one a hospital steward, were cut up while giving assistance to wounded Moros by the wounded, and by those

feigning death for the purpose of getting his vengeance. I personally ordered every assistance given wounded Moros, and that food and water should be sent them and medical attendance. In addition friendly Moros were at once directed to proceed to mountain for this purpose. I do not believe that in this or in any other fight any American soldier wantonly killed a Moro woman or child, or that he ever did it except unavoidably in close action. Action was most desperate, and was impossible for men fighting literally for their lives in close quarters to distinguish who would be injured by fire. In all actions against Moros we have begged Moros again and again to fight as men and keep women and children out of it. I assume entire responsibility for action of the troops in every particular, and if any evidence develops in any way bearing out the charges will act at once.[42]

By defending themselves as much as their men had, Moro women had—according to Wood's logic—failed to conform to the gendered expectations of female behavior and thereby forfeited the right to be treated as women. The claim that they had been wearing trousers, were armed like the men, and were seemingly willing to sacrifice their children's lives only served to further emphasize their savagery and lack of civilization. Wood's misrepresentation of religious martyrdom also failed to acknowledge that the Moros had entrenched themselves on Bud Dajo as an act of desperation to defend their faith and community—not because they were seeking death. In the face of imminent defeat, the *parang sabil* ethos valorized a willingness to die for a just cause, and anyone familiar with William Barrett Travis's famous letter from Alamo might in fact have found many similarities between these culturally diverse expressions of a heroic commitment to "never surrender or retreat."

The fact was that the American forces had trapped the Moros on Bud Dajo, and explicit orders had been given not to let anyone escape and not to take any prisoners. Women and children were in trenches with the men because the entire summit of the mountain—crater as well as rim—was saturated with artillery fire, and there was literally nowhere safe to hide. Once the Americans reached the summit, machine guns were deliberately trained on the huts and other structures, and the troops had subsequently swept the entire area inside the crater, killing anyone left alive. On several occasions, Moro women along with children had been killed while trying to surrender on Bud Dajo—most brutally when a large group emerged from the last *cotta* on the afternoon of March 7, only to be gunned down by Burke and the machine-gun crew on the south summit. During the night between March 7 and March 8, Koehler's advance party had also opened fire on the mother of Agil, who came down the west trail with the *datu*'s infant son. The woman was killed, but the child survived and was taken down to camp and handed over to local Moros.[43]

Wood's claim that wounded Moros were offered water and medical attention was also highly misleading, as were the stories that the Americans had allowed the dead to be buried by their own relatives. In the morning of March 8, for instance, one officer described how

> the houses were burned, the barricades and parapets destroyed and the wounded given water and food, and the troops were then withdrawn to allow the relatives and friends to go to the assistance of the wounded and to bury the dead, it being sacrilegious for us to touch their dead.[44]

None of this was true. Apart from the small group of women and children that were photographed, there were no survivors, and no one came to bury the dead. According to Islamic tradition and Moro custom, burial was supposed to take place within a day of death, and because a corpse was considered unclean, there were elaborate rituals of bathing and purification before interment.[45] Moreover, a proper burial entailed the recital of prayers at the grave, including annual feasts as part of Ramadan, yet none of this was possible at the summit of the mountain with its thousand corpses in varying stages of decay. So the dead on Bud Dajo were left unburied, and although they were considered to be martyrs, they were never fully put to rest. On March 8 the Americans had simply abandoned Bud Dajo, leaving behind a charred killing ground; a soldier who visited the summit a few days later was horrified: "The scene was sickening, the corpses having been only half interred in the trenches, while the foul smell nearly knocked me down. I saw all I wanted to in a very few minutes. . . ."[46]

Summaries of Wood's message were quickly released to the press both in Manila and in the United States, on the assumption that the troubling reports had now been answered in full. When Taft forwarded Wood's explanation to President Roosevelt, he thus gave it his full endorsement:

> It seems to me to show most clearly that the unfortunate loss of life of the men, women, and children among the Moros was wholly unavoidable, in view of their deliberate use of their women and children in actual battle and their fanatical and savage desire that their women should perish with them if defeat were to come.[47]

As might be expected, Roosevelt readily accepted Wood's denial of "wanton slaughter," informing Taft that "this answer is, of course, entirely satisfactory."[48]

———

Not everyone was so receptive to Wood's arguments, and Mark Twain noted that

> Doctor Wood will find that explaining things is not in his line. He will find that where a man has the proper spirit in him and the proper force at his command, it is easier to massacre nine hundred unarmed animals than it is to explain why he made it so remorselessly complete.[49]

Several newspapers similarly questioned the justification provided by Wood and called for an official explanation, including the *Times-Democrat*:

> No time should be lost and no effort spared by the authorities at Washington for securing a full, complete and comprehensive report of the recent merciless and apparently unprovoked slaughter of natives in the Philippine Islands. On the face of the meager details thus far received the killing of nine hundred men, women and children on Mount Dajo was a frightful atrocity.[50]

The newspaper coverage was indeed making politicians ask questions, and on March 14, Texas senator Charles Allen Culberson submitted a resolution for all reports and communication related to the Bud Dajo expedition to be placed before the Senate.[51] The following day, Vice President Charles W. Fairbanks shared the recent communication between Taft and Wood, along with President Roosevelt's final approval, but if he hoped this would satisfy the critical voices, he was sorely mistaken.[52] Augustus Octavius Bacon, a Democrat senator from Georgia, repeated the request for all official communication to be shared, insisting that "the particular thing which it seems to me the Senate would desire to know would be what was the occasion for this unfortunate massacre of men, women, and children."[53] There was a clear sense of frustration among the Democrats about the lack of official communication on Bud Dajo—like everyone else, politicians knew only what was reported in the press, as Bacon described:

> So far as concerns any information conveyed to us through the press, there has been nothing tending to show what was the provocation on the part of these people which led to this wholesale slaughter—and I use this language, Mr. President, which under other circumstances might be considered extreme, because we are told in the press that none escaped, and when none escaped, regardless of age, sex, or participation, it can not be correctly designated, whether justifiable or not, by any other language, certainly none less comprehensive, than the word "slaughter."[54]

This line of criticism did not sit well with the Republicans, and Henry Cabot Lodge of Massachusetts objected to Bacon, who, Lodge said, "got up and began to talk about massacres and slaughters before he knew anything official whatsoever."[55] Lodge instead called for caution and asked his fellow senators to be patient:

> Until we know the facts it seems to me just as well not to enter into a condemnation of the American soldiers and the American officers who have been charged with it. We know nothing direct, as a matter of fact, except the dispatch from General Wood, and when we do know the facts then it will be time enough to talk about massacres, if the facts justify it, which I do not believe for one moment they will.[56]

After a brief back-and-forth, the matter was put aside for the time being, for no reply to the original resolution had yet been given by the War Department.

In the House of Representatives, meanwhile, the president's acceptance of Wood's explanation prompted spirited interventions by Democrat representatives. William Atkinson Jones of Virginia stood up to express his disappointment that the president would approve of a massacre that "shocked the humane and moral sensibilities of every right-thinking American citizen."[57] More damning, however, was Jones openly disputing the truth of Wood's account:

> General Wood, who it seems did not make the ascent of the mountain until the butchery had been ended for the very lack of more victims, tells us that he is convinced there was "no man, woman, or child wantonly killed"—they were all, he says, "unavoidably" killed. The women were killed because they wore trousers, and the children being used as shields by the men naturally suffered a like fate. Then to silence forever any carping critics at home he adds "they apparently desired that none be saved." This is probably the only side of this pitiful story that will ever be given the American people. The lips of every Moro are sealed in death, and we are asked to accept General Wood's statement that the women and children were killed simply because they did not desire to be saved. For one I decline to be satisfied with such an incredible story....[58]

Jones then proceeded to read from the editorial of the day's *Washington Post*, titled "A War for Civilization," which compared Wood and the slaughter in Jolo to a range of historical tyrants, including the Spanish commanders Pizzaro and Cortez, whose brutality in sixteenth-century Peru and Mexico, respectively, was legendary. Wood had acted no better than a Roman proconsul, the editorial claimed, and had in fact delivered on the order given by "Hell-Roaring" General Smith only a few years before. The entire affair made the newspaper question the very future of American rule in the Philippines:

> There is no authority in the Constitution to shoot civilization into savages on the other hemisphere. If it must be done, there are empires and kingdoms over

there that believe in it and are accustomed to it. Let them do it. If we cannot govern the Moros without murdering women, better that we withdraw and let them govern themselves.[59]

Putting down the newspaper, Jones delivered his closing remarks before the House, to the applause of his fellow Democrats:

Mr. Chairman, excuse it as we may, the revolting story of the massacre of Mount Dajo will go down into history as the blackest stain upon the American name. A thousand years of honorable, humane, noble, and Christian conduct on the part of our American soldiery will not suffice to blot out that stain.[60]

During Jones's speech, a creative correspondent in the press gallery had been inspired to write a few verses about Bud Dajo, based on Alfred, Lord Tennyson's famous poem "The Charge of the Light Brigade."[61] Being an old acquaintance of Representative John Sharp Williams, the minority leader, the writer sent his freshly composed poem by messenger to the floor, just as Jones was wrapping up. Williams was getting ready to speak on a completely different subject, namely the Republican caucus, but decided on the spur of the moment to read out the poem, which was, he explained, just "handed to me." Titled "The Charge of the Wood Brigade—or what the heathen call 'The Massacre of Mount Dajo,'" it included the following verses:

> *Chased them from everywhere,*
> *Chased them all onward,*
> *Into the crater of death*
> *Drove them—six hundred!*
> *"Forward the Wood brigade;*
> *Spare not a one," he said;*
> *"Shoot all six hundred!"*

> *"Forward the Wood brigade!"*
> *Was there a man afraid?*
> *Not tho' a soldier knew*
> *Heathen had blundered.*

Savages can't reply,
Heathen can't reason why
Women and children die;
Forced in the crater of death,
Forced with six hundred.

. . .

Cannon to right of them,
Cannon to left of them,
Cannon in front of them,
Volleyed and thundered.
Stormed at with shot and shell,
While child and mother fell,
They that had loved so well!
Thrust into jaws of death,
Trapped into mouth of hell,
Not a babe left of them—
Left of the six hundred.[62]

The poem was more effective in rendering the suffering of the Moros at Bud Dajo as real and worthy of empathy for an American audience than any of the numerous newspaper accounts had been. The correspondents in the gallery eagerly transcribed the verses, and when Williams finished, loud applause broke out among the Democrats. Although Republicans and the expansionist press subsequently mocked the poem as "doggerel verse," it was widely disseminated and reprinted in many of the Democrat-leaning newspapers.[63] The number six hundred had evidently stuck, even among Wood's critics, and the reports that far more Moros had been killed were never again brought up. Although Wood had failed to keep a lid on the story, he had succeeded in substantially downplaying the number of Moros killed.

Following the debates in the Senate and the House, the press coverage became even more heated: While the *New York Times* reported indignantly "Wood's Battle Called Murder in Congress," the *Boston Globe* reprinted the poem under the headline "Massacre of Dajo Hill."[64] Even as Jones's poem was slammed in the expansionist press, the president's approval of Wood's explanation was given full coverage, and the *New York Times* headline, for instance, loudly proclaimed: "No Wanton Slaughter of Moros."[65] Other commentators took a more cautious approach as they sought to balance expressions of regret over the killing of women and children while studiously avoiding saying anything that could be perceived as critical of either the president or the army. The report in the *Semi-Weekly Gazette*—"Heavy Loss to Both Sides"—thus implied a sense of equivalence that could in truth be achieved only by ignoring the fact that even the more conservative estimates had twenty-seven Moros killed for each US dead.[66] A *Harper's Weekly* editorial, on the other hand, suggested that Wood deserved "condolences" rather than "congratulations," but ultimately came down firmly in support of the general:

> The exploit which General Wood has reported must not be misjudged nor condemned merely because it wasn't nice. War is not nice, even at its best. To the victors at Dajo Hill we offer our respectful and sympathetic thanks for having completed what seems to have been a warrantable job of extermination.[67]

In other words, there was no attempt to deny the circumstances of the massacre, which was simply accepted as unavoidable and even desirable. "The extermination of the Moro outlaws in their stronghold on the island of Jolo was a necessity and in the long run it was humanity [i.e., humane]," the Republican newspaper *Philadelphia Press* insisted.[68]

Meanwhile, in the Philippines, Wood received the latest cablegrams from the United States on March 16 and for the first time learned the full extent of the controversy that his actions had sparked back home, as he noted in his diary: "Press dispatches from the United States indicate that the Administration is being vigorously attacked on sensational charges incident to fight at Mount Dajo."[69]

TWELVE

Fake News

We learned that a private cable, sent directly from Zamboanga to Washington by an unknown man, accused the troops of savagery and cruelty and accused them of having unnecessarily massacred all the women and children. This denunciation was gleefully welcomed by the President's critics, who were only too happy to use Wood to attack him indirectly. Mr. [William Randolph] Hearst, the leader of the opposition, brought the matter to the Senate with fake outrage and demanded an explanation. I had lunch that day at the military club with Wood who said with a laugh that during the next expedition he would be happy to invite some senators to join the assault with the troops to help them personally investigate the conduct of the troops.

Réginald Kann, Manila[1]

D ESPITE HIS BLUSTER, GENERAL WOOD WAS MORE CONCERNED than he was letting on, and soon after, he ordered a search of all telegrams that had been sent from Zamboanga to track down what he perceived to be a leak. Yet in none of the messages sent by Wright, DeRackin, and other correspondents from Zamboanga was the killing of women and children mentioned. In his diary, Wood noted: "Can find no evidence of any telegram bearing out statements made by press."[2] On March 18, Wood thus wrote a cablegram to Taft, triumphantly dismissing all reports of "wanton slaughter" as deliberate falsehoods:

> Sensational cables sent to the United States relating to the Mount Dajo fight were made up in Manila. There has been no reference in any cable from Mindanao to the killing of women and children. On receipt of Colonel Andrews's condensed report from me in Washington, the American newspapers cabled for details. The reporters here had no other information than was contained in my report to Colonel Andrews and supplied sensational features.[3]

The story behind the mysterious leak was in fact less dramatic than Wood made it out to be. Contrary to Wood's claims, the unofficial report was not "made up" but was evidently based on someone's firsthand knowledge of what had occurred at Bud Dajo. Notably, when the account was published in the American newspapers, it also described how General Bliss had made a reconnaissance of the island a week before the attack. No other reports mentioned this, and only two civilians had been present at both the reconnaissance and the assault on Bud Dajo: Wright and his stenographer. Neither of Wright's two messages, which Wood later examined, contained any mention of women and children, leaving the stenographer, who remains anonymous, as the only possible source. In his second telegram, Wright mentioned that his stenographer had left Zamboanga early, and it would accordingly seem that he reached Manila two days later with fresh news about the attack.[4] Given the time difference between Manila and the West Coast, eyewitness accounts from Bud Dajo could thus be published in the US by the evening of March 10, having been sent by the Associated Press along with the other correspondents' news stories. On the evening of March 9, reporters in Manila had already talked to an unnamed officer and a civilian who had come straight from Jolo and who described the early stages of the operation.[5]

The report itself did not actually contain any accusation of "wanton slaughter" and instead simply explained the killing of women and children as a result of them being "mingled with the warriors" so that "it was impossible to discriminate and all were killed in the fierce onslaught."[6] There was in truth nothing sensationalist about the account, which was explanatory rather than accusatory. It was only because Wood himself had deliberately left out any mention of women and children in his official report that the story subsequently attracted so much attention. Yet Wood remained convinced that the controversy was the result of deliberate distortions:

> Everything shows that on receipt in Washington of Andrews's condensation of my report to him that American papers cabled here for details. There was nothing here except my official report, and the horrors and sensations were added by local writers.[7]

It never seemed to occur to Wood that no "horrors and sensations" had to be invented for the massacre at Bud Dajo.

Wood now set out to ensure that he would not be blindsided by any new and potentially embarrassing revelations. In Zamboanga, Colonel Duncan was preparing the official military report on the Bud Dajo expedition, which included individual reports from each of the column commanders.[8] Knowing that any reports relating to Bud Dajo were likely to be closely scrutinized, Wood sent instructions "to caution Colonel Duncan to have his reports complete in every particular, as they would have to be transmitted to Washington."[9] Duncan was furthermore directed to hold off on submitting the final report. Wood had, once again, ensured that he alone would be able to control the narrative, and he sat down to write a preliminary report for the governor-general of the Philippines, Henry Clay Ide.[10]

Wood's third account of the Bud Dajo expedition differed little from his earlier reports and simply elaborated on his previous claims that the Moros had been given every opportunity to surrender and that the killing of women and children had been unavoidable. In providing more details about the circumstances surrounding the massacre, Wood made a number of new claims that can only be described as deliberate distortions of the truth. In order to defend Scott from the accusations made by DeRackin, Wood insisted that he had instructed Scott "to use every possible effort to get these people off the mountain without a fight." However, Wood had been in the US for his surgery at the time that Scott was dealing with the people on Bud Dajo, and no such instruction had in fact been given. Wood actually wrote to Scott personally, mentioning this issue:

> You need have no anxiety about the reports concerning Mount Dajo. My official report stated that the delay in the attack on Mount Dajo was in accordance with my specific instructions to that end; I have also written to the same effect, stating that the delay was incident to making every effort to get them out without a fight, knowing as we did that once the fight was on we should have to kill nearly all of them.[11]

In his report, Wood also stated that by early March "it was the general opinion of all good Moros, as well as of Americans, that this situation had reached a point which must be immediately dealt with."[12] This conveniently left out the fact that Reeves had been building the case for the attack since mid-February and that the connection between the Moros on Bud Dajo and the unrest was based mostly on rumors. Wood furthermore claimed that everything had been done to avoid a confrontation:

> Operations had been delayed for practically an entire day in order that Captain Reeves, the governor, might make a final effort to induce these people to come off the mountain without a fight. It was thought that the presence of a large reinforcement of troops would indicate clearly what was coming. They were exceedingly defiant, and it was learned that they had all taken an oath to stand together. Jokanain and Calbi had made a final effort to induce the people to come off the mountain, but without success.[13]

However, the attempt to bribe Adam to let the Americans reach the summit would most definitely have resulted in a fight, and Wood did not seem to understand that the Moro chiefs used as intermediaries had long since given up on negotiating with their former followers.[14] Wood nevertheless insisted that the Moros "had had ample opportunity to surrender, and knew absolutely that they would be received unharmed if they did so." Considering the precedent set during the punitive campaigns of preceding years, this was again a rather liberal interpretation of the facts. Although the Americans as a rule encouraged women and children to surrender before attacking a *cotta*, they did not give any quarter once the fighting started. Wood's claim was also not borne out by the events at Bud Dajo.

Another instance of blatant dishonesty on the part of Wood was his assertion regarding the killing of women and children: "It was learned that a number of women and children had been killed. I inspected a portion of the rim of the crater, but saw no women or children among the dead, although I know a number were killed." Yet Kann's photos clearly show women among the dead in the trenches on the southern summit, as well as Wood himself being present just nearby (see figures 12 and 14). Wood noted that "this, although very regrettable, was unavoidable" and repeated his earlier claim that the women had been indistinguishable from the men and were simply caught in the line of fire—yet again ignoring the actual circumstances of the assault.

Having completed the report, Wood went to see Ide, as he noted in his diary: "Called on Governor-General at half past 4 and suggested to him the propriety of the Commission either approving or disapproving the action of the troops, and presented my report to him."[15] Wood effectively presented Ide with a fait accompli. Ide and the commission could hardly disapprove of an action that the US president had already commended, and Wood thus effectively forced the governor-general to publicly state his support and endorse the account presented in the report. It had been a busy day for Wood, but he still found time that evening to send a telegram to Secretary of War Taft suggesting that Major Scott, who was then in the US, would be able to provide "more detailed information concerning facts leading to Mount Dajo fight."[16] At this point, Taft and Wood were working closely together, on both sides of the Pacific, to mobilize support and make sure that the story could be contained.

———✦———

Taking the long westward route from the Philippines, Scott had only just landed in New York on March 10 and had no idea of what had occurred in Jolo after he left:

> Arriving in New York, I went over to call on General Wade, commanding at Governor's Island, and while talking to him in his office his aide, Colonel Glasgow, came in and announced the news of a big battle with the Moros at Joló in which fifty soldiers and six hundred Moros had been killed, with many more wounded. The hallway downstairs was full of newspaper correspondents seeking someone who could tell them anything about Jolo. I bade the general goodbye and, being in civilian clothes, slipped unnoticed through the crowd of reporters and bought a paper on Broadway, giving an account of the fight.[17]

One of the pieces of news that would have been particularly unwelcome to the former governor of Jolo was the accusation that the entire affair was caused by his soft approach—made by DeRackin from Zamboanga but circulated by the Associated Press and printed anonymously. "I saw at once that New York was no place for me," Scott reasoned, "and that the newspaper men would rout me out at once if I went home; so I told a friend in Yonkers that I had come to stay with him until the clouds rolled by."[18] Scott's attempt to lay low did not work for long, however, and on March 19 he was summoned to Washington by Taft "as necessary for the public service," just as Wood had recommended.[19] In his subsequent meeting with the secretary of war, Scott provided what information he could:

> I told him I had left everybody at peace there in December, and I did not know what had happened in the meantime but supposed that the Moros had got excited again over the payment of the head-tax and had gone up on Bud Daho for the third time, and that the fight had probably occurred in getting them down. He told me to get what I had told him typewritten, to be taken over to

the cabinet meeting at eleven o'clock; I got two stenographers at work on it and handed it to him just in time. I had talked rather freely to him as secretary of war, far more freely than if I had been talking to the press.[20]

Soon after, Scott wrote a letter to Wood, reassuring the general that the whole affair would eventually blow over.[21] Scott also enclosed a few newspaper clippings, including one that described a sermon given at the Madison Square Presbyterian Church by Reverend C. H. Parkhurst, who was an ardent social reformer.[22] While speaking on the relationship between Christian nations and "heathens" on March 18, Parkhurst criticized the president's congratulatory telegram to Wood and the general attitude toward the people of the Philippines:

Consider, also, the easy and self-satisfied way in which we regard the mowing down of the savages and semi-savages in the Philippine Islands when they stand in the way of the national purpose of which after eight years of "benevolent assimilation" we have just had a most startling and heart-rending example in the bombarding to death of six hundred men, women and children collected in a crater in the Moro Islands.[23]

The massacre was a deeply shameful act, Parkhurst insisted, adding that "it was no more a 'brilliant feat of arms' than smoking bees out of a hive or rats out of a nest."[24] Parkhurst did not, of course, know just how accurate his analogy was.

———

Roosevelt and Wood's supporters were now getting ready to fight back, and Taft had carefully briefed Ohio congressman Charles H. Grosvenor, who came to the House of Representatives on March 19 armed with an entire file of "official documents."[25] Grosvenor took the floor to denounce the criticism leveled at Roosevelt earlier that week and argued that what had happened at Bud Dajo was tragic but unavoidable: the situation in Jolo had become "intolerable," and there was "no alternative" for the US Army to get "this band of pirates" off the mountain. "As to the statement that no prisoners were taken," he continued, "this seems to be wholly gratuitous and untrue. . . ."[26] Despite the several reports to the contrary, Grosvenor insisted that there had in fact been many Moro survivors:

> Now, it is but fair to suppose that when the full facts are known it will be found that quite a number of prisoners were taken and a great many wounded cared for in the hospitals and by the medical officers of the Army, and that among these prisoners will be a great number of women and children.[27]

Grosvenor then asked to enter into the record a series of documents "as illustrative of the whole condition that our troops found when they made the assault."[28] When John Sharp Williams objected and queried the nature of the documents in question, Grosvenor lost his composure. "I have not relinquished the floor," he shouted, before assuming his attack on Williams and the Democrats:

> It is greatly to be regretted that gentlemen should have given out to the world and a charge be made upon the floor of Congress that involves the honor and integrity of the United States Army, and that has assailed the intelligence and wisdom of the President by inference necessarily, and planted a hostile feeling in the charge made. I will show you that this wonderful victory ought to have a vote of Congress rather than the implied censure of Congress.[29]

The documents that Grosvenor eventually entered into the *Congressional Record*, which ensured that they would be officially published, consisted of excerpts from several Spanish accounts of the Moros, one of which dated back to 1667, but also Dr. Joseph Montano's account of the *juramentado*, as well as Henry Savage Landor's travelogue from 1904.[30] The aim was evidently to prove that the Moros of Jolo were irredeemable fanatics or, as Grosvenor put it, "a body of professional criminals, organized for murder." Invoking the authority of these accounts, Grosvenor renewed his defense of the US Army and its assault on Bud Dajo: "Will it be said that any more force was used than necessary? I deny it. Is it to be said that there should be gentler means? I point out that gentler means would have been unavailing."[31] The representative from Ohio finished his lengthy speech by asserting that Wood's assault had been "skilfully done, successfully done," claiming once more that a considerable number of women and children had survived. Even if this turned out not to be the case, Grosvenor argued, "let the fault fall upon the men who made it impossible to destroy the nest of vipers without the incidentals that were required."[32] In the final calculation, Grosvenor thus placed the blame for any "incidental" killing of women and children squarely on the Moros themselves.

"I catch some of the usual phrases of jingoism," Williams scoffed as he took the floor to reply.[33] He knew well that his poem channeling Tennyson had been mocked by the Republicans at every opportunity, and he addressed the issue head-on:

> The gentleman objects to treating the matter poetically. Prosaically treated, then, it is reduced to the loss of 18 killed on one side and on the other side the loss of 600 people, part of whom were women and children. These are the bare facts.[34]

Williams then proceeded to unpack the contradictions of the different accounts that had been provided by various official sources: first it was reported that all six hundred of the enemy were killed, with no mention of wounded or prisoners. Then it was admitted that women and children had also been killed—the latter supposedly because they had been used as shields by the Moros themselves. But then another explanation was offered, namely that the women and children had been killed by long-range artillery fire and that their deaths had been accidental:

> Which of the two explanations is going to be taken? Or, is it true that later on we will have still a third one? Perhaps when American sentiment demands it there will be prisoners and perhaps wounded reported. And if hereafter prisoners and wounded are to be reported, why were they not reported in the official report of the battle, giving the casualties on our side and the casualties on the other?[35]

Grosvenor interjected and repeated his claim that there had been prisoners taken at Bud Dajo, but Williams dismissed this, mocking his opponent in his concluding remarks:

We can not change our opinions upon the mere supposition, the mere predic-
tion of the chief prophet of the Republican party that there, perhaps, "may be"
prisoners, that there, perhaps, "may be" wounded to be reported later "officially," and now only unofficially suggested by him.[36]

That was the end of what turned out to be the last debate on Bud Dajo to
take place in the House of Representatives.

———

While Grosvenor and Williams were debating, Reverend Edward Abbott,
who was a member of the Anti-Imperialist League, published a letter in
the *Boston Daily Advertiser* in which he decried the hypocrisy of American
imperial policy. In referring to Roosevelt's by-then-infamous telegram to
Wood, Abbott offered a historical analogy—steeped in the rhetoric of the
pulpit:

> A little more than 40 years ago Abraham Lincoln, standing on the field of Get-
> tysburg, amidst the graves of men who in a true sense had "upheld the honor" of
> "the American flag," reminded us how "our fathers brought forth upon this con-
> tinent a new nation, conceived in liberty and dedicated to the proposition that
> all men are created equal . . . that government of the people by the people for the
> people should not perish from the earth." Is anybody prepared to measure the
> distance from the Declaration of Independence and the field of Gettysburg to
> the Massacre of Dajo?[37]

Abbott's poignant question nevertheless fell on deaf ears, and much of the
criticism was drowned out as the latest message from Wood was reported
with glee throughout the expansionist press—headlines included "'Fake'
News of Jolo" and "False News from Manila."[38] Wood's dismissal of the
stories as lies was taken as the final word in the matter, and the lurid reports of the slaughter of women and children were reported as untrue. The
story of Bud Dajo was transformed into a celebration of American rule in
the Philippines, and the resulting headlines completely whitewashed the
massacre: one newspaper reported Wood's cablegram under the heading
"No Women or Children Killed," while another suggested that "Troops

Saved Women."[39] Taking a cue from the president, any and all critique of
the handling of the Mount Dajo affair was furthermore portrayed as essentially unpatriotic and a betrayal of the troops. A *New York Sun* editorial
asked rhetorically "Why Do These Democrats Hate the Army?," and the
New York Sun went one step further, writing that "John Williams will go
out of his way to spit on American soldiers."[40]

———

Meanwhile, Taft and the War Department had been busy mobilizing
further support for Wood. On March 21, Taft put before the Senate a
cablegram from Governor-General Ide, as well as a three-page memorandum written by Major Scott, both of which were immediately released to
the press.[41] Ide's cablegram had the clearest message and was published
in full:

> Newspaper reports from Manila announcing wanton slaughter of women and
> children at Mount Dajo extremely sensational and in all essential details false.
> The situation occupied by Moro outlaws on crater of volcano, 2,100 feet high,
> was exceedingly difficult and required great display of heroism on the part of
> the Army, Navy, Filipino, and Moro constabulary, who rendered most valiant
> service. Some women and children were killed and wounded by preliminary
> shelling at distance. Moros were outlaws and fanatics and refused to surren-
> der to the last, attempting repeatedly to murder our forces who were rescuing
> wounded Moros. Moro Sultan and leading datos rendered great assistance, and
> the surrounding population entirely in sympathy with the course taken to re-
> move gang of cutthroats who were preying upon community, retreating as occa-
> sion required to what they supposed to be impenetrable fastness.
>
> There was no killing of anyone except such as was indispensable to end intol-
> erable situation. Attack not ordered until every resource looking into peaceable
> adjustment exhausted. Troops and officers deserving of highest praise.[42]

This was little more than a rephrasing of Wood's previous explanations, yet
because it came from the office of the highest American civil authority in
Manila, Ide's message was presented as an official exoneration. Scott's longer memorandum provided more context and crucially painted a portrait

of Wood as an exemplary and benign colonial administrator. "The policy of General Wood in that archipelago," Scott insisted, "has always been to bring about peace and order as gently and with as little loss of life as possible."[43] The expansionist papers eagerly seized upon these latest interventions in the debate, and the resulting headlines made it clear that many considered Wood and the army to have been completely vindicated:

IDE ACQUITS TROOPS OF KILLING MORO WOMEN
SAYS SULTAN AND POPULACE INDORSE OUR ARMY'S ACTIONS
WOOD A PEACEMAKER—SCOTT[44]

Some of the headlines were outright implausible—the *Democrat and Chronicle* ran with "Battle Humane," while the *Punxsutawney News* managed to turn Wood into a savior: "Tried to Spare the Women."[45]

If Taft and the government had managed to convince most of the public that there was nothing to the story of Bud Dajo, the critics were far from satisfied, and many questions remained unanswered. On March 22, Charles Allen Culberson pointed out in the Senate that the official correspondence that had so far been released was incomplete and that in some instances reports had been condensed.[46] A new resolution was accordingly passed, once again directing the War Department to submit "full copies of all reports and all other communications" to the Senate.[47] Beyond the walls of the Capitol, however, the critical press was less patient. There were numerous inconsistencies in the official account, and some papers suggested that there had been a deliberate cover-up and that incriminating telegrams had been withheld.[48] Under the heading "Wanted—A Straight Story," the *Washington Post* pointed out many of the same contradictions that Representative Williams had previously mentioned in the House.[49] Ide's claim that Moro women were accidentally killed by long-range shells, for instance, was essentially incompatible with Wood's explanation that they had been killed in hand-to-hand fighting because they wore trousers and were indistinguishable from the men.

From the very moment that the reports about Bud Dajo had first reached the US, journalists and politicians had in fact been calling for a full account of what happened. However, the physical distance between the

imperial metropole and the Philippines enabled the government to maintain a near-complete control of the flow of information. In the absence of
any new evidence, there was ultimately little that the critics could do. On
March 26, Taft put before the Senate all communication relating to Bud
Dajo, in compliance with Culbertson's latest resolution.[50] Yet these documents merely consisted of telegrams and messages from the period between
March 9 and March 20, most of which had already been published in the
press.[51] This was the last time that any material relating to Bud Dajo was
officially released. Although Taft and the War Department had technically
complied with the letter of the resolutions, they never published any evidence that would allow for a more critical scrutiny of what had occurred
in Jolo.

In the end, Taft and the expansionist press were successful in shaping the
story of Bud Dajo. Even the papers that were usually critical of the Roosevelt administration eventually accepted the logic of the official narrative.
Three weeks after the news of Bud Dajo had first reached the US, an editorial in *Harper's Weekly* thus summarized what had by then become the
accepted view of the so-called Battle of Mt. Dajo:

> There were women and children killed. That was deplorable, of course. The lat-
> est dispatches say they were killed at long range by shell-fire, and add that many
> were left alive. It was a bad mess, but at the same time it was a difficult, danger-
> ous, and, apparently, a necessary job well done.[52]

Public interest in the subject soon waned, and without the political attention, which had driven much of the original outrage and debate, the occasional news piece about Bud Dajo in the following weeks and months
failed to gain much attention, much less spark any debate. By the time that
San Francisco was hit by a major earthquake, on April 18, 1906, instantly
becoming the dominant news story, distant events in the Philippines had
already disappeared from the front pages.

By the end of March, Wood could breathe more easily, and his aide, Captain McCoy, indeed made light of Bud Dajo when writing to a friend:

The Jolo Moros gave us a very fierce little fight, just to vary the monotony. Like every other fierce little scrap down there we have the feeling this will be about the last of the sort, but severe lessons don't seem to teach the Sulu much.[53]

The attempt to downplay the matter nevertheless obscured the fact that Wood and his staff had been genuinely worried about the possibility of an official investigation, as McCoy admitted in another letter: "The newspapers have been making a great deal of fuss about the poor Moros, but it has all passed over without any courts of inquiry or courts-martial."[54] Already in his March 13 message, Wood had shown that he was not entirely confident of how his explanation would be received and even seemed to admit the possibility that new "evidence" might prove him wrong. The general had good reasons to be cautious in his wording of the message to Taft—he was one of the most controversial officers in the US Army and had numerous enemies in the press and in the world of politics. Wood had in fact previously instructed Langhorne to collect evidence in case there was an investigation:

Send copies all papers, letters, etc. on file in re Daho Moros. Secure from Reeves full information as to conditions which made action Mount Daho necessary, especially Scott's efforts to get the people off the mountain without fighting.[55]

The deliberate attempt to build the case for the expedition against Bud Dajo retrospectively had already begun on March 5, when Captain Langhorne wrote a formal request to Wood for military assistance:

Sir; I have the honour to inform you that the assistance of troops have been found necessary in Jolo in order to arrest a large party of lawbreakers who have taken possession of the summit of Mount Daho. These people are committing depredations on friendly Moros, and the native headmen and local civil authorities have found it impossible to cope with the situation. For this reason the assistance of troops is formally requested. The garrison of Jolo is found to be insufficient, hence the request for additional troops from Zamboanga and other points.[56]

Considering that the operation against Bud Dajo was already well underway by March 5, this request was both absurd and redundant, and was in truth little more than an attempt to a create a paper trail and provide a formal pretext for the assault. Wood was keenly aware that any misstep on his part might be seized upon by his critics, so his every move was made with political optics in mind. Even as late as mid-May, the issue was still haunting Wood, who evidently felt the need to explain himself to the president:

> I see most of the blackguards in public as well as private life have let up on the Mount Dajo business. The officers and men appreciate very much your attitude in this instance. Work of this kind, while calling for a high degree of courage and dash on the part of the troops, has its disagreeable side, which is the unavoidable killing of women and children; but it must be done, and disagreeable as it is, there is no way of avoiding it. The sex of a charging fanatical mass, well-armed and determined to kill, is not a matter for determination at the time. In fact, no part of such an aggregation can be given any protection or consideration from those who are ordered to destroy it.[57]

On April 14, 1906, Wood handed over the governorship of the Department of Mindanao and Sulu to General Bliss during a ceremony in Zamboanga, months after he should formally have done so. Now all that remained for Wood was to submit the official report of the Bud Dajo expedition. Most of Colonel Duncan's official report, which also included reports from the officers who commanded the main columns as well as the artillery and naval contingents, had actually been written in the days immediately after the expedition. Yet Duncan sat on it for several weeks, at Wood's request, and handed it over to Wood personally only when the general visited Zamboanga in April.[58] Duncan, Bundy, Lawton, and Koehler made no reference whatsoever to the killing of women and children in their respective reports. The only mention was to be found in the final observations that Duncan had evidently added much later in response to the criticism in the United States:

> In conclusion, it is a matter of great regret to all who participated in this expedition that some women and children were inadvertently killed during the fight

on the summit of the mountain. It is not believed that a woman or child was intentionally killed by anyone, even though in many instances the women are said to have fought like demons; for the American soldier is of that superior type of manhood that would never willingly lift an avenging hand against woman or child.[59]

It would indeed appear that Duncan had modeled this part of his report closely on Wood's own explanations. In the final words of the official report of the Bud Dajo expedition, Duncan placed the responsibility for the massacre squarely on the Moros themselves:

> It will readily and clearly be seen that the Moros had every opportunity to remove all their women and children, and that to them and their fanaticism should be laid the injury and death of every woman and child.[60]

Altogether, Wood took more than two weeks before he finally dispatched Duncan's report by boat to Washington, where it was eventually received by Taft on May 20—two and a half months after the massacre.[61] By this point, however, there were no longer any demands for a full account of what had happened, and Taft simply filed the 130-odd-page report in the official records, effectively burying the story of Bud Dajo.[62]

———◆———

The day before Wood formally stepped down as governor of the Moro Province, he held a meeting with Sultan Jamalul Kiràm II and the most important Moro chiefs onboard the ship *Sabah*, anchored in Jolo harbor. The purpose of this meeting was ostensibly to mark the transfer of governorship, yet Wood was mainly concerned with securing the approval of the Moro elites in case there were further queries concerning the assault on Bud Dajo. Prompted by Wood, the sultan and various leaders all readily agreed that the Americans had acted correctly by defeating the people on the hill, yet in the end the general did not elicit the unequivocal statements of support that he expected. When Wood asked Jokanain a leading question about whether the expedition had had a positive effect on the situation in the island, the *datu* responded cautiously: "I do not know what to say; if I say it was a good thing, it would not be right, because there were a good many people killed; if I say it was not a good thing, that would be wrong, because there were bad people killed there; so I don't know what to say."[63] Before the meeting came to an end, Wood reminded the assembled chiefs that they were responsible for the actions of their followers, and he warned of the consequences should any one of them choose to challenge the Americans:

> If you look back over the last three years, where is Hassan, where is Pala, where is Peruka Utig, and others, and all those men on the hill, what has become of them? They are all dead. And in the future, all the men who make trouble will be dead, too.

Considering that little more than a month had passed since the slaughter at Bud Dajo, Wood's parting words were in many ways a fitting summary of his tenure in the Moro Province. Whatever the Sultan and Moro chiefs had been comfortable telling Wood to his face, they ultimately presented Scott with a very different story when he returned in the summer of 1906:

> Arriving back in Jolo, I found Jokanain, Calbi and Indanan much displeased over the Bud Dajo fight. They all said "that fight would never have happened if you had been there. . . ."[64]

THIRTEEN

The Stories They Told

You have most likely seen by the papers that we had a battle. The little line or so that is in the paper never can tell the story for it was something awful. I have seen sights that I never expected to see.

I will try and write about this trouble but I never can tell all.

John C. Schweiger, writing to his parents
from Jolo, March 18, 1906[1]

IKE SOLDIERS ELSEWHERE—IN DIFFERENT WARS AT DIFFERENT times—some of the Americans who participated in the assault on Bud Dajo struggled to describe their experience and explain to friends and family back home what they had been through. For instance, Captain Lawton wrote a friend shortly after his return from Jolo, claiming that "the desperate nature of the fighting, and the horrible scenes enacted are beyond description. No human pen could do them justice."[2] However, this apparent case of "veteran's aphasia" did not prevent Lawton from writing several pages, describing in great detail the assault and the violence of the aftermath. The fact was that most of the officers and men who had fought their way to the summit of Bud Dajo were only too willing to share their stories—and where Wood and the Roosevelt administration had been deliberately cautious about the information released, the soldiers were surprisingly frank and entirely unconstrained in what they divulged in letters written to friends and family back home. Local newspapers that did not have the benefit of their own correspondents in Washington or Manila would furthermore publish private letters sent from the Philippines in lieu of foreign news. On May 24, 1906, for instance, the *Melvern Review*, based in the town of Melvern, Kansas (population 500), published a letter received by a Mrs. John Long from her cousin, Archie Johnson, who served with the 6th Infantry in the Philippines—here reproduced in full:

Jolo, Jolo, P.I., March 29, '06
Dear Cousin Claire,

We have left Cebu and are in the most southern part of the islands, on a little island south of Mindanao spelled "Jolo" but pronounced "Holo." I am getting along fine as a silk, still getting three square meals a day and getting fat, I am cook now. I get $24.00 a month, but I don't like to cook for sixty men very well—too much work. We get lots of fine fish here of all kinds, right out of the bay.

  Say, did you see anything in the papers about the fight we had at Jolo? We killed 1,200 Moros and lost 23 men killed and 52 wounded. It was a terrible sight. They were on top of a high mountain—2,100 feet high—the mountain slanted up about like this /‾\ with a crater at the top, and it was hard to climb. They had it well fortified, but we finally got to top. They were firing at us all the way up. We had two cannons that threw explosive shells right in among them, and tore heads, arms and legs off. We had two machine guns that shoot four hundred times a minute. When they opened up on the Moros they fell just like wheat before a sickle, and there were six companies of the sixth infantry firing at them at the same time. It took us three days to take them. Out of 1,200 on the mountain only five were left, two women and three little kids, and they were wounded. The "niggers" were piled up in some of the trenches six feet deep, and scattered all around over the ground: men, women and children. Just think seeing 1,200 lying around dead. I never want to see such a sight again. Every once in a while I would see one of our men fall, but we kept on going.

There was one old, gray headed woman lying there with a piece of sugar cane in her mouth. She was eating it just as a shell took the top of her head off. All such sights as that. I am going to get some pictures of the battlefield and I will send you one. These people think that if they die fighting they will go to heaven on a gray horse, so I guess there will be quite a bunch of them.

The fight was on the 6th, 7th and 8th of March. The papers state 600 Moros were killed. But the officers made a small report so there would not be much said about it in the states.

The mountain is only five and one half miles from here. Before the fight they would come down and burn our targets at the range and steal our flags. When they saw us coming they yelled, "Come on, you Americano—," and called us names. They thought we could not get up it at all, but we did.

I expect I will be home in about six months. Tell the folks all hello. If I get in any more fights I am going to try to dodge all the bullets. So good bye.

Archibald Johnson
Co, E. 6th Inf't., Manila, P.I.[3]

The stories told privately by the officers and men of the Bud Dajo expedition differed from the carefully curated official narrative only in that they were more honest—honest about the racialized dehumanization of the Moros, honest about the indiscriminate violence of the massacre, and honest about the actual number of men, women, and children who had been killed.[4] That is not to say that the soldiers were always truthful, and exaggeration and sensationalism were at the heart of the stories that were being shared among the soldiers, even while the assault on Bud Dajo was still ongoing. "Weird stories from all parts of the battle-field were told the writer the last night of the combat," Wright later recounted:

> The Moro women fought more desperately than the men. One could not tell them from the men. One horrible photograph I have shows a woman with hair cut short. One saw a Filipino [constabulary] cut a Moro woman in two with one slash of a bolo. Others saw Moros kill their own children or use them as shields in the fight.... A Moro woman threw her baby at a soldier, and then made at him with a barong. She was shot down. A Moro threw his baby on a row of bayonets, and as it stuck on one he jumped and killed the soldier behind the bayonet.[5]

These stories underscored Moro savagery, thereby justifying American violence, and some were ludicrously embellished, as the soldier who claimed that the Moros "throwed their own children, even tore their children apart and threw the pieces."[6] The circulation of such violent tales, usually shared only around the campfire or among veterans, seemed to reflect a desire to both shock and impress.[7] When Colonel Duncan, for instance, was later interviewed by a local newspaper in the US, the story of Bud Dajo had been turned into an exotic tale worthy of Edgar Rice Burroughs or H. G. Wells:

> I broke up their fortifications and killed scores of them with my artillery. I told my interpreter to beg them for heaven's sake to surrender, as I had no alternative, but to kill them. But they leaped up naked on the fortifications beating tom-toms, smacking their bare limbs and grimacing fearfully. They were absolutely without fear. I would not say they were courageous, because they fought merely like so many wild animals.[8]

Despite the graphic details shared by soldiers, however, neither their families and friends nor the wider public seems to have thought much of the violence committed by Americans. The father of Robert E. Ricketts, 6th Infantry, thus told a newspaper about a letter received from his son describing the assault on Bud Dajo:

He said that dead Moros were piled four and five deep in the trenches and that from the first stockade to the summit of the mountain the route of the troops was marked by the dead bodies of the slain. Seven of his regiment were killed and about twenty-five wounded falling all around him. "I am proud of that boy!," added Mr. Ricketts, "but I wish he was home."[9]

When Private Townsend's letter to his mother, describing the slaughter on the southern summit, was subsequently published in a local newspaper, it was introduced by the following comment:

The American soldier is apt to be a cheerful chap in almost any circumstances or conditions. He is most cheerful, however, when there is prospect of a fight, and the possibility of losing his life does not seriously disturb him. If he were otherwise he would not be a good soldier. . . . The letter of this Morristown boy written to his mother from the Island of Mindanao three weeks after the fight, is interesting as showing the adventurous spirit of the young soldier. Several thousand miles from home, wounded, in hospital, he writes with cheerfulness and naivete. . . .[10]

The soldiers, as it turned out, were very much aware that the Bud Dajo expedition had been reported in the American press, and it soon became known that there had been widespread critique of the killing of women and children.[11] From April onward, their letters thus began to directly address the accusations of "wanton slaughter," complaining that they were being unfairly maligned by people with no real knowledge or experience of the Philippines. One soldier wrote a friend:

In regard to the last fight with the Moros at Jolo, we see that the papers in the states are giving us an awful raking over for the wholesale slaughter of women and children. Now could these same people, would have been so misinformed, have been eye witnesses to that fight, they would certainly have another story to tell.[12]

Private Burke, who had operated the machine gun at the top of the southern summit, had nothing but scorn for the people who criticized US

military conduct at Bud Dajo and for what was assumed to be their misplaced sympathy for the Moros:

> Our beloved people will probably be horrified and will say, "Don't hurt our lit-
> tle brown brothers: we must educate them," and all that sort of thing, but if
> they would attend to the heathen in the states and let us deal with the savages
> as they do with us things would fare far better both here and there. This kind
> of warfare has been carried on since 1898 and is no nearer the end. Why? That
> is the question, to which there are several answers. The main one is two-thirds
> of the people (women especially, who are at the head of the army) are under
> the delusion that the Filipinos and Moros are actually human beings; and for
> every American soldier who is slashed in the back with a bolo or is captured and
> tortured to death, the culprit should be patted on the back and called "our little
> brown brother."[13]

Some of the participants in the expedition engaged directly with the
press back in the US, and Captain Lawton, for instance, wrote a long letter
to the editor of the *Sun* in May 1906:

> I feel that I owe it to myself and the officers of my command to refute the state-
> ments and insinuations made by those misguided philanthropists who, in utter
> ignorance of conditions and circumstances in this far-off country, have taken on
> themselves to sit in judgement and "roast" in most scathing terms officers and
> men who but did their duty under most trying circumstances, and who feel that
> applause, at least, rather than censure, is their due.[14]

Lawton's attempt to explain the circumstances surrounding what he referred to as a "battle," however, was thoroughly misleading. First, he insisted that the men and officers of the expedition did not know there were
any women and children at Bud Dajo, right up until the point when they
reached the summit and engaged in desperate hand-to-hand combat. This
was a highly implausible claim that completely contradicted the account
made by Wood and other officers to the effect that they had begged the
Moros to send out their women and children prior to the attack. During

the fighting, Lawton continued, it was impossible to distinguish between sexes, and he even implied that he would have been court-martialed for gross negligence if he had prevented his men from killing women. Again, this was a fanciful counterfactual claim that bore no correlation whatsoever to the way that the Americans had been fighting in the southern Philippines for years. Finally, Lawton explained, the children had been killed only because they had been used as shields by their own parents:

> These Moros were fanatics of the worst kind. They were determined either to conquer or die, and if it was die, the women must go with them, and the babies, too. Such was their cult, such their dictum, carried out to the letter.
>
> No man, woman or child faltered. All fought to the last breath. Their stoicism was sublime, their courage filled us with wonder and admiration, but their fate was inevitable.[15]

The letter was published in the *Sun* on July 9, along with a strong endorsement by the editor:

> The American soldiers in the Philippines, and wherever else, have the confidence, respect and thorough cordial good will of all but a negligible quantity of their countrymen. They are as humane as they are fearless; and they must not think that any howling of Bedlam dervishes can make the country unjust to its defenders.[16]

A week later, Ensign Henry D. Cooke, who was with the naval detachment on the eastern summit of Bud Dajo, returned to the United States on sick leave, and he was shortly after interviewed by a local Philadelphia newspaper. Asked about the claims made by Captain Lawton, Cooke was hesitant to speak: "I think it would be presumptuous of me to talk about that battle, when my superior officers have given their versions."[17] The journalist nevertheless pressed him:

> "But there remains a public concern as to whether women and children were shot down coldly," he was reminded.

"Well, as to women and children," he answered, "I never saw one of them till after it was all over. Then I saw some lying dead, and I saw twenty who were captives."[18]

Cooke was evidently not comfortable sharing too much, let alone bragging about it, but he eventually opened up, and when Lawton's description of the suicidal Moros was read out, he concurred: "'This is quite true,' approved Mr. Cooke. 'We were fighting fanatics, whose religion was that by dying they would come to reward after death. Yes, like the Japanese, no doubt.'"[19] The reference to the Japanese was evidently an allusion to reports during the Russo-Japanese War (1904–1905) that their soldiers preferred to die by their own hand rather than being captured by the enemy.[20] The journalist interviewing Cooke added another, and by now inevitable, point of comparison: "That was the enemy—Moslems with the idea of resist or die, such as those Kitchener dealt with on the field at Omdurman."[21]

One of the more unusual ways in which the American soldiers in the Philippines responded to the criticism at home was through poems and songs. The initial condemnation of the massacre had of course been made in the form of poetry from the floor of the House of Representatives, namely the much-ridiculed verses about "The Wood Brigade." However, what was to become the single most popular piece of writing about Bud Dajo was the poem "The Fight at Dajo," written by Alfred E. Wood, a relatively unknown correspondent with links to the army in the Philippines, and first published in the *Cablenews Manila* on May 11, 1906. The poem included the following verses:

There are twenty dead who're sleeping near the slopes of Bud Dajo,
'Neath the shadow of the crater where the bolos laid them low,
And their comrades feel it bitter, and their cheeks grow hot with shame,
When they read the sneering comments which have held them up to blame.
. . .
Though [the Moros] had robbed and slain and ravaged, though their crimes
had mounted high,

Though 't is true that naught became them like the death they chose to die,
One would think to read the papers that the troops who scaled their fort,
Were a lot of brutal ruffians shooting girls and babes for sport.[22]

The poem gives a clear sense of the bitterness and betrayal experienced by the soldiers who had expected the support and respect of the American public. The maudlin verses evidently struck a note with the officers and men of the Bud Dajo expedition, and at the headquarters of the 6th Infantry in Zamboanga, Duncan had it reprinted and distributed among the troops. One officer, who had been at Bud Dajo, sent a copy to the editor of the *Minneapolis Messenger* with the following comments:

> The army as a whole and especially the men who took part in the fight will be surprised and humiliated if the general public believe the untrue reports in regards to the wanton destruction of women and children. We believe that the army will be given full credit when the truth is known.[23]

Once the poem reached the US, it received even greater circulation: it was printed in newspapers and magazines and even in book form a few years later, when it was included in Burton Egbert Stevenson's *Poems of American History* under the title "The Fight at Dajo."[24] The poem appears to have inspired at least two popular songs, which both seized upon the motif of the dying soldier at Bud Dajo: "The Soldier Boy's Last Toast" (1908) and "He Is Sleeping Where Mount Dajo Frowning Looks on Jolo Bay" (1910).[25] These songs drew on familiar themes of sacrifice and sentimental patriotism that harked back to the Civil War and simply changed the lyrics slightly to make the songs more topical. Soon after, the vaudeville-inspired song "If a Lady's Wearin' Pantaloons" first began circulating in the United States. Seemingly a light comedic tune, filled with colloquial slang as was typical of American popular entertainment at the time, the song was also known by another title: "The Ladies in the Trenches: A Soldier Song of the Sulu Isles." The first verse and chorus were as follows:

If a lady wearin' pantaloons is swingin' wit' a knife,
Must I stop an' cross-examine as ter sex?

"Air you Datto Mudd, his ownself, Ma'am, or air you jest his wife?
Kindly answer 'fore I reach yer solar plex."
If a lady wearin' britches is a-hidin' in the ditches,
An' she itches fer me ears as souvenirs,
Must I arsk before I twists 'er, "Air you Miss or air you Mister?"
How shell a bashful man decide th' dears?
[Chorus:]
Ladies, if yer wearin' o' yer husband's pantaloons—
(Mercy! How you makes a soldier blush!)
You will have ter take th' chances w'ich is tagged to husband's pantses,
Or stay ter home an' make th' babies hush!
We ain't no clarryvoyants; if yer wearin' pantaloons
We must take you as we find you when th' guns begin their tunes;
An' we cannot be caressin' though you puzzle us distressin',
When yer wearin' o' yer husband's pantaloons.[26]

Although these verses might seem more at home in Ade's comical musical, they were in fact a cheery tune about the killing of Moro women at Bud Dajo, and later verses made explicit reference to the soldiers charging a mountain while dodging *bolos* and *krises*. The killing of women, even more so than children, had proven to be hugely damaging to army morale; with its titillating play on cross-dressing, the American soldiers' concerns about their own masculinity were clearly exposed in the song.[27] Sixty years later, when the killing of Vietnamese women by US soldiers once again became a point of debate in the United States, an old veteran of the Philippine campaigns still remembered the lyrics and still defended the soldiers' actions:

Well, the average American male, conditioned in the tradition of gallantry, who always walks next to the curb when he promenades with a flower of Southern womanhood, recoils at the idea of shooting or hand-grenading a lady, but if she's in uniform which does not disclose her sex, and she's trying to shoot or hand grenade him, I suppose he has no recourse but to fight back.[28]

FOURTEEN

An Operation, Not an Aberration

We guess the Moros who were wiped out by General Wood's command were bad folks, and since they were all killed, we are anxious to believe that they needed killing. But of course it was a dirty job to clean them out. In our Indian wars, which lasted down to twenty or thirty years ago, it was sometimes necessary to exterminate a band of Indians, as this band of Moros was exterminated. It was done, faithfully, by as good soldiers and officers as we ever had, and it was hard, dangerous, inglorious work—a kind of rat-killing.

Life, March 29, 1906[1]

O N MARCH 16, 1906, THE *NEW YORK WORLD* PUBLISHED A CAR-toon by C. R. Macauley that showed Taft and Roosevelt, the latter in his Rough Rider uniform and carrying his signature club, draping the American flag over small corpses, with a sign that says "Jolo." The caption read: "Covering it up."[2] If there was a cover-up in the aftermath of the Bud

Dajo expedition, however, it was a cover-up in broad daylight. For sure, there was a very selective release of information by both Wood and the Roosevelt administration, in conjunction with patently inaccurate statements.[3] The circumstances that led to the assault, the killing of women and children, the number of Moro casualties, and the treatment of the wounded and the dead were all grossly misrepresented in official communications. Much of the information that had been withheld nevertheless emerged that very summer through unofficial channels as correspondents and officers on leave from the Philippines began arriving back in the United States. In the months following the expedition to Jolo, dozens of letters and eyewitness accounts were furthermore published in newspapers all over the country, and the explicit and uncensored accounts of Archie Johnson, Mahoney, Townsend, and dozens of participants in the massacre were thus available for everyone in America to read.

Hamilton M. Wright returned from his visit to the Philippines in May 1906 and immediately began publishing a series of highly sensational articles about the "Battle of Mt. Dajo." These accounts appeared, incongruously, among his other journalistic output, which presented the Philippines as a land of boundless opportunity for American investors. The barely concealed boosterism of articles with titles such as "In the Land of the Big Cigar" or "In the Rich Cagayan Valley" was thus interrupted by the tabloid hyperbole of "Hurling Babies on Bayonets Moros Greet Death on Mt. Dajo."[4] Pitched as exclusive exposés by a special correspondent, Wright's lurid pieces were accompanied by a selection of his own photographs from Bud Dajo, some ten in total, as well as fanciful line drawings of the desperate struggle on the mountain. Despite the poor black-and-white reproduction of the photos, the bodies of dead Moros are still clearly visible, scattered all over the crest and among the fortifications on the eastern summit (see figure 15). Though framed as a hard-won victory by the Americans over fanatic "outlaws," the extent of the slaughter was quite explicit.[5] In the end, however, neither the images nor the many detailed accounts produced any response whatsoever, and it would indeed appear that the story had lost its ability to shock the American public. Yet the salient point remains: What had happened at Bud Dajo was not some dark secret—it was, in other words, not knowledge that lacked.[6] More than the lies and omissions, what ultimately enabled the whitewashing of the massacre was the ideological narrative that framed the violence. The same day that the troops returned to Zamboanga from Jolo, a soldier addressed this very point in a letter home:

> The slaughter of so many may appear to those at home to be terrible, but these people want to die when they have made up their minds to it and nothing but death will satisfy them. It is hoped here that this may prove to be the final settling of the matter of how absurd it is to stand against the Government in its desire to promote the welfare of these poor, ignorant people, and while it seems to be a queer way to show them that we want to be good and kind, it is the only way.[7]

The fact was that the Bud Dajo Massacre was exceptional only in its scale, and General Wood unique only in his ambition. Although there were some Americans who, like W. E. B. Du Bois, Mark Twain, and Moorfield Storey, clearly recognized what happened at Bud Dajo as an atrocity, there were far more who saw nothing but a military victory to celebrate or, at best, a tragic but necessary part of the civilizing mission. Apart from the widespread support for Wood among Republicans and the expansionist press, Roosevelt also received a number of personal messages congratulating him on the victory at Bud Dajo. For instance, former Union Army officer Grenville M. Dodge wrote Roosevelt and compared the critique of Wood to the Powder River Expedition in 1865, when Dodge had been ordered to cease his pursuit of Arapaho Indians after US troops had killed a number of women and children.[8] Dodge lamented the fact that he had been hindered in completing the job:

> Supposed that Wood had surrounded these men and made them surrender? That would only be giving them another opportunity. There is no question that in fighting savages there is nothing that subdues them except severe punishment which they can all see and appreciate.[9]

Wood and the other officers of the expedition received similar letters, and an old army friend wrote Captain McCoy from New York: "I wish I could have been with you on the last Jolo expedition. You certainly 'civilized' a big bunch. A few more expeditions should materially 'pacify' the country."[10] Support for Wood and the army also came from high-ranking figures such as Dean C. Worcester, who was a member of the Philippine Commission and the secretary of the interior:

> My opinion is that the troops in Jolo did the only possible thing and the entirely proper thing and I do not care who knows what my opinion on this subject is. . . . It was no more possible to avoid killing women and children here than it was to avoid killing them in the Wounded Knee fight in the United States.[11]

When contemporary critics compared Bud Dajo to Wounded Knee, and Wood to Jacob "Howling Wilderness" Smith, they did so on the assumption that such massacres were self-evidently unjustifiable.[12] An editorial in the *Index*, for instance, insisted that the killing of women and children was inherently un-American:

> It is not pleasant to think of the United States—the land of freedom and liberty—entering the butchering business. Yet that is what we have done. Someone is responsible for this bloody work and the public should make it clear that murdering practically defenseless men, women and children is not in accord with American ideas.[13]

However, this was not a commonly held view, as reflected by Worcester, but also expressed in the pages of *Manila Times*, which was politically closely aligned with the US administration in the Philippines:

> Too much criticism has been made over this assault by the press of the East. It was necessary to tranquilize the island: The men killed were professional murderers; the women killed were their pals and fought just as fiercely as did the men. They refused to surrender after the height had been gained by the Americans. There was nothing else to do but annihilate the band. Their deaths were a blessing to the world, and the soldiers who had the unpleasant business in hand are entitled to only praise, not censure, from the people of the United States. In point of fact they did nothing that has not been done in every Indian fight between the Atlantic and the Pacific, because men in battle cannot distinguish

whether those who are trying to kill them are men or women. It is a case of life and death, and certainly it is better for a murderous Moro to be killed than an American soldier.[14]

By situating Bud Dajo within a time-honored tradition of Indian fighting, the massacre was not denied so much as justified. In private correspondence with a friend, Leonard Wood himself cited the precedent set by the first settlers in North America:

> I have been amused by some of the various criticisms which have been made. Some gentlemen, of rather limited military experience, seem to think that the mountain could have been surrounded and the people starved into surrender. . . . There was nothing to do but to take the place, and it was taken very gallantly. I believe that some of our own hard-playing ancestors dealt with the Pequot Indians in a somewhat similar manner, and a great deal less provocation.[15]

Drawing a direct line from the Pilgrims to Bud Dajo, Wood thus invoked the kind of redemptive violence that was a defining feature of America's founding myth, with the obvious implication that the violence deployed against the Moros was both reasonable and justifiable. It might be noted that the way the Pequot Indians were "dealt with" included the killing of five hundred men, women, and children during the assault on their main village of Mistick in 1637, which was surrounded and burned to the ground. Just seven survivors were reported, and the Pequot tribe was afterward considered to be extinct.[16]

For commentators outside the United States, the parallels between America's policy toward its own indigenous population and the Moros were only too obvious, and one German newspaper explained how "the American government now realized that it is impossible to restore peace on the island without eradicating the Moros, and since then they have been hunted down like the Indians once were."[17] The German ambassador in Washington, Hermann Speck von Sternburg, wrote to President Roosevelt after he learned of the Bud Dajo expedition, congratulating him on the "brilliant fighting" and "first class sharpshooting."[18] The ambassador finished his message with what might have been mistaken for a touch of envy: "How Wood must have enjoyed the work!"[19] Roosevelt wrote back to Speck: "It is just the kind of fighting which I knew would appeal to you."[20] Considering the German reputation for brutality in colonial warfare and a bloody record that included the first genocide of the twentieth century, perpetrated against the Herero in South West Africa, it would appear that Roosevelt and Sternburg were both fairly candid about what "the kind of fighting" actually entailed.[21]

The truth was that the assault on Bud Dajo was just one of many punitive expeditions and so-called pacification campaigns that took place throughout the Western empires in Africa and Asia during the turn of the century. In 1906 alone, there were at least five major colonial conflicts within the British, Dutch, and German imperial spheres. At the exact same time that the operation against Bud Dajo was taking place, the British were fighting an Islamic revolt in northern Nigeria, and on March 10 at the village of Satiru several thousand warriors and civilians were killed by colonial troops. The commanding officer insisted that it was essential that "so dangerous a body of fanatics should be not merely defeated but annihilated."[22] Just a few months later, the British faced an uprising in Natal in South Africa, following the introduction of a poll tax, which, much like the cedula in Jolo, led to widespread resistance among the Zulu. The uprising, led by chief Bambatha, was brutally suppressed, and at the final battle of Mome Gorge the entire rebel force was wiped out. As many as four thousand Zulus were killed, whereas the British forces suffered just eighteen dead.[23] The same year, a Dutch expeditionary force to Bali massacred the entire royal household and its retinue of almost one thousand people, who were performing a traditional ritual known as the *puputan*.[24] Similarly, during the suppression of the Maji Maji Rebellion by German colonial troops in East Africa in 1906, large swaths of the land were laid waste and hundreds of thousands among the local population died as a result of scorched-earth tactics.[25] In German South West Africa, the Nama rebellion was also put down with horrific losses of human life, even as the genocide against the Herero was still ongoing.

While the rules of war were inscribed in international law, in Geneva in 1864 and at the Hague Conventions in 1899 and 1907, "uncivilized" people were explicitly excluded from attempts to minimize the cruelty of modern warfare.[26] The same was the case for the so-called Lieber Code, or General Order 100, which regulated US military conduct but which in practice was interpreted so as to facilitate violence, especially in conflicts with "savages."[27] The absence of the restraints of conventional rules of war was explicitly described by Callwell as a distinctive element of colonial war because "operations are sometimes limited to committing havoc which the laws of regular warfare do not sanction."[28] For Réginald Kann, himself a veteran of numerous "small wars," it was certainly self-evident that the Moros on Bud Dajo could not be accorded the protections of the law: "It is also true that the soldiers finished off the wounded, as is always done in a merciless war against fanatics who neither give nor ask for quarter and for whom the Geneva Convention does not exist."[29]

This was at any rate a moot point since the legal context of the Bud Dajo expedition was never questioned and never became an issue. The war in the Philippines had officially ended in 1902, which meant that subsequent military operations in the South were technically considered as taking place during "peacetime." When anticolonial resistance could be construed as criminality, its suppression became a matter of law and order, and this was indeed one of the key reasons that the Moros on Bud Dajo had been officially labeled as "outlaws." Any level of violence could thus be justified in the name of preserving the peace and protecting law-abiding citizens, whether it was directed at indigenous people or colonized subjects, as described by the *Weekly Republican* in April 1906:

The suppression of crime is often attended with unpleasant circumstances, especially when crime is of a violent and defiant nature. This has been the case in our own country in which the Modocs were almost entirely exterminated and the Apache and Sioux were seriously depleted in numbers. It has been the case in Africa where Dervishes of the Soudan have been slaughtered and in the Malays where head hunters have been slain by hundreds. It will always be the case where such criminals have to be handled, and there is afforded no occasion whatever by this incident in Jolo, for our anti-imperialistic friends to raise a cry of American tyranny.[30]

Despite the deep-seated suspicion of European imperialism that under-wrote American exceptionalism, the parallels between settler violence and colonial warfare were increasingly difficult to deny. In fact, it proved impossible for the press in the United States not to view events in other European colonies through the lens of their own experience in the southern Philippines. When in May 1906 it was reported that rebels in Natal had been massacred by British colonial forces, the *Lancaster Intelligencer* made the now familiar case that such violence was unfortunate yet unavoidable—and in the final calculation even beneficial:

> The British troops in Natal have just been having a wholesale killing of Zulus similar to our recent killing of fanatical Moros in the Philippines. The Zulus are said to have fought with fanatical frenzy, having been fully persuaded by their witch doctors that they were bullet-proof and insisting upon perforation as the only conclusive proof to the contrary. In this case the fanatics attacked the troops posted upon a hill, while in our abattoir operations in the Moro country the process was reversed, and the hilltop had a hole in it, where women and children were mixed in in a manner altogether horrible and sickening.
>
> It must be confessed that the imperial progress of the English-speaking portion of enlightened humanity and Christian civilization proceeds rather awkwardly. It would be much more pleasant and creditable if these frequent blotches of gore upon the record could be avoided, and many find it difficult to believe that they could not be; but there are the stubborn facts of savagery and fanaticism confronted by benevolent assimilation with the most improved killing machinery, and casualties are bound to follow.[31]

This was a remarkable acknowledgment of the type of violence involved in colonial warfare—memorably described as "abattoir operations"—yet at the same time also an admission of its perceived necessity. If Indian killing in America's past provided a historical context and justification for the violence at Bud Dajo, European imperialism and colonial warfare provided a contemporary framework that was both practical and ideological. The moral alignment of manifest destiny and the civilizing mission even forced some Americans to reconsider their previous condemnation of European colonial violence, as outlined in a highly revealing editorial in the *Manila Times*:

Attention may well be directed to the unpleasant necessities which are sometimes forced upon troops engaged in such warfare. Within the past few years we
can find several instances in which we have criticized in others what appeared to
us at the time as wanton cruelties and inhumanities.

In Cuba, for instance, the concentration system of the Spaniards aroused all
our indignation and provoked sweeping denunciations. Later, however, when
confronted with the same problems as those that faced Spain, we adopted the
same tactics.

So also with the Dutch in Java. The reports that the troops there were slaugh-
tering women and children provoked loud outcry of barbarity. But in the affair
at Mount Dajo we practised the same inhumanities which led us to condemn
the Dutch soldiery. As we now know, the exigencies of the situation called for
such apparently ruthless tactics.

If our insular or colonial experiences have taught us nothing more, they
ought to prove helpful in giving us larger tolerance for other nations bearing
"the white man's burden." They have shown that circumstances sometimes force
upon us a resort to tactics which are deplorable but unavoidable. And hereafter,
when we hear of alleged barbarities on the part of civilized nations in their dealing with savage peoples, we should be able to pass fairer judgement upon them
and allow for extenuating circumstances.[32]

The "concentration system" referred to here was the strategy of forcefully
relocating the local population to camps, first resorted to by the Spanish
under General Weyler in Cuba in 1896 and soon after adopted by both the
Americans in the Philippines and the British in South Africa.[33] The allusion to the Dutch slaughter of women and children concerned the infamous
Van Daalen expedition during the Aceh War in 1904, where the colonial
forces of the Netherlands had massacred thousands of civilians under circumstances very similar to Wood's earlier expeditions in Jolo.[34] Notably,
a photographer captured scenes of the Dutch troops as they posed on the
ramparts of the village of Koetö Réh, with corpses strewn everywhere, in
trenches and on the ground. In several of the images, surviving infants
can be seen among the bodies—much as they can in the photos from Bud
Dajo.[35] Indeed, the photos taken at the two massacres bear an uncanny resemblance.[36] The Dutch colonial press also recognized the similarities when

reporting on Bud Dajo, noting sarcastically how the Americans had done exactly what they criticized others for just two years earlier.[37]

———————

At the annual meeting of the Anti-Imperialist League in December 1906, Moorfield Storey revisited Bud Dajo in his presidential address:

> Incidents in our career of conquest like the massacre of Mt. Dajo in which men, women and children perished by a common death, have helped to swell the feeling of disgust with our enterprise. Unhappily in such exploits we are not alone. I have found in the newspapers the account of a victory won by the Dutch over the natives of Bali in which "the followers of the native princes numbering in all 400 men were killed while the Dutch lost four killed and ten wounded." The British in Natal slaughtered 575 Zulus without losing a man, while it is said that the Germans have in a year reduced the Herero nation from 80,000 souls to 2000, mostly women and children. What a record of cowardly murder the superior races are making, for is it not cowardly to mow down with modern arms men who can make no effective resistance. What page of human history is blacker than that which the "superior races" are writing now, and to think that America is leading in this barbarism.[38]

Yet Storey's view was shared by only a minority, and most Americans could instead take succor in the belief that the massacre at Bud Dajo had really been a battle and that it was after all justified by the precedents set by other imperialist powers as much as by the example of the Pilgrims. A week after Storey's speech, President Roosevelt was awarded the Nobel Peace Prize for his role in negotiating a peace between Russia and Japan, thus bringing an end to the Russo-Japanese War.[39] This was the same Roosevelt who privately reasserted his support for Wood long after the details of the massacre had emerged:

> I thrilled with indignation over the infamous attacks upon Wood and our troops, and I took, as you saw, the earliest opportunity not only in a message to Wood but in a message to Congress, to show that I intended to stand by Wood and our troops right up to the limit.[40]

Considering the level of violence unleashed at Bud Dajo, it is difficult to imagine what, exactly, he deemed the limit to be.

———————

In Scott's final report on the state of Jolo for 1906, he insisted that the expedition against Bud Dajo had been necessary and that the turbulent Moros had finally been pacified:

> Much as the necessity to reduce the Daho Moros by force of arms was to be regretted, still that it did exist was recognized by the wisest and most influential of the Moros, and the carrying out of the reduction until all resistance ceased, has been for the benefit of the Moro people.... It is believed that the inhabitants of this island during the past year have experienced a change of heart; that they are beginning to understand the benevolent intentions of the Americans toward them, and are willing to respond.[41]

Scott's declaration of "civilizing mission accomplished," however, was both naive and premature—the Moros were far from beaten, and Bud Dajo was not the last massacre in the bloody history of US rule in the southern Philippines.

In 1908 and 1909, a Moro named Jikiri caused widespread unrest throughout the Sulu Archipelago as he and his followers carried out numerous raids and acts of piracy, targeting both Chinese traders and European settlers. After an extensive hunt involving US military forces and naval gunboats, Jikiri was eventually tracked down and killed after a desperate fight; like Hassan before him, Jikiri was reported as dying in a hail of bullets.[42] According to Moro tradition, Jikiri was a sort of Robin Hood figure who had been cheated by Chinese merchants and wronged by the Americans, and who had bravely chosen to die a hero's death rather than accept injustice.[43]

In 1909, John J. Pershing had succeeded Bliss as commander of the Mindanao Division and governor of the Moro Province. The veteran officer continued the slow work of developing the region and maintaining US presence without provoking too many confrontations with the Moros. In 1911, however, there was a spate of *juramentado* attacks in Jolo, and on at least one occasion one of Pershing's subordinates revived the time-honored tradition of burying the corpses of Moros with pigs. The same year, Pershing also ordered the complete disarmament of all Moros, which caused widespread resentment among a people for whom carrying a bladed weapon was a key symbol of honor and status. As unrest quickly spread across Jolo, Pershing was preparing a punitive campaign to enforce disarmament at the point of the bayonet, but political intervention from Manila forced him to take a more conciliatory approach. In December of 1911, hundreds of Moros—men, women, and children—retreated to the top of Bud Dajo once again, and it appeared as if a rerun of the 1906 massacre was inevitable. Surrounding the mountain and cutting off all the trails, Pershing nevertheless took a very different approach to Wood, whose troubled record he was keen not to repeat. Pershing wrote his wife that "I would not want to have that on my conscience for the fame of Napoleon."[44] In the end he did not have to, and over the course of several weeks the Moros came down from Bud Dajo in small groups and surrendered. In the end, just twelve Moros were killed while the Americans had three wounded—a very different outcome than five years before.[45]

Pershing's reputation as a peacemaker has nevertheless been vastly exaggerated—often in direct comparison to the bellicose Wood.[46] Ever since his first campaigns in Mindanao a decade before, Pershing had proven himself quite willing to resort to violence when he thought it was necessary, and his view of the Moros was certainly little different than that of his predecessors. In his annual report for 1911, for instance, he thus argued that the population of Jolo had to learn "that murderers and outlaws have no destiny under civilized government save extermination."[47] The reality of such a policy became apparent in 1913, when several hundred Moro warriors entrenched themselves on Bud Bagsak, a mountain near Lake Siet. In June, US forces and detachments of Philippine Scouts under Pershing's command launched a four-day attack on the Moro fortifications, which ended with the complete annihilation of the defenders. Although there were no women and children among the Moros at Bud Bagsak, the disparity in casualties was no less striking than it had been at Bud Dajo: Pershing's forces suffered fourteen dead and twenty-five wounded, whereas it was estimated that some four hundred Moros were killed.[48] This time around, the American forces had also been equipped with the very latest weaponry, including hand grenades. A poster based on a painting titled "Knocking Out the Moros" was produced by the US Army in the 1950s, imaginatively depicting a desperate hand-to-hand fight between American soldiers and armor-clad and sword-wielding Moro warriors. The caption:

> The four-day battle of Bagsak Mountain on Jolo Island in the Philippines took place from 11 to 15 June 1913. Americans of the 8th Infantry and the Philippine Scouts, personally lead [sic] by Brigadier General John J. Pershing, brought to an end years of bitter struggle against the Moro pirates. These Bolo men, outlaws of great physical endurance and savage fighting ability, were well organized under their Datus or chiefs. They had never been conquered during several centuries of Spanish rule in the Philippines. The U.S. Army .45-caliber pistol was developed to meet the need for a weapon with enough striking power to stop fanatical charges of lawless Moro tribesmen in hand-to-hand fighting.[49]

FIFTEEN

The Most
Illuminating Thing

Like the gun, the camera has been part of the technology of subjugation, furnishing images to relay the workings of a prior and
seemingly unassailable will. Colonial photographs seem like trophies of conquest. And to see them—even today—is to come in
contact with this violence.

Vicente L. Rafael, *White Love and Other*
Events in Filipino History (2000)[1]

D URING THE RESEARCH FOR THIS BOOK, THE IDENTITY OF THE PHO-
tographer who produced the image of the trench at Bud Dajo eluded
me (see figure 13). Over time, it became almost an obsession—my white
whale, if you will—and the one missing piece that prevented me from completing the story of the massacre. Despite the fact that the image is today
all over the internet, there is very little concrete information regarding its
provenance; most of the surviving copies are mass-produced postcards or
later reproductions, rather than original prints made from the negative. For

instance, the photograph in the Library of Congress, which comes from the John J. Pershing Papers, is a heavily cropped copy, which was itself made from another photographic reproduction.[2] The copy in the National Archives is also a later reprint of low quality from the Army Signal Corps collection.[3] A high-resolution version of the image, with two vertical creases, which is available online, appears to be an original print but has no identifiable provenance.[4]

I knew for sure that two photographers were present at Bud Dajo, namely the French lieutenant Réginald Kann and the American writer Hamilton M. Wright, who each took a dozen images between March 6 and March 8, 1906. They both published a selection of their photographs along with accounts of the massacre, and I could trace their movements during the assault with a high degree of accuracy. I was furthermore able to track down original prints of their images in the private papers of officers who participated in the Bud Dajo expedition, now held in US archives.[5] Kann could easily be ruled out because he was present on the southern summit with Bundy's column and furthermore used a Kodak film camera: if the story told by Erving Winslow was correct, the photograph had been taken with an older type of camera with glass-plate negatives. Wright, on the other hand, seemed to fit the bill: he was present at the top of the eastern trail and took photographs of the big trench with the tree trunk—albeit from the opposite side. However, he also employed a small camera that used film, and he tended to copyright his photographs with a caption on the negative. The trench photo had furthermore not been published in any of Wright's many articles about the massacre. After months of intensive research, it eventually became clear to me that there must have been a third person with a camera at Bud Dajo. I was able to purchase copies of the original image, yet I could not get any closer to identifying their maker.

My first breakthrough came during a heady research trip to the US in early 2022, during which I attended a conference and visited three different archives. The papers of John R. White are held in the Knight Collection, University of Oregon Library, and I always suspected that he might have had a copy of the photograph, although it is not included in his 1928 memoirs, *Bullets and Bolos*. Going through the boxes of photos in White's collection, I found an entire set of Kann's images and many other photos related to both Bud Dajo and White's career elsewhere in the Philippines. However, the photo of the trench was not among them. I then ordered and went through all the other boxes with photographs in the White collection (thirty-four in total), and in the middle of photos of giant red pine from his time as a superintendent of the Sequoia National Park in the 1930s, I finally found the trench photo, which had clearly been misplaced. Not only was there an original print of the trench photo; there was also a version made from what appeared to be a broken negative, as well as an image from Bud Dajo taken six weeks after the massacre (see frontispiece and figures 13 and 20). It was thus clear that the story of the broken negative was true and that the photographer was furthermore someone who was not just visiting Jolo in March 1906 but had spent a longer time in the region and was perhaps even based there permanently.

Later during the same trip, I was fortunate enough to be able to consult Mike G. Price's private collection of historical postcards and photographic prints from the Philippines—probably the single largest collection of its kind anywhere in the world. Mike, who has been collecting since the 1960s, has an unparalleled knowledge of the history of photography in the Philippines during the American period and has several thousand photos and postcards from Jolo alone, including dozens of different versions of the photo of the trench at Bud Dajo. Mike had not been able to discover the identity of the photographer but had over the years collected a vast amount of information about local photography studios in Jolo and Zamboanga during the first decades of the twentieth century. Among the list of names, one in particular stood out: Aeronaut Gibbs. Mike had done a bit of research and found out that Gibbs was a retired US soldier who worked out of his own studio in Jolo. The name struck a chord with me, and when I searched the hundreds of newspaper articles I had collected during my research, one result came up: an eyewitness described Aeronaut Gibbs as being present on the eastern summit of Bud Dajo on the morning of March 8. When I looked further, I discovered that Gibbs had taken photographs for J. L. Travis, who was mentioned in Leonard Wood's diary as also being present at Bud Dajo. I had finally found my man. I could now finish the story of the photograph titled "After the Battle at Mt. Daho" that was sent to W. E. B. Du Bois in 1907.

Very little is known about the life and background of Aeronaut Gibbs. Richard Henry Gibbs was born in Nebraska in 1876, and after his young wife died in 1899, probably during childbirth, he joined the US Army and was soon deployed to the Philippines as a private in the Signal Corps.[6] It was here that he first learned photography and began specializing in balloon reconnaissance, earning the informal title of "aeronaut."[7] Gibbs was evidently a bit of a daredevil; in 1904 he ascended in a balloon to a height of nine thousand feet over Manila before jumping out with a parachute to the amazement of hundreds of spectators.[8] While stationed in Manila, Gibbs also worked as a staff photographer for the weekly newspaper *Philippines Gossip*, and he eventually left the army to take up photography for a living. By 1906, he had moved to Jolo and set up what was soon to become a highly successful photography studio outside the walled city, adopting the trade name Aeronaut Gibbs. A contemporary account describes him as a colorful character whose arrival made a big impression:

> I wonder where he ever found that first name, it sounds romantic but unusual. He wandered in here about a month ago on a transp[ort] steamer with a 4×5 camera and an unlimited supply of gall, with no return ticket and now he is almost a millionaire, post cards six for a dollar, and he can't make 'em fast enough.[9]

Although cameras were becoming cheaper and more common, there was still a huge market for photographic postcards among the local American soldiers and officials as well as visiting tourists.[10] Gibbs's was thus just one of the numerous small studios of varying degrees of professionalism that sprang up all over the Philippines, and throughout the world, during this period. A surviving copy of a 1906 ad for Gibbs's studio offers "A Fine Line of Moro Views—Developing for Amateurs—Printing Done for Amateurs—When in Need of Any of the Work Come and See Me!"[11] Enough people evidently came to the studio to buy his images, have their own negatives developed, or sit for a portrait, and his business flourished. Gibbs remained in Jolo until 1918, when he returned to the US and set up a small portrait studio in Seattle, where he eventually passed away in 1935.[12] Other than a few dozen copyrighted photographic postcards, however, Aeronaut Gibbs never left much of a trail in the archives. That is, apart from the photo of the trench at Bud Dajo—arguably the most famous image from the US occupation of the southern Philippines—for which he was never credited.[13]

In March 1906, Gibbs was commissioned by writer J. L. Travis to take photos in Jolo for a special issue of the *Far Eastern Review*, which was aimed at demonstrating the progress made by the Americans in the southern Philippines.[14] Travis was in Zamboanga on March 6 and joined Wood when he left for Jolo to oversee the progress of the attack on Bud Dajo. Once in Jolo, Travis brought Gibbs along, and it was accordingly more or less by accident that the photographer happened to be in Bundy's camp at Position 2 on March 7, when the first wounded were brought down. As a former soldier, Gibbs was able to move about freely, and the first photo he took was of the wounded Captain White, who was lying under a tent cover along with three other soldiers. Later, Gibbs took two more images of wounded Americans being transported on the back of mules on their way to Jolo—the injured men swathed in blankets and bandages, while the mule drivers wait patiently for the camera (see figure 18).[15]

Early the following morning, Gibbs went to Position 3 and climbed up to the eastern summit with his heavy old-fashioned camera—around the same time that Wright did. Both photographers were thus present at the big trench early on March 8, and Wright described how Gibbs had given some water to a dying Moro woman and even placed her dead baby in her lap.[16] Having tried to succor the woman in her dying moments, as Wright described it, it is nevertheless evident that Gibbs decided to photograph her and the scene before him. It was then around 9:30 a.m., and the men of Lawton's column were resting after the very last Moros at the top of Bud Dajo had been killed.[17] In order to prove that Moro women had been fighting alongside their men in the trenches, it seems likely that Gibbs—or perhaps one of the soldiers—exposed her right breast for the camera. Had the woman been white, this would have been considered a morally repugnant transgression, but not so in the colonial world of the Philippines, where the bodies of brown women were commonly objectified and openly sexualized in popular postcards.[18] Considering that the Moro woman is at the very center of the composition, the eroticization of her corpse was certainly no accident.

The smell of death hung in the air, mixed with the acrid smoke from the burning houses in the crater, as Gibbs cautiously positioned the legs of the stand among the corpses and rubble covering the ground. Judging from images of the time, his camera was probably of a type similar to the Rochester Optical Pony Premo No. 6 4×5.[19] First, he opened the camera box and extended the bellows, which could be adjusted for focus based on the approximate distance to the object. Having opened the shutter, the image now appeared upside down on a removable sheet of ground (matte) glass at the back of the camera, and the final adjustments could be made to frame the scene as desired. Captain Lawton himself can be seen standing with a spear on the far left, and the soldiers seem perfectly at ease in front of the camera. This was indeed just one of about two dozen images taken during the assault on Bud Dajo. Being satisfied with the composition, Gibbs closed the shutter and inserted a wooden plateholder that contained a 4×5 inch gelatin dry plate covered by a slide, which kept it protected from light. Once the plateholder was in place, the slide was removed, and the silver halides in the gelatin emulsion would be exposed inside the camera box and ready to capture any light once the shutter was opened.

We can imagine the quietude in the moment the photo was taken: a few muffled voices, the crackling of the smoldering hut in the background, and perhaps the rhythmic singing of jungle birds in the surrounding trees—interrupted by a metallic "click" as Gibbs pressed the release for the timed shutter. In a split-second, the scene of the "Battle of Mt. Dajo" was captured: the Moros suspended in death and the men who killed them forever staring into the camera. Gibbs then reinserted the slide to cover the exposed plate, and he extracted the plateholder, which now contained the negative. He would have to bring this back to his studio, which had the requisite facilities to finally develop the image and make a photographic print.

The Moros on Bud Dajo were thus shot twice—first by the soldiers and then by Gibbs. These were not essentially distinct actions, and the same racialized logic that justified the indiscriminate slaughter of men, women, and children also justified the soldiers being photographed as they posed with the bodies like hunters with their prey. An image only of the dead provided no narrative and might in fact represent nothing more than a tragedy. By including both the dead Moros *and* the living American soldiers within the same frame, the meaning of the photo was transformed through the explicit juxtaposition of the vanquished and the victorious. It became, in short, a trophy photo—part of a distinct genre of what has been described as "staged triumphalism."[20]

The word *massacre*, it may be noted, is derived from French and was originally used to describe the butchery and slaughter of animals, and was also associated with hunting and the killing of quarry; it was in the latter context that the term was used in the sixteenth century more specifically to describe the head or antlers of a stag taken as a trophy after a hunt.[21] A historical definition of *massacre* might thus include the indiscriminate killing of humans *as if* they were animals—and the treatment of their remains as trophies. The word, in fact, denotes the explicit dehumanization of the victims. Since the Moros were dehumanized through a discourse of racial othering and equated with hornets, rats, and mad dogs fit only for extermination, the hunting analogy is entirely explicit—and the word "massacre" entirely appropriate.[22]

Gibbs, Wright, and Kann were not passive bystanders innocently documenting events in which they played no part. They were all embedded with the American expeditionary force, practically and ideologically—Kann had furthermore operated the mountain gun at Position 1 and carried messages between Koehler and Duncan, effectively erasing any distinction between observer and participant.[23] The very presence of the photographers normalized the violence they recorded, and many of the images were taken with the cooperation of the soldiers themselves. The deterrent message of the assault itself was furthermore amplified through the subsequent circulation of the photo, and although there are no records of the image being specifically shown to Moros in Jolo, it was widely disseminated, and it is inconceivable that they were unaware of its existence.[24] By staging the scene of the trench, Gibbs turned the massacre into a spectacle and became an active participant.

Wright and Kann planned to use their photos as illustrations for commissioned articles, but Gibbs was a commercial photographer, working out of his studio in Paseo de Arolas. The image of the trench at Bud Dajo proved very popular among the soldiers of the garrison in Jolo, and Gibbs soon began producing and selling it as both prints and postcards. Written mirror-wise in black on the negative, so that it would show up as white on the final print, the photographer added a simple caption: "After the Battle of Bud Dajo—1600 Moros were killed." Just three weeks after the Bud Dajo expedition, a soldier stationed in Jolo mentioned the existence of photos taken during the assault, which he promised to send to his cousin in Kansas, and a number of veterans subsequently did so.[25] Paper prints could be made directly from the glass negative, but they could also be reproduced on prefabricated postcard stock, and it would appear that Gibbs did both. The existence of the photograph eventually came to General Wood's attention, and when he visited Jolo on April 13, in preparation for handing over the province to Tasker Bliss, he went to see Gibbs in his studio. This was when the incident described by Erving Winslow took place:

> When General Wood heard that the photograph had been taken at the scene of the slaughter he made a call upon the photographer to ask to see the plate, casually letting it fall upon the ground, so that it broke, and then gave the photographer eight or 10 pesos for compensation for the "accident."[26]

When Wood had "accidentally" broken the negative of the photo from Bud Dajo, he presumed that would be the end of the matter and that no potentially incriminating images would ever appear. But the entrepreneurial Gibbs was not so easily deterred; while he already had complete prints made from the original, he also pieced the broken negative together and made a new complete print from the fragments—a print in which the fractures showed up in the image like a broken mirror. This, too, was sold as a postcard and soon turned up in Manila and even farther afield. In May a US official in Japan reported the following:

> I have just ascertained that a school-teacher named Miller, now in Japan on leave, has a photograph in his possession of the Dajo fight, in which is shown a half-naked female corpse, with a gash in the breast, and lying near the bodies of several infants. American soldiers are standing near, gazing at them, and due to light and shade the female corpse looks like that of a white woman. Miller has shown the picture to several people and boasted that he intended to sell it (of course at a long figure) for use in the next Presidential campaign. His remarks

on the subject of the fight have not been complementary to our people, and he claims that it was a massacre.[27]

The real concern over the image was evidently not the violence it depicted as much as the fact that the dead Moro woman might be mistaken for a white woman. Whereas the massacre of Moro men, women, and children was justifiable, a racial "misreading" of such an image would be damaging to both Wood and his supporters, including President Roosevelt. The official in Japan thought the image sufficiently troubling to personally inform Wood's staff:

> If I had received this information in time, I would have attempted to secure the photo. I am told that it has the appearance of having been taken from a broken negative which had been restored. Miller also stated that his photo and that in possession of a solder were the only ones in existence. It may be possible to destroy them and attempt should be made upon the return of Miller. . . .[28]

Nothing ever came of this, but Wood's attempt to get rid of the evidence had clearly failed, and the image was now circulating outside of military circles and well beyond the Philippines. Gibbs produced several different versions of the photo, including a cropped print in which only the woman and the surrounding corpses could be seen.[29] The other photos that Gibbs had taken at Bud Dajo—of the wounded being transported on mules, for instance— were also turned into postcards. Although Gibbs did register some of his photos for copyright, he did not do so with his best-selling image of the trench at Bud Dajo—most likely to avoid getting in trouble with Wood and the military authorities.[30] In 1908 a postcard manufacturer, Charles W. McDonald of San Francisco, copyrighted a cropped version of the image with the caption: "Annihilation of one thousand men, women and children near the walled city of Jolo, March 1906."[31] The reproduction was of a poor quality and never gained wide circulation, yet the fact that copyright was registered reflects the commercial value attributed to what was essentially an atrocity photo. Altogether, more than a dozen different versions of the image, of varying quality, were produced in 1906 and during the following years.[32] Two of Kann's photos were also reproduced as postcards, but they never reached the same scale of circulation.[33]

The photos made by Gibbs, Wright, and Kann were evidently treasured by the veterans of the Bud Dajo expedition as well as by American soldiers and colonial officials elsewhere in the Philippines—both individually and collectively, privately and publicly. For instance, Kann sent prints of his images to several of the officers of the expedition, including Wood and White, both of whom kept them in photo albums along with other images as mementos of their time in the Philippines.[34] For the Americans, the images from Bud Dajo did not represent an atrocity but rather testified to the progress and success of the civilizing mission. In Wood's album, official portraits, picturesque landscapes, and colonial domestic scenes thus sit side by side with photographs from the massacre because the former was perceived to be predicated on the latter. Wood was clearly not disturbed by the slaughter of the Moros as captured in the trench photo, only by the possibility that it might be "misinterpreted." Wood was far from unique in this respect, and William Cameron Forbes, the commissioner of Commerce and Police in the American government in the Philippines, also had Gibbs's photograph in his album of family photographs, as did many others.[35] Edgar A. Stirmyer, a US officer stationed in Zamboanga, inserted copies of Wright's photographs among his own snapshots of his wife, small child, and Filipino nanny, as well as a deeply nostalgic tableau in which a small palm had been turned into a Christmas tree.[36] The proximity of idyllic scenes of settler life in the tropics and harrowing images of a massacre within carefully curated albums remains a visceral testament to the normality of extreme violence as a ubiquitous feature of American imperialism in the southern Philippines at the dawn of the twentieth century.

John R. White also kept several albums in which photographs of landscapes and banal tourist scenes were intermingled with multiple copies of both Kann's and Gibbs's images. As opposed to Wood's album, however, White's was heavily annotated, and every single picture was inscribed with personal notes, identifying individuals and providing what amounted to a running commentary. In Kann's photos from the top of the southern trail, White thus marked with an X the spot where he had been positioned when wounded and where he had later received medical aid. White even sent a postcard of Gibbs's photos of himself, taken as he was lying wounded at

Position 2, to acquaintances in the US a few months after the expedition.[37] Through his written notes, White turned the photos from Bud Dajo into a visual narrative of his own suffering—a process of self-fashioning that involved the explicit erasure of the Moros as victims.

Photographs played a central role in how the Americans who participated in the Bud Dajo expedition later remembered the event.[38] None of them ever expressed any sense of shame or guilt, yet they were clearly affected by the loss of their comrades. One officer's wife wrote the following to her father from Jolo, after the troops returned to the garrison:

> There were four officers wounded, but none seriously. They all speak of the fight with horror, and say they never want to go through anything like it again.... I hope we will never have to go through such a time again. All day Wednesday and Thursday morning I could see the pack mules coming, bringing the wounded and dead, and I never, never, want to see a pack mule again.[39]

In personal correspondence, several soldiers similarly revealed that they were haunted by what they had *seen* at Bud Dajo—though not by what they had *done*. One soldier stated that "the sight of the dead and dying as we took possession of the Moro stronghold is one that I will never forget," and another soldier similarly explained that "I have seen sights that I never expected to see."[40] Archie Johnson, as already mentioned, wrote to his cousin "I never want to see such a sight again."[41] The soldiers were apparently able to perpetrate a massacre without compunction, only to be horrified when confronted by the grim spectacle of its aftermath.[42] The horror of what they had witnessed, however, did not lessen the value of the photographs, which served as a means by which to communicate experiences that words alone could not describe.[43] Sharing and circulating the image within military networks, and among veterans, allowed the men of the Bud Dajo expedition to reminisce about their time in the Philippines, share stories, and maintain a sense of group identity.[44] One medical officer sent an entire set of Gibbs's photos to his father in Kentucky, as the local newspaper reported:

> Noel Jean received several pictures sent by his son Lieut. Jean, surgeon in U.S. army. They were taken immediately after the big fight on Dajo mountain, in

which several American soldiers were killed and wounded. . . . The pictures show the wounded soldiers being carried off the field of battle, the field hospitals, the scene of the fight, and other pictures of the battle. They are valued highly by Mr. Jean, as several other relics that his son has sent him recently.[45]

The images thus provided a sense of connection between people divided by thousands of miles and had sentimental value as such—regardless of the violence they depicted. Soon after the 19th Infantry Regiment returned to the US, in June 1907, the regimental chaplain, S. J. Smith, started giving lectures about Bud Dajo with a stereopticon, or "magic lantern," which projected images.[46] Far from being a source of shame or embarrassment, the photos had become part of the regimental commemoration of the "Battle of Mount Dajo."

DeKalb County History Center, in Illinois, today has an enlarged print of the trench-photo, which had been framed in a local studio and presented as a gift by Ralph Meigs, who was at Bud Dajo with the naval detachment, to another veteran.[47] On the back of the photo, all the different units that participated in the expedition were carefully listed. The image was evidently regarded as a valuable gift between veterans and was intended to be displayed. In White's private papers, at the Knights Library, University of Oregon, there are three of the images by Gibbs in a very large 9 × 12 format: the original photo of the trench, a print made from the broken image, as well as another scene of the aftermath. These prints were obviously made by Gibbs himself and of such a size that White must have acquired them with the intention of hanging them on his wall. The larger print that W. E. B. Du Bois had wanted—"framed and put upon the walls of my recitation room"—did indeed exist, but it had adorned the wall of one of the officers who participated in the massacre.

———————

Several of the veterans of Bud Dajo carried wounds from the fight, which they referred to as mementos, and Private Mahoney, for instance, noted how "I have got a scar on my cheek now to remember that day on Mt. Dajo."[48] When President Roosevelt wrote to Gordon Johnston's family, reassuring them that their son's wounds were not serious, he added that it was in fact "just such a wound as a man is proud to have."[49] Wounds, of a certain kind, were accordingly seen as a sign of masculinity and functioned as a sort of embodied souvenir.[50] At times, the different forms of visual and material mementos were brought together in a single frame. A photograph, likely taken by Gibbs in his Jolo studio, shows a shirtless man with his back to the camera revealing two thick scars running horizontally across his back and onto the left upper arm (see figure 19).[51] The man is Ernest J. Packard, Troop I, 4th Cavalry, who was severely wounded at the top of Bundy's trail on March 7, during the fighting where White was also wounded.[52] One of his friends described Packard as having been "boloed across the back and cut one lung in two," yet evidently he survived, albeit losing the use of his right arm. The composition is reminiscent of contemporary medical photographs of combat wounds, but the *barong* that inflicted the wounds is also included on a stand in the forefront of the image. The physical scars that Packard carried as a reminder of Bud Dajo and the material trophy of the *barong* were thus combined in this image, which itself constituted a visual souvenir and was subsequently reproduced and sold as a postcard.[53] The juxtaposition of the savage-looking weapon and the wounds it had inflicted on an American body furthermore invoked the stereotypical image of the ferocious Moro, effectively reversing the roles of perpetrator and victim at Bud Dajo.

Other souvenirs gathered from the bloody ground of Bud Dajo were more macabre, and Gibbs's photo of the trench had a companion piece that combined the material and the visual trophy in the most striking manner. By the time that Wood broke the glass negative in April 1906, Gibbs had realized that there was a real market for photographs from the massacre, and he decided to return to the summit of Bud Dajo and get more images. The site had already become a hunting ground for soldiers and visitors looking for souvenirs, and Gibbs went out with a small detachment of cavalry toward the end of April.[54] The result of Gibbs's return to Bud Dajo was as grim as the original photograph. Taken from the opposite side of the same trench at the top of Lawton's trail, it is the mirror image of the one taken on the morning of March 8. Titled "Six Weeks After the Battle of Dajo," the composition is almost identical, with fourteen US cavalry troopers and officers, including one man in civilian dress, posing for the camera on either side of the tree trunk traversing the trench. Three of the troopers are hold-ing their Krag carbines, but everyone else appears unarmed; the trooper closest to the camera, on the right, strikes a particularly photogenic pose, with his hands resting on a stick and his hat at a jaunty angle. Where the bodies of the Moros used to be, overflowing the sides of the trench, there is now nothing to see but debris: blasted tree stumps, pieces of bamboo, and broken wood and shrubs. However, on the tree trunk between the troop-ers is irrefutable evidence of the desperate struggle that had taken place just weeks before: twenty-one human skulls neatly arranged in a row (see figure 20).

In order to create the drama befitting an image of the slaughter ground of Bud Dajo, Gibbs and his party evidently decided to collect the remains of the dead Moros, who, contrary to Wood's claims, had neither been taken away by relatives nor properly interred.[55] Even at this altitude, the heat and insects had done their job effectively, and six weeks after the massacre there had been nothing but bones left under the thin layer of dirt with which the soldiers hastily covered the bodies before leaving on March 8. It was hardly coincidental that the number of skulls matched the twenty-one US casual-ties from the assault on Bud Dajo, and Gibbs's second image thus tells the story of a score settled and of dead comrades avenged.

The treatment of the Moros' remains stands in stark contrast to how the Americans dealt with their own dead. Gibbs had in fact photographed the twenty-one US casualties as they were about to be repatriated for proper burial (see figure 21). The picture was taken on the wharf of Jolo harbor, and a canvas cloth had been pulled back to reveal the wooden coffins stacked on top of each other in three rows of seven. On the end panel of each of the twenty-one crates the individual's name, rank, unit, and coun-try were carefully written. Whereas the dead soldiers were treated with the utmost respect and privacy, the Moros were fully exposed to the camera's gaze and reduced to a faceless tangle of bodies or row of laughing skulls.[56] If Gibbs's first photo of the trench at Bud Dajo was a trophy image, the sec-ond one was doubly so—a trophy photo of trophy skulls. When the party left the summit, they took some of the skulls with them as souvenirs. This appears to have inspired others, and a few months later, the *Manila Times* reported that the skulls of Bud Dajo victims are now being peddled on the streets of Jolo. Many a soldier's barrack is decorated with the ghastly relics. . . . There seems to be an unlimited supply. After the battle of Dajo the authorities made some effort to burn up the Moro dead by saturating the bodies with petroleum; but it could not be done. The hill-top is covered with the bleaching bones.[57]

When Scott returned to Jolo, he tried to put a stop to the macabre hunt for souvenirs on Bud Dajo, but seemingly to no avail, After a journalist complained about the presence of unburied bodies in July, Bliss ordered Scott's successor to "clean the place up . . . before more tourists are allowed to climb the hill."[58] Perhaps the collecting of Moro remains was too reminiscent of the taking of human trophies such as scalps back in the US—a practice usually associated with the alleged barbarism of Native Americans but in truth a characteristic feature of settler violence.[59] As early as 1623, the Plymouth colonists had displayed the severed head of the Neponset warrior Wituwamat on a pole outside their fort, and the mutilation of the enemy's body, and collecting of body parts, had been a recurring aspect of the "Indian Wars." This was moreover not a uniquely American tradition, and the colonial wars of all the European imperial powers offered numerous examples of the mutilation of the corpses of indigenous people—as a tool of colonial control or to satisfy demands for skulls to populate medical collections or adorn the gentleman's smoking room.[60] Robbing indigenous graves and scouring battlefields for human trophies was as much a distinguishing feature of colonial warfare as was the looting of artifacts.[61]

In October 1906, after the famous ornithologist Alexander Edgar Mearns and several American botanists visited the summit of Bud Dajo, Wood found himself forced to reissue the order "prohibiting the removal of any bones from Dajo."[62] Almost four decades later, a very similar order was issued by the commander in chief of the Pacific Fleet when American troops started collecting skulls and other trophies from the Japanese dead after the Battle of Guadalcanal, in World War II.[63] Mearns was known for having collected the skulls of Moros during previous campaigns in the southern Philippines, and although there was supposedly a distinction between scientific collecting and trophy taking, the desecration of the enemy's remains was in practice indistinguishable.[64] When the skulls of the Moros killed at Bud Dajo were removed and turned into trophies and decorative objects, the process of dehumanization that began with the order for their extermination was complete.

The postcard that Gibbs produced from his second photograph proved as popular as the first. One of the troopers who accompanied Gibbs, and was in the scene, subsequently sent it home to his family with a brief comment written in the margin: "Do I look natural? 'E' Trop 4. Cavalry."[65] A brief note written on another copy of this postcard reveals something of what the image meant to US soldiers stationed in the southern Philippines at the time: "A few good Moros 6 weeks after battle of Dajo."[66]

———◆———

In Mike G. Price's collection, one of the postcards of the trench at Bud Dajo has a few lines scribbled on the back, almost certainly written by Gibbs himself to an acquaintance:

> I would not send you this grisly reminder of Bud Dajo, but the very grotesque-
> ness of death makes it loose [sic] some of its terror. At this fight just four miles
> from Jolo, nine hundred and forty some Moros were slain (no wounded). The
> only survivor a little girl, I am going to try and get a picture of her, but she is
> very shy. She can be seen in the extreme left hand corner of this card.[67]

The reference to the girl is intriguing. At the edge of the corpse-filled trench, a woman can on closer inspection be seen sitting among the American troops in the upper left corner of the photograph (see figure 13). She has a piece of cloth covering her hair, and a small child—the girl Gibbs referred to—is sitting on her lap. The little girl's features are indiscernible, but her small legs are resting on a tree branch jutting out from the side of the trench, right next to one of the many dead bodies covering the ground. The woman's face is half-turned to the left, and her eyes are fixed on the soldier sitting right next to her with a rifle held in his lap, menacingly pointed in her direction. The vague outline of a second child can be discerned just behind the woman. Whereas the soldiers' gaze is locked with the camera, as they proudly pose for the shot, the huddled figures of the survivors appear lost in a sea of bodies, many of whom would have belonged to their relatives. Although the story never made it into the official reports, Lawton had in fact described how the little girl was found by the Americans in the morning of March 8, before the assault on the last *cotta*:

> As we were preparing to finish our work on the mountain a soldier came up from the crater holding by the hand a little Moro girl, some seven or eight years old, very pretty, with long black hair, dressed with all the gaudy finery and color which characterize the dress of the Moros.
>
> She was prattling away to the soldier in her strange tongue wholly unconcerned by the horror of her surroundings, and came up to us tripping lightly, almost laughingly, over the dead bodies of her people. She had spent the night in the depths of that dark crater alone—for all were dead but she.[68]

Lawton here seems to have been carried away by a poetic turn of phrase: there were evidently other survivors. Kann's and Wright's photographs show at least two women and some six children in the trenches on the eastern summit, and one woman and two boys on the southern (see figures 11 and 16). It was, however, the little girl mentioned by Lawton who captured the Americans' imagination. The girl had been orphaned by the massacre and ended up as a sort of mascot for the Jolo garrison, spending most of her time around the barracks, and this is where Gibbs subsequently managed to photograph her.[69] In fact, she soon became something of a local attraction, and at least a dozen different photos exist, several of which were later turned into postcards. The real name of the destitute girl was never recorded, and instead she became known only by the massacre that made her an orphan: "Miss Bud Dajo."[70] (See figure 24.)

In 1907 a large exhibition was organized in Norfolk, Virginia, to commemorate the founding of the first settlement in Jamestown three hundred years before—and, by extension, to celebrate the greatness of the United States at the beginning of the twentieth century. Among the many attractions of the Jamestown Ter-Centennial Exposition, visitors could see "seventy-seven Filipinos of five tribes—Tagalogs, Moros, Bagobos, Visayans and Ilocanos" in the mock village of the Philippine Reservation—including what one report described as "two survivors of the Mount Dajo battle."[71]

Photos of the "savage Moros" at the Jamestown Exposition indeed show a little girl with a striking similarity to "Miss Bud Dajo," and it is thus very likely that the girl was brought to the US and ended up in a human zoo exhibit.[72] The display of different types of "primitive" people, to the wonder and amusement of a largely white audience, was a key feature of the world's fairs and exhibitions that gained popularity during the second half of the nineteenth century.[73] Apart from the Philippine village, the 1907 exposition also boasted a selection of amusement rides, a Japanese tea garden, the Millers Brothers Ranch 101 Wild West Show, a display of Gatling guns, and "enlarged photographs of Moro campaign, 1903."[74] At the end of the exposition, the participants returned to the Philippines, and, it would appear, the girl known as "Miss Bud Dajo" returned to her former life. In 1911 a newspaper report mentioned that "there is running around Jolo now a little waif girl bearing the name of the mountain, who is said to have been the only survivor."[75] What later happened to her remains unknown.

The fascination that "Miss Bud Dajo" evidently held for Americans is reminiscent of earlier episodes in the country's history of settler violence. Following the Massacre of Tallushatchee in 1813, during which US militia forces slaughtered almost two hundred Red Stick Creeks, Andrew Jackson "adopted" one of the survivors, a boy he named Lyncoya. Something similar happened at Wounded Knee in 1890, when Brigadier General Leonard W. Colby seized an infant girl who had been found next to her dead mother several days after the massacre and brought her home to his wife. Given the historical context, "adoption" is of course misleading, and rather than simply being a benign act of charity, the adoption of Native American children was part and parcel of a broader US policy of genocidal assimilation. The redemptive symbolism of adopting the children of a vanquished enemy has a deep history, and by fetishizing the survivors of colonial massacres, Americans could effectively reframe their own violence and turn it into a sentimental narrative of benevolence in which the white man assumed the role of savior.[76] When Leonard Wood died, in 1927, newspapers claimed that he was widely mourned by the Moros "as he won their confidence after conquering them at the bloody battle of Bud Dahu."[77] More striking, however, was the claim that he had personally looked after children who survived the massacre:

It is learned that since that decisive affray the late governor general had been privately supporting two Moro children found there immediately after the encounter and picked up for dead by American troops. They later recovered and Wood took them under his care.[78]

None of this was true, but such fabrications in the obituaries for Leonard Wood ensured that he was remembered as the savior of Bud Dajo.[79] The reality was that nobody adopted the little Moro girl after Bud Dajo, and instead her likeness was commercialized and distributed as a postcard. One of the postcards in Price's collection appears to be a copy that Gibbs himself sent to the same acquaintance as the picture of the trench, as indicated by the inscription on the back:

This is the girl I spoke to you about. She is the only survivor of the Bud Dajo fight, it is a shame that they did not make a clean sweep of it for she is the dirtiest kid of a dirty lot in Jolo.[80]

Rather than sympathy, the image of the pitiful child instilled nothing but contempt in the photographer.

SIXTEEN

Afterimage

As to the Bud Dajo photograph showing dead Moros in trench.
I have a copy of this but it is too grisly. I think I can dig up one or
two photos of Bud Dajo.

John R. White to his publisher, 1928[1]

DESPITE HIS BEST EFFORTS, GENERAL WOOD FAILED TO PREVENT
Gibbs's photo from reaching the public eye, and on June 23, 1906,
the image of the trench at Bud Dajo was published for the first time in
Harper's Weekly, one of the most popular magazines in the US. Printed in
half size on a single page, the photo was included with another of Gibbs's
photos, this one showing a wounded American soldier being transported
on a mule following the assault (see figure 18). The caption provided
what had by then become a familiar account of "outlaws" and "savages"
defeated in "battle" against American soldiers—implicitly depriving the
Moros and their resistance of any legitimacy and reducing the massacre
to a morally unambiguous story. Describing the fortifications at the summit as a "death-trap" further emphasized the dangers and hardship of the
American soldiers tasked with fighting the "outlaws," as did details of the

"insurmountable difficulties," which were taken almost verbatim from Wood's first telegram of March 9.

The textual framing of the photograph of the trench, combined with the other image of the wounded soldier, fundamentally changed its meaning: the dead woman was clearly visible, but it was the single wounded soldier, looking into the camera, in the second image who would have elicited sympathy from the reader. Yet again, it was the Americans who were made out to be the real victims of Bud Dajo, and instead of being evidence of an atrocity, Gibbs's photograph functioned as a visual representation of the "white man's burden."[2] In the end, Wood had nothing to fear from the dissemination of the image: the racialized logic of American imperialism allowed the indiscriminate killing of women and children to be presented as an act of self-defense. Squeezed in between news stories about the recent assassination attempt on the king and queen of Spain, the aftereffects of the San Francisco earthquake, a report from the night shift at a telephone exchange, and an advertisement for Miller High Life ("the champagne of bottled beer"), the photo from Bud Dajo had effectively been rendered harmless.

Exactly one year after the massacre, in March 1907, the popular French journal *Le Tour Du Monde* ("around the world") published a two-part article by Réginald Kann describing his experiences in the Philippines.[3] Crucially, Kann's article was accompanied by a dozen photographs that he had taken with a Kodak camera, including the very graphic scenes of the dead Moros on the southern summit (see figures 7, 8, 11, 12, and 14). The article, however, was not widely read outside France, and the images did not reach the American press or public.[4] Kann was entirely supportive of Wood and the conduct of the US Army, and he ended the article on a sentimental note:

> It was not without regret that I left the Philippines, where thanks to fortunate circumstances and the kindness of the authorities I had been able to gather precious information and spend some of the most exhilarating hours of my life.[5]

Kann remained active as a war correspondent and participated in numerous conflicts before being killed in 1925 while covering the Rif War in Morocco.

None of the officers or men of the Bud Dajo expedition ever suffered any adverse consequences for their participation in the massacre—on the contrary. Three men were awarded the Medal of Honor for their actions, namely Gordon Johnston, Joseph Cecil, and Joseph Fitz.[6] Additionally, the officers of all the different branches of the army and navy involved in the operations received commendations for having distinguished themselves, including Duncan, Bundy, Koehler, Lawton, Schindel, McGlachlin, Worcester, and Cooke. Meanwhile, Captain White was awarded the Constabulary medal of valor.[7] Ten army certificates for unusual bravery were furthermore awarded to noncommissioned officers and privates of the Bud Dajo expeditionary force.[8]

The year after the Bud Dajo expedition, Joseph Duncan became chief of staff for the Pacific Department, and in 1911 he was finally promoted to brigadier general, as had been his ambition.[9] When he died, in 1912, the obituary in the *Army and Navy Journal* eulogized him as "a great white soul" and, once more, justified the massacre at Bud Dajo:

> None of the large number of those who knew Gen. Duncan in the army and outside the army could for a moment believe that he would have sanctioned any war upon women, but they knew well that his experience as an Indian fighter in the frontier days had taught him that sharp and decisive action is the best and surest way to meet attacks of the insensate savage.

Leonard Wood was made chief of staff of the US Army in 1910, and a few years later both Hugh L. Scott and Tasker H. Bliss in turn occupied the same position. A number of the officers and men of the Bud Dajo expedition also saw active service during World War I, including Omar Bundy, who commanded the 2nd Division of the US Army in France. Edward P. Lawton retired from the army in 1908 and set up a fruit plantation in Puerto Rico before being appointed as the military attaché to the American Embassy in Switzerland.[10] Once John R. White recovered from his wound, he was appointed superintendent of the Iwahig Penal Colony in Palawan.[11] Over time, Bud Dajo became just another exotic name in the service records of the officers and men who had participated in the expedition; there was certainly no dishonor attached to it, and at least one veterans' group was named after it.[12] After the world war, Bud Dajo was listed among the defining moments in the glorious history of the US Army, which could trace its history back to the Civil War:

> The achievement of the old Army from the close of the civil to that of the Spanish-American war is one of the brightest pages in American history, filled as it is with adventure, heroic display of courage, fortitude and suffering, in the subjugation of the many hostile tribes of Indians, outlaws and all-round hard cases from the ragged edges of civilization, whose brutal orgies or murder and rapine vied with that of his redskins brother, to be finally subdued as were the Indian by the old Army in the reclamation of the great American desert.
>
> But this rough school produced men, some of them alive today, that scaled the wall of Peking, China, and the crater of Bud Dajo, San Juan Hill, and, last but not least, the subjugation of the Hun during our recent world war.[13]

As a proud part of the army's history, Bud Dajo could even be used to sell products, and the chemical company DuPont de Nemours invoked "The Scaling of Bud Dajo" in an advertisement for gunpowder, which had an illustration of soldiers of the 6th Infantry climbing the mountain while Moros are seen pouring gunfire and rolling large stones at them.[14] A better example of Wood's success in managing the narrative of Bud Dajo could hardly be conceived.

In the years following the massacre, Gibbs's photo kept circulating as a postcard and would from time to time appear in various publications, usually without much context.[15] In 1920, when Wood was running for the Republican nomination for president, journalist and civil-rights activist Oswald Garrison Villard referred to the image in an article in which he argued that the general was eminently unsuited for the role of president:

> I have an interesting photograph taken at the battle of Mount Dajo showing the bodies of dead women and children in the Moro stronghold killed by American

soldiers of General Wood's command who stand by, rifles in hand. There is no doubt that General Wood is a very able soldier, in peace-time at least. . . .[16]

Wood did not win the nomination, as it turned out, and instead he returned to the Philippines as governor-general, a role that he occupied until his death. The copy of the photo in Villard's possession was one of the many postcards still in circulation, and he later included it in his autobiography, *Fighting Years: Memoirs of a Liberal Editor.*[17] Interestingly, the only memoir to be published by a participant in the assault on Bud Dajo was John R. White's *Bullets and Bolos*, which appeared in 1928. The Bud Dajo expedition was recounted as just one of many exciting adventures that White experienced during his career in the Philippine Constabulary, which included fighting tropical diseases and hunting bandits in Luzon. As might be expected, White's own experience was thus at the center of the narrative, and the detailed account of Bud Dajo focused on his reconnaissance of the southern trail and culminated when he was wounded in the knee at Adam's *cotta* on March 7. In the book, White's begrudging respect for the Moros was couched in crass Orientalist stereotypes that ultimately served only to emphasize the paternalism of the Englishman's colonial vision:

> Poor gallant gentlemen of Sulu, with your brilliant carmine, orange, and green jackets, your tight-fitting trousers, your wavy krises, and razor barongs, your turbans and jaunty fezzes, your bastard Mohammedanism and contempt for the unbeliever, your fairy boats on a fairy sea amid fairy isles—you are, after all, a picturesque people fit for better things than to fill moldering graves on the summits of your beautiful mountains. I'm afraid that you needed the lesson that even Sulu courage and daredevilry could not prevail against American numbers and science.[18]

Despite the fact that White himself had copies of Gibbs's photograph, it is noteworthy that the only image from Bud Dajo to be included in his memoir was one taken during Pershing's expedition in 1911. The photograph showed American troops on the *cotta* at the eastern summit—without a single Moro in sight, dead or alive.[19] A few years later, White, who had by then achieved the rank of colonel and superintendent of the

Sequoia National Park, was interviewed for the *Overland Monthly and Out West Magazine*. White was sharing his memories of the Philippines and reminiscing about General Wood, as the interviewer described:

> The Colonel showed me another personal letter from General Wood, remark-ing: "I'll never forget when I first met the General; I was a young captain at the time, in the Islands. I thought I knew something about fighting Moros. We had just returned from an expedition in the Island of Sulu (the Isle that made the Sultan famous) where we had rounded up 600 bad Moro brigands and had converted them into 600 perfectly good Moros."
>
> "With what result?" I interrupted inquisitively.
>
> "Six hundred dead Moros," was the casual reply, without so much as blink-ing an eyelash.[20]

A quarter of a century after Bud Dajo, White had evidently lost none of his disdain for the Moros. However, the passing of time did seem to mod-ify some attitudes, and the writer Vic Hurley, who more than anyone else helped popularize the story of the American occupation of the southern Philippines, provided a very different account in his classic work *The Swish of the Kris* from 1938:

> By no stretch of the imagination could Bud Dajo be termed a "battle." Cer-tainly the engaging of 1,000 Moros armed with *krises*, spears, and a few rifles by a force of 800 Americans armed with every modern weapon was not a matter for publicity. The American troops stormed a high mountain peak crowned by fortifications to kill 1,000 Moros with a loss to themselves of twenty-one killed and seventy-three wounded! The casualty lists reflect the unequal nature of the battle.[21]

In 1939 the American experience fighting Moros in the southern Phil-ippines received the Hollywood treatment in the adventure movie *The Real Glory*, based on a novel by Charles L. Clifford and starring Gary Cooper, David Niven, and Andrea Leeds.[22] Ostensibly set in 1906, the film nevertheless reflected a historical context in which the Philippines was about to be granted independence following the Tydings-McDuffie

Act of 1934. The plot thus revolved around the desperate need for American officers to train the Philippine Constabulary to protect "good" Filipinos against "bad" Moros, portrayed as villainous slave-raiding pirates. Notably, the film included a scene in which Cooper's character, the heroic Lieutenant Canavan, threatens a captured *juramentado* with a pig skin in a scene obviously inspired by the burials that took place in Jolo in 1903. The depiction of the frenzied and half-naked Muslim charging suicidally at the Americans while brandishing a curved sword is one that has left an indelible impression.[23]

In March 1906, when Bud Dajo still dominated the headlines, Mark Twain had attended a sending-off luncheon for the powerful publisher and then-editor of *Harper's Weekly*, George Harvey, who was about to depart for Europe. Inevitably, the conversation had touched on the massacre, as Twain described:

> Harvey said he believed that the shock and shame of this episode would eat down deeper and deeper into the hearts of the nation and fester there and produce results. He believed it would destroy the Republican party and President Roosevelt. I cannot believe that the prediction will come true, for the reason that prophecies which promise valuable things, desirable things, good things, worthy things, never come true. Prophecies of this kind are like wars fought in a good cause—they are so rare that they don't count.[24]

One reason that Harvey's prophecy never came true and that Bud Dajo failed to make much of an impact on American politics at all was— ironically—that Mark Twain himself never spoke about it in public and furthermore decided against publishing his comments on the affair. Although selections from his autobiography appeared in installments in the *North American Review* later in 1906, Twain reserved his more controversial pieces for a future autobiography that would be published only after his death. As a result, his withering account of the massacre was not made public until 1924, more than a decade after his death, and even then it was not published in full.[25]

Similar to Harvey, Moorfield Storey and the Anti-Imperialist League mistakenly assumed that the massacre would "shock and shame" American politicians and the public. In January of 1907, hundreds of copies of Gibbs's photograph were produced and sent to members of the US Senate.[26] Just a single newspaper, the *Baltimore Sun*, wrote about the story, in a brief notice tucked away on page 11: "Senators and Representatives today received in the mail from some anonymous source sheets of paper showing a halftone picture of Filipino men, women and children killed at the battle of Mount Dajo, lying in a trench."[27] Other than W. E. B. Du Bois, not a single person reacted, and the utter failure of the attempt to use the image had a decidedly dampening effect on the activities of the Anti-Imperialist League, which did not again invoke Bud Dajo. By this point, anti-imperialism had in fact lost much of its political appeal, and the league soon slipped into obsolescence before eventually being disbanded in 1920. Meanwhile, Du Bois went on to write some of the most poignant critiques of Western imperialism, especially in Africa, but he never returned to the photo of Bud Dajo. Yet even as interest in American atrocities in the Philippines waned, the work against racial injustice in the US continued.

In 1909, Storey and Du Bois helped found the National Association for the Advancement of Colored People, which was to become the biggest civil-rights organization in the country and for which Storey served as the first president. The following year, Du Bois set up the organization's official publication, the *Crisis*, which included a regular column documenting instances of lynching across the country. As early as 1891, journalist and later cofounder of the NAACP, Ida B. Wells, had published a photographic postcard as well as an illustration of lynchings in her pamphlet *A Red Record*.[28] At the time, she affirmed the belief that knowledge of racial violence would in and of itself be sufficient to mobilize public outrage:

> The very frequent inquiry made after my lectures by interested friends is "What can I do to help the cause?" The answer always is: "Tell the world the facts." When the Christian world knows the alarming growth and extent of outlawry in our land, some means will be found to stop it.[29]

This was also Du Bois's conviction, and as a sociologist he was committed to scientific research as a means to carefully expose the injustices suffered by African Americans in the South. In 1899, however, an event took place not far from Atlanta that seriously undermined his belief that truth would speak for itself.[30] A black farmer named Sam Hose had been accused of killing his white employer over a dispute about wages, and as the authorities searched for the suspect, it was rumored that Hose had also raped the employer's wife. Du Bois wrote a letter in which he warned against the violence likely to follow if the baseless accusations of rape were allowed to circulate unchallenged. He then went to see Joel Chandler Harris, editor of the *Atlanta Constitution*, to have it published. On his way to the newspaper offices, Du Bois nevertheless found out that he was already too late: Hose had been captured, and a white mob had tortured and killed him, putting some of his burned fingers on display in the nearby meat market. "Something died in me that day," Du Bois later explained:

> I didn't deliver my letter. I turned back to the University and said: Now, there's no use simply telling these people how many Negroes have been arrested and what has been done to them, last year and this next year, and what should be done, and criminal treatment, and how many people have died. . . . These people aren't going to pay any attention to that.[31]

"The cure," Du Bois realized, "wasn't simply telling people the truth, it was inducing them to act on the truth."[32] A more activist approach was required, he now argued: "You've got to begin propaganda and tell the people when you know something is wrong, you've got to do something about it."[33] The propaganda that Du Bois had in mind included a more deliberate use of images and especially of the photographic postcards sold as souvenirs after lynchings.

Du Bois's strategic vision found its most striking expression in a supplement to the July 1916 edition of the *Crisis* titled "The Waco Horror," which had been written by suffragette and investigative journalist Elizabeth Freeman.[34] The illustrated supplement provided an unflinching account of the lynching of seventeen-year-old Jesse Washington, who had been accused of the rape and murder of a white woman two months earlier. Thousands of spectators had flocked to Waco, Texas, and watched as a mob beat, stabbed, and castrated Washington before they hoisted him in chains from a tree and burned him alive. Crucially, the supplement included four photographs of Washington's mutilated and charred body as it was slowly reduced to ashes in front of the crowd. Some 42,000 copies of the special supplement were printed and circulated to NAACP supporters, as well as members of Congress and President Woodrow Wilson. As a result, the lynching gained unprecedented attention nationally, and although no arrests were made and racial violence continued with undiminished ferocity in the South, the publication of the photos marked a watershed in the ongoing antilynching campaign.[35] What proved so shocking about these images was not just the horrific violence they exposed but also the smiling faces of the white spectators who posed for the camera next to the remains of Washington. The strategy that Du Bois had first suggested in 1907, after he saw the photo of the trench at Bud Dajo, had finally been put into practice. In his editorial in the *Crisis*, he wrote the following:

> We make no apology for including in this number a detailed account with pictures of perhaps the most horrible lynching that has taken place in the United States. We know that those who so hate the evil of this world that they are unwilling to be disturbed by it will question our taste, but as we have already questioned theirs on numerous occasions there is here, at least, no chance for misunderstanding.[36]

Conclusion

American Amnesia

ODAY, THERE REMAIN BUT FEW VISIBLE TRACES OF THE BUD DAJO
Massacre in the United States. The military training facility in Missouri
still carries Leonard Wood's name, and the three recipients of the Medal
of Honor awarded after the 1906 expedition are still venerated in the pantheon of American heroes. The efforts to rescind the twenty Medals of Honor
awarded after the Wounded Knee Massacre or the debates about military
bases named after Confederate generals have no counterpart when it comes
to Bud Dajo. Instead, the "Battle of Mount Dajo" has simply become part
of military tradition and, in the case of the 4th US Cavalry, even embedded
in the regimental coat of arms: on the crest above the shield and regimental
motto, "Paratus Et Fideles" ("Prepared and Loyal"), a stylized green volcano,

with a red reversed kris in the crater, was thus added after 1906 to represent the Bud Dajo expedition and the defeat of the Moros. The regimental insignia and coat of arms of the 4th Field Artillery Regiment, which incorporated the 28th Battery Field Artillery, similarly included both a kris and a crescent in reference to the regiment's service against the Moros. Bud Dajo was not simply honored with medals awarded to individual soldiers or the insignia of the individual regiments: on the US Army flag, the eleven campaign streamers for the Philippine-American War include one that reads "Jolo 6–8 March 1906." To this day, the massacre in which a thousand men, women, and children were killed thus remains proudly displayed as part of the US military tradition. It is indeed no accident that the streamer with a blue ribbon and two red stripes symbolizing the assault on Bud Dajo is displayed on the Army flag alongside campaigns such as "Pine Ridge November 1890–January 1891" and "Tet Counteroffensive 30 January–1 April 1968"—the labels of which carefully conceal the massacres they represent.

Although Leonard Wood is today no longer celebrated as a great American hero in the way that he once was, there are still those who find it difficult not to invoke ameliorating factors to justify US colonial violence in the southern Philippines. In his 2014 book, *Teddy Roosevelt and Leonard Wood: Partners in Command*, the late John S. D. Eisenhower essentially justified the brutality of Wood's approach to fighting the Moros:

> Wood could hardly be blamed for the deaths of women, because many of them would don black clothing and, showing no signs of their gender, fight with the men to the death. Thus, it was only the children who were unjustly killed. As a rule, Wood's losses in Americans would be only a handful. His tactics were shocking to many Americans, but they were effective.[1]

More than a hundred years after this argument was first made, by Wood himself, it would seem that it is still possible to blame the Moros at Bud Dajo for their own deaths.

———

A key reason for the historical amnesia surrounding Bud Dajo is a profound reluctance on the part of many Americans to face an uncomfortable past—an instinct shared by most former imperialist powers, it might be added. In December 1969 the journalist Jonathan Schell, who covered the war in Vietnam, wrote an impassioned reflection on the significance of the My Lai photos, which had then only just been published:

> When others committed them, we looked on the atrocities through the eyes of the victims. Now we find ourselves, almost against our will, looking through the eyes of the perpetrators, and the landscape seems next to unrecognizable. The victims are indistinct—almost invisible. A death close to us personally seems unfathomably large, but their deaths dwindle in our eyes to mere abstractions. We don't know what kind of lives they led or what kind of things they said to each other. We are even uncertain of the right name of the village we are said to have annihilated.[2]

The unspoken understanding is that the "we" that Schell addressed was an overwhelmingly white American public for whom the very idea that "our boys" might do horrible things was largely inconceivable. It was certainly not a "we" that included the people at the receiving end of US foreign policy, for whom the identity of the perpetrators would have been quite self-evident. The prevalence of an exceptionalist narrative in the Western world indeed makes it difficult for many people to acknowledge atrocities carried out in their name or in the name of progress. Instead, a range of different strategies are deployed to manage the historical narrative and deny or deflect from those aspects of the past that do not so easily conform to a comforting patriotic myth.

There is, in fact, an entire vocabulary explicitly designed to gloss over the violence and brutality of conquest and warfare, rendering it more palatable and less likely to cause concern or invite criticism. Whereas some euphemisms have a distinctly military origin, like "pacification," "collateral damage," and "hearts and minds," others have a longer history and are more overtly political, including "manifest destiny," "benevolent assimilation," and Rudyard Kipling's insidious, oxymoronic "savage wars of peace." When a conflict is cast in starkly ideological terms, whether it is "civilization versus barbarism," "freedom versus communism," or the so-called War on Terror, there is no question about who the "good guys" are, and it is taken for granted that the ends justify the means. Wars of conquest become just wars, and atrocities become defendable.

As the case of My Lai shows, many people have an implicit sympathy with their own troops, regardless of the circumstances. Whereas the Viet Cong or NVA were considered to be innately barbaric, a normative assumption concerning the civilized behavior of young American men means that the slaughter of hundreds of unarmed civilians has been explained—or rather, explained away—by a variety of external and supposedly mitigating factors: the frustration of jungle warfare, the cruelty of the enemy, or even tautological clichés about the brutality of modern war. Even critical scholars have found it difficult to maintain an analytical distance; in an article titled "An American Atrocity," Claude Cookman, for instance, described the men who carried out the My Lai Massacre as "angry, frightened, and struggling to stay alive in March 1968."[3] It goes without saying that the same analytical generosity is rarely accorded the Viet Cong or the NVA. In this case, a sympathetic reading of My Lai transforms the massacre into what has been described as a "tragedy without villains."[4]

When atrocity cannot be denied, it is most commonly explained as an "isolated episode" and blamed on a small group or a single individual— the proverbial "bad apple." Examining historical atrocities through a legal framework, as "war crimes," for instance, further serves to narrow the focus to issues of personal culpability. That is indeed what happened in the case of Lieutenant Calley after My Lai, which was conveniently rewritten as the misguided actions of a single rogue officer who lost control of his troops, and in no way reflective of the American way of war in Vietnam more generally. When journalist Nick Turse, in his 2012 book *Kill Anything That Moves*, argued that the My Lai Massacre was in fact the norm rather than the exception, the backlash from conservative military historians was immediate.[5] In their indignant response, Gary Kulik and Peter Zinoman insisted that "military atrocities must be studied as specific events that occur in particular contexts, often as the result of a unique set of circumstances," thus effectively ruling out the possibility of ever uncovering systemic violence.[6] It goes without saying that any historical event should be studied in its particular context, yet to use a methodological approach explicitly designed to preclude structural factors would appear to be, at the very least, intellectually dubious.

In most accounts of the My Lai Massacre, the figure of helicopter pilot Hugh Thompson Jr. is also invoked as a corollary to Calley's "bad apple." During the massacre, Thompson landed his helicopter and along with his crew saved several Vietnamese villagers, at one point even threatening to open fire on the US soldiers engaged in the killing. Thompson was subsequently one of just a few witnesses who spoke out, and he eventually testified against Calley during the trial. By focusing on the heroic actions of Thompson and his crew, however, the slaughter carried out by US troops is downplayed and the massacre at My Lai thereby transformed into a redemptive narrative. In his 2017 book, *My Lai: Vietnam, 1968, and the Descent into Darkness*, historian Howard Jones concludes that the entire massacre could best be understood as a matter of personal character traits:

> We have to accept that there remains a crucial difference between William Calley and Hugh Thompson. Perhaps this difference involves "character"—however we define it. I suggest it embodies a notion of decency that was most noticeably missing at My Lai. Thompson, Lawrence Colburn, and Glenn Andreotta leave us room for hope because, unlike Calley (and others), they did not lose sight of ordinary human decency. And that, in the end, is a form of heroism.[7]

There should be no doubt that Thompson and his crew did something genuinely heroic at My Lai, which deserves to be recognized. Yet at the same time it seems obscene when the My Lai Massacre is reduced to a matter of "decency" and ultimately turned into a story of American heroism. This moral sleight of hand might make for a more edifying narrative, but it makes for poor history. When asked whether Americans had ever come to terms with the Vietnam War, writer Michael Herr replied:

> We're not a great introspective people. It is not in our nature. We're very ignorant of our history. We're great perverters of our tradition.[8]

This particular dynamic is, of course, not unique to the Vietnam War, for the very myth of American exceptionalism is largely predicated on a disavowal of the systematic destruction and dispossession of Native Americans upon which the nation was founded. In fact, the very same arguments used to absolve American troops of full responsibility for the My Lai Massacre is also used to condone the exterminatory violence of the "Indian Wars" in the American West. In a textbook published by Oxford University Press in 2019, *In Harm's Way: A History of the American Military Experience*, for instance, historians Gene Allen Smith, David Coffey, and Kyle Longley question whether it is appropriate to describe Wounded Knee as a "massacre" because, as they claim, there is no evidence of intent on the part of the US Army and no formal order was given to perpetrate one.[9] In fact, their argument goes, this was not a "massacre": the Lakota were armed, refused to lay down their weapons, and then fired "the first lethal volleys"—a claim first made by the US Army in 1890 to justify its actions but that has since been debunked.[10] In the end, the three authors' argument amounts to little more than bothsidesism dressed up as historical analysis:

> Clearly, army leaders' decision to employ a heavy-handed approach to an already explosive situation set the stage for disaster. Sending in the long-aggrieved 7th Cavalry to disarm potential veterans of the Battle of Little Bighorn only exacerbated tensions, and the fact that many of the troopers were raw recruits who had never been exposed to combat conditions no doubt played a role, as it did at My Lai seventy-eight years later.
>
> What happened at Wounded Knee was nothing more than what had happened dozens of times throughout the brutal history of the Indian Wars. It was the result of perpetual misunderstanding, mistrust, and mistakes, of one culture exercising overwhelming advantage over another, of failure of leadership. Once a preventable exchange became a full-blown firefight, not enough was done to stop it or to protect innocents. In this regard neither side was blameless. Was Wounded Knee a massacre? Like so much about the Indian Wars, there is no easy answer. The situation was far too complex to boil down to a single word.[11]

Deliberately obfuscating the facts, and with a generous use of the passive tense to dissipate any sense of agency or causality, *In Harm's Way* thus presents a narrative in which Wounded Knee becomes an "inevitable tragedy" for which no one can ultimately be held responsible. Contemporaries, of course, had no problem recognizing what happened at Wounded Knee for what it was—including US Army major general Nelson A. Miles, who described it as "the most abominable military blunder and a horrible massacre of women and children."[12] The archaeologist Warren K. Moorehead similarly referred to the "Wounded Knee massacre" in 1891, adding with some emphasis: "for it really was a massacre."[13] To the Lakota survivors, there was certainly nothing complex about it: "We tried to run," Louise Weasel Bear remembered, "but they shot us like we were a buffalo."[14] Smith, Coffey, and Longley conveniently omit Bud Dajo in their historical survey but have the following to say about US military operations in the Philippines, which by the authors' own account cost the lives of between two hundred thousand and one million civilians between 1899 and 1902:

> The Philippine experience proved largely a success for the United States, with the military developing sound counterinsurgency practices and positive nation-building programs.[15]

Apart from the outright denial of atrocity, which is what the argument in *In Harm's Way* amounts to, there is also a more oblique type of liberal historical whitewash, one that acknowledges atrocity but, again, only as a singular episode and only as an exception to a supposedly benign rule. Introducing his short film on the 1864 Sand Creek Massacre, popular documentary filmmaker Ken Burns makes a strong case for a more nuanced engagement with the past:

> Being an American means reckoning with a history fraught with violence and injustice. Ignoring that reality in favor of mythology is not only wrong but also dangerous. The dark chapters of American history have just as much to teach us, if not more, than the glorious ones, and often the two are entwined.[16]

Although Burns correctly insists on using the term *massacre* for what happened at Sand Creek, his vision of the past is nevertheless a highly simplistic one, neatly arranged into national "triumphs" and "failings." The centuries-long genocide of the Native American population is never mentioned, and the Sand Creek Massacre is instead reduced to an isolated event—or what Burns refers to simply as a "dark chapter" or a "shameful moment."[17] This is not a reckoning with the past as much as a form of historiographical containment, which only admits to a momentary failure in an otherwise celebratory narrative of American exceptionalism. Such a discourse has its obvious parallel in European imperial nostalgia, which can be sustained only by either ignoring or minimizing the grim facts of colonial violence and exploitation in Africa, Asia, and across the globe.

Ultimately, the historical ignorance described by Michael Herr cannot be considered merely as an absence of knowledge but should rather be understood as a deliberate choice. And it is this self-inflicted amnesia that, time and again, allows people to insist that "this is not who we are" when confronted by Western atrocities. What happened in March 1906, however, was not an isolated episode any more than Wounded Knee and My Lai were. Instead, the Bud Dajo Massacre should be recognized as a key moment along the blood meridian that runs through American history.

———◆———

Sadly, this story does not end with My Lai, and if many aspects of the Bud Dajo Massacre seem eerily familiar to twenty-first-century readers, there is a good reason for that.[18] In the wake of the attacks of September 11, 2001, and as part of the so-called Global War on Terror, the representation of Muslims as a particularly insidious threat—against whom extreme forms of violence are not only permissible but necessary—has become a staple of political discourse in the United States and in the West more generally.[19] The language may have changed slightly, and the bogey of the *juramentado* replaced by that of the suicide bomber, yet the protection of the law can today be suspended at will, and Muslim civilians killed with impunity, just as they could in 1906.[20] In 2005 Leonard Wood's biographer, Jack McCallum, summarized the general's tenure in the southern Philippines in terms that foreshadowed Donald Trump's feverish rhetoric a decade later:

> Wood, in Mindanao, got involved in fighting—the first time in United States history—got involved in fighting with fundamentalist Islamic terrorists, who were basically making hash of the southern part of the Philippines. He more

or less succeeded in his battle with those people—he certainly didn't put them
down since they're still there.[21]

To describe the Moros of the Sulu Archipelago who fought the Americans
at the beginning of the twentieth century as "fundamentalist Islamic terrorists" is both analytically inept and deeply anachronistic, yet it is far from
an uncommon view. James R. Arnold's popular history *The Moro War*, published in 2011, explicitly framed the US experience in the southern Philippines as a precursor to the "Global War on Terror," claiming that "the
post-9/11 war against terrorists is not the first time the United States has
battled such ferocious foes."[22] Trump's Pershing anecdote is thus merely the
most egregious expression of the prevalent belief that the past can—quite
literally—be weaponized in the present.[23]

Ultimately, the much-touted anecdote about the use of pigs' blood to
fight Muslims does not exist in a vacuum. When looking at the infamous
trophy photos from the Abu Ghraib prison in Iraq, or the images of the
so-called Kill Team in Afghanistan, it is accordingly difficult not to recognize them as modern iterations of the same dehumanizing impulse that
framed Gibbs's photograph from Bud Dajo.[24] Whereas the actual history
of US atrocities in the southern Philippines has been largely forgotten, the
racialized logic that underpinned the violence of March 1906 has not.

———————

Like Aeronaut Gibbs, who pieced together the broken negative, I have used
the incomplete fragments of the past to reconstruct what happened in
March 1906—the story that Wood and the US government tried so hard
to bury. In doing so, I have sought to resist the numbness that comes with
the passing of time and instead recover something of the grim epiphany first
experienced by W. E. B. Du Bois when he saw the photograph from Bud
Dajo. There is, of course, something deeply intrusive and unsettling about
looking at an image of atrocity "through the eyes of the perpetrators."[25]
And yet it is precisely the disorienting shift in vantage point, evocatively described by Jonathan Schell, that makes the photograph so illuminating. The
image is not just evidence of a massacre—in the way that we might consider
a crime-scene photo—but is itself an artifact of violence. The photograph

of the trench inadvertently captured more than Gibbs intended and thus revealed more than he ever imagined.[26] After all, this was the image for which the US soldiers posed to celebrate their victory and which they subsequently kept as a souvenir—to preserve their memories and share their experience. This is the image that they would send home to their families and loved ones, and that would be widely disseminated as a popular postcard. In fact, it is only because of the photograph that the Bud Dajo Massacre has not been lost in time and forgotten entirely. Its very existence is testament to the ugly truth it reveals, and if we refuse to look, however uncomfortable it may be, we become complicit in its erasure.[27]

In Joseph Conrad's novella "Heart of Darkness," Kurtz, the fallen imperial hero, initially writes a report for the "International Society for the Suppression of Savage Customs," providing a visionary blueprint for the civilizing mission in Central Africa.[28] The idealism of the report is nevertheless undercut by a postscript, scrawled in an unsteady hand, calling simply for the slaughter of the "natives." That was, in Conrad's view, the true logic of Western imperialism, and although the story was ostensibly about the Congo Free State, the author reminded his readers that "all Europe contributed to the making of Kurtz."[29] The image from Bud Dajo, I would argue, might appropriately be seen as a visual counterpart to Kurtz's "exposition of a method":

> It was very simple, and at the end of that moving appeal to every altruistic sentiment it blazed at you, luminous and terrifying, like a flash of lightning in a serene sky: "Exterminate all the brutes!"[30]

Epilogue

Jolo 2022

DURING EVERY RESEARCH PROJECT THAT I HAVE WORKED ON OVER the past twenty years, I have made a point of visiting the place I was writing about—whether it was a tiny village and former haunt of "Thugs" in India's Chambal Valley, the cantonment town of Sialkot in Pakistan, or the site of the Jallianwala Bagh massacre in Amritsar. Understanding the topography and walking the paths plotted by century-old maps is as important as hours spent in the archive and is frankly indispensable if you want to get a real sense of the place and events that you are trying to reconstruct. For me, Bud Dajo was no different, but the problem was that Jolo is generally considered to be a dangerous place. For the past fifty years, Moro separatist movements have battled the armed forces of the Philippines in Mindanao and Sulu, and Jolo was until recently also one of the hot spots in the "Global War on Terror" in southeast Asia. A number of Islamic militant groups, including the ISIS-affiliated Abu Sayyaf Group, have been involved in kidnappings of Westerners, several of whom have ended up being killed; the island's reputation is well-illustrated by writer Matthew Thompson's aptly titled 2015 article "Don't Go to Jolo."[1] This was obviously not a place for a hapless historian to wander around.

Every embassy and foreign-office website warned against visiting the southern Philippines, and despite my best efforts, I found it impossible to find anyone who could help me. I had almost given up when I came across a Filipino travel blog that included the email contact for the provincial tourist office of the Sulu region. That is how I met Jainab Abdulmajid, who turned out to be incredibly helpful. She seemed to understand intuitively why I wanted to visit Jolo, and much to my surprise, she responded that it would not be a problem and that she was happy to help arrange a visit to Bud Dajo. It still took several years, and a global epidemic, before I was finally able to board a plane for Manila in March 2022, but by that point I had completed most of the research, and visiting the site of the massacre seemed to be a fitting way to end the book.

When I explained what I was doing to my taxi driver in Manila, he immediately knew what I was talking about, and—like almost every other person I met in the Philippines—he brought up the press conference in 2016, when then-president Rodrigo Duterte criticized Obama while brandishing the photo of the trench. The driver also mentioned the Balangiga Massacre and the subsequent US retribution, which occurred on the island of Samar in 1901, during the Philippine-American War. The Muslim South was not involved in the Filipino struggle for independence, but a shared history of armed resistance against the Americans has led to a postindependence reconfiguration of historical memory in which Bud Dajo and Balangiga have been folded into the same nationalist narrative. Although Duterte used the photo from Bud Dajo mainly as a political prop, this televised moment resonated with a lot of people, in Manila as much as Jolo, who saw it as a sort of public reckoning in which the Philippines finally called out their former colonial oppressor. Even in the Philippines, I couldn't help but notice, Bud Dajo is essentially remembered through the photograph, and the image and the event are in truth inseparable.

Early next morning, I flew to Zamboanga, where I was met by Jainab and two policemen, Mac and Lid, who would serve as my bodyguards during the duration of my stay in the South. Both foreign and Filipino visitors in Sulu are routinely provided with armed escorts by either the army or the police, and Jainab, as it turned out, was extremely well-connected and had secured all necessary permission from the authorities. Bud Dajo is one of the defining moments in the history of the region, and, like everyone else whom I met in Jolo, Jainab was genuinely enthusiastic about my project and eager to help with the research.

There is a forty-minute flight between Zamboanga and Jolo, but instead we took the popular overnight ferry, following the very same route that Colonel Duncan's expeditionary force did in 1906. I couldn't sleep in the stifling heat and spent most of the journey with Mac and Lid on the open rear deck, where a light breeze made the night more bearable. The moon cast a silvery reflection on the still waters of the Sulu Sea as we sailed through the dark past fishing boats and the faint lights from distant islands. Just before dawn, Jolo came into view, and among its many mountains I soon recognized the distinct outline of Bud Dajo, visible through a white haze. I had seen numerous photographs and read hundreds of historical accounts, yet nothing could have prepared me for the experience of finally seeing the mountain in person, its summit shrouded by clouds.

Once we disembarked, I was quickly shaken out of my historical revelries. In Jolo the military and the police are virtually indistinguishable, and on the pier we were met by a fifteen-man police escort in full combat gear, carrying an assortment of assault rifles (including an FN Minimi). As we left in Jainab's car, there were several policemen on motorcycles in front, while others followed behind in Toyota pickup trucks. Leaving the harbor, our convoy passed the iconic old Spanish lighthouse, which is now a small mosque, and as we drove through Jolo town, I recognized many of the historical landmarks of what Landor in 1904 described as "the prettiest and cleanest little settlement." Today, Jolo is neither pretty nor clean, but a noisy and bustling town where scooters and motorcycle taxis vie for space in the narrow streets; the government neglect and the lack of investment in the region are difficult to ignore. Local elections were going on, and among the many colorful posters I noticed one that encouraged people to vote for John S. Schuck III—a direct descendant of Leonard Wood's interpreter more than a century ago. I was put up in the Peacekeepers Inn in Asturias, familiar to all foreign-aid workers and visitors to the island, with Mac and Lid in the room next to mine. There were always at least half a dozen heavily armed policemen outside, and the police headquarters was just down the street.

———◆———

In Jolo, everyone knows about Bud Dajo and about the photograph. It is, moreover, a distinctly local narrative, steeped in the traditional *kissas* and preserved through family memories. Datu Adam's descendants, for instance, are still ashamed of what has been remembered as his shameful betrayal, and people were surprised and even incredulous when I told them that Adam had actually died fighting on the mountain. One of the most memorable experiences I had in Jolo was when Jainab took me to meet Edmund Gumbahali, whose great-grandfather, Panglima Hawani, escaped from Bud Dajo as a young boy while the rest of the family perished. The family used to keep the rifle his great-grandfather brought down from Bud Dajo, but it was lost in the 1970s, when President Marcos declared martial law.[2]

When the attack had begun, Edmund told me, the walls of the *cottas* were high enough to cover a man standing upright, yet at the end they had been all blown to pieces by the American guns, thus exposing the Moro warriors. On the first day, most of the men were killed, and on the second day only the young boys and old men were able to fight. On the last day, only the women and children were left alive, hiding inside the mosque at the bottom of the crater. There was only water from the spring to soothe the children's hunger, and the women were singing to drown out the noise of the American guns. Although Edmund was proud that the Moro warriors had fought the Americans, and did not lament their death, the killing of women and children was deeply painful: "It haunts our memories until today," he explained. "When you just look at it as a battle, you don't understand. It is only when you go inside the crater, where the women and children died, that you understand. The story is within."

In 1999 Filipino filmmaker Sari Lluch Dalena went to Jolo with a small
film crew to recreate the Bud Dajo Massacre for the camera as part of a documentary project, "Memories of a Forgotten War," codirected with Camilla
Griggers. At the time, there was intensive fighting between the Philippine
Army and the Moro National Liberation Front (MNLF), but a temporary
ceasefire provided a brief opportunity for Sari to film in one of the villages
in the foothills of Bud Dajo. Because of the difficult conditions, as well as
budgetary constraints, Sari ended up relying on locals to play the parts of
the Moros, and she was accordingly able to work much of the local oral tradition into her script, including the stories of Edmund's great-grandfather.

According to Edmund, a wedding was taking place when the attack on
Bud Dajo occurred, and Sari painstakingly recreated the intricate cere-
monies of a Moro marriage ritual, which is brutally interrupted by the exploding shells from the American artillery. Later, the film shows women
and children cowering inside the mosque in the crater, saying their prayers,
while the bodies of dead warriors are scattered on the ground outside. In
the final scene, the camera slowly pans over the dead bodies, a profusion of
contorted arms and legs, the bridal finery covered in blood. As the camera
comes to rest on the bride's ghostly face, covered in the traditional white
rice-water paint, the image fades into the old photograph of the trench.

When I met Sari in Quezon City, Manila, she told me the remarkable
story of what had happened off-screen during the filming of this last scene.
Once she cried "cut," the women who had played the parts of the dead
Moros slowly got up, but the girl who was the bride could not be revived.
She seemed to be in a trance-like state but soon after became frantic, and
Sari was worried that she might be having an epileptic fit. The girl was taken
to a nearby house, and while the crew and villagers anxiously waited, a local
imam came and began a ritual of exorcism. There was singing and chanting
that lasted all through the night, and at one point a second imam had to be
brought in when several of the other actors also seemed to fall into a trance.

Things had settled down next morning, and Sari fully expected that she
and the crew would be told to leave. Instead, the village elders thanked Sari
for having caused the incident—during the episode, the girl had apparently
revealed things about the Bud Dajo Massacre that the locals believed only
someone who had been there could have known. According to the imam,

the girl and other actors had actually been possessed by the spirits of the dead martyrs, which was considered to be a great honor. Sari was left deeply affected by the experience but completed the film, which had revealed in such a remarkable way how the violent history of Bud Dajo refused to remain confined to the past—just like the spirits of the dead.[3]

———————

One of the people I met in Jolo was Professor Hanbal Bara, from the Mindanao State University, Sulu, who has lived and taught in the region his entire life. As a young man, he told me, he used to listen to the *kissas* about Bud Dajo, which were broadcast on the local radio every Sunday. In 1974, however, the tapes were lost when Jolo town was completely razed by the Philippine army, during fighting with members of the MNLF. Before their death, one of the fighters was said to have written a message in his own blood on the wall of a ruined building: "We choose martyrdom in the name of Allah [*parang sabil*], for the defence of our homeland, our people and our religion." The religious language of defiance that framed the standoff at Bud Dajo has thus continued to inform the Moro struggle for independence through the history of postindependence Philippines. When I asked Bara how people in Jolo today viewed the events of 1906, he said that Bud Dajo has become a symbol of their continuing struggle for independence: "Tausūg [Moro] dignity is not sanctified until the sovereignty of Sulu is achieved." The relationship between the government in Manila and the Muslim South is still deeply fraught, and there are many who to this day consider the army as an occupying force in Mindanao and Sulu—a view that the deployment of US troops in the region has done little to dispel. Since the establishment of the Bangsamoro Autonomous Region in Muslim Mindanao (BARMM) in 2019, there have been signs of improvement, although much remains to be done, not least in terms of acknowledging a painful history of violence.

The continued presence of US troops in Jolo has indeed kept memories of the colonial period alive—and kept the anger fresh. When we talked about the possibility of an American apology for the 1906 massacre, Bara mentioned the $90 million that President Obama in 2016 had pledged to help clear Laos of unexploded ordnance, but he also referred to

German reparations to Namibia in recognition of the Herero and Nama Genocide in the early twentieth century. It was clear to me that among the descendants of the victims of the Bud Dajo Massacre, and among the people of Mindanao and Sulu more generally, there is a sense of having been forgotten—and a real need for their suffering to be known and acknowledged. "Americans need to know," Bara insisted. This reminded me of something Edmund had said about his great-grandfather's escape from Bud Dajo: on the last day, before the final American attack, his father (Edmund's great-great-grandfather) handed him a rifle and told him to escape down the side of the mountain through the jungle—"so that there is someone to tell our story." I have carried these words with me since.

———◆———

Finally, the time had come for me to climb Bud Dajo. While Jainab and my police escort stayed behind in Jolo town, I was to be the guest of Lieutenant Colonel E. Abolencia, Commanding Officer of the 21st Infantry (Invincible) Battalion, who had just recently established a forward position at the top of the mountain. Following a meet-and-greet at the Brigade headquarters in Talipao, where a replica of the Sultan's Palace (Astana Darul Jambangan) had been built, we drove in a large convoy of military vehicles to the site of what the Americans in 1906 referred to as Position 2. Today, Bud Dajo and its foothills are covered by a thick tropical rain forest, all but impenetrable apart from the narrow trails that run up the south, west, and east slopes. Abolencia and I and about twenty-five soldiers set out on foot to climb the mountain by the south trail, along the very same route taken by Captain White and the Philippine Constabulary forces during the assault.

We began climbing up the muddy trail lined by thick undergrowth, with the triple canopy of the surrounding jungle blocking out the sun above us. Although there was no visible wildlife, the jungle was never quiet, and the shrill white noise of cicadas filled the humid air, oscillating between a pleasant hum and occasionally rising to a deafening crescendo. From time to time, some unseen bird could be heard from high up in the trees, joining the insect chorus. The rough path went straight up along a narrow hogback ridge, which fell away precipitously on either side, making it feel like I was walking along the edge of a cliff. Occasionally, I would catch a glimpse through an opening in the leaves, revealing the treetops in the valley far below. From the southern trailhead, the path climbs to about 2,000 feet above sea level at the very summit. This is not much for a mountain, yet the trail was 45–65 degrees most of the way, and the steep ascent made the elevation seem much more dramatic. I didn't look at the back of the man in front of me but at the back of his boots, and at times I had to scramble on all fours, grabbing on to muddy roots to pull myself up.

We had started out in an orderly column, but soon the detachment was stretched out along the entire extent of the trail as exhaustion began to set in; the men took off their helmets and slung their rifles more comfortably across their shoulders. I had been exercising regularly for months to make sure I was fit for this climb, but both the heat and humidity hovered in the nineties. It took every bit of my strength not to embarrass myself in front of the soldiers, who, unlike me, were also carrying body armor, rifles, and ammunition, in addition to heavy backpacks and radio equipment, etc. It took us little more than an hour to climb the south trail, which was considerably less than the American forces took in 1906—but then we did not have to climb any palisades or dodge rifle fire. As we broke out of the jungle on the southern summit, where Adam's *cotta* once stood, the dramatic view exposed the entire island before us, with the surrounding mountains in the distance framed by the Sulu Sea.

As I sat on the summit, trying to catch my breath, I realized that I was more or less in the same spot where Réginald Kann had taken his photograph of the trench and fortifications, and where White had been wounded. Now, however, the rim had been leveled to make space for a helicopter landing pad. So much of the landscape of Bud Dajo and its surroundings was clearly recognizable from the images I had seen and the accounts I had read, yet there were few obvious traces of the massacre itself. During World War II, the Japanese had occupied Jolo and subsequently entrenched themselves on the mountain. When the Americans recaptured the island, tons of bombs were dropped directly on Bud Dajo to flush out the Japanese troops, and a contemporary photo shows US soldiers later going over the hillside with flamethrowers. Since then, Bud Dajo has served as a refuge for different armed militants from time to time, and one officer told me that a camp belonging to the Abu

Sayyaf Group had been discovered on the mountain as recently as 2021. For more than a century, a succession of conflicts has been waged on Bud Dajo, yet over time all traces have been covered up by the jungle.

After a brief rest, we descended into the crater to see the newly installed marker commemorating the massacre. There had actually been an earlier commemoration of the Bud Dajo Massacre, in the centenary year of 2006, which was organized by local grassroots organizations and NGOs and was also attended by a number of foreign humanitarian workers. Several hundred people had climbed Bud Dajo at the time, including Jonathan Rudy of the Mennonite Central Committee, as part of a "Pagtibaw Sajahitra," or "peace pilgrimage." I had talked to Jon, who described the commemoration, during which he argued that there could be no healing without an acknowledgment of the historical facts: "It's not healing if it leaves out remembering. We need to know about the truth; we need truth telling."[4] As an American, he told me, he had apologized for the massacre and had also helped put up a marker:

A TRIBUTE TO MORE THAN A THOUSAND TAUSUGS
WHO FELL AS MARTYRS TO THE
BUD DAHU BATTLE, MARCH 5–8, 1906
LET THE MEMORIES OF OUR ANCESTORS
BE THE LEGACY FOR THOSE GENERATIONS
WHO WILL CONTINUE TO WORK FOR PEACE AND JUSTICE.[5]

The marker was only temporary and has long since disappeared, and although there have been numerous calls for an official commemoration of the Bud Dajo Massacre, the Philippine government has so far ignored them. Ironically, it is the armed forces that have done the most in this regard.

Just a week before my visit, a permanent marker had been put up in a clearing inside the crater, and there were still flower wreaths and large banners with historical photographs, including the photo of the trench, extended from the surrounding trees.[6] The inscription of the marker read:

This marker commemorates the Battle of Bud Dahu' fought between the Bangsa Sug and the American Forces from March 6 to 8, 1906 on the fortified slopes and ridges of the cloud-capped mountain named Dahu'. This historic clash represents one of the most dramatic and notable defiance of, and armed resistance against, American rule in the Philippines.

The more than nine hundred Tausug men, women and children defenders of Bud Dahu' fought gallantly with their kris, spears and occasional rifles, and bravely withstood artillery bombardments, sniper shots and the onslaught of heavy machine gun fire from the six hundred American Soldiers who laid siege on the mountain.

After three days of fierce fighting, however, the indomitable courage of the Bangsa Sug of Bud Dahu' was overwhelmed by the superior weapons of the Americans, and the battle turned into a massacre, which was denounced by some quarters in the United States of America, as an ignominious victory by the American army in Jolo.

The famous American writer Mark Twain called the battle "a slaughter," referring to the use of superior force by the American Soldiers on poorly-armed men, and the killing of their women and children in the process. Twain reserved his most emphatically melancholic words for the fallen children of the massacre: "We see the small forms. We see the terrified faces. We see the tears. We see the small hands clinging in supplication to the mother; but we do not see those children that we are speaking about. We see in their places the little creatures whom we know and love."

To the very end, the undaunted defenders of Bud Dahu' chose honorable death over the cowardice of surrender and condemnation to servitude of their children—a trait that the Bangsa Sug of today has cherished and preserved for their land, nation and religion.

The initiative for setting up the marker came from Abolencia himself, who had been working closely with the civil authorities, and the memorial can perhaps be seen as a symbol of the changing role of the Philippine Army in the South. BARMM is still in a transitional phase, and it would be naive to assume that conditions in Jolo are stable, yet most of the locals with whom I talked seemed hopeful about the future. Just a few years ago it would indeed have been inconceivable for the Philippine Army to be engaged in a local historical commemoration in this manner.

Following the obligatory group photo in front of the marker, Abolencia had me plant a mahogany sapling inside the crater, replete with a small tag bearing my name. Afterward, we went to the spring, which still runs in a stream through the crater before plunging down the deep ravine that divides the east and south summit; drinking from the clear water as it emerged from the muddy ground somehow seemed like the obvious thing for me to do. The entire basin is now covered in jungle, with tall mangosteen trees and large groves of thick bamboo, and apart from a few footpaths it is all but impenetrable.

Eventually, we climbed back up onto the ridge and reached the camp, which is located at the approximate site of the original *cotta* at the top of the western trail. The soldiers would spend several weeks at a time on top of Bud Dajo, and although they slept in simple hammocks strung up between the trees and covered by tarpaulin, there were also small huts with working toilets, as well as a makeshift kitchen. In the center of the camp, at the highest point of the summit, a lookout with a bamboo railing and a pergola had been built, including a bamboo bench in the shape of a heart. In my mind I had often imagined what visiting Bud Dajo would be like. However, nothing could have prepared me for the surreal experience of sitting in a wicker chair with a hand-painted sign that said "21IB ♥ you" while listening to the standard fare of Filipino karaoke hits as the men of the forward position indulged in some light R & R. Utterly exhausted, I watched the sun set over Jolo as the clouds began rolling in like giant waves, soon drowning out the view in a thick wet mist. By nightfall, the summit was completely engulfed, and the sharp lights around the perimeter of the camp revealed only a sea of white.

A one-man pup tent had been set up for me, and someone's child had generously given up a couple of *Frozen-* and *Minions*-themed fleece blankets for my comfort. I nevertheless found it impossible to spend the night cooped up; I hadn't traveled this far only to see the inside of a tent, and it was hot and humid. Instead, I made a makeshift bed on a wooden bench right on the edge of the precipice and stretched out under my waterproof poncho. I did not sleep much that night, although it mattered little. At night, the sound of cicadas was less intense and provided an almost pleasant backdrop to the staccato rhythm of some exotic bird's song. A pale distant glow from the lights in Jolo was visible through the mist, and the trees swayed in a constant gentle breeze, shedding thick droplets from their leaves like the aftermath of a heavy shower. If the spirits of the dead were still haunting Bud Dajo, as Edmund had told me they did, they left me alone.

Next morning, the mist still clung to the summit, and it rained a little. I had previously been able to see clean across the crater, toward the tree line where Lawton's trench would have been, but now visibility was reduced to a few dozen feet. After a simple breakfast, consisting of rice and fried bananas, Abolencia and a small detachment prepared to take me to the east ridge. We set out along the ridge, moving in a clockwise direction, and I realized just how difficult the terrain was to navigate around the summit. The trail was covered in thick, slippery mud, and I constantly had to steady myself to avoid falling over the many roots that grew unobstructed across the path—at one point I grabbed a vine hanging from a tree only to find my entire palm covered in little cactus-like spikes. From time to time, we halted to communicate our progress to the different smaller positions that were scattered all around the slopes of Bud Dajo. Although there was no real sense of danger, as far as I was concerned, our movement was conducted with all the caution of a military operation. Eventually, we reached the east summit, at the top of Lawton's trail.

The soldiers were taking a break and had dropped their heavy backpacks and rifles on the ground. The mist was slowly dissipating, and the light morning rain had stopped. I walked a bit by myself along the narrow trail, trying to see if I could locate any of the original fortifications on the ridge, now overgrown and covered in thick foliage. In a small clearing, I noticed two small traditional Moro gravestones protruding from the soil—old and weathered, they were almost invisible among the fallen leaves. There were no traces of the trench, which had been covered up many years ago, along with its grim contents, but I realized I had found what I was looking for. Whoever erected these small markers knew the story.

As I stood at the exact spot where the photo was taken, at the summit of the eastern trail of Bud Dajo, I was reminded of the conclusion to the story told by Edmund's great-grandfather. After the Americans had seized the crest on the third day of the attack, almost all the Moros were dead:

According to people, a bright light descended on Bud Dajo—brighter than the sun. Seeing this light, the dying Moros began to rise. One young woman, who was badly wounded, said: "Oh, my longed-for. It was not our fate to be together on earth, but I shall wait for you in the afterlife." Dying, her lover answered: "I feel the same grief and if it was not our fate to be together on earth, I shall wait for you at the fallen tree that leads as a bridge to the afterlife." After this promise had been made between the lovers, they finally expired. Had they been sticks, the number of Americans and Moros who were killed were enough to make a broom. That is the story of the fight at Bud Dajo between the Moros and the Americans.[7]

Yet there was more to this tragic tale. In May 1906 the Manila-based correspondent Alfred E. Wood wrote an article about the assault on Bud Dajo for the *St. Louis Post-Dispatch*, which was based mainly on information provided by Hamilton Wright. This was in fact the only account to mention Aeronaut Gibbs, and it would appear that Wright was present when Gibbs first came upon the scene at the trench that overflowed with "heaps of dead":

One woman, whose side had been torn open by a shell splinter, asked Aeronaut Gibbs to bring her baby, which lay dead a short distance away, killed by the same explosion. He laid it on her lap, and went down the hill and brought her some clean water. She then asked him if he would drag her husband over to her, so that they could be sure of going to heaven together. He did so, and she seemed pleased, but she would not have her wound dressed. If that was done and she lived, she would not die fighting the infidel and would go to a different heaven from her husband and her baby.[8]

It is impossible not to connect this account to the photograph that Gibbs subsequently took—centered as it was on the woman with her dead child in her lap. Yet somehow this eyewitness account by an American writer present at the massacre also corresponds to the local oral history that still

circulates among the Moros in Jolo today. This rare convergence of the colonial text and local voices ultimately hints at a different vantage point from
which to view the photograph of the trench at Bud Dajo. The words dissolve
the camera's frozen gaze and allow us to imagine the woman released from
the photograph's frame, even in death.

Notes

Prologue: A Negative Made on the Spot

1. Du Bois to Storey, October 21, 1907, in Herbert Aptheker (ed.), *The Correspondence of W. E. B. Du Bois* (Amherst: Massachusetts University Press, 1973), 1:136.

2. The pamphlet was Moorfield Storey, *The Philippine Policy of Secretary Taft* (Boston: Anti-Imperialist League, 1904).

3. "A Brave Feat of Arms," folder: Printed matter, 1906, box 7, Moorfield Storey Papers, LOC.

4. "Brave Feat of Arms."

5. "Brave Feat of Arms." See also Roosevelt to Wood, March 10, 1906, folder 2, box 3, Leonard Wood Papers, LOC.

6. Kristin L. Hoganson, *Fighting for American Manhood: How Gender Politics Provoked the Spanish-American and Philippine-American Wars* (New Haven, CT: Yale University Press, 2000); Karen Wonders, "Hunting Narratives of the Age of Empire: A Gender Reading of Their Iconography," *Environment and History* 11, no. 3 (2005): 269–291.

7. See Jorge Lewinski, *The Camera at War: A History of War Photography from 1848 to the Present Day* (London: W. H. Allen, 1978).

8. See Karl Jacoby, "Of Memory and Massacre: A Soldier's Firsthand Account of the 'Affair on Wounded Knee,'" *Princeton University Library Chronicle* 64, no. 2 (2003): 333–362; and Jeffrey Ostler, *The Plains Sioux and US Colonialism from Lewis and Clark to Wounded Knee* (Cambridge: Cambridge University Press, 2004). The classic account is, of course, Dee Brown, *Bury My Heart at Wounded Knee: An Indian History of the American West* (New York: Holt, Rinehart & Winston, 1970).

9. Christina Klein, "'Everything of Interest in the Late Pine Ridge War Are Held by Us for Sale': Popular Culture and Wounded Knee," *Western Historical Quarterly* 25, no. 1 (Spring 1994): 45–68; Richard E. Jensen, R. Eli Paul, and John E. Carter, *Eyewitness at Wounded Knee* (Lincoln: University of Nebraska Press, 2011).

10. Frederic Remington, "The Opening of the Fight at Wounded Knee," *Harper's Weekly*, January 24, 1891.

11. See also Ned Blackhawk, *Violence over the Land: Indians and Empires in the Early American West* (Cambridge, MA: Harvard University Press, 2008).

12. For an introduction to the subject, see Christopher Capozzola, *Visualizing Cultures: Photography & Power in the Colonial Philippines* (Massachusetts Institute of Technology,

2017). See also Benito M. Vergara Jr., *Displaying Filipinos: Photography and Colonialism in Early 20th Century Philippines* (Quezon City: University of the Philippines Press, 1995); and David Brody, *Visualizing American Empire: Orientalism and Imperialism in the Philippines* (Chicago: University of Chicago Press, 2010).

13. Daniel Foliard, *The Violence of Colonial Photography* (Manchester: Manchester University Press, 2022). See also Teju Cole, "When the Camera Was a Weapon of Imperialism (And When It Still Is)," *New York Times Magazine*, February 6, 2019, www.nytimes.com/2019/02/06/magazine/when-the-camera-was-a-weapon-of-imperialism-and-when-it-still-is.html.

14. Vicente L. Rafael, *White Love and Other Events in Filipino History* (Durham, NC: Duke University Press, 2000).

15. See James Allen, Hilton Als, John Lewis, and Leon F. Litwack, *Without Sanctuary: Lynching Photography in America* (Santa Fe: Twin Palms, 2000); and Amy Louise Wood, *Lynching and Spectacle: Witnessing Racial Violence in America, 1890–1940* (Chapel Hill: University of North Carolina Press, 2009).

16. Shawn Michelle Smith, *Photography on the Color Line: W.E.B. Du Bois, Race, and Visual Culture* (Durham, NC: Duke University Press, 2004).

17. Du Bois to Storey, October 21, 1907, 1:136.

18. Anti-Imperialist League to Du Bois, October 25, 1907, W.E.B. Du Bois Papers (MS 312), Special Collections and University Archives, University of Massachusetts Amherst Libraries.

19. Anti-Imperialist League to Du Bois, October 25, 1907.

20. Christina L. Twomey, "Framing Atrocity: Photography and Humanitarianism," in *Humanitarian Photography: A History*, ed. Heide Fehrenbach and Davide Rodogno (Cambridge: Cambridge University Press, 2015), 47–63.

21. John Peffer, "Snap of the Whip/Crossroads of Shame: Flogging, Photography, and the Representation of Atrocity in the Congo Reform Campaign," *Visual Anthropology Review* 24, no. 1 (Spring 2008): 55–77.

22. Mark Twain, *King Leopold's Soliloquy: A Defense of His Congo Rule* (Boston: P. R. Warren, 1905), 68.

23. "Recalls Mount Dajo Massacre—Pictures of Filipino Dead Sent to Congressmen," *Baltimore Sun*, January 17, 1907.

Acknowledgments

1. Donald J. Trump speech on February 19, 2016, at the North Charleston Convention Center, https://youtu.be/ZBVKO5_em6U.

2. See, for instance, "Donald Trump Cites Dubious Legend About Gen. Pershing, Pig's Blood and Muslims," *Politifact*, February 23, 2016, www.politifact.com/factchecks/2016/feb/23/donald-trump/donald-trump-cites-dubious-legend-about-gen-pershi; "The Real Story Behind Donald Trump's Pig's Blood Slander," *Time*, February 24, 2016; and "Trump Said to Study General Pershing: Here's What the President Got Wrong," *Washington Post*, August 18, 2017. For a more informed intervention, see Paul A. Kramer, "An Enemy You Can Depend On: Trump, Pershing's Bullets, and the Folklore of the War on Terror," *Asia-Pacific Journal* 15, no. 4 (2017): 3–9.

3. "Director's Statement," *Apocalypse Now Redux* (DVD), Francis Ford Coppola (dir.), American Zoetrope (1979, 2001).

Introduction: "Slaughter" Is a Good Word

1. Mark Twain, *Mark Twain's Autobiography, with an Introduction by Albert Bigelow Paine* (New York: Harper & Brothers, 1924), 2:188–189.

2. See Jim Zwick, ed., *Mark Twain's Weapons of Satire: Anti-Imperialist Writings on the Philippine-American War* (Syracuse, NY: Syracuse University Press, 1992).

3. See, for instance, A. G. Hopkins, *American Empire: A Global History* (Princeton, NJ: Princeton University Press, 2018).

4. Amy Kaplan and Donald E. Pease, eds., *Cultures of United States Imperialism* (Durham, NC: Duke University Press, 1993); Paul A. Kramer, *The Blood of Government: Race, Empire, the United States, and the Philippines* (Chapel Hill: University of North Carolina Press, 2006).

5. *Congressional Record—Senate*, January 9, 1900, 704.

6. "Mark Twain Home, an Anti-Imperialist," *New York Herald*, October 16, 1900.

7. "Mark Twain Home."

8. Mark Twain, "To the Person Sitting in Darkness," *North American Review* 172 (February 1901): 176. See also Richard E. Welch Jr., "American Atrocities in the Philippines: The Indictment and the Response," *Pacific Historical Review* 43, no. 2 (1974): 233–253; and Christopher J. Einolf, *America in the Philippines, 1899–1902: The First Torture Scandal* (New York: Palgrave Macmillan, 2014).

9. Michael C. Hawkins, *Making Moros: Imperial Historicism and American Military Rule in the Philippines' Muslim South* (DeKalb: Northern Illinois University Press, 2013).

10. Oli Charbonneau, *Civilizational Imperatives: Americans, Moros, and the Colonial World* (Ithaca, NY: Cornell University Press, 2020), 159–161; Karine V. Walther, *Sacred Interests: The United States and the Islamic World, 1821–1921* (Chapel Hill: University of North Carolina Press, 2015), 193–198.

11. See Oli Charbonneau, "Visiting the Metropole: Muslim Colonial Subjects in the United States, 1904–1927," *Diplomatic History* 42, no. 2 (2018): 204–227; and Michael C. Hawkins, *Semi-civilized: The Moro Village at the Louisiana Purchase Exposition* (Ithaca, NY: Cornell University Press, 2020).

12. "The Iron Hand in the Philippines," *Lancaster (PA) Daily Intelligencer*, March 10, 1906.

13. Twain, *Mark Twain's Autobiography*, 192.

14. "Killing Women and Children in Jolo," *Literary Digest*, March 24, 1906, 433. See also Richard E. Welch Jr., "'The Philippine Insurrection' and the American Press," *Historian* 36, no. 1 (November 1973): 34–51.

15. See, for instance, "Our Exploit in the Philippines," *Washington Post*, March 13, 1906.

16. Twain, *Mark Twain's Autobiography*, 192–194. The headlines are from *New York Herald*, March 11, 1906.

17. The article was later published as a pamphlet: Moorfield Storey, *The Moro Massacre* (Boston: Anti-Imperialist League, 1906).

18. Storey, *The Moro Massacre*.

19. Twain, *Mark Twain's Autobiography*, 199. A "battue" is a shooting party in which the game is driven by beaters toward the hunters, and Twain is here using it in a manner similar to "turkey shoot" or "shooting fish in a barrel."

20. *Congressional Record—House*, March 15, 1906, 3895.

21. The literature on My Lai is extensive, but see Michael Bilton and Kevin Sim, *Four Hours in My Lai* (New York: Penguin, 1992); and Kendrick Oliver, *The My Lai Massacre in American History and Memory* (Manchester: Manchester University Press, 2006).

22. "Cameraman Saw GIs Slay 100 Villagers," *Plain Dealer* (Cleveland), November 20, 1969.

23. "The Massacre at My Lai," *Life*, December 5, 1969.

24. Oliver, *My Lai Massacre*, 134.

25. Patrick Hagopan, "Vietnam War Photography as a Locus of Memory," in *Locating Memory: Photographic Acts*, ed. Annette Kuhn and Kirsten McAllister (New York: Berghahn, 2006), 201–222.

26. The only time that Bud Dajo was brought up in the context of the My Lai Massacre was a brief reference in an article by Douglas Robinson of the *New York Times*; see "My Lai Slayings Recall Army Massacre of Sioux, Filipinos," *Morning Call* (Allentown, PA), November 28, 1969.

27. *Apocalypse Now* (film), Francis Ford Coppola (dir.), American Zoetrope (1979). The movie was filmed in the Philippines, and the helicopters used in the famous scene featuring Wagner's *Ride of the Valkyries* were deployed to fight the Moro National Liberation Front (MNLF) in the South during the middle of the production. See Eleanor Coppola, *Notes: On the Making of Apocalypse Now* (London: Faber and Faber, 1995), 26.

28. *The US Army/Marine Corps Counterinsurgency Field Manual* (Chicago: University of Chicago Press, 2007), 392; Brian McAllister Linn, *The Philippine War, 1898–1902* (Lawrence: University Press of Kansas, 2000).

29. Joshua Gedacht, "'Mohammedan Religion Made It Necessary to Fire': Massacres on the American Imperial Frontier from South Dakota to the Southern Philippines," in *Colonial Crucible: Empire in the Making of the Modern American State*, ed. A. W. McCoy and F. A. Scarano (Madison: University of Wisconsin Press, 2009), 397–409; Michael C. Hawkins, "Managing a Massacre: Savagery, Civility, and Gender in Moro Province in the Wake of Bud Dajo," *Philippine Studies* 59, no. 1 (2011): 83–105; Walther, *Sacred Interests*, 211–220; Charbonneau, *Civilizational Imperatives*, 105–109.

30. The photo from Bud Dajo is also discussed in Nerissa Balce, *Body Parts of Empire: Visual Abjection, Filipino Images, and the American Archive* (Ann Arbor: University of Michigan Press, 2016), 71–73; Silvan Niedermeier, "Intimacy and Annihilation: Approaching the Enforcement of US Colonial Rule in the Southern Philippines Through a Private Photograph Collection," *InVisible Culture: An Electronic Journal for Visual Culture* 25, "Security and Visibility" (2017), http://ivc.lib.rochester.edu/intimacy-and-annihilation-approaching-the-enforcement-of-u-s-colonial-rule-in-the-southern-philippines-through-a-private-photograph-collection; and Jeremy Adelman, "Don't Look Away: Photography and Humanitarianism," *Aeon*, September 12, 2017, https://aeon.co/essays/does-photography-make-us-act-or-inure-us-to-despair.

31. Anyone studying Bud Dajo, it should be acknowledged, is indebted to Fulton's pioneering work; see *Honor for the Flag: The Battle for Bud Dajo—1906 and the Moro Massacre* (Bend, OR: Tumalo Creek, 2011).

32. Kramer, *Blood of Government*, 218–220.

33. See also William Stout, "The Filipino Massacre," *Dark Horse Presents #23* (Dark Horse Comics, 1988), 1–5.

34. Daniel Immerwahr, *How to Hide an Empire: A History of the Greater United States* (New York: Farrar, Straus and Giroux, 2019), 105–106. See also Immerwahr's hagiographic essay on

Pershing: "One Record of General Pershing's Quite Cordial Relationship with Filipino Muslims," *Slate*, August 18, 2017.

35. Ronald K. Edgerton, *American Datu: John J. Pershing and Counterinsurgency Warfare in the Muslim Philippines, 1899–1913* (Lexington: University Press of Kentucky, 2020).

36. Andrew J. Bacevich, "What Happened at Bud Dajo: A Forgotten Massacre—and Its Lessons," *Boston Globe*, March 12, 2006. See also Danny Sjursen, "A Picture (of a War Crime) Is Worth a Thousand Words," AntiWar.com, October 1, 2019, https://original.antiwar.com /Danny_Sjursen/2019/09/30/a-picture-of-a-war-crime-is-worth-a-thousand-words.

37. See also the Epilogue.

38. *Journal of Perpetrator Research*, https://jpr.winchesteruniversitypress.org.

39. See Robert Harriman and John L. Lucaites, *No Caption Needed: Iconic Photographs, Public Culture and Liberal Democracy* (Chicago: University of Chicago Press, 2011).

40. Karl Jacoby, "'The Bloody Ground': Nineteenth-Century Frontier Genocides in the United States," in *The Cambridge World History of Genocide*, ed. Ned Blackhawk, Ben Kiernan, Benjamin Madley, and Rebe Taylor (Cambridge: Cambridge University Press, 2023), 3:410.

41. See also Michel-Rolph Trouillot, *Silencing the Past: Power and the Production of History* (Boston: Beacon, 1995).

42. *Congressional Record—House*, March 15, 1906, 3895. See David W. Grua, *Surviving Wounded Knee: The Lakotas and the Politics of Memory* (Oxford: Oxford University Press, 2016); and Bilton and Sim, *Four Hours in My Lai*. Of course, Bud Dajo is not the only "forgotten" atrocity; see, for instance, Suhi Choi, "Silencing Survivors' Narratives: Why Are We Again Forgetting the No Gun Ri Story?," *Rhetoric & Public Affairs* 11, no. 3 (2008): 367–388.

43. Ricardo Roque and Kim A. Wagner, eds., *Engaging Colonial Knowledge: Reading European Archives in World History* (Basingstoke: Palgrave Macmillan, 2012).

44. See also Saidiya Hartman, "Venus in Two Acts," *Small Axe* 12, no. 2 (2008): 1–14; and Katherine McKittrick, "Mathematics Black Life," *Black Scholar* 44, no. 2 (2014): 16–28.

45. I have to acknowledge a debt to the remarkable work of Joshua Oppenheimer, who in the context of the Indonesian genocide of 1965–1966 has shown with great poignancy how the perpetrator's own words can be used to destabilize and ultimately unravel their narratives. See *The Act of Killing* (documentary), Joshua Oppenheimer (dir.), Final Cut for Real, DK Film, 2012; and *The Look of Silence* (documentary), Joshua Oppenheimer (dir.), Final Cut for Real, Making Movies Oy, Piraya Film A/S, Spring Films, 2014. See also James Dawes, *Evil Men* (Cambridge, MA: Harvard University Press, 2013).

46. On the ethics of studying and reproducing images of atrocity and suffering, see Dora Apel, "On Looking: Lynching Photographs and Legacies of Lynching After 9/11," *American Quarterly* 55, no. 3 (September 2003): 457–478; Susan A. Crane, "Choosing Not to Look: Representation, Repatriation, and Holocaust Atrocity Photography," *History and Theory* 47, no. 3 (2008): 309–330; Christina Sharpe, *In the Wake: On Blackness and Being* (Durham, NC: Duke University Press, 2016); and Temi Odumosu, "The Crying Child: On Colonial Archives, Digitization, and Ethics of Care in the Cultural Commons," *Current Anthropology* 61, no. 22 (2020): 289–302.

47. See John Berger, "Photographs of Agony," in *About Looking* (New York: Pantheon, 1980), 3–40; Susan Sontag, *Regarding the Pain of Others* (New York: Farrar, Straus and Giroux, 2003); K. Hannah Holtschneider, "Victims, Perpetrators, Bystanders? Witnessing, Remembering and the Ethics of Representation in Museums of the

Holocaust," *Holocaust Studies* 13, no. 1 (2007): 82–102; Jane Lydon, "'Behold the Tears': Photography as Colonial Witness," *History of Photography* 34, no. 3 (2010): 234–250; and Carolyn J. Dean, "Atrocity Photographs, Dignity, and Human Vulnerability," *Humanity: An International Journal of Human Rights, Humanitarianism, and Development* 6, no. 2 (2015): 239–264.

48. *Congressional Record—House*, March 19, 1906, 3986.

Chapter 1: In the Path of God

1. Theodore Roosevelt, *The Winning of the West* (New York: G. P. Putnam's Sons, 1889–1896), 3:45–46.

2. Roosevelt, *Winning of the West*, 3:45–46.

3. Roosevelt, 3:45.

4. See Richard Slotkin, *Regeneration Through Violence: The Mythology of the American Frontier, 1600–1860* (Middletown, CT: Wesleyan University Press, 1973); and Gail Bederman, *Manliness & Civilization: A Cultural History of Gender and Race in the United States, 1880–1917* (Chicago: University of Chicago Press, 1995).

5. See Patrick Brantlinger, "Kipling's 'The White Man's Burden' and Its Afterlives," *English Literature in Transition, 1880–1920* 50, no. 2 (2007): 172–191.

6. Brantlinger, "Kipling's 'The White Man's Burden,'" 172.

7. Rudyard Kipling, "The White Man's Burden," *McClure's* 12, no. 4 (February 1899): 290–291.

8. Stuart Creighton Miller, *"Benevolent Assimilation": The American Conquest of the Philippines, 1899–1903* (New Haven, CT: Yale University Press, 1982).

9. Paul A. Kramer, "Empires, Exceptions, and Anglo-Saxons: Race and Rule Between the British and United States Empires, 1880–1910," *Journal of American History* 88, no. 4 (2002): 1315–1353.

10. David J. Silbey, *A War of Frontier and Empire: The Philippine-American War, 1899–1902* (New York: Hill & Wang, 2008).

11. The classic account is Peter G. Gowing, *Mandate in Moroland: The American Government of Muslim Filipinos, 1899–1920* (Quezon City, Philippines: New Day, 1983), but for a more updated history, see Charbonneau, *Civilizational Imperatives*. For a broad narrative overview, see Robert A. Fulton, *Moroland: The History of Uncle Sam and the Moros, 1899–1920* (Bend, OR: Tumalo Creek, 2007).

12. Walther, *Sacred Interests*, 174–178.

13. Michael Salman, *The Embarrassment of Slavery: Controversies over Bondage and Nationalism in the American Colonial Philippines* (Berkeley: University of California Press, 2001).

14. Roosevelt to Chaffee, May 5, 1902, quoted in Edgerton, *American Datu*, 6.

15. See Samuel K. Tan, *Sulu Under American Military Rule, 1899–1913* (Quezon City, Philippines: University of the Philippines, 1968); and Arnold Henry Savage Landor, *The Gems of the East: Sixteen Thousand Miles of Research Travel Among Wild and Tame Tribes of Enchanting Islands* (New York: Harper & Brothers, 1904), 169.

16. Najeeb Saleeby, *The History of Sulu* (Manila: Bureau of Printing, 1908), 133.

17. Landor, *Gems of the East*, 169.

18. Cesar Andres-Miguel Suva, "In the Shadow of 1881: The Death of Sultan Jamalul Alam and Its Impact on Colonial Transition in Sulu, Philippines from 1881–1904," *TRaNS: Trans-Regional and -National Studies of Southeast Asia* 8, no. 2 (2020): 85–99.

19. For a comprehensive analysis, see Cesar Andres-Miguel Suva, "Nativizing the Imperial: The Local Order and Articulations of Colonial Rule in Sulu, Philippines 1881–1920" (PhD thesis, Australian National University, 2015).

20. Wallace to Sultan, January 19, 1903, in "Report of General Wood as to Abrogation Bates Treaty, December 16, 1903," Exhibit T in *Annual Reports of the War Department for the Fiscal Year Ended June 30, 1903*, vol. 5: *Report of the Philippine Commission* (Washington, DC: Government Printing Office, 1903), 513. See also Walker to Wallace, February 14, 1903, 536; and Dunn to Wallace, February 26, 1903, 536–538 (hereafter Report of General Wood, December 16, 1903).

21. Report of Massin, February 11, 1903, Report of General Wood, December 16, 1903, 539; "Moros of Jolo Aroused by Imprisonment of Leaders," *St. Louis Republic*, March 22, 1903.

22. Landor, *Gems of the East*, 169–170.

23. Barrows to Worcester, March 14, 1903, quoted in E. F. Ugarte, "'The Demoniacal Impulse': The Construction of Amok in the Philippines" (PhD thesis, University of Western Sydney Nepean, 1999), 127–128.

24. "Juramentados," Report of General Wood, December 16, 1903, 542.

25. "Why 'Juramentados' Were Buried with Hog," *Washington Times*, December 21, 1903.

26. There is an extensive literature on the subject of *juramentado*. See Thomas M. Kiefer, "Parrang Sabbil: Ritual Suicide Among the Tausug of Jolo," *Bijdragen tot de Taal-, Land- en Volkenkunde*, 1ste Afl (1973): 108–123; Eduardo Ugarte, "Muslims and Madness in the Southern Philippines," *Pilipinas* 19, nos. 1–2 (1992): 1–23; Isagani R. Medina, "A Historical Reconstruction of the Juramentado/Sabllallah Ritual," *Anuaryo/Annales: Journal of History* 11, no. 1 (1993): 19–39. The most comprehensive study is Ugarte, "Demoniacal Impulse.'"

27. Charbonneau, *Civilizational Imperatives*, 3.

28. "Moros Are Fatalists," *Hawaiian Star*, November 1903.

29. Report by Sumner, June 30, 1903, Appendix II in *Annual Report of Major General George W. Davis, United States Army, Commanding Division of the Philippines from October 1, 1902 to July 26, 1903* (Manila, P.I., 1903), 38–40; "From the Philippines," *Albuquerque Citizen*, May 26, 1903; "The Juramentado," *Pensacola (FL) News*, October 2, 1903.

30. See "With the Sulus," *Topeka (KS) State Journal*, August 4, 1899.

31. Medina, "Historical Reconstruction," 20–21, 34.

32. Jialin Christina Wu, "Disciplining Native Masculinities: Colonial Violence in Malaya, 'Land of the Pirate and the Amok,'" in *Violence, Colonialism, and Empire in the Modern World*, ed. Philip Dwyer and Amanda Nettelbeck (Basingstoke: Palgrave Macmillan, 2018), 175–195. See also "Fearful Tale of 'Amok' from the North of Borneo," *Manila Times*, March 26, 1905; and Hugh Lenox Scott, *Some Memories of a Soldier* (New York: Century, 1928), 315.

33. Quoted in Wu, "Disciplining Native Masculinities," 185.

34. Dean C. Worcester, "The Malay Pirates of the Philippines," *Century* 56, no. 5 (1898): 690–702. Scott, *Some Memories of a Soldier*, 312–320; John R. White, *Bullets and Bolos: Fifteen Years in the Philippine Islands* (New York: Century, 1928), 293–298. See also David Kloos, "A Crazy State: Violence, Psychiatry, and Colonialism in Aceh, Indonesia, ca. 1910–1942," *Bijdragen tot de Taal-, Land- en Volkenkunde/Journal of the Humanities and Social Sciences of Southeast Asia* 170, no. 1 (2014): 25–65; and Sloan Mahone, "The Psychology of Rebellion: Colonial Medical Responses to Dissent in British East Africa," *Journal of African History* 47, no. 2 (2006): 241–258.

35. Elizabeth Kolsky, "The Colonial Rule of Law and the Legal Regime of Exception: Frontier 'Fanaticism' and State Violence in British India," *American Historical Review* 120, no. 4

(October 2015): 1218–1246; Mark Condos, "Fanaticism and the Politics of Resistance Along the North-West Frontier of British India," *Comparative Studies in Society and History* 58, no. 3 (2016): 717–745.

36. Winston S. Churchill, *The Story of the Malakand Field Force: An Episode of Frontier War* (London: Longmans, Green, 1898), 40–41.

37. John Foreman, *The Philippine Islands* (London: S. Low, Marston, 1899), 158.

38. "Why 'Juramentados' Were Buried with Hog."

39. Landor, *Gems of the East*, 170–171.

40. Medina, "Historical Reconstruction," 23; Kiefer, "Parrang Sabbil," 113.

41. Barrows to Worcester, March 14, 1903, quoted in Ugarte, "'Demoniacal Impulse,'" 128.

42. "Why 'Juramentados' Were Buried with Hog."

43. "Why 'Juramentados' Were Buried with Hog."

44. "Why 'Juramentados' Were Buried with Hog."

45. "Amok," *Singapore Free Press and Mercantile Advertiser*, June 7, 1901.

46. "The Passing Throng," *New-York Daily Tribune*, June 30, 1903.

47. Kim A. Wagner, "Calculated to Strike Terror: The Amritsar Massacre and the Spectacle of Colonial Violence," *Past & Present* 233, no. 1 (2016): 185–225.

48. Kim A. Wagner, *The Skull of Alum Bheg: The Life and Death of a Rebel of 1857* (Oxford: Oxford University Press, 2018).

49. "Blowing from Guns at Peshawur," *Daily News* (NY), November 5, 1857.

50. William Howard Russell, *My Diary in India, in the Year 1858–9* (London: Routledge, Warne, and Routledge, 1860), 2:43.

51. Quoted in Kolsky, "Colonial Rule of Law," 1237.

52. Wagner, "Calculated to Strike Terror."

53. Wagner, "Calculated to Strike Terror." See also Wu, "Disciplining Native Masculinities," 178.

54. The best analysis of this kind of violence is to be found in the work of Lee-Ann Fujii: "The Puzzle of Extra-lethal Violence," *Perspectives on Politics* 11, no. 2 (2013): 410–426; and the posthumously published *Show Time: The Logic and Power of Violent Display*, ed. Martha Finnemore (Ithaca, NY: Cornell University Press, 2021).

55. Scott, *Some Memories of a Soldier*, 315.

56. Joshua Gedacht, "Holy War, Progress, and 'Modern Mohammedans' in Colonial Southeast Asia," *Muslim World* 105, no. 4 (2015): 446–471.

57. Asma Afsaruddin, *Striving in the Path of God: Jihād and Martyrdom in Islamic Thought* (New York: Oxford University Press, 2013).

58. See Stephen Frederic Dale, "Religious Suicide in Islamic Asia: Anticolonial Terrorism in India, Indonesia, and the Philippines," *Journal of Conflict Resolution* 32, no. 1 (1988): 37–59; James Siegel, "Victory Without Surrender: The Jihad in Aceh," *Archipel* 87, no. 1 (2014): 29–62; and Mark Condos, "Licence to Kill: The Murderous Outrages Act and the Rule of Law in Colonial India, 1867–1925," *Modern Asian Studies* 50, no. 2 (2016): 479–517.

59. "Parang Sabil Kan Abdulla Iban Putli' Isara" ("The Parang Sabil of Abdulla and his wife Putli' Isara"), 3.5, Philippine Epics and Ballads Archive, Rizal Library, Ateneo de Manila University, http://epics.ateneo.edu. See also Calbi A. Asain, "The Tausug Parang Sabil Kissa as Literary, Cultural, and Historical Materials," *Journal of History*, 52 no. 1 (2006): 245–281; and Gerard Rixhon, "Levels of Discourse in the Tausug Parang Sabil Epic," in *Old Ties and New Solidarities: Studies on Filipino Communities*, ed. Charles J-H. Macdonald and Guillermo Mangubat Pesigan (Quezon City: Ateneo de Manila University Press, 2000), 12–23. For

a broader introduction to *kissas*, see Gerard Rixhon, *Voices from Sulu: A Collection of Tausug Oral Traditions* (Quezon City: Ateneo de Manila University Press, 2010).

60. Thomas M. Kiefer, "Reciprocity and Revenge in the Philippines: Some Preliminary Remarks About the Tausug of Jolo," *Philippine Sociological Review* 16, nos. 3/4 (1968): 124–131; Kiefer, "Modes of Social Action in Armed Combat: Affect, Tradition and Reason in Tausug Private Warfare," *Man* 5, no. 4 (1970): 586–596.

61. "Parang Sabil Kan Abdulla Iban Putli' Isara," verses 71–73. The song has 180 verses, and this and the following quotations have been edited for clarity.

62. The *kris* and *barong* are traditional bladed weapons in Sulu, the former known for its flame-shaped blade, whereas the latter is more like a machete, with a leaf-shaped blade.

63. "Parang Sabil Kan Abdulla Iban Putli' Isara," verse 116.

64. Kiefer, "Parrang Sabbil," 119.

65. Kiefer, 116.

66. J. Montano, "Voyage aux Philippines," *Le Tour du Monde* 47 (1884): 130. The photograph is available online: https://gallica.bnf.fr/ark:/12148/btv1b53136580p?rk=858373;2.

67. Medina, "Historical Reconstruction," 33. See also Julia A. Clancy-Smith, *Rebel and Saint: Muslim Notables, Populist Protest, Colonial Encounters* (Berkeley: University of California Press, 1994); and Jonathan Krause, "Islam and Anti-colonial Rebellions in North and West Africa, 1914–1918," *Historical Journal* 64, no. 3 (2021): 674–695.

68. Saleeby to Barrows, April 1, 1903, quoted in Ugarte, "'Demoniacal Impulse,'" 155–156.

69. Quoted in Kiefer, "Parrang Sabbil," 112.

70. Report by Wallace, June 30, 1903, Appendix IV-B in *Annual Report of Major General George W. Davis*, 112.

71. Report by Wallace, June 30, 1903, 111–113.

72. Report by Wallace, June 30, 1903.

73. Barrows to Worcester, March 14, 1903, quoted in Ugarte, "'Demoniacal Impulse,'" 128.

74. Najeeb Saleeby, *The Moro Problem: An Academic Discussion of the History and Solution of the Problem of the Government of the Moros of the Philippine Islands* (Manila: E. C. McCullough, 1913), 24.

75. Report by Wallace, June 30, 1903, 101–102.

76. Landor, *Gems of the East*, 174–175.

Chapter 2: One Clean-Cut Lesson

1. Henry O. Dwight, "Our Mohammedan Wards," *Forum* 29 (March 1900): 27–28.

2. See Hermann Hagedorn, *Leonard Wood, a Biography* (New York: Harper & Brothers, 1931); and Jack C. Lane, *Armed Progressive: General Leonard Wood* (Lincoln: University of Nebraska Press, 2009).

3. Mark Twain Project, *Autobiography of Mark Twain*, 1:408–409, marktwainproject.org.

4. Quoted in Fulton, *Moroland*, 192.

5. Scott, *Some Memories of a Soldier*, 273.

6. See Donna J. Amoroso, "Inheriting the 'Moro Problem': Muslim Authority and Colonial Rule in British Malaya and the Philippines," in *The American Colonial State in the Philippines: Global Perspectives*, ed. Julian Go and Anne L. Foster (Durham, NC: Duke University Press, 2003), 118–147; and Oli Charbonneau, "The Permeable South: Imperial Interactivities in the Islamic Philippines, 1899–1930s," in *Crossing Empires: Taking US History into Transimperial Terrain*, ed. K. L. Hoganson and J. Sexton (Durham, NC: Duke University Press, 2020), 183–202. On the transimperial circulation of colonial military knowledge and expertise, see

also Volker Barth and Roland Cvetkovski, eds., *Imperial Cooperation and Transfer, 1870–1930: Empires and Encounters* (London: Bloomsbury, 2015); Christoph Kamissek and Jonas Kreienbaum, "An Imperial Cloud? Conceptualising Interimperial Connections and Transimperial Knowledge," *Journal of Modern European History* 14, no. 2 (2016): 164–182; and especially Tom Menger, "The Colonial Way of War: Extreme Violence in Knowledge and Practice of Colonial Warfare in the British, German and Dutch Colonial Empires, c. 1890–1914" (PhD thesis, University of Cologne, 2021).

7. Lord Roberts had won the Victoria Cross as a young man in India, during the 1857 uprising, and Kitchener had recently commanded the British forces in Soudan and during the war in South Africa.

8. McCoy to family, May 8, 1903, quoted in Andrew J. Bacevich, *Diplomat in Khaki: Major General Frank Ross McCoy and American Foreign Policy, 1898–1949* (Lawrence: University Press of Kansas, 1989), 26.

9. Hagedorn, *Leonard Wood*, 2:49.

10. McCoy to family, May 28, 1903, quoted in Bacevich, *Diplomat in Khaki*, 26.

11. McCoy to family, June 24, 1903, quoted in Bacevich, *Diplomat in Khaki*, 27.

12. Wood to Roosevelt, August 3, 1903, quoted in Hagedorn, *Leonard Wood*, 2:4–5.

13. See Isabel V. Hull, *Absolute Destruction: Military Culture and the Practices of War in Imperial Germany* (Ithaca, NY: Cornell University Press, 2006); and Menger, "Colonial Way of War."

14. C. E. Callwell, *Small Wars: Their Principles and Practice*, 3rd ed. (London: HMSO, 1906), 72. *Small Wars* was first published in 1896 and revised in 1899 and again in 1906.

15. Kim A. Wagner, "Savage Warfare: Violence and the Rule of Colonial Difference in Early British Counterinsurgency," *History Workshop Journal* 85 (Spring 2018): 217–237.

16. Callwell, *Small Wars*, 24.

17. Wood diary, August 24, 1903, quoted in Hagedorn, *Leonard Wood*, 2:8.

18. Wood diary, August 24, 1903, 2:8.

19. Wood diary, August 24, 1903, 2:9.

20. Letter from Wood to his wife, quoted in Hagedorn, *Leonard Wood*, 2:10. The performative demonstration of modern firearms was a common strategy and considered as an effective means to subduing recalcitrant "natives" throughout the European empires. See Chris Vaughan, "'Demonstrating the Machine Guns': Rebellion, Violence and State Formation in Early Colonial Darfur," *Journal of Imperial and Commonwealth History* 42, no. 2 (2014): 286–307; and Ryan Patterson, "'To Form a Correct Estimate of Their Nothingness When Compared with It': British Exhibitions of Military Technology in the Abyssinian and Ashanti Expeditions," *Journal of Imperial and Commonwealth History* 44, no. 4 (2016): 551–572.

21. Hagedorn, *Leonard Wood*, 2:12.

22. See Salman, *Embarrassment of Slavery*.

23. See Hagedorn, *Leonard Wood*, 2:16–17.

24. McCoy, quoted in Hagedorn, *Leonard Wood*, 2:16–17.

25. Scott, *Some Memories of a Soldier*, 316–317.

26. "Buried Moro with a Pig," *Sun* (NY), December 8, 1903.

27. "Buried Moro with a Pig."

28. Scott, *Some Memories of a Soldier*, 298.

29. Biroa was tried before a Moro court and fined 25 dollars for the murder, which he promptly paid; Scott, *Some Memories of a Soldier*, 306.

30. Scott to Davis, November 4, 1903, quoted in Fulton, *Moroland*, 191.

31. "Ballad written and sung by Jolo Moros," folder: Letters re. Philippines: January–December, 1907, box 57, Hugh Lenox Scott Papers, LOC, 1.

32. General Orders No. 1, November 11, 1903, folder: Letters re. Philippine Is. (Jolo), 1903 (3), box 55, Hugh Lenox Scott Papers, LOC.

33. See Helmut Walser Smith, "The Logic of Colonial Violence: Germany in Southwest Africa (1904–1907) and the United States in the Philippines (1899–1902)," in *German and American Nationalism: A Comparative Perspective*, ed. Hartmut Lehmann and Hermann Wellenreuther (New York: Berg, 1999), 205–231; and Benjamin Claude Brower, *A Desert Named Peace: The Violence of France's Empire in the Algerian Sahara, 1844–1902* (New York: Columbia University Press, 2009).

34. McCoy to Carpenter, December 2, 1903, quoted in Hagedorn, *Leonard Wood*, 2:21.

35. Bullard diary, quoted in Fulton, *Moroland*, 244.

36. Wood diary, November 25, 1903, quoted in Fulton, *Moroland*, 197.

37. Wood diary, 204.

38. Wood diary, 204.

39. Scott, *Some Memories of a Soldier*, 331.

40. Walther, *Sacred Interests*, 202–211. See also Fulton, *Moroland*, 182–184.

41. Wood to Taft, December 16, 1903, Report of General Wood, December 16, 1903, 490.

42. Wood to Taft, December 16, 1903, 489.

43. "Report for the past year [1903–4], June 30, 1904," folder: Official file: Philippines—July, 1904, box 55, Hugh Lenox Scott Papers, LOC.

44. Scott, *Some Memories of a Soldier*, 349.

45. Scott, 350.

46. Renato T. Oliveros, "Islam in the Moro-American War (1899–1913): Implications on Mindanao, the Philippines" (PhD thesis, Temple University, 2005), 262–270; Sajed S. Ingilan, "Tausug's Identity in Parang Sabil: A Critical Discourse Analysis," *CMU Journal of Science* 22, no. 1 (January–December 2018): 37–43.

47. Robert L. Bullard, "The Calibre of the Revolver," *Journal of the Military Service Institution for the United States* 36 (1905): 300–304.

48. Bullard, "Calibre of the Revolver," 302.

49. "Report for the Department of Mindanao, July 1, 1904," *Annual Reports of the War Department for the Fiscal Year Ended June 30, 1904*, vol. 3: *Report of the Philippine Commission* (Washington, DC: Government Printing Office, 1904), 271. See also "Shotguns to Fight Moros," *Scranton (PA) Republican*, December 22, 1904. This is the origin of the myth of the Colt .45 pistol, which, however, was developed only much later, in 1911.

50. "With Taft Party in the Philippines," *Courier* (Cedar Falls, IA), November 15, 1905. The evidence for the informal use of dum-dum bullets among the US military in the southern Philippines is extensive, and another account described how "all soldiers outside the lines are supposed to be armed with heavy revolvers or rifles, and many of these are supplied with dumdum and 'doctored' bullets, for the Moro will fight as long as he can stand and does not mind having a few holes in his body." "When a Sulu Runs Amok," *Atlanta Constitution*, February 25, 1906.

51. In 1902 there were accusations of the use of expanding bullets by American troops in the Philippines; see, for instance, "Use of 'Dum-Dums,'" *Baltimore Sun*, May 21, 1902.

52. "Statement on the General Question of the 'Stopping Power' of Modern Small-Bore Bullets, by Surgeon-Colonel Stevenson, M.D." (December 14, 1897), Departmental Committee on Small Arms report no. 17: Further Trial of Dum Dum Bullets and of Bullets to R.L.

Designs Nos 9063B and 9063B (London, 1898), M2685, 1898, Asian and African Studies
Reading Room, British Library.

53. Perry L. Miles, *Fallen Leaves: Memories of an Old Soldier* (Berkeley, CA: Wuerth,
1961), 113.

54. See Maartje Abbenhuis, Branka Bogdan, and Emma Wordsworth, "Humanitarian Bullets and Man-Killers: Revisiting the History of Arms Regulation in the Late Nineteenth Century," *International Review of the Red Cross* 920–921 (November 2022): 1689.

55. Quoted in Hagedorn, *Leonard Wood*, 2:43.

56. See Oli Charbonneau, "'A New West in Mindanao': Settler Fantasies on the US Imperial Fringe," *Journal of the Gilded Age and Progressive Era* 18, no. 3 (2019): 304–323.

57. Quoted in "Editorial Comment," *Mindanao Herald*, November 2, 1907.

Chapter 3: A State of Unrest, 1904–1905

1. Charles to Slocum, January 21, 1905, folder: Letters re. Philippines: January–March,
1905, box 56, Hugh Lenox Scott Papers, LOC.

2. Butu to Scott, July 5, 1904, folder: Letters re. Philippines, July, 1904, box 55, Hugh Lenox
Scott Papers, LOC; "Report of Field Operations . . . from December 26th, 1904 to January
15th, 1905," folder: Letters re. Philippines: January–March, 1905, box 56, Hugh Lenox Scott
Papers, LOC.

3. Butu to Scott, July 5, 1904.

4. Report by Habib Mura, August 2, 1904, folder: Letters re. Philippines: August–December,
1904, box 56, Hugh Lenox Scott Papers, LOC; Scott conference with Moro chiefs, August
12, 1904, folder: Letters re. Philippines: August–December, 1904, box 56, Hugh Lenox Scott
Papers, LOC.

5. "Report of Field Operations . . . from December 26th, 1904 to January 15th, 1905."

6. Report by Salahuddin, August 2, 1904, folder: Letters re. Philippines: August–December,
1904, box 56, Hugh Lenox Scott Papers, LOC.

7. See Scott conference with Moro chiefs, August 12, 1904.

8. Scott conference with Moro chiefs, August 12, 1904.

9. Scott conference with Moro chiefs, August 12, 1904.

10. Meeting between Scott and Usap, August 17, 1904 (incomplete document), folder: Letters re. Philippines: August–December, 1904, box 56, Hugh Lenox Scott Papers, LOC.

11. Meeting between Scott and Usap, August 17, 1904.

12. Report by Salahuddin, August 2, 1904.

13. Report by Salahuddin, August 2, 1904.

14. Unga to Scott (via Schuck), August 4, 1904, folder: Letters re. Philippines: August–
December, 1904, box 56, Hugh Lenox Scott Papers, LOC.

15. See also Fulton, *Moroland*, 134; and "Scene of the Moro Massacre," *Army and Navy
Register*, April 14, 1906.

16. "Report of Field Operations . . . from December 26th, 1904 to January 15th, 1905."

17. "Report of Field Operations . . . from December 26th, 1904 to January 15th, 1905."

18. "Report of Field Operations . . . from December 26th, 1904 to January 15th, 1905."

19. "Report of Field Operations . . . from December 26th, 1904 to January 15th, 1905."

20. Report by Jaji, August 1, 1904, folder: Letters re. Philippines: August–December, 1904,
box 56, Hugh Lenox Scott Papers, LOC.

21. "Report of Field Operations . . . from December 26th, 1904 to January 15th, 1905."

22. Report by Mansang, August 1, 1904, folder: Letters re. Philippines: August–December, 1904, box 56, Hugh Lenox Scott Papers, LOC.

23. "Report of Field Operations . . . from December 26th, 1904 to January 15th, 1905."

24. Dorey to Langhorne, January 8, 1905, folder: Letters re. Philippines: January–March, 1905, box 56, Hugh Lenox Scott Papers, LOC.

25. Annual report, from September 2nd, 1904, ending June 30th, 1905, folder: Official file: Philippines—June–August, 1905, box 56, Hugh Lenox Scott Papers, LOC.

26. Thomsen to Hepler, January 17, 1905, folder 15, box 2, Robert Fulton Research Collection, Knight Library, University of Oregon.

27. Charles to Slocum, January 9, 1905, folder: Letters re. Philippines: January–March, 1905, box 56, Hugh Lenox Scott Papers, LOC.

28. "Report of Field Operations . . . from December 26th, 1904 to January 15th, 1905."

29. Scott, *Some Memories of a Soldier*, 389–390.

30. See Thomas M. Kiefer, *The Tausug, Violence and Law in a Philippine Moslem Society* (New York: Holt, Rinehart and Winston, 1972), 77–79; and Jeffrey Wheatley, "US Colonial Governance of Superstition and Fanaticism in the Philippines," *Method and Theory in the Study of Religion* 30 (2018): 21–36.

31. Belief in bullet magic was a recurring feature in a number of revivalist and anticolonial movements, including the Ghost Dance movement in the US, the so-called Boxer Rebellion in China, and later also in German East Africa during the Maji-Maji Rising. See Kim A. Wagner, "Rebellion, Resistance, and the Subaltern," in *The Oxford World History of Empire*, ed. Peter Fibiger Bang, Walter Scheidel, and C. A. Bayly (Oxford: Oxford University Press, 2020), 416–436. See also John S. Galbraith, "Appeals to the Supernatural: African and New Zealand Comparisons with the Ghost Dance," *Pacific Historical Review* 51, no. 2 (1982): 115–133; Dominic J. Capeci Jr. and Jack C. Knight, "Reactions to Colonialism: The North American Ghost Dance and East African Maji-Maji Rebellions," *Historian* 52, no. 4 (1990): 584–601; and Paul A. Cohen, *History in Three Keys: The Boxers as Event, Experience, and Myth* (New York: Columbia University Press, 1997).

32. "Report of Field Operations . . . from December 26th, 1904 to January 15th, 1905." For comparative African examples, see Arthur Abraham, "Bai Bureh, the British, and the Hut Tax War," *International Journal of African Historical Studies* 7, no. 1 (1974): 99–106; and Sean Redding, "A Blood-Stained Tax: Poll Tax and the Bambatha Rebellion in South Africa," *African Studies Review* 43, no. 2 (2000): 29–54.

33. "Report of Field Operations . . . from December 26th, 1904 to January 15th, 1905."

34. Wood endorsement of "Report of Field Operations," February 21, 1905, folder: Letters re. Philippines: January–March, 1905, box 56, Hugh Lenox Scott Papers, LOC.

35. Scott, *Some Memories of a Soldier*, 377.

36. Annual report, from September 2nd, 1904, ending June 30th, 1905.

37. Scott, *Some Memories of a Soldier*, 379.

38. Scott, "History of the Third Squadron 14th Cavalry from Its Organization (April 15th, 1901) to September 12th, 1905," folder: Official file: Philippines—1905, Sept., box 56, Hugh Lenox Scott Papers, LOC.

39. "They Made the Place a Shambles," *Victoria Daily Times*, February 1, 1905.

40. "They Made the Place a Shambles."

41. Wood to Scott, March 2, 1905, folder: Letters re. Philippines: January–March, 1905, box 56, Hugh Lenox Scott Papers, LOC.

42. Wood to Scott, March 2, 1905. The proposed strategy was very much part and parcel of the doctrine developed during campaigns against the Native Americans, in which predawn attacks on camps and villages were favored. See John Grenier, *The First Way of War: American War Making on the Frontier, 1607–1814* (Cambridge: Cambridge University Press, 2005); and Karl Jacoby, *Shadows at Dawn: An Apache Massacre and the Violence of History* (New York: Penguin, 2009).

43. Scott to Wood, March 9, 1905, folder: Letters re. Philippines: January–March, 1905, box 56, Hugh Lenox Scott Papers, LOC.

44. Scott to Wood, March 9, 1905. The change in currency was a reference of the shift from Spanish silver currency to American dollars. See Willem G. Wolters, "From Silver Currency to the Gold Standard in the Philippine Islands," *Philippine Studies* 51, no. 3 (2003): 375–404.

45. Scott to Wood, March 9, 1905.

46. Scott to McCoy, March 25, 1905, folder: Letters re. Philippines: January–March, 1905, box 56, Hugh Lenox Scott Papers, LOC.

47. Scott, "History of the Third Squadron."

48. Scott.

49. Scott to Langhorne, May 28, 1905, folder: Official file: Philippines—April–May, 1905, box 56, Hugh Lenox Scott Papers, LOC.

50. On the conditions prevailing in Jolo, see, for instance, Report by Habib Mura, August 2, 1904.

51. Scott to Wood, April 17, 1905, folder: Official file: Philippines—April–May, 1905, box 56, Hugh Lenox Scott Papers, LOC.

52. Scott to Wood, April 17, 1905.

53. Callwell, *Small Wars*, 228–229.

54. Scott to Wood, April 17, 1905.

55. Scott to Wood, April 19, 1905.

56. Scott, "History of the Third Squadron."

57. Report by Wood, May 22, 1905, folder: Official file: Philippines—April–May, 1905, box 56, Hugh Lenox Scott Papers, LOC.

58. Wood diary, May 1, 1905, folder 1, box 3, Leonard Wood Papers, LOC.

59. Horace P. Hobbs, *Kris and Krag: Adventures Among the Moros of the Southern Philippine Islands* (self-published 1962, revised as *Kris and Krag: The Moro Campaigns*, 1964, https://emu.usahec.org/alma/multimedia/245537/20182903MN000263.pdf), 138.

60. Scott, "History of the Third Squadron."

61. Scott.

62. Scott.

63. Wood diary, May 3, 1905, folder 1, box 3, Leonard Wood Papers, LOC.

64. Wood diary.

65. Scott, "History of the Third Squadron."

66. Hobbs, *Kris and Krag*, 139–141.

67. Hobbs, 142–143.

68. Hobbs, 145–151.

69. See, for instance, "General Chronology of 1905: May 13," *Anaconda (MT) Standard*, December 31, 1905.

70. "General Wood's Third Sulu Expedition," *Monticellonian* (Monticello, AR), November 23, 1905.

71. Report by Wood, May 22, 1905.

72. See Hagedorn, *Leonard Wood*, 2:60–61.

73. Wood diary, May 18–19, 1905, folder 1, box 3, Leonard Wood Papers, LOC.

74. Scott to Langhorne, May 28, 1905.

75. Scott to Langhorne, May 28, 1905.

Chapter 4: The People on the Hill, 1905

1. Annual report, from September 2nd, 1904, ending June 30th, 1905.

2. Indanan, conference on board *Sabah* at Jolo, April 13, 1906, folder 2, box 3, Leonard Wood Papers, LOC (hereafter "*Sabah* conference, April 13, 1906").

3. *Sabah* conference, April 13, 1906.

4. *Sabah* conference, April 13, 1906.

5. Sawajaan interview, June 12, 1905, Exhibit B in Reeves to Langhorne, March 31, 1906, folder 1, box 37, Leonard Wood Papers, LOC.

6. Sawajaan interview, June 12, 1905.

7. Sawajaan interview, June 12, 1905.

8. Sawajaan interview, June 12, 1905.

9. Scott, *Some Memories of a Soldier*, 379–380.

10. Michael Schuck Montemayor, *Captain Herman Leopold Schuck: The Saga of a German Sea Captain in 19th-Century Sulu-Sulawesi Seas* (Honolulu: University of Hawaii Press, 2006).

11. Schuck statement, March 29, 1906, Exhibit C in Reeves to Langhorne, March 31, 1906, folder 1, box 37, Leonard Wood Papers, LOC.

12. Schuck statement, March 29, 1906.

13. Schuck statement, March 29, 1906.

14. Annual report, from September 2nd, 1904, ending June 30th, 1905.

15. In August 1905, Secretary of War William Howard Taft visited Jolo as part of a diplomatic mission, accompanied by dozens of correspondents; see Fulton, *Honor for the Flag*, 85–87.

16. Scott, *Some Memories of a Soldier*, 376.

17. Annual report, from September 2nd, 1904, ending June 30th, 1905.

18. Howard to Scott, May 30, 1905, folder: Official file: Philippines—April–May, 1905, box 56, Hugh Lenox Scott Papers, LOC. See also Report by Habib Mura, August 2, 1904.

19. Scott to Wood, March 9, 1905.

20. "Dain ha Kastilaq pa biaqhaqun" ("From the Spanish Period to the Present"), 3.2, Philippine Epics and Ballads Archive, Rizal Library, Ateneo de Manila University, http://epics.ateneo.edu.

21. Charbonneau, *Civilizational Imperatives*, 74–77.

22. Astrid S. Tuminez, "This Land Is Our Land: Moro Ancestral Domain and Its Implications for Peace and Development in the Southern Philippines," *SAIS Review of International Affairs* 27, no. 2 (Summer–Fall 2007): 77–91.

23. Indanan, *Sabah* conference, April 13, 1906.

24. "Annual report for the District of Sulu, from July 1st, 1905, to June 30th, 1906," folder: Official file 1906, box 57, Hugh Lenox Scott Papers, LOC.

25. Indanan, *Sabah* conference, April 13, 1906.

26. Reeves to Scott, January 10, 1906, folder: Letters re. Philippines: January–March, 1905, box 56, Hugh Lenox Scott Papers, LOC. This letter is misdated but is clearly from 1906, not 1905.

27. Stefan Eklöf Amirell, "Pirates and Pearls: Jikiri and the Challenge to Maritime Security and American Sovereignty in the Sulu Archipelago, 1907–1909," *International Journal of Maritime History* 29, no. 1 (2017): 44–67.

28. See also Scott, *Some Memories of a Soldier*, 370.

29. Schuck statement, March 29, 1906.

30. Schuck statement, March 29, 1906.

31. Schuck statement, March 29, 1906.

32. Sawajaan interview, December 4, 1905, Exhibit A in Reeves to Langhorne, March 31, 1906, folder 1, box 37, Leonard Wood Papers, LOC.

33. Schuck statement, March 29, 1906.

34. Quoted in Suva, "Nativizing the Imperial," 121.

35. Quoted in Suva, "Nativizing the Imperial," 121.

36. Schuck statement, March 29, 1906.

37. Schuck statement, March 29, 1906.

38. Jokanain, *Sabah* conference, April 13, 1906.

39. Butu, *Sabah* conference, April 13, 1906.

40. Schuck statement, March 29, 1906.

41. Statement by Fim Janarin, attached to Sawajaan interview, December 4, 1905, Exhibit A in Reeves to Langhorne, March 31, 1906, folder 1, box 37, Leonard Wood Papers, LOC.

42. Sawajaan interview, December 4, 1905, Exhibit A in Reeves to Langhorne, March 31, 1906, folder 1, box 37, Leonard Wood Papers, LOC.

43. Schuck statement, March 29, 1906.

44. "Annual report for the District of Sulu, from July 1st, 1905, to June 30th, 1906."

45. Scott, *Some Memories of a Soldier*, 380.

46. Schuck statement, March 29, 1906.

47. Scott to Langhorne, December 5, 1905, folder 1, box 37, Leonard Wood Papers, LOC.

48. Scott memorandum, March 20, 1906, Senate Document Number 278, 59th Congress, 1st Session, 2–5.

49. Schuck statement, March 29, 1906.

50. Schuck statement, March 29, 1906.

51. Schuck statement, March 29, 1906.

52. Sawajaan interview, December 4, 1905.

53. McCoy letter to mother, March 10, 1906, folder: Family Correspondence 1906, box 4, Frank R. McCoy Papers, LOC.

54. Schuck statement, March 29, 1906.

55. Wood diary, December 31, 1905, folder 1, box 3, Leonard Wood Papers, LOC.

56. Reeves to Scott, January 17, 1906, folder: Letters re. Philippines: January–March, 1905, box 56, Hugh Lenox Scott Papers, LOC.

57. Hayudin, *Sabah* conference, April 13, 1906.

58. Hayudin, *Sabah* conference, April 13, 1906.

59. Jokanain, *Sabah* conference, April 13, 1906.

60. Reeves to Langhorne, March 1, 1906, folder 1, box 37, Leonard Wood Papers, LOC.

61. Wood, *Sabah* conference, April 13, 1906.

62. "Kissa Bunuq ha Bud Dahuq" ("The Story of the Battle of Bud Dajo"), 3.6, Philippine Epics and Ballads Archive, Rizal Library, Ateneo de Manila University: http://epics.ateneo .edu. The complete *kissa* contains 207 verses, and the ones reproduced here have been edited. Thanks to Calbi Asian for help with the translation. Although the song was not recorded until

late in the twentieth century, there is evidence to show that it was performed as early as 1909; see "Traditions, Customs and Commerce of the Sulu Moros," *Mindanao Herald*, February 3, 1909, 21–25. See also "Ballad written and sung by Jolo Moros," folder: Letters re. Philippines: January–December, 1907, box 57, Hugh Lenox Scott Papers, LOC.

Chapter 5: They Will Probably Have to Be Exterminated

1. Wood diary, September 26, 1905, folder 1, box 3, Leonard Wood Papers, LOC.

2. Wagner, "Savage Warfare."

3. G. W. Steevens, *With Kitchener to Khartoum* (Edinburgh: William Blackwood and Sons, 1898), 264.

4. Wood diary, September 29–30, 1905, folder 1, box 3, Leonard Wood Papers, LOC.

5. Wood diary, January 9, 1906, folder 1, box 3, Leonard Wood Papers, LOC.

6. Wood diary, January 9, 1906.

7. Wood diary, January 31, 1906, folder 1, box 3, Leonard Wood Papers, LOC.

8. Wood diary, January 31, 1906.

9. Wood to Roosevelt, May 14, 1906, folder 1, box 37, Leonard Wood Papers, LOC.

10. Wood to Corbin, February 12, 1906, folder 2, box 3, Leonard Wood Papers, LOC. See also John M. Thompson, *Great Power Rising: Theodore Roosevelt and the Politics of US Foreign Policy* (Oxford: Oxford University Press, 2019), 117–118.

11. "Troops Enroute to Philippines," *Arizona Sentinel* (Yuma), February 28, 1906. See also "Extra Troops for the Philippines," *Mindanao Herald*, January 20, 1906.

12. See "Confidential Memorandum for Heads of Departments prepared under the instructions of the Division Commander," February 21, 1906, folder 2, box 3, Leonard Wood Papers, LOC.

13. Wood to Roosevelt, February 21, 1906, quoted in Hagedorn, *Leonard Wood*, 2:74.

14. Roosevelt to Wood, April 2, 1906, Theodore Roosevelt Papers: Series 2: Letterpress Copybooks, 1897–1916, vol. 62, 1906, Mar. 12–Apr. 12, LOC.

15. Reeves to Scott, January 17, 1906. See also Roosevelt to Wood, January 17, 1906, Theodore Roosevelt Papers: Series 2: Letterpress Copybooks, 1897–1916, vol. 62, 1906, Mar. 12–Apr. 12, LOC.

16. Stedje to Reeves, February 1, 1906, Exhibit D in Reeves to Langhorne, March 31, 1906, folder 1, box 37, Leonard Wood Papers, LOC.

17. Stedje to Reeves, February 1, 1906.

18. "Annual report for the District of Sulu, from July 1st, 1905, to June 30th, 1906."

19. See *Sabah* conference, April 13, 1906.

20. "Annual report for the District of Sulu, from July 1st, 1905, to June 30th, 1906."

21. See Laura Ann Stoler, "In Cold Blood: Hierarchies of Credibility and the Politics of Colonial Narratives," *Representations* 37 (1992): 151–189; Mike G. Vann, "Fear and Loathing in French Hanoi: Colonial White Images and Imaginings of 'Native' Violence," in *The French Colonial Mind*, ed. M. Thomas (Lincoln: University of Nebraska Press, 2011), 2:52–76; and Kim A. Wagner, "'Treading Upon Fires': The 'Mutiny'-Motif and Colonial Anxieties in British India," *Past & Present* 218, no. 1 (2013): 159–197.

22. Langhorne to Wood, February 9, 1906, folder 1, box 37, Leonard Wood Papers, LOC. I have not been able to locate Reeves's original report to Langhorne.

23. Langhorne to Wood, February 9, 1906.

24. Langhorne to Wood, February 9, 1906.

25. Langhorne to Wood, February 9, 1906.

26. Wood to Langhorne, February 17, 1906, folder 1, box 37, Leonard Wood Papers, LOC.

27. Wood to Langhorne, February 17, 1906, quoted in Wayne Wray Thompson, "Governors of the Moro Province: Wood, Bliss, and Pershing in the Southern Philippines, 1930–1913" (PhD thesis, University of California, San Diego, 1975), 83. The original letter appears to be missing from the Wood Papers, LOC.

28. Benjamin Madley, *An American Genocide: The United States and the California Indian Catastrophe, 1846–1873* (New Haven, CT: Yale University Press, 2016); Jeffrey Ostler, *Surviving Genocide: Native Nations and the United States from the American Revolution to Bleeding Kansas* (New Haven, CT: Yale University Press, 2019).

29. Quoted in Russell F. Weigley, *The American Way of War: A History of United States Military Strategy and Policy* (Bloomington: Indiana University Press, 1977), 158.

30. Callwell, *Small Wars*, 159.

31. See also Sven Lindqvist, *Exterminate All the Brutes* (London: New Press, 1997).

32. Wood to Ide, February 25, 1906, folder 2, box 3, Leonard Wood Papers, LOC (hereafter "Wood diary"). See also Wood to Roosevelt, February 25, 1906, Wood diary.

33. Wood diary, February 25, 1906.

34. Scott M. Cutlip, *The Unseen Power: Public Relations. A History* (Hillsdale, NJ: Lawrence Erlbaum, 1994), 76.

35. Cutlip, *Unseen Power*, 76.

36. Cutlip, 77, 78. Cutlip incorrectly claims that Wright worked for Leonard Wood.

37. "Opportunities in the Orient," *Sacramento Sun*, January 25, 1906.

38. "Sultan of Sulu Explains Mystery of His Harem," *Evansville (IN) Press*, August 13, 1906.

39. Wood diary, February 28, 1906.

40. Wood diary, February 28, 1906.

41. Wood diary, March 1, 1906.

42. Reeves to Langhorne, March 1, 1906.

43. Reeves to Langhorne, March 31, 1906, folder 1, box 37, Leonard Wood Papers, LOC.

44. Reeves to Langhorne, March 31, 1906.

45. Reeves to Langhorne, March 1, 1906.

46. Wilcox to Langhorne, February 28, 1906, folder 5, box 38, Leonard Wood Papers, LOC.

47. "The Taking of Mount Dajo," *Stevens Point (WI) Journal*, May 14, 1906. The two sketches mentioned, drawn by First Lieutenant A. Poillon, 14th Cavalry, are in File 1108562, RG 94, entry 25, AGO Document File, 1890–1917, NARA.

48. Reeves to Langhorne, March 1, 1906.

49. Reeves to Langhorne, March 1, 1906.

50. Schuck statement, March 29, 1906.

51. Reeves to Langhorne, March 1, 1906.

52. Reeves to Langhorne, March 31, 1906.

53. Scott to Wood, March 9, 1905, folder: Letters re. Philippines: January–March, 1905, box 56, Hugh Lenox Scott Papers, LOC.

54. Wilcox to Langhorne, February 28, 1906.

55. See Wagner, "Calculated to Strike Terror."

56. Wilcox to Langhorne, February 28, 1906.

57. Wilcox to Langhorne, February 28, 1906.

58. See William Gallois, "Dahra and the History of Violence in Early Colonial Algeria," in *The French Colonial Mind*, ed. Martin Thomas (Lincoln: University of Nebraska Press, 2011), 2:3–25; and Tom Menger, "Concealing Colonial Comparability: British Exceptionalism, Imperial Violence, and the Dynamiting of Cave Refuges in Southern Africa, 1879–1897," *Journal of Imperial and Commonwealth History* 50, no. 5 (2022): 860–889.

59. See White, *Bullets and Bolos*, 190–191, 216, and 305; and Karl Jacoby, "'The Broad Platform of Extermination': Nature and Violence in the Nineteenth Century North American Borderlands," *Journal of Genocide Research* 10, no. 2 (2008): 255.

60. Wilcox to Langhorne, February 28, 1906.

61. Bliss to Wood, March 1, 1906, folder 5, box 38, Leonard Wood Papers, LOC.

62. Wood diary, March 2, 1906. In his diary, Wood misrepresented Reeves's message as "requesting assistance." See Wood diary, March 3, 1906.

63. See Wood's instructions of February 12 and 21, 1906, Wood diary.

Chapter 6: March 2–5, 1906

1. Colonel Joseph W. Duncan, *Report of Engagement with the Moro Enemy on Bud-Dajo, Island of Jolo, March 5th, 6th, 7th and 8th, 1906* (hereafter "Duncan Report"), 1. A copy of the report can be found in folder 6, box 217, Leonard Wood Papers, LOC. The complete report with maps is file 1108562, RG 94, entry 25, AGO Document File, 1890–1917, NARA (College Park, MD).

2. Joseph W. Duncan, "The Fight at Bud Dajo," in *Year Book: Eighth Annual Reunion Army of the Philippines* (Kansas City: Camp Louis A. Craig, August 1907), 59.

3. See also Ron Field and Richard Hook, *Spanish-American War 1898* (London: Brassey's, 1998); and Alejandro de Quesada and Stephen Walsh, *The Spanish-American War and Philippine Insurrection 1898–1902* (London: Osprey, 2012).

4. See Vic Hurley, *Jungle Patrol: The Story of the Philippine Constabulary* (New York: E. P. Dutton, 1938).

5. White, *Bullets and Bolos*, 300.

6. "Report on Bud Dajo, March 6–7–8, 1906 by Captain John R. White," folder 2, box 19, John R. White Papers, Special Collections and University Archives, Knight Library, University of Oregon (hereafter "White Report"), 1.

7. Appendix N, *List of Appendices Accompanying Colonel Duncan's Report of Engagement with the Moro Enemy*. See also Wood diary, March 3, 1906.

8. Duncan Report, 3. Wigwag flags functioned similarly to Morse code, and words were spelled by waving two flags in different patterns, one in each hand.

9. Duncan Report, 2.

10. Duncan, "Fight at Bud Dajo," 59.

11. Wood diary, March 3, 1906.

12. Réginald Kann, "Voyages et Combat dans le Sud des Philippines," *Le Tour Du Monde* 13, n.s. no. 12 (March 23, 1907): 137. All translations are by the author (with help from Mark Condos).

13. Joseph J. Matthews, *Reporting the Wars* (Minneapolis: University of Minnesota Press, 1957), 131.

14. See Wood diary, February 5, 1906.

15. Kann, "Voyages et Combat," 133.

16. Kann, 137.

17. Duncan Report, 5–6.

18. Kann, "Voyages et Combat," 137.

19. Wood diary, March 2, 1906. See also previous day's entry.

20. Wood to Bliss, March 2, 1906, folder 4, box 38, Leonard Wood Papers, LOC.

21. Wood to Bliss, March 2, 1906.

22. Duncan Report, 4. See also "Arkansan Tells of Battle at Jolo," *Daily Arkansas Gazette* (Little Rock), May 12, 1906.

23. Duncan subsequently met with Wilcox, who at this point was completely excluded from any decision making. See Duncan Report, 4–5; and Duncan, "The Fight at Bud Dajo," 61.

24. Duncan, "Fight at Bud Dajo," 60.

25. File 1108562, RG 94, entry 25, AGO Document File, 1890–1917, NARA.

26. Duncan Report, 4.

27. Duncan, "Fight at Bud Dajo," 60.

28. Kann, "Voyages et Combat," 137.

29. White, *Bullets and Bolos*, 301.

30. Duncan Report, 5.

31. Duncan Report, 4–5.

32. Duncan Report, 5.

33. Duncan, "Fight at Bud Dajo," 61.

34. "Kissa Bunuq ha Bud Dahuq," verses 146–147 and 151.

35. Butu, *Sabah* conference, April 13, 1906.

36. Indanan, *Sabah* conference, April 13, 1906.

37. Duncan Report, 6–7.

38. "Report of Captain C. C. Farmer," Appendix G, *List of Appendices Accompanying Colonel Duncan's Report of Engagement with the Moro Enemy*, 51. An American trooper was shot and killed on this trail on March 7, but it was nevertheless left out of Duncan's plan of operations.

39. Duncan Report, 7.

40. Duncan Report, 9; "Report of Captain Edward P. Lawton," Appendix D, *List of Appendices Accompanying Colonel Duncan's Report of Engagement with the Moro Enemy* (hereafter "Lawton Report"), 26. Like Duncan's report, the appendices can be found in folder 6, box 217, Leonard Wood Papers, LOC; or file 1108562; RG 94, entry 25, AGO Document File, 1890–1917, NARA.

41. Kann describes his Kodak camera in *Journal d'un Correspondant de Guerre en Extrême-Orient: Japon, Mandchourie, Corée* (Paris: Calmann-Lévy, 1905), 139.

42. Duncan Report, 7–8. According to local tradition, the defenders at Bud Dajo also included Hadji Apas, Jalali, Sali, and Abtuq, in addition to the historical figures of Sahiron, Adam, Agil, and Imam Harip; see "Kissa Bunuq ha Bud Dahuq."

43. Duncan Report, 8–9.

44. Duncan Report, 8–9.

45. "In Hotel Corridors," *Salt Lake Tribune*, June 26, 1907.

46. See also Michael Taussig, "Culture of Terror—Space of Death: Roger Casement's Putumayo Report and the Explanation of Torture," *Comparative Studies in Society and History* 26, no. 3 (July 1984): 467–497.

47. "Voice of the People," *Eau Claire (WI) Leader*, May 3, 1906; White Report, 1.

48. Miller, *"Benevolent Assimilation,"* 220.

49. Quoted in Brown, *Bury My Heart*, 86–87.

50. See Katharine Bjork, *Prairie Imperialists: The Indian Country Origins of American Empire* (Philadelphia: University of Pennsylvania Press, 2018); and Stefan Aune, *Indian Wars Everywhere: Colonial Violence and the Shadow Doctrines of Empire* (Berkeley: University of California Press, 2023).

51. "Col. Duncan Quits Helena," *Helena (MT) Independent,* July 30, 1907.

52. Langhorne to Wood, August 23, 1905, quoted in Fulton, *Moroland,* 292.

53. White, *Bullets and Bolos,* 304–305.

54. White, 304.

55. White, 304.

56. White, 305.

57. "Report of Captain L. M. Koehler," Appendix C, *List of Appendices Accompanying Colonel Duncan's Report of Engagement with the Moro Enemy* (hereafter "Koehler Report"), 17. Kann took a photo of Rivers as he was being helped into his saddle to return to Jolo and the garrison hospital; see Kann, "Voyages et Combat," 144.

58. Lawton Report, 26.

59. "Report of Captain E. F. McGlachlin," Appendix E, *List of Appendices Accompanying Colonel Duncan's Report of Engagement with the Moro Enemy* (hereafter "McGlachlin Report"), 42.

60. Duncan, "Fight at Bud Dajo," 63.

61. Duncan Report, 14.

62. McGlachlin Report, 44.

63. White Report, 2. White, *Bullets and Bolos,* 305–306.

64. White Report, 2.

65. Duncan Report, 11.

66. White, *Bullets and Bolos,* 306.

67. White Report, 2.

68. White, *Bullets and Bolos,* 306–307.

69. White Report, 3.

70. Duncan Report, 15.

71. See also Duncan Report, 24.

72. White, *Bullets and Bolos,* 307; White Report, 3.

Chapter 7: March 6

1. "Kissa Bunuq ha Bud Dahuq," verses 135–136.

2. Duncan, "Fight at Bud Dajo," 64.

3. Lawton Report, 27.

4. "Letter from Soldier," *Journal and Tribune* (TN), October 7, 1906.

5. "Letter from Soldier."

6. Lawton Report, 28; "Letter from Soldier."

7. "Letter from Soldier."

8. Duncan Report, 20–21.

9. Duncan Report, 20–21. The time of the message recorded in Duncan's report appears to be inaccurate.

10. Koehler Report, 18.

11. Koehler Report, 18.

12. Koehler Report, 19.

13. Koehler Report, 19.

14. Koehler Report, 20.

15. White, *Bullets and Bolos*, 307.

16. White Report, 3–4.

17. White, *Bullets and Bolos*, 308.

18. White, 308.

19. White Report, 4.

20. White Report, 4–5.

21. White Report, 4–5.

22. McGlachlin Report, 43.

23. McGlachlin Report, 45.

24. "Taking of Mount Dajo."

25. "Taking of Mount Dajo."

26. McGlachlin Report, 43.

27. Hamilton Wright, "The Awful Slaughter of 1,000 Moro Bandits—Men, Women, and Children," *Leslie's Weekly*, May 10, 1906.

28. Duncan Report, 18.

29. Duncan Report, 19.

30. Duncan Report, 21.

31. Duncan subsequently informed Bundy that Wetherill had reached the summit on the east trail "this afternoon," when in fact it had been reached before 9 a.m.; see Duncan Report, 20 and 22.

32. Duncan Report, 22.

33. Duncan Report, 23.

34. Koehler Report, 20–21.

35. Kann, "Voyages et Combat," 140.

36. Kann, 140.

37. Kann, 140.

38. White Report, 5.

39. Kann, "Voyages et Combat," 141.

40. White Report, 5.

41. White, *Bullets and Bolos*, 309. See also interview with Vinton B. Hill in Wayne L. Sanford, "Battle of Bud Dajo: 6 March 1906," *Indiana Military History Journal* 7, no. 1 (January 1982): 8, 10.

Chapter 8: Morning, March 7

1. "Kissa Bunuq ha Bud Dahuq," verses 180, 189, 192, and 194.

2. "Report of Major Omar Bundy," Appendix A, *List of Appendices Accompanying Colonel Duncan's Report of Engagement with the Moro Enemy* (hereafter "Bundy Report"), 6.

3. Bundy Report, 2; Appendix N, *List of Appendices Accompanying Colonel Duncan's Report of Engagement with the Moro Enemy*, 57.

4. Bundy Report, 6.

5. McGlachlin Report, 44.

6. White Report, 5.

7. White Report, 5.

8. White, *Bullets and Bolos*, 309.

9. White Report, 5–6.

10. White Report, 5–6.

11. "Fought in Volcano's Crater," *Cincinnati Enquirer*, April 26, 1906. The "Battle Above the Clouds" is a reference to the Battle of Lookout Mountain, November 24, 1863, during the US Civil War.

12. Sanford, "Battle of Bud Dajo," 10–11.

13. "Taking of Mount Dajo."

14. White Report, 6–7.

15. Sanford, "Battle of Bud Dajo," 11.

16. White Report, 7.

17. White Report, 7–8.

18. Bundy Report, 6.

19. "Taking of Mount Dajo."

20. "Voice of the People."

21. White, *Bullets and Bolos*, 311.

22. White Report, 8. See also Kann, "Voyages et Combat," 141.

23. "Arkansan Tells of Battle at Jolo."

24. White Report, 8.

25. "Taking of Mount Dajo."

26. Sanford, "Battle of Bud Dajo," 11. See also Kann, "Voyages et Combat," 141.

27. White Report, 8.

28. "Arkansan Tells of Battle at Jolo."

29. "Letter from the Philippine Islands," *Morristown (TN) Gazette*, June 6, 1906.

30. "Voice of the People." Mahoney was probably referring to the .38 caliber Colt M1902.

31. "In the Fight," *Kentucky Advocate* (Danville), April 30, 1906.

32. White Report, 8–9.

33. "Letter from the Philippine Islands."

34. "Taking of Mount Dajo."

35. "Killed and Wounded, Bud-Dajo Expedition, March 1906," Appendix I, *List of Appendices Accompanying Colonel Duncan's Report of Engagement with the Moro Enemy*, 54–56.

36. Bundy Report, 7.

37. Bundy Report, 7–8.

38. Kann, "Voyages et Combat," 142.

39. "Letter Concerns Mt. Daho Battle," *York (PA) Daily*, April 25, 1906.

40. The photograph was reproduced in Kann, "Voyages et Combat," 139.

41. Mike G. Price collection.

42. Kann, "Voyages et Combat," 141; "Arkansan Tells of Battle at Jolo."

Chapter 9: Afternoon, March 7

1. "Kissa Bunuq ha Bud Dahuq," verses 196–197.

2. Lawton to Duncan, March 7, 1906, folder 1, box 38, Leonard Wood Papers, LOC. This file includes Lawton's original message, written in pencil on yellow notepaper.

3. Wood diary, March 3, 1906.

4. "Report of Midshipman J. H. Hayward," Appendix F, *List of Appendices Accompanying Colonel Duncan's Report of Engagement with the Moro Enemy*, 48.

5. Wood diary, March 7, 1906.

6. See also Langhorne note on Bud Dajo, March 15, 1906, folder 1, box 38, Leonard Wood Papers, LOC (hereafter "Langhorne Note, March 15, 1906"). Langhorne never produced a formal report but described his involvement in this "note."

7. Wood diary, March 7, 1906.

8. Lawton Report, 29.

9. Wright, "Awful Slaughter."

10. Wright, "Awful Slaughter."

11. McGlachlin Report, 44.

12. Wright, "Awful Slaughter."

13. Kann, "Voyages et Combat," 141–142.

14. McGlachlin Report, 45.

15. "Report of 2nd Lieutenant Leighton Powell," Appendix H, *List of Appendices Accompanying Colonel Duncan's Report of Engagement with the Moro Enemy* (hereafter "Powell Report"), 52–53.

16. Koehler Report, 21–22.

17. "From a Winfield Boy—Who Was in the Fierce Fight on Jolo Mountain," *Winfield (KS) Daily Courier*, June 6, 1906.

18. "Revised List of Casualties Place Number of Killed at Twenty-One; Wounded, Sixty-Four," *Mindanao Herald*, March 17, 1906.

19. "Mowed Down: Slaughter of Women and Children at Mt. Dajo May Be Investigated," *Leavenworth (KS) Times*, June 29, 1906. Despite the headline, nothing further came of this.

20. Kann, "Voyages et Combat," 142.

21. Sanford, "Battle of Bud Dajo," 12.

22. Powell Report, 53.

23. "A Letter from Jolo," *Garnet (KS) Journal Plaindealer*, April 27, 1906.

24. Langhorne Note, March 15, 1906.

25. Lawton Report, 30.

26. Langhorne Note, March 15, 1906.

27. Lawton Report, 30.

28. Lawton Report, 31.

29. "Letter from Soldier."

30. Kann, "Voyages et Combat," 142.

31. "Voice of the People."

32. Lawton Report, 31.

33. Lawton Report, 32–33; Langhorne Note, March 15, 1906.

34. Lawton Report, 41.

35. Wright, "Awful Slaughter."

36. *Army and Navy Gazette*, January 7, 1899.

37. "Voice of the People."

38. "History of the Nineteenth Infantry," *El Paso Sunday Times*, June 28, 1908.

39. "History of the Nineteenth Infantry."

40. Lawton Report, 32.

41. Langhorne Note, March 15, 1906.

42. Lawton Report, 32. See also Langhorne Note, March 15, 1906.

43. See the Epilogue.

44. Lawton Report, 32.

45. "History of the Nineteenth Infantry."

46. Wright, "Awful Slaughter." See also "Thrilling Days in Philippines," *Honolulu Advertiser*, April 6, 1937. Wright's dramatic description of the fall of Bud Dajo and its moral effect on
the Moros of Jolo was, of course, pure conjecture.

47. Langhorne Note, March 15, 1906.

48. Wright, "Awful Slaughter."

Chapter 10: The End, March 8

1. "History of the Nineteenth Infantry."

2. Wright, "Awful Slaughter."

3. Wright.

4. McCoy letter to mother, March 10, 1906.

5. Lawton Report, 34.

6. "History of the Nineteenth Infantry."

7. "Voice of the People."

8. McCoy letter to mother, March 10, 1906.

9. Lawton Report, 35.

10. Bundy Report, 9.

11. Wright, "Awful Slaughter."

12. Wright.

13. Kann, "Voyages et Combat," 142. As early as 1906, the accessions of the State Historical
Society of Wisconsin list in the collection a "Lime box from the scene of the battle between
United States troops and Moros at the crater of Bud-Dajo, Jolo, P.I." *Bulletins of Information—
State Historical Society of Wisconsin* 1, nos. 1–32, 1894–1906 (Madison: State Historical Soci-
ety of Wisconsin, 1906), 99.

14. Edward P. Lawton, *A Saga of the South* (Ft. Myers Beach, FL: Island, 1965), 293.

15. "Arkansan Tells of Battle at Jolo."

16. See, for instance, Quartermaster Receipt, September 7, 1905, in Scott Papers, box 56,
LOC; and Scott, *Some Memories of a Soldier*, 370. There is a substantial literature on the
subject; see James Hevia, "Looting Beijing: 1860, 1900," in *Tokens of Exchange: The Problem
of Translation in Global Circulations*, ed. Lydia H. Liu, Stanley Fish, and Fredric Jameson
(Durham, NC: Duke University Press, 1999), 192–213; Michael Carrington, "Officers, Gentlemen and Thieves: The Looting of Monasteries During the 1903/4 Younghusband Mission
to Tibet," *Modern Asian Studies* 37, no. 1 (2003): 81–109; and Dan Hicks, *The Brutish Museums: The Benin Bronzes, Colonial Violence and Cultural Restitution* (London: Pluto, 2020).

17. Bundy Report, 9.

18. Hamilton Wright, "The Fight in the Crater," *Sunday Times: Chattanooga* (TN), June 3,
1906. Whereas the Krag Jorgensen rifles were likely stolen from US forces, the M1893 Mauser
had been the standard arm of the Spanish Army, and many ended up with Filipino insurgents
and the Moros after 1898.

19. Wright, "Fight in the Crater." See also "Last Confederate Rifle Used in War,"
Times-Dispatch, August 1, 1907. The discovery of the rifle was later attributed to 1st Lieutenant C. U. Leonori, 19th Infantry; see "Confederate Gun Far Afield," *Kansas City Star*, May
17, 1914.

20. This rifle is today kept in the American Civil War Museum in Richmond, Virginia (catalogue number: 0985.03.00209); see https://acwm.pastperfectonline.com/we
bobject/94448040-F43F-472A-8336-109188417477. The University of Michigan Museum
of Anthropological Archaeology has a *barong* with sheath said to have been collected from the

battlefield of Bud Dajo: 8375-a/b (original acquisition number M15-1). The knife was acquired from H. L. Brown, who served with the Hospital Corps at Bud Dajo, which would seem to confirm the provenance (thanks to Jim Moss at UMMAA). At the Field Museum of Natural History in Chicago there are currently two Moro swords known as *kampilans* (N.253029 and N.253030) that, according to the catalog index, are both "said to be captured at Bud Dajo battle, Jolo Island." See https://collections-anthropology.fieldmuseum.org/catalogue/1161228 and https://collections-anthropology.fieldmuseum.org/catalogue/1161229.

In 1940 the Illinois State Museum had two similar *kampilans* on loan from Dr. H. E. Stafford, formerly of the Army Medical Corps, who had lived in the Philippines for some forty years. Stafford provided the following information about their provenance: "Both were captured at 'Bud Dajo' the famous battle at the mountain by that name. . . . The one with the red rag on it was being used by a Moro who was bayoneted in the chest by a soldier and he was trying to pull himself farther on the bayonet so as to reach the infidel with this sword. The Moros are fanatical fighters and as hard to kill as a carabao. One reason why the army adopted the large .45 automatic so the larger bullet would shock them to a stop. The Moros used to use a red and white spotted bandana-like cloth to indicate they had killed. Both [swords] had blood on them. I have had them for thirty years or more if I remember correctly." Stafford to Kable, August 25, 1939, ISM. (Thanks to Brooke Morgan and DeeAnn Watt at the ISM.) The two swords are no longer in the Illinois State Museum, but there are likely many more objects taken from Bud Dajo in various collections throughout the United States.

21. Lawton Report, 36. See also Duncan Report, 42.

22. Wood Report, April 22.

23. Kann, "Voyages et Combat," 142.

24. Koehler Report, 23.

25. "Kissa Bunuq ha Bud Dahuq," verses 202–203 and 206–207. See also "Kissa Bud Dahu" in Oliveros, "Islam in the Moro-American War," 271. The horse is the Burāq, similar to the one in the story of Abdulla and Isara.

Chapter 11: Telegram Blackout

1. Kann, "Voyages et Combat," 143.

2. Kann, 143.

3. Wood diary, March 9, 1906.

4. "A Soldier on the Spot," *Ocala (FL) Evening Star*, May 22, 1906.

5. Robert L. Bullard, *Personalities and Reminiscences of the War* (Garden City: Doubleday, Page, 1925), 12.

6. "Censorship is Re-Established," *Mindanao Herald*, March 10, 1906.

7. "Editorial Comments," *Mindanao Herald*, March 10, 1906.

8. Wood to Andrews, March 9, 1906, folder 1, box 37, Leonard Wood Papers, LOC. For the condensed message forwarded to Washington, DC, see *Pursuant to Senate Resolution No. 95, Copies of All Reports and Other Communications Between the War Department and the Officials of the Philippine Islands Respecting the Recent Attack by Troops of the United States on Mount Dajo* (March 19, 1906), Senate Document Number 276, 59th Congress, 1st Session (Washington, DC: Government Printing Office, 1906), 1–3.

9. Constabulary losses were three dead and fourteen wounded, which meant that the total casualties of the Bud Dajo expeditionary force were twenty-one killed and seventy-three wounded; see "Killed and Wounded, Bud-Dajo Expedition, March 1906," Appendix I, *List of Appendices Accompanying Colonel Duncan's Report of Engagement with the Moro Enemy*, 54–56.

10. Wood to Andrews, March 9, 1906.

11. Wood to Andrews, March 9, 1906.

12. In addition to Wood's report, brief telegrams were dispatched by the Constabulary and Signal Corps commanders to their respective headquarters, briefly communicating their casualties; see Greene to Signals, Manila, March 9, 1906; and Scott to Conrad, March 9, folder 1, box 37, Leonard Wood Papers, LOC. On March 10, Cooke, who was wounded, sent a message to Navy headquarters in Cavite, reporting on the involvement and casualties of the sailors from the *Pampanga*; see Cooke to Senior Officer, Cavite, March 10, 1906, folder 1, box 37, Leonard Wood Papers, LOC.

13. Wright to Reys, March 9, 1906, folder 1, box 37, Leonard Wood Papers, LOC.

14. Wright to Hillbert, March 10, 1906, folder 1, box 37, Leonard Wood Papers, LOC.

15. DeRackin to *Cablenews American*, March 9, 1906, folder 1, box 37, Leonard Wood Papers, LOC.

16. "Editorial Comment," *Mindanao Herald*, March 24, 1906.

17. Cook to Coulter, March 9, 1906; Kinghorne to *Commercial Pacific*, March 9, 1906, folder 1, box 37, Leonard Wood Papers, LOC.

18. Wright, "Awful Slaughter." See also "Letter from Soldier."

19. See "Explains Shooting of Women," *New Ulm (MN) Review*, June 6, 1906; "Letter from the Philippines," *Californian* (Salinas), April 24, 1906; "From a Winfield Boy"; and "Letter from the Philippine Islands," *Melvern (KS) Review*, May 24, 1906.

20. "Letter from the Philippine Islands." Private Mahoney's claim of three thousand, on the other hand, was very clearly an exaggeration; see "Voice of the People." See also "Forced to Shoot Down the Women," *San Francisco Examiner*, October 19, 1906.

21. "Letter from Jolo."

22. "Letter from the Philippines."

23. "Explains Shooting of Women."

24. Langhorne Note, March 15, 1906.

25. Senate Document Number 276, 59th Congress, 1st Session, 1–3, 1–2.

26. See, for instance, "Killed 600 Moros," *Abilene (TX) Daily Chronicle*, March 10, 1906.

27. "18 Americans and 600 Moros Slain in Battle," *Los Angeles Record*, March 9, 1906; "600 Mad Moros Killed—Not One Escaped from Fort," *Cablenews*, March 10, 1906.

28. Twain, *Mark Twain's Autobiography*, 189.

29. "18 Americans and 600 Moros Slain in Battle."

30. "Fierce Fight with Moros," *Hawaiian Star*, March 9, 1906.

31. AP news report, dated Manila, night of March 10, printed in numerous US newspapers—see, for instance, "Nine Hundred Killed in Four Days' Fight with Armed Outlaws," *Raleigh (NC) Times*, March 10, 1906. Manila was twelve hours ahead of Eastern Standard Time and fifteen hours ahead of Pacific Standard Time.

32. "Philippines Battle," *Daily Telegraph* (UK), March 12, 1906.

33. George Ade, *The Sultan of Sulu: An Original Satire in Two Acts* (New York: R. H. Russell, 1903), 14.

34. See, for instance, *Democrat and Chronicle* (NY), March 9, 1906; and *Philadelphia Inquirer*, March 10, 1906.

35. "Benevolent Assimilation," *Time's Tribune* (PA), March 14, 1906.

36. "No Moro Survived," *Washington Post*, March 11, 1906.

37. Wood diary, March 10, 1906.

38. Wood to Roosevelt, March 13, 1906, Wood diary.

39. See "General Wood's Report," *Topeka (KS) Daily Capital*, March 10, 1906; and "Secretary Taft Tells of the Group and Its People," *New York Tribune*, March 10, 1906.

40. Taft to Wood, March 12, 1906, *Complete Copies of All Communication That Have Been Received in or Sent from the War Department Pertaining to the Recent Attack by Troops of the United States on Mount Dajo* (March 26, 1906), Senate Document Number 289, 59th Congress, 1st Session (Washington, DC: Government Printing Office, 1906), 3.

41. See also "Hearst Not Guilty," *Mindanao Herald*, April 28, 1906.

42. Wood to Taft, March 13, 1906, folder 1, box 37, Leonard Wood Papers, LOC. See also *Congressional Record—Senate*, March 15, 1906, 3838; and *An Account of the Engagement on Mount Dajo Between United States Forces and a Band of Moros* (March 15, 1906), Senate Document Number 622, 59th Congress, 1st Session (Washington, DC: Government Printing Office, 1906), 1–2.

43. Koehler Report, 22.

44. "Fought in Volcano's Crater." See also Wright, "Awful Slaughter"; and Wood in March 18, 1906, report.

45. See Kiefer, *Tausug*, 130–131; and Rixhon, *Voices from Sulu*, 142–143. See also S. Barter and I. Zatkin-Osburn, "Shrouded: Islam, War, and Holy War in Southeast Asia," *Journal for the Scientific Study of Religion* 53, no. 1 (2014): 187–201.

46. "Soldier on the Spot." See also "Buffalo Nurse in Philippines," *Buffalo Courier*, September 5, 1906.

47. Taft to Roosevelt, March 13, 1906, *Congressional Record—Senate*, March 15, 1906, 3838.

48. Roosevelt to Taft, March 14, 1906, *Congressional Record—Senate*, March 15, 1906, 3838. President Roosevelt further insisted that the American soldiers who fought at Bud Dajo "are entitled to the heartiest admiration and praise of all those of their fellow citizens who are glad to see the honor of the flag upheld by the courage of the men wearing the American uniform." *Congressional Record—Senate*, March 15, 1906, 3838.

49. Twain, *Mark Twain's Autobiography*, 198.

50. "Our Prowling Constabulary," *Times-Democrat* (LA), March 11, 1906.

51. *Congressional Record—Senate*, March 14, 1906, 3765.

52. *Congressional Record—Senate*, March 15, 1906, 3838. See also *Account of the Engagement on Mount Dajo*, 1–2.

53. *Congressional Record—Senate*, March 15, 1906, 3839.

54. *Congressional Record—Senate*, March 15, 1906, 3839.

55. *Congressional Record—Senate*, March 15, 1906, 3839.

56. *Congressional Record—Senate*, March 15, 1906, 3839.

57. *Congressional Record—House*, March 15, 1906, 3895.

58. *Congressional Record—House*, March 15, 1906, 3895.

59. "A War for Civilization," *Washington Post*, March 15, 1906.

60. "War for Civilization."

61. The backstory of the poem is described in "Nine Days of Fame," *Colony (KS) Free Press*, July 11, 1907.

62. *Congressional Record—House*, March 15, 1906, 3896.

63. See, for instance, "Satire on 'Charge of Wood's Brigade,'" *Washington Post*, March 16, 1906. See also "Nine Days of Fame."

64. "Massacre of Daho Hill," *Boston Globe*, March 16, 1906.

65. "No Wanton Slaughter of Moros," *New York Times*, March 15, 1906.

66. "Heavy Loss to Both Sides," *Semi-Weekly Gazette* (Hutchinson, KS), March 14, 1906.

67. Editorial, *Harper's Weekly*, March 24, 1906, 399.

68. Quoted in "Crushing the Moro Outlaws," *Sioux City (IA) Journal*, March 15, 1906.

69. Wood diary, March 16, 1906.

Chapter 12: Fake News

1. Kann, "Voyages et Combat," 144.

2. Wood diary, March 16, 1906.

3. Wood to Taft, March 18, 1906, *Complete Copies of All Communication That Have Been Received in or Sent from the War Department Pertaining to the Recent Attack by Troops of the United States on Mount Dajo* (March 26, 1906), Senate Document Number 289, 59th Congress, 1st Session (Washington, DC: Government Printing Office, 1906), 6. See also "'Fake' News of Jolo," *Hartford Courant*, March 20, 1906; and "Reports of Battle Were Exaggerated," *Star Press* (IN), March 20, 1906.

4. "Women and Children Killed in Onslaught," *Altoona (PA) Tribune*, March 12, 1906, refers to "an unofficial report from Jolo."

5. "Scene of the Fight," *Cablenews*, March 10, 1906.

6. AP news report, dated Manila, night of March 10, 1906.

7. Wood diary, March 18, 1906. See also Langhorne to Wood, March 26, 1906, folder 1, box 37, Leonard Wood Papers, LOC. Langhorne seemed to assume that DeRackin was behind the "unofficial report."

8. Parts of the report had been written as early as March 8; see Lawton Report, 24.

9. Wood diary, March 18, 1906.

10. Wood to Ide, March 18, 1906, folder 3, box 38, Leonard Wood Papers, LOC.

11. Wood to Scott, June 25, 1906, folder: Official file 1906, box 57, Hugh Lenox Scott Papers, LOC.

12. Wood to Ide, March 18, 1906.

13. Wood to Ide, March 18, 1906.

14. Reeves to Langhorne, March 1, 1906, folder 1, box 37, Leonard Wood Papers, LOC.

15. Wood diary, March 18, 1906.

16. Wood to Taft, March 18, 1906, 6.

17. Scott, *Some Memories of a Soldier*, 384.

18. Scott, 384.

19. Ainsworth to Scott, March 19, 1906, *Complete Copies of All Communication That Have Been Received in or Sent from the War Department Pertaining to the Recent Attack by Troops of the United States on Mount Dajo* (March 26, 1906), Senate Document Number 289, 59th Congress, 1st Session (Washington, DC: Government Printing Office, 1906), 6.

20. Scott, *Some Memories of a Soldier*, 384–385.

21. Scott to Wood, March 19, 1906, folder 3, box 38, Leonard Wood Papers, LOC.

22. Scott to Wood, March 19, 1906.

23. "Parkhurst Denounces Roosevelt's Cablegram," *New York Times*, March 19, 1906.

24. "Parkhurst Denounces Roosevelt's Cablegram."

25. *Congressional Record—House*, March 19, 1906, 3981.

26. *Congressional Record—House*, March 19, 1906, 3980.

27. *Congressional Record—House*, March 19, 1906, 3981.

28. *Congressional Record—House*, March 19, 1906, 3981.

29. *Congressional Record—House*, March 19, 1906, 3981.

30. *Congressional Record—House*, March 19, 1906, 3981–3985.

31. *Congressional Record—House*, March 19, 1906, 3985.

32. *Congressional Record—House*, March 19, 1906, 3985.

33. *Congressional Record—House*, March 19, 1906, 3985.

34. *Congressional Record—House*, March 19, 1906, 3985.

35. *Congressional Record—House*, March 19, 1906, 3986.

36. *Congressional Record—House*, March 19, 1906, 3986.

37. "Letter to the Editor," *Boston Daily Advertiser*, March 20, 1906.

38. See also "'Fake' News of Jolo"; and "Reports of Battle Were Exaggerated."

39. "No Women or Children Killed," *Daily Arkansas Gazette* (Little Rock), March 20, 1906; "Troops Saved Women," *Cedar Falls (IA) Gazette*, March 27, 1906.

40. "The Great Yazoo Jester," *Sun* (NY), March 21, 1906. See also the cover of *Judge*, April 14, 1906.

41. *Congressional Record—Senate*, March 21, 1906, 4073. The files are *Additional Information of an Official Character with Reference to the Recent Engagement of American Forces with Moro Outlaws on Mount Dajo* (March 21, 1906), Senate Document Number 278, 59th Congress, 1st Session (Washington, DC: Government Printing Office, 1906), 1–5.

42. Ide to Taft, March 20, 1906, Senate Document Number 278, 59th Congress, 1st Session, 5.

43. Scott memorandum, March 20, 1906, Senate Document Number 278, 59th Congress, 1st Session, 2–5. Scott also gave a number of interviews; see, for instance, "Killing of Moros," *Washington Post*, March 20, 1906.

44. "Ide Acquits Troops of Killing Moro Women," *New York Times*, March 21, 1906.

45. "Battle Humane," *Democrat and Chronicle* (NY), March 21, 1906; "Tried to Spare the Women," *Punxsutawney (PA) News*, March 21, 1906.

46. *Congressional Record—Senate*, March 22, 1906, 4093–4094.

47. *Congressional Record—Senate*, March 22, 1906, 4093–4094.

48. "Country Wants an Explanation," *Fort Payne (AL) Journal*, March 21, 1906; "Grave Inconsistency in Official Record," *St. Louis Post-Dispatch*, March 25, 1906; "Over-Explained," *Wilkes-Barre (PA) Leader*, April 5, 1906.

49. "Wanted—A Straight Story," *Washington Post*, March 23, 1906.

50. *Congressional Record—Senate*, March 23, 1906, 4156; *Congressional Record—Senate*, March 26, 1906, 4254.

51. *Complete Copies of All Communication*, 1–11.

52. Editorial, *Harper's Weekly*, March 31, 1906, 435.

53. McCoy to Manly, March 27, 1906, folder: General Correspondence May–August 1906, box 11, Frank R. McCoy Papers, LOC.

54. McCoy to Winter, March 27, 1906, folder: General Correspondence May–August 1906, box 11, Frank R. McCoy Papers, LOC. For rumors concerning a formal investigation, see "The Mount Dajo Fight," *Midland Daily Telegraph* (Coventry, UK), March 19, 1906.

55. McCoy to Langhorne, March 19, folder 1, box 37, Leonard Wood Papers, LOC. See also Langhorne to Wood, March 26, 1906; and Reeves to Langhorne, March 31, 1906, folder 1, box 37, Leonard Wood Papers, LOC.

56. Langhorne to Wood, March 5, 1906, folder 1, box 37, Leonard Wood Papers, LOC.

57. Wood to Roosevelt, May 14, 1906, folder 1, box 37, Leonard Wood Papers, LOC.

58. See also telegram from Duncan to McCoy, March 18, 1906, folder: General Correspondence March–April 1906, box 11, Frank R. McCoy Papers, LOC.

59. Duncan Report, 58.

60. Duncan Report, 60.

61. Wood diary, April 26, 1906; "Army and Navy News," *Evening Star*, May 20, 1906.

62. See file 1108562; RG 94, entry 25, AGO Document File, 1890–1917, NARA.

63. Jokanain, *Sabah* conference, April 13, 1906.

64. Scott, *Some Memories of a Soldier*, 386. The best evidence of what the Moros thought of the massacre at Bud Dajo is to be found in the *kissas* and local stories that still circulate; see the Epilogue.

Chapter 13: The Stories They Told

1. "Explains Shooting of Women."

2. "History of the Nineteenth Infantry." Another soldier, Hartmann, used the exact same expression; see "He Fought at Jolo," *Parsons (KS) Daily Eclipse*, August 7, 1906. The incommunicability of the experience of war is one of the key themes examined by Samuel Hynes in his classic book *The Soldier's Tale: Bearing Witness to Modern War* (London: Pimlico, 1998).

3. "Letter from the Philippine Islands."

4. See also "Voice of the People"; "From a Winfield Boy"; and "Letter from Jolo." For a discussion of the derogatory language used in the Philippines, see Paul A. Kramer, "Race-Making and Colonial Violence in the US Empire: The Philippine-American War as Race War," *Diplomatic History* 30, no. 2 (2006): 193–194.

5. Wright, "Awful Slaughter." See also "Soldier on the Spot."

6. "He Fought at Jolo."

7. It should be noted that Wright did in fact publish these stories in *Leslie's Weekly*. See Wright, "Awful Slaughter."

8. "Hero of Moro Slaughters," *Omaha Daily Bee*, August 13, 1907. Leonard Wood's own son later wrote a fictional short story about Bud Dajo; see Leonard Wood Jr., "A Woman of the Tropics," *Harvard Advocate* 96, no. 1 (September 26, 1913): 46–48.

9. "He Could Not Remain Behind When Comrades Charged up Dajo Hill," *Topeka (KS) Daily Capital*, June 29, 1906.

10. "A Soldier Boy's Letter," *Tennessean* (Nashville, TN), June 18, 1906.

11. "Letter From the Philippine Islands." See also "In the Fight."

12. "He Fought at Jolo."

13. "Letter from Jolo."

14. "On Mount Bud-Dajo," *Sun* (NY), July 9, 1906.

15. "On Mount Bud-Dajo."

16. Editorial, "The Fight on the Mountain," *Sun* (NY), July 9, 1906.

17. "Engineer Tells of Jolo Battle," *Philadelphia Inquirer*, July 16, 1906.

18. "Engineer Tells of Jolo Battle."

19. "Engineer Tells of Jolo Battle."

20. See, for instance, "Suicide of Japs Thrill Nation," *Chicago Tribune*, July 4, 1904.

21. "Engineer Tells of Jolo Battle."

22. "The Fight at Dajo," *Cablenews Manila*, May 11, 1906. See also "Soldier Correspondent Sends the First Complete Story of Battle Between Filipinos and Americans," *St. Louis Post-Dispatch*, May 13, 1906.

23. "The Fight at Dajo Crater," *Minneapolis Messenger*, August 30, 1906.

24. Burton Egbert Stevenson, ed., *Poems of American History* (Boston: Houghton Mifflin, 1908), 645–646. See also *Life*, August 16, 1906; and *Army and Navy Register*, August 25, 1906.

25. Thomas P. Walsh, *Tin Pan Alley and the Philippines: American Songs of War and Love, 1898–1946, a Resource Guide* (Lanham, MD: Scarecrow, 2013), 212–214, 221.

26. There are several different versions of the song, but this is taken from Damon Runyon, *The Tents of Trouble* (New York: Desmond FitzGerald, 911), 76–78, which is the earliest recorded version. See also Edward Arthur Dolph, *"Sound Off": Soldier Songs from Yankee Doodle to Parley Voo* (New York: Cosmopolitan, 1929).

27. See Bederman, *Manliness & Civilization*; and Hoganson, *Fighting for American Manhood*.

28. "Paul Flowers' Greenhouse," *Commercial Appeal* (Memphis, TN), December 18, 1965. See also Heather Marie Stur, *Beyond Combat: Women and Gender in the Vietnam War Era* (Cambridge: Cambridge University Press, 2011).

Chapter 14: An Operation, Not an Aberration

1. *Life*, March 29, 1906, 380. The editorial comment was accompanied by a small vignette showing the caricatured heads of four Moros hanging from a bamboo pole. The chapter title is from Ronald Ridenhour's pithy summary of the My Lai Massacre; see David L. Anderson, ed., *Facing My Lai: Moving Beyond the Massacre* (Kansas City: University Press of Kansas, 1998), 56.

2. "Covering It Up," *New York World*, March 16, 1906. See also Abe Ignacio, Enrique de la Cruz, Jorge Emmanuel, and Helen Toribio, *The Forbidden Book: The Philippine-American War in Political Cartoons* (San Francisco: T'boli, 2004).

3. For a comparative study, see Truda Gray and Brian Martin, "My Lai: The Struggle over Outrage," *Peace & Change* 33, no. 1 (2008): 90–113.

4. "In the Land of the Big Cigar," *San Francisco Chronicle*, March 18, 1906; "In the Rich Cagayan Valley," *Nashville Banner*, May 5, 1906; "Hurling Babies on Bayonets Moros Greet Death on Mt. Dajo," *Wilkes-Barre (PA) Leader*, May 4, 1906.

5. In the book that Wright published after his return to the United States, there is only a brief mention of the massacre, although he states that between 1,200 and 1,400 Moros had been killed. See Hamilton M. Wright, *A Handbook of the Philippines* (Chicago: A. C. McClurg, 1907), 155.

6. Raoul Peck makes this point in *Exterminate All the Brutes* (documentary), Raoul Peck (dir.), HBO Documentary Films, Velvet Films, Sky Documentaries, ARTE France, 2020.

7. "Fought in Volcano's Crater."

8. Dodge to Roosevelt, March 17, 1906, Theodore Roosevelt Papers: Series 1: Letters and Related Material, 1759–1919, 1906, March 13–May 18, LOC.

9. Dodge to Roosevelt, March 17, 1906.

10. Walther to McCoy, April 24, 1906, folder: General Correspondence March–April 1906, box 11, Frank R. McCoy Papers, LOC.

11. Worcester to Catherine C. Worcester, June 28, 1906, quoted in Rodney J. Sullivan, *Exemplar of Americanism: The Philippine Career of Dean C. Worcester* (Ann Arbor: University of Michigan Center for South and Southeast Asian Studies, 1991), 149.

12. See, for instance, "Benevolent Assimilation," *Time's Tribune* (PA), March 14, 1906; and "A War for Civilization," *Washington Post*, March 15, 1906. See also Heather Cox Richardson, *Wounded Knee: Party Politics and the Road to an American Massacre* (New York: Basic Books, 2010).

13. "Editorial Comment: The Massacre at Jolo," *Index*, March 17, 1906.

14. *Manila Times*, quoted in "The Dajo Fight," *Salt Lake Telegram*, April 24, 1906. The comparison between Moros and Native Americans was also emphasized in a cartoon in the *New York Times* that showed Uncle Sam forcing a Moro, who was holding a small American flag, to sing "Yankee Doodle" at the point of a bayonet. Next to the Moro, a Native American who has already undergone the same treatment is furtively looking on; see *New York Times*, March 18, 1906.

15. Wood to Higginson, May 6, 1906, quoted in Hagedorn, *Leonard Wood*, 2:65–66.

16. Ben Kiernan, *Blood and Soil: A World History of Genocide and Extermination from Sparta to Darfur* (New Haven, CT: Yale University Press, 2007), 225–236.

17. "Ausland," *Berliner Börsen-Zeitung*, Marts 13, 1906.

18. Sternburg to Roosevelt, March 12, 1906, Theodore Roosevelt Papers: Series 1: Letters and Related Material, 1759–1919, 1906, January 27–March 12, LOC.

19. Sternburg to Roosevelt, March 12, 1906.

20. Roosevelt to Sternburg, March 12, 1906, Theodore Roosevelt Papers: Series 2: Letterpress Copybooks, 1897–1916, vol. 62, 1906, March 2–13, LOC.

21. Hull, *Absolute Destruction*; Susanne Kuß, *German Colonial Wars and the Context of Military Violence* (Cambridge, MA: Harvard University Press, 2017).

22. Quoted in R. A. Adeleye, "Mahdist Triumph and British Revenge in Northern Nigeria: Satiru 1906," *Journal of the Historical Society of Nigeria* 6, no. 2 (1972): 205.

23. Shula Marks, *Reluctant Rebellion: The 1906–1908 Disturbances in Natal* (Oxford: Clarendon, 1970); Jeff Guy, *Remembering the Rebellion: The Zulu Uprising of 1906* (Scottsville, South Africa: University of KwaZulu-Natal Press, 2006).

24. Margaret J. Wiener, *Visible and Invisible Realms: Power, Magic, and Colonial Conquest in Bali* (Chicago: University of Chicago Press, 1995); see also Emmanuel Kreike, "Genocide in the Kampongs? Dutch Nineteenth Century Colonial Warfare in Aceh, Sumatra," *Journal of Genocide Research* 14, nos. 3–4 (2012): 297–315.

25. James Giblin and Jamie Monson, eds., *Maji Maji: Lifting the Fog of War* (Leiden: Brill, 2010).

26. Frédéric Mégret, "From 'Savages' to 'Unlawful Combatants': A Postcolonial Look at International Humanitarian Law's 'Other,'" in *International Law and Its Others*, ed. A. Orford (Cambridge: Cambridge University Press, 2006), 265–317; Wagner, "Savage Warfare."

27. See Will Smiley, "Lawless Wars of Empire? The International Law of War in the Philippines, 1898–1903," *Law & History Review* 36, no. 3 (August 2018): 511–550; and Helen Kinsella, "Settler Empire and the United States: Francis Lieber on the Laws of War," *American Political Science Review* 117, no. 2 (2023): 629–642. Thanks also to Justin F. Jackson for sharing his research on General Order 100 and US violence during the Philippine war.

28. Callwell, *Small Wars*, 42. See also Elbridge Colby, "How to Fight Savage Tribes," *American Journal of International Law* 21, no. 2 (1927): 279–288.

29. Kann, "Voyages et Combat," 144. General Lothar von Trotha, the German officer responsible for the war of extermination against the Herero in South West Africa, expressed the very same view when called upon to defend his actions: "That a war in Africa cannot be waged exclusively according to the Geneva Conventions is self-evident." Quoted in Menger, "Colonial Way of War," 8.

30. "The Facts of the Case," *Weekly Republican* (IN), April 5, 1906. Considering the widespread practice of collecting human crania by American and European colonial officers, the use of "head hunters" to describe indigenous people is somewhat ironic.

31. "Light and Shadow," *Lancaster (PA) Intelligencer*, May 9, 1906. See also "Voice of the People."

32. "The Alleged Barbarities at Mount Dajo," *Manila Times*, March 17, 1906.

33. See, for instance, Jonathan Hyslop, "The Invention of the Concentration Camp: Cuba, Southern Africa and the Philippines, 1896–1907," *South African Historical Journal* 63, no. 2 (2011): 251–276; and Jonas Kreienbaum, "Deadly Learning? Concentration Camps in Colonial Wars Around 1900," in *Imperial Cooperation and Transfer, 1870–1930: Empires and Encounters*, ed. Volker Barth and Roland Cvetkovski (London: Bloomsbury, 2015), 219–235.

34. Menger, "Colonial Way of War," 130–143, 274–292.

35. Paul Bijl, *Emerging Memory: Photographs of Colonial Atrocity in Dutch Cultural Remembrance* (Amsterdam: Amsterdam University Press, 2015); Paul Bijl, "Saving the Children? The Ethical Policy and Photographs of Colonial Atrocity During the Aceh War," in *Photography, Modernity and the Governed in Late-Colonial Indonesia*, ed. Susie Protschky (Amsterdam: Amsterdam University Press, 2015), 103–130.

36. For similar examples from other empires, see Foliard, *Violence of Colonial Photography*; and Michelle Gordon, "Viewing Violence in the British Empire: Images of Atrocity from the Battle of Omdurman, 1898," *Journal of Perpetrator Research* 2, no. 2 (2019): 65–100.

37. "De Slachting de Jolo," *Locomotief* (Dutch East Indies), March 3, 1906. See also "Brieven uit de Nieuwe Wereld," *Soerabaijasch Handelsblad* (Dutch East Indies), April 26, 1906. In Britain the press paid only a passing interest to the Bud Dajo expedition and subsequent debates in the US; see, for instance, "Philippine Fight," *Daily Telegraph* (UK), March 20, 1906.

38. "Anti-Imperialists Meet," *Boston Evening Transcript*, December 3, 1906.

39. "Nobel Peace Prize Awarded President," *Washington Times*, December 10, 1906.

40. Roosevelt to Dodge, March 19, 1906, Theodore Roosevelt Papers: Series 2: Letterpress Copybooks, 1897–1916, vol. 62, 1906, March 12–April 12, LOC.

41. "Annual report for the District of Sulu, from July 1st, 1905, to June 30th, 1906."

42. Vic Hurley, *The Swish of the Kris: The Story of the Moros* (New York: E. P. Dutton, 1936), 198–207.

43. "Kissaq Kan Parang Sabil Jikiri" ("The Story of the Fight of Jikiri"), 3.4, Philippine Epics and Ballads Archive, Rizal Library, Ateneo de Manila University, http://epics.ateneo .edu. See also Scott, *Some Memories of a Soldier*, 370.

44. Quoted in Fulton, *Honor for the Flag*, 183.

45. A number of photographs of the trenches on Bud Dajo were taken following the standoff in 1911; see Mike G. Price Collection.

46. See Edgerton, *American Datu*.

47. *Annual Report of Brigadier General John J. Pershing, US Army, Governor of the Moro Province, for the Year Ending June 30, 1911* (Zamboanga: Mindanao Herald, 1911), 26. Thanks to Oli Charbonneau for sharing this reference.

48. Fulton, *Moroland*, 434.

49. This poster is likely a key source for the story of the 1911 Colt .45 pistol, which was not in fact developed for use against Moros.

Chapter 15: The Most Illuminating Thing

1. Rafael, *White Love*, 77.

2. "Trench at Bud Dajo," Library of Congress, www.loc.gov/resource/ds.04272.

3. National Archives ref. 111-SC-83648. The Burns Archive in New York has what appears to be an original print, and there is also a copy in the Frank West Papers in the Huntington Library, San Marino, California.

4. According to Robert A. Fulton, this print comes from the John R. White Papers, Knight Library, University of Oregon, but I was unable to locate it there. The late Jim Zwick, who wrote extensively about Mark Twain and American anti-imperialism, thought that the photographer might have been a soldier in the Signal Corps; see private correspondence between Zwick and Mike G. Price. Fulton, on the other hand, suggests that it was an unidentified civilian who accompanied Hamilton Wright; see *Honor for the Flag*, 194n16.

5. Edgar A. Stirmyer Photograph Collection, USAHEC; John R. White Papers, Knight Library, University of Oregon; Leonard Wood Papers, LOC. The photographs in the National Archives are from the papers of Captain E. F. McGlachlin.

6. "The Army," *Army and Navy Register*, April 4, 1903. Gibbs's biography, such as it is, has been reconstructed with the help of Mike G. Price.

7. "He Will Ascend," *Manila Times*, July 25, 1904.

8. "A Balloon Ascension," *Sterling (IL) Standard*, September 20, 1904.

9. Text on envelope with Aeronaut Gibbs studio letterhead, Jolo, circa 1906, Mike G. Price Collection.

10. Ignacio, de la Cruz, Emmanuel, and Toribio, *Forbidden Book*. See also Janet Hoskins, "Postcards from the Edge of Empire: Images and Messages from French Indochina," *SPAFA Journal* 18, no. 1 (2008): 19–25; Patricia Goldsworthy, "Images, Ideologies, and Commodities: The French Colonial Postcard Industry in Morocco," *Early Popular Visual Culture* 8, no. 2 (2010): 147–167; Felix Axter, "'. . . Will Try to Send You the Best Views from Here': Postcards from the Colonial War in Namibia (1904–1908)," in *German Colonialism, Visual Culture, and Modern Memory*, ed. Volker Langbehn (New York: Routledge, 2010), 67–82.

11. Advertisement for "Aeronaut Gibbs, Photographer," in pamphlet for Jolo Agriculture Fair, October 12–15, 1906, folder: Official File Philippines 1906, box 57, Hugh Lenox Scott Papers, LOC.

12. Information provided by Mike G. Price.

13. My reconstruction of the staging, making, and afterlife of the photograph of the trench at Bud Dajo is indebted to an extensive body of scholarship, including that of John Berger, Susan Sontag, and Judith Butler, but see also Joshua Oppenheimer, "Misunderstanding Images: *Standard Operating Procedure*, Errol Morris," in *Killer Images: Documentary Film, Memory and the Performance of Violence*, ed. Joram Ten Brink and Joshua Oppenheimer (New York: Columbia University Press, 2012), 311–324; Joey Brooke Jakob, "Beyond Abu Ghraib: War Trophy Photography and Commemorative Violence," *Media, War & Conflict* 10, no. 1 (2017): 87–104; S. Koole, "Photography as Event: Power, the Kodak Camera, and Territoriality in Early Twentieth-Century Tibet," *Comparative Studies in Society and History* 59, no. 2 (2017): 310–345; Foliard, *Violence of Colonial Photography*; S. Protschky, "Burdens of Proof: Photography and Evidence of Atrocity During the Dutch Military Actions in Indonesia (1945–50)," *Journal of the Humanities and Social Sciences of Southeast Asia/ Bijdragen tot de Taal-, Land- en Volkenkunde* 176, nos. 2–3 (2020): 240–278; and Wendy Lower, *The Ravine: A Family, a Photograph, a Holocaust Massacre Revealed* (New York: Houghton Mifflin Harcourt, 2021).

14. *Far Eastern Review* 2, no. 13 (May 1906). The special issue had a portrait of General Wood on the cover with the following caption: "First American Governor of the Moro Province, Philippine Islands, Whose Progressive Administration of Civil Affairs Has Opened up that Country to Immigration, and Industrial, Commercial and Agricultural Development."

15. There are copies of these images in folder 1, photo box 1, John R. White Papers, Special Collections and University Archives, Knight Library, University of Oregon; and in the Mike G. Price Collection. See also Hugh Lenox Scott, "The Skilled Packer," *Journal of the US Cavalry Association* 17 (July 1906–April 1907), 518–520; and Bowers Davis, "Mount Dajo Expedition," *Infantry Journal* 25 (July–December 1924), 250–256.

16. "Soldier Correspondent."

17. In the photo, the light falls from behind the soldiers, from the upper left corner, which is consistent with morning light on the eastern summit of Bud Dajo. Robert A. Fulton claims that the image was taken in the evening of March 7, when the trench was first taken, but that is incorrect. See Fulton, *Honor for the Flag*, 140.

18. See Nerissa S. Balce, "The Filipina's Breast: Savagery, Docility, and the Erotics of the American Empire," *Social Text* 24, no. 2 (June 2006): 89–110; and Jennifer Yee, "Recycling the 'Colonial Harem'? Women in Postcards from French Indochina," *French Cultural Studies* 15, no. 1 (2004): 5–19.

19. Thanks to Michael Pritchard for his expert advice on this matter.

20. See Joshua Oppenheimer and Michael Uwemedimo, "Show of Force: A Cinema-Séance of Power and Violence in Sumatra's Plantation Belt," in *Killer Images: Documentary Film, Memory and the Performance of Violence*, ed. Joram Ten Brink and Joshua Oppenheimer (New York: Columbia University Press, 2012), 287–310, 395. See also Linda Kalof and Amy Fitzgerald, "Reading the Trophy: Exploring the Display of Dead Animals in Hunting Magazines," *Visual Studies* 18, no. 2 (2003): 112–122; and Matthew Brower, "Trophy Shots: Early North American Photographs of Nonhuman Animals and the Display of Masculine Prowess," *Society & Animals* 13, no. 1 (2005): 13–32.

21. Thanks to Mark Condos for bringing this to my attention.

22. Captain White was later to lament that "despite fumigatory legislature, patience, and constructive administration, a good many Americans were to be stung to death before the buzzing Mohammedan swarms calmed down." White, *Bullets and Bolos*, 190–191. See also Jacoby, "'Broad Platform of Extermination.'"

23. Kann, "Voyages et Combat," 140. The articles later written by Kann and Wright clearly revealed them to be little more than mouthpieces for the American military administration rather than critical journalists.

24. Mike G. Vann, "Of Pirates, Postcards, and Public Beheadings: The Pedagogic Execution in French Colonial Indochina," *Historical Reflections* 36, no. 2 (Summer 2010): 39–58.

25. "Doings in the Philippines," *Kentucky Advocate* (Danville), August 17, 1906.

26. "A Brave Feat of Arms," *Daily Democrat—Johnstown* (PA), January 22, 1907.

27. Shuster to Wood, May 23, 1906, folder: General Correspondence May–August 1906, box 11, Frank R. McCoy Papers, LOC. Thanks to Oli Charbonneau for bringing this letter to my attention.

28. Shuster to Wood, May 23, 1906.

29. See, for instance, "Trench at Bud Dajo," Library of Congress, LOT 8850, www.loc.gov /item/2013649095.

30. *Catalogue of Copyright Entries—Part 4: Engravings, Cuts, and Prints; Chromos and Litographs; Photographs; Fine Arts* (Washington: Government Printing Office, 1907), 482.

31. The postcard is H116090, *Catalogue of Copyright Entries—Part 4: Engravings, Cuts, and Prints; Chromos and Lithographs; Photographs; Fine Arts*, new series, 3, nos. 1–53, January–December, 1908 (Washington: Government Printing Office, 1908), 392.

32. See Mike G. Price Collection.

33. Mike G. Price Collection.

34. See, for instance, inscription on photos in folder 1, photo box 1, John R. White Papers, Special Collections and University Archives, Knight Library, University of Oregon.

35. Thanks to Patricia Irene Dacudao and Mico Aquino for identifying this copy of the photograph.

36. Figure 6 in Niedermeier, "Intimacy and Annihilation."

37. Folder 1, photo box 1, John R. White Papers, Special Collections and University Archives, Knight Library, University of Oregon.

38. Silvan Niedermeier, "Imperial Narratives: Reading US Soldiers' Photo Albums from the Philippine-American War," *Rethinking History: The Journal of Theory and Practice* 18, no. 1 (2014): 28–49; Martha Langford, *Suspended Conversations: The Afterlife of Memory in Photographic Albums* (Montreal: McGill-Queen's University Press, 2001).

39. "Illinois Woman's Impression of the Battle of Mt. Dajo," *St. Louis Post-Dispatch*, April 29, 1906. See also Wright, "Awful Slaughter," which mentions Lawton being "distraught."

40. "Letter Concerns Mt. Daho Battle." See also "Explains Shooting of Women."

41. "Letter from the Philippine Islands."

42. For an excellent discussion, see Ron Eyerman, "Perpetrator Trauma and Collective Guilt: The My Lai Massacre," in *Memory, Trauma, and Identity* (New York: Palgrave Macmillan, 2019), 167–194. See also Ditte Marie Munch-Jurisic, *Perpetrator Disgust: The Moral Limits of Gut Feelings* (Oxford: Oxford University Press, 2023).

43. "History of the Nineteenth Infantry." See also Silvan Niedermeier, "'If I Were King'—Photographic Artifacts and the Construction of Imperial Masculinities in the Philippine-American War (1899–1902)," in *SpaceTime of the Imperial*, ed. Holt Meyer, Susanne Rau, and Katharina Waldner (Berlin: Walter de Gruyter, 2016), 100–131.

44. See also Tarak Barkawi, *Soldiers of Empire* (Cambridge: Cambridge University Press, 2017), Chapter 7; Megan MacKenzie, "Why Do Soldiers Swap Illicit Pictures? How a Visual Discourse Analysis Illuminates Military Band of Brother Culture," *Security Dialogue* 51, no. 4 (2020): 340–357; and Erik Linstrum, *Age of Emergency: Living with Violence at the End of the British Empire* (Oxford: Oxford University Press, 2023), Chapter 2.

45. "Doings in the Philippines."

46. "War Pictures at the Post," *El Paso Herald*, December 12, 1907; "Anniversary of Battle of Mount Dajo," *El Paso Herald*, March 11, 1908.

47. Personal correspondence with Rob Glover—and with many thanks to DeKalb County History Center.

48. "Voice of the People." See also White, *Bullets and Bolos*, 313.

49. Roosevelt to Johnston, March 10, 1906, Theodore Roosevelt Papers: Series 2: Letterpress Copybooks, 1897–1916, vol. 62, 1906, March 2–12, LOC.

50. M. R. Higonnet, "Souvenirs of Death," *Journal of War and Culture Studies* 1, no. 1 (2008): 65–78.

51. There is an original print in the collection of the Sulphur Springs Valley Historical Society, Chiricahua Regional Museum and Research Center, Willcox, Arizona. The image was later also turned into a postcard.

52. "Letter from Jolo."

53. One soldier later sent the photograph home to his mother, falsely claiming that it was of him and the wounds he received when a Moro woman attacked him from behind: "One Boy's Experience," *Arkansas City Daily News*, May 12, 1907.

54. See "Soldier on the Spot"; and "A Letter from the Philippines," *Ellis (KS) Review,* June 7, 1907.

55. A remarkable parallel to this image may be found in one of the earliest and most famous photographs from a colonial conflict, namely a picture taken by Felice Beato during the suppression of the 1857 Uprising in India. The image is of the aftermath of the assault on Lucknow, and it shows a large building pockmarked by bullet holes. At the time, it was not technically possible to capture military action on camera, and to provide more drama to his composition, Beato had the skulls and skeletons of dead rebels disinterred and arranged in the foreground. See Sean Willcock, "Aesthetic Bodies: Posing on Sites of Violence in India, 1857–1900," *History of Photography* 39, no. 2 (2015): 142–159.

56. See also Jan Tomasz Gross and Irena Grudzinska Gross, *Golden Harvest: Events at the Periphery of the Holocaust* (Oxford: Oxford University Press, 2016).

57. "Not Proven," *Mindanao Herald*, October 13, 1906.

58. Quoted in Fulton, *Honor for the Flag*, 160.

59. James Axtell and William C. Sturtevant, "The Unkindest Cut, or Who Invented Scalping," *William and Mary Quarterly* 37, no. 3 (July 1980): 451–472.

60. See Merrick Burrow, "The Imperial Souvenir: Things and Masculinities in H. Rider Haggard's *King Solomon's Mines* and *Allan Quatermain*," *Journal of Victorian Culture* 18, no. 1 (2013): 72–92; Simon Harrison, *Dark Trophies: Hunting and the Enemy Body in Modern War* (Oxford: Berghahn, 2012); Wagner, *Skull of Alum Bheg*; and Jeremiah Garsha, "The Head of Chief Mkwawa and the Transnational History of Colonial Violence, 1898–2019" (PhD thesis, University of Cambridge, 2020).

61. See Elise Juzda, "Skulls, Science, and the Spoils of War: Craniological Studies at the United States Army Medical Museum, 1868–1900," *Studies in History and Philosophy of Biological and Biomedical Sciences* 40, no. 3 (2009): 156–167; Tom Arne Midtrød, "Calling for More Than Human Vengeance: Desecrating Native Graves in Early America," *Early American Studies* 17, no. 3 (2019): 281–314; and Krystle Stricklin, "With a Skull in Each Hand: Boneyard Photography in the American Empire After 1898," in *Imperial Islands: Art, Architecture, and Visual Experience in the US Insular Empire After 1898*, ed. Joseph R. Hartman (Honolulu: University of Hawai'i Press, 2022), 62–81.

62. Wood diary, October 11, 1906, folder 3, box 3, Leonard Wood Papers, LOC.

63. Paul Fussell, *Wartime: Understanding and Behavior in the Second World War* (New York: Oxford University Press, 1989), 117. See also Simon Harrison, "Skull Trophies of the Pacific War: Transgressive Objects of Remembrance," *Journal of the Royal Anthropological Institute* 12, no. 4 (2006): 817–836.

64. Kermit Roosevelt, *The Long Trail* (New York: Review of Reviews, Metropolitan Magazine, 1921), 44–45. See also the brilliant study of Mearns in Amy Kohout, *Taking the Field: Soldiers, Nature, and Empire on American Frontiers* (Lincoln: University of Nebraska Press, 2023). I have not been able to identify any skulls taken from Bud Dajo in modern collections of human remains, although it is almost certain that some were sent back to the United States.

65. Mike G. Price Collection.

66. Mike G. Price Collection.

67. Mike G. Price Collection.

68. "History of the Nineteenth Infantry."

69. Inscription on the back of postcard in Mike G. Price Collection. Writing on another copy of the same image claims that the girl "stays in town now with the soldiers."

70. The motif appears to have become so popular that the label "Miss Bud Dajo" was simply added to various images of Filipino girls to sell as postcards. The real "Miss Bud Dajo" is nevertheless quite distinct and easily recognizable. Thanks to Mike G. Price for his thoughts on this matter.

71. "Filipinos at the Exposition," *Atlanta Constitution*, April 22, 1907; *See! See! See! Guide to Jamestown Exposition, Historic Virginia and Washington* (Washington, DC: Byron S. Adams, 1907), 18.

72. See "Philippine Children in the Philippine Concession, Jamestown Exposition, Virginia," Keystone-Mast Collection, UC Riverside, California Museum of Photography, http://imgzoom.cdlib.org/Fullscreen.ics?ark=ark:/13030/kt0q2nb9jb/z1&order=2&brand=oac4. The girl might be seen sitting with one arm resting on the wheel of the cart, with a piece of paper in her hand.

73. See Charbonneau, "Visiting the Metropole"; and Hawkins, *Semi-civilized*.

74. *The Official Blue Book of the Jamestown Ter-centennial Exposition, A. D. 1907* (Norfolk, VA: Colonial, 1909), 401.

75. "A Brush with Our Mohammedans," *Indianapolis News*, December 29, 1911.

76. See also Bijl, "Saving the Children?"

77. "Filipinos Mourn Loss of Governor," *Santa Barbara (CA) Daily News*, August 8, 1927.

78. "Filipinos Mourn Loss of Governor."

79. The story probably originated in an episode that took place during the Second Jolo Expedition in 1903; see Wood diary, November 16, 1903, cited in Hagedorn, *Leonard Wood*, 2:21.

80. From text on the back of a postcard of "Miss Bud Dajo," Mike G. Price Collection.

Chapter 16: Afterimage

1. White to Shuster, March 14, 1928, folder 2, box 19, John R. White Papers, Special Collections and University Archives, Knight Library, University of Oregon.

2. See also "Victims of Moro Bullets," *Nebraska State Journal* (Lincoln), March 12, 1906.

3. Réginald Kann, "Voyages et Combat dans le Sud des Philippines," *Le Tour Du Monde* 13, n.s. no. 11 (March 16, 1907), 121–132, and no. 12 (March 23, 1907), 133–143. Kann's account of the Bud Dajo expedition is in the second article.

4. One American newspaper printed two line drawings based on Kann's photos; see "Narrative of the Mt. Dajo Fight," *Leavenworth (KS) Times*, May 13, 1906. The publication of Kann's article was also reported in the German press; see "Kämpfe auf den Philippinen," *General-Anzeiger der stadt Mannheim und Umgebung* (Germany), April 22, 1907.

5. Kann, "Voyages et Combat," 144.

6. *Medal of Honor Recipients, 1863–1978* (Washington, DC: US Government Printing Office, 1979), 370, 371, 374.

7. "Bravery in the Philippines," *Leavenworth (KS) Times*, January 8, 1908.

8. "In the Ranks," *Army and Navy Life* 13 (July–December 1907): 252.

9. "Honors for Six Officers," *Leavenworth (KS) Post*, June 10, 1907.

10. Lawton, *Saga of the South*, 282.

11. White, *Bullets and Bolos*, 313.

12. "Spanish War Veterans Ready for Encampment," *Pittsburgh Press*, August 31, 1913. It may be noted that in 1955, Gibbs's photo was formally included in the *Congressional Record* during a hearing on veterans' pensions—not as evidence of the massacre, but as proof of the hardship suffered by American soldiers; see *Hearings Before the Subcommittee on the Spanish War of the Committee on Veterans' Affairs, House of Representatives, Eighty-Fourth Congress*

First Session on H. R. 707, 714, 754, 2407, 2867, 2998, 3708, 4069, 4210, 4684, 4945, 5055, 5056, 5058, 5246, H. J. Res. 65, 94, 110, 115, 124, 151, 183, 190, 249, 281—miscellaneous bills relating to benefits for veterans (and their dependents) who served in the general period of the Spanish War, April 21 and 22 (Washington, DC: Government Printing Office, 1955), 623–629.

13. "Gallant Record of Our Army," *Sunday Star* (Washington, DC), February 8, 1920.

14. *Army and Navy Register* 61 (1924): 1263.

15. See, for instance, John Dill Ross, *Sixty Years: Life and Adventure in the Far East* (New York: E. P. Dutton, 1911), facing 2:338. An American photographer, J. D. Givens, also included the image, and several other photographs from Bud Dajo, in a book of photographs he published in several different editions, *Scenes Taken in the Philippines, Japan and on the Pacific— Relating to Soldiers* (n.p., 1910, 1912, and 1914). See Elizabeth Rita Bryer, "Scramble for Photographs of Empire: Complicating Visions of the Philippine American War (1899–1913)" (PhD thesis, University of Toronto, 2019). The photograph of the trench at Bud Dajo plays a central role in an obscure novel written by Presbyterian minister Frank Gates Ellett; see *A Modern Hamilton* (Detroit: Frank H. West, 1912).

16. Oswald Garrison Villard, "The Truth About Leonard Wood," *Nation*, May 29, 1920.

17. Oswald Garrison Villard, *Fighting Years: Memoirs of a Liberal Editor* (New York: Harcourt, Brace, 1939), 156.

18. White, *Bullets and Bolos*, 312.

19. See chapter epigraph. See also "The Conquest of the Moro," *Army and Navy Register*, April 20, 1912.

20. George Woods Hicks, "Colonel John R. White: Keeper of Your National Playground, Says 'Any Man Can Succeed—If He Wants To!,'" *Overland Monthly and Out West Magazine* 90, no. 3 (April 1932): 78.

21. Hurley, *Swish of the Kris*, 186. See also Robert Frothingham, *Around the World— Friendly Guide for the World Traveler* (Boston: Houghton Mifflin, 1925), 179–180.

22. *The Real Glory* (film), Henry Hathaway (dir.), Samuel Goldwyn Productions, 1939.

23. See, for instance, Vivienne Angeles, "Moros in the Media and Beyond: Representations of Philippine Muslims," *Contemporary Islam* 4 (2010): 29–53; Reeva Spector Simon, *Spies and Holy Wars: The Middle East in 20th-Century Crime Fiction* (Austin: University of Texas Press, 2010); and Dag Tuastad, "Neo-Orientalism and the New Barbarism Thesis: Aspects of Symbolic Violence in the Middle East Conflict(s)," *Third World Quarterly* 24, no. 4 (2003): 591–599.

24. Twain, *Mark Twain's Autobiography*, 197.

25. Zwick, *Mark Twain's Weapons of Satire*, 168–170. For the unexpurgated text, see mark twainproject.org, *Autobiography of Mark Twain*, 1:403–409.

26. The photo was also reprinted in a small newspaper, the *Daily Democrat—Johnstown* (PA), on January 22, 1907.

27. "Recalls Mount Dajo Massacre—Pictures of Filipino Dead Sent to Congressmen," *Baltimore Sun*, January 17, 1907. The image was later reproduced in an article in the *International Socialist Review*, although it had little relevance to the text; see "Untold Tales of the Navy by Ex-Marines in the US Navy," *International Socialist Review* 13, no. 5 (November 1912): 405.

28. Ida B. Wells, *A Red Record: Tabulated Statistics and Alleged Causes of Lynchings in the United States, 1892–1893–1894* (Chicago: Donohue & Henneberry, 1895), 39, 55.

29. Wells, *Red Record*, 101.

30. See also W. E. B. Du Bois, *Dusk of Dawn: An Essay Toward an Autobiography of a Race Concept* (New York: Oxford University Press, 2007 [1940]), 34–35.

31. W. E. B. Du Bois, "My Evolving Program for Negro Freedom" (originally published 1944), *Clinical Sociology Review* 8, no. 1 (1990): 44; "Oral History Interview of W. E. B. Du Bois by William Ingersoll (1960)," W. E. B. Du Bois Papers (MS 312), Special Collections and University Archives, University of Massachusetts Amherst Libraries, 148–149.

32. Ingersoll interview with Du Bois, 146–147.

33. Ingersoll, 147.

34. Elizabeth Freeman, "The Waco Horror," Supplement, *Crisis*, July 1916, 1–8.

35. See Wood, *Lynching and Spectacle*, 182; and Amy Helene Kirschke, *Art in Crisis: W. E. B. Du Bois and the Struggle for African American Identity and Memory* (Bloomington: Indiana University Press, 2009), 74–75.

36. Editorial, *Crisis*, July 1916, 135.

Conclusion: American Amnesia

1. John S. D. Eisenhower, *Teddy Roosevelt & Leonard Wood: Partners in Command* (Columbia: University of Missouri Press, 2014), 113.

2. Jonathan Schell (unsigned), "Notes and Comments: Talk of the Town," *New Yorker*, December 20, 1969, 69.

3. Claude Cookman, "An American Atrocity: The My Lai Massacre Concretized in a Victim's Face," *Journal of American History* 1 (June 2007): 155.

4. Arthur M. Schlesinger Jr., *The Bitter Heritage: Vietnam and American Democracy, 1941–1966* (Boston: Houghton Mifflin, 1967), 32. See also Oliver, *My Lai Massacre*, 5.

5. Nick Turse, *Kill Anything That Moves: The Real American War in Vietnam* (New York: Metropolitan, 2013); Peter Zinoman and Gary Kulik, "Misrepresenting Atrocities: *Kill Anything That Moves* and the Continuing Distortions of the War in Vietnam," *Cross-Currents: East Asian History and Culture Review* 12 (2014): 162–198.

6. Zinoman and Kulik, "Misrepresenting Atrocities," 164.

7. Howard Jones, *My Lai: Vietnam, 1968, and the Descent into Darkness* (New York: Oxford University Press, 2017), 353.

8. Eric James Schroeder, "Interview with Michael Herr: 'We've All Been There,'" *Writing on the Edge* 1, no. 1 (1989): 43.

9. Gene Allen Smith, David Coffey, and Kyle Longley, *In Harm's Way: A History of the American Military Experience* (New York; Oxford University Press, 2020), 57.

10. For just one example, see Ostler, *Plains Sioux*.

11. Smith, Coffey, and Longley, *In Harm's Way*, 57.

12. Quoted in Grua, *Surviving Wounded Knee*, 31.

13. Warren K. Moorehead, "The Indian Messiah and the Ghost Dance," *American Antiquarian and Oriental Journal* 13 (January–November 1891): 165.

14. Quoted in Brown, *Bury My Heart*, 444.

15. Smith, Coffey, and Longley, *In Harm's Way*, 317, 319.

16. Ken Burns, "Being American Means Reckoning with Our Violent History," *Washington Post*, November 22, 2021.

17. Burns, "Being American Means Reckoning."

18. Derek Gregory, *The Colonial Present: Afghanistan. Palestine. Iraq* (Oxford: Blackwell, 2004); Laura Ann Stoler, *Duress: Imperial Durabilities in Our Times* (Durham, NC: Duke University Press, 2016).

19. Mahmood Mamdani, *Good Muslim, Bad Muslim* (New York: Pantheon, 2004); Kramer, "Enemy You Can Depend On."

20. Mégret, "From 'Savages' to 'Unlawful Combatants'"; Natsu Taylor Saito, "Colonial Presumptions: The War on Terror and the Roots of American Exceptionalism," *Georgetown Journal of Law and Modern Critical Race Perspectives* 1 (2009): 67–110; Talal Asad, "Thinking About Terrorism and Just War," *Cambridge Review of International Affairs* 23, no. 1 (2010): 3–24.

21. "Leonard Wood: Rough Rider, Surgeon, Architect of American Imperialism," www.c-span.org/video/?190324-1/leonard-wood-rough-rider-surgeon-architect -american-imperialism. In the book, McCallum describes the *juramentado* as "suicidal Islamic radicals." See Jack McCallum, *Leonard Wood: Rough Rider, Surgeon, Architect of American Imperialism* (New York: New York University Press, 2005), 214.

22. James R. Arnold, *The Moro War: How America Battled a Muslim Insurgency in the Philippine Jungle, 1902–1913* (New York: Bloomsbury, 2011). See also Charles Byler, "Pacifying the Moros: American Military Government in the Southern Philippines, 1899–1913," *Military Review* (May–June 2005): 41–45; and Miguel J. Hernández, "Kris vs. Krag," *Military History* 23 (2006): 58–65.

23. Max Boot is another notable exponent of this particular genre of historical illiteracy; see Max Boot, *The Savage Wars of Peace: Small Wars and the Rise of American Power* (New York: Basic Books, 2004).

24. See Susan Sontag, "Regarding the Torture of Others," *New York Times Magazine*, May 23, 2004; Dora Apel, "Torture Culture: Lynching Photographs and the Images of Abu Ghraib," *Art Journal* 64, no. 2 (2005): 88–100; and Errol Morris and Philip Gourevitch, *Standard Operating Procedure: A War Story* (New York: Penguin, 2008). See also Mark Boal, "The Kill Team: How US Soldiers in Afghanistan Murdered Innocent Civilians," *Rolling Stone*, March 28, 2011, www.rollingstone.com/politics/politics-news/the -kill-team-how-u-s-soldiers-in-afghanistan-murdered-innocent-civilians-169793.

25. See Crane, "Choosing Not to Look."

26. I am here referring to what Christopher Pinney describes as the "margins of excess." See Christopher Pinney, "Introduction: 'How the Other Half...,'" in *Photography's Other Histories*, ed. Christopher Pinney and Nicolas Peterson (Durham, NC: Duke University Press, 2003), 1–14. Elizabeth Edwards also speaks of "an energy at the edge of the frame"; see Edwards, "Interpreting Photographs: Some Thoughts on Method," in *Framing the Interpreter*, ed. Anxo Fernández-Ocampo and Michaela Wolf (New York: Routledge, 2014), 19–26.

27. See Wendy Kozol, "Battlefield Souvenirs and the Affective Politics of Recoil," *Photography and Culture* 5, no. 1 (2012): 21–36; and Molly Rogers, "Twice Captured: The Work of Atrocity Photography," in *The Routledge Companion to Photography Theory*, ed. Mark Durden and Jane Tormey (New York: Routledge, 2020), 228–242.

28. Joseph Conrad, "Heart of Darkness," in *Youth: A Narrative, and Two Other Stories* (Edinburgh: William Blackwood, 1902), 49–182.

29. Conrad, "Heart of Darkness," 133.

30. Conrad, 134.

Epilogue: Jolo 2022

1. Matthew C. Thompson, "Don't Go to Jolo," *Sydney Review of Books*, June 5–December 15, 2015, https://sydneyreviewofbooks.com/essay/dont-go-to-jolo. See also Patricio N. Abinales, "The Good Imperialists? American Military Presence in the Southern Philippines in Historical Perspective," *Philippine Studies* 52, no. 2 (2004): 179–207.

2. According to Edmund, there used to be an old man who cultivated a few crops inside the crater of Bud Dajo, and he had allegedly found gold coins and bits of kitchen utensils and other artifacts from the massacre, including pieces of burned rice, which were subsequently used as medicine.

3. According to Jainab, a similar incident took place during a local reenactment of the massacre in 2006.

4. Initiatives for International Dialogue, "Bud Dahu: Healing and Justice Is Sought for a 100-Year Old Injustice," March 29, 2006, https://iidnet.org/bud-dahu-healing-and -justice-is-sought-for-a-100-year-old-injustice.

5. Conversation with Jon Rudy, June 2023.

6. The photos displayed at Bud Dajo were the same as those shown by Rodrigo Duterte in 2016, which is to say that they included Gibbs's photo but also an image from Erzerum in 1895, along with a photograph taken during the US bombardment of Japanese positions on the mountain in 1945.

7. This version of the story was recorded by anthropologist Thomas Kiefer at some point in the twentieth century; see Oliveros, "Islam in the Moro-American War," 277–278.

8. "Soldier Correspondent."

Bibliography

Abbreviations

LOC   Library of Congress, Manuscripts Division (Washington, DC)
NARA   National Archives (College Park, MD)
USAHEC US Army Heritage and Education Center (Carlisle, PA)

Newspapers and Periodicals

Abilene (TX) Daily Chronicle
Albuquerque Citizen
Altoona (PA) Tribune
Anaconda (MT) Standard
Arizona Sentinel (Yuma)
Arkansas City Daily News
Army and Navy Life
Army and Navy Register
Atlanta Constitution
Baltimore Sun
Berliner Börsen-Zeitung
Boston Daily Advertiser
Boston Evening Transcript
Boston Globe
Buffalo Courier
Cablenews Manila
Californian (Salinas)
Cedar Falls (IA) Gazette
Chicago Tribune
Cincinnati Enquirer
Collier's
Colony (KS) Free Press
Commercial Appeal (Memphis, TN)
Courier (Cedar Falls, IA)

Crisis
Daily Arkansas Gazette (Little Rock)
Daily Democrat—Johnstown (PA)
Daily News (NY)
Daily Telegraph (UK)
Democrat and Chronicle (NY)
Eau Claire (WI) Leader
El Paso Herald
El Paso Sunday Times
Ellis (KS) Review
Evansville (IN) Press
Evening Star
Far Eastern Review
Fort Payne (AL) Journal
Garnet (KS) Journal Plaindealer
*General-Anzeiger der stadt Mannheim
    und Umgebung* (Germany)
Harper's Weekly
Hartford Courant
Hawaiian Star
Helena (MT) Independent
Honolulu Advertiser
Index
Indianapolis News

Journal and Tribune (TN)

Judge

Kansas City Star

Kentucky Advocate (Danville)

Lancaster (PA) Daily Intelligencer

Leavenworth (KS) Post

Leavenworth (KS) Times

Leslie's Weekly

Life

Literary Digest

Locomotief (Dutch East Indies)

Los Angeles Record

Manila Times

Melvern (KS) Review

Midland Daily Telegraph (Coventry, UK)

Mindanao Herald

Minneapolis Messenger

Monticellonian (Monticello, AR)

Morning Call (Allentown, PA)

Morristown (TN) Gazette

Nashville Banner

Nation

Nebraska State Journal (Lincoln)

New Ulm (MN) Review

New York Daily Tribune

New York Herald

New York Times

New York Times Magazine

New York Tribune

New York World

New Yorker

Ocala (FL) Evening Star

Omaha Daily Bee

Overland Monthly and Out West Magazine

Parsons (KS) Daily Eclipse

Pensacola (FL) News

Philadelphia Inquirer

Philadelphia Press

Pittsburgh Press

Punxsutawney (PA) News

Raleigh (NC) Times

Sacramento Sun

Salt Lake Telegram

Salt Lake Tribune

San Francisco Chronicle

San Francisco Examiner

Santa Barbara (CA) Daily News

Scranton (PA) Republican

Semi-Weekly Gazette (Hutchinson, KS)

Singapore Free Press and Mercantile Advertiser

Sioux City (IA) Journal

Slate

Soerabaijasch Handelsblad (Dutch East Indies)

St. Louis Post-Dispatch

St. Louis Republic

Star Press (IN)

Sterling (IL) Standard

Stevens Point (WI) Journal

Sun (NY)

Sunday Star (Washington, DC)

Sunday Times: Chattanooga (TN)

Sydney Review of Books

Tennessean (Nashville, TN)

Time

Times-Democrat (LA)

Time's Tribune (PA)

Topeka (KS) Daily Capital

Topeka (KS) State Journal

Victoria Daily Times

Washington Post

Washington Times

Weekly Republican (IN)

Wilkes-Barre (PA) Leader

Winfield (KS) Daily Courier

York (PA) Daily

Archival Material

Library of Congress, Manuscript Division (Washington, DC)

    Tasker H. Bliss Papers

    Frank R. McCoy Papers

    John J. Pershing Papers

    Theodore Roosevelt Papers

    Hugh Lenox Scott Papers

Moorfield Storey Papers

Leonard Wood Papers

Special Collections and University Archives, University of Massachusetts Amherst Libraries (Amherst, MA)

W. E. B. Du Bois Papers

Knight Library, University of Oregon (Eugene, OR)

John R. White Papers

Robert Fulton Research Collection

National Archives (College Park, MD)

File 1108562; RG 94, Entry 25, AGO Document File, 1890–1917

U.S. Army Heritage and Education Center (Carlisle, PA)

Edgar A. Stirmyer Collection

Rizal Library Special Collection, Ateneo de Manila University (Manila)

William C. Forbes Collection

Philippine Epics and Ballads Archive: http://epics.ateneo.edu

Printed Government Documents

An Account of the Engagement on Mount Dajo Between United States Forces and a Band of Moros (March 15, 1906). Senate Document Number 622, 59th Congress, 1st Session. Washington, DC: Government Printing Office, 1906, 1–2.

Additional Information of an Official Character with Reference to the Recent Engagement of American Forces with Moro Outlaws on Mount Dajo (March 21, 1906). Senate Document Number 278, 59th Congress, 1st Session. Washington, DC: Government Printing Office, 1906, 1–5.

Annual Report of Brigadier General John J. Pershing, US Army, Governor of the Moro Province, for the Year Ending June 30, 1911. Zamboanga: Mindanao Herald Publishing Company, 1911.

Annual Report of Major General George W. Davis, United States Army, Commanding Division of the Philippines from October 1, 1902 to July 26, 1903. Manila, P.I., 1903.

Complete Copies of All Communication That Have Been Received in or Sent from the War Department Pertaining to the Recent Attack by Troops of the United States on Mount Dajo (March 26, 1906). Senate Document Number 289, 59th Congress, 1st Session. Washington, DC: Government Printing Office, 1906, 1–11.

Congressional Record—House, March 15 and 19, 1906.

Congressional Record—Senate, March 14, 15, 21–23, and 26, 1906.

Hearings Before the Subcommittee on the Spanish War of the Committee on Veterans' Affairs, House of Representatives, Eighty-Fourth Congress First Session on H. R. 707, 714, 754, 2407, 2867, 2998, 3708, 4069, 4210, 4684, 4945, 5055, 5056, 5058, 5246, H. J. Res. 65, 94, 110, 115, 124, 151, 183, 190, 249, 281—miscellaneous bills relating to benefits for veterans (and their dependents) who served in the general period of the Spanish War, April 21 and 22, 1955. Washington, DC: Government Printing Office, 1955.

Pursuant to Senate Resolution No. 95, Copies of All Reports and Other Communications Between the War Department and the Officials of the Philippine Islands Respecting the Recent Attack by Troops of the United States on Mount Dajo (March 19, 1906). Senate Document Number 276, 59th Congress, 1st Session. Washington, DC: Government Printing Office, 1906, 1–3.

Report of Engagement with the Moro Enemy on Bud-Dajo, Island of Jolo, March 5th, 6th, 7th and 8th, 1906 (by Colonel Joseph W. Duncan), and *List of Appendices Accompanying Colonel*

Duncan's Report of Engagement with the Moro Enemy: file 1108562; RG 94, entry 25, AGO document file, 1890–1917, NARA (see also Folder 6, Box 217, Leonard Wood Papers, LOC).

"Report of General Wood as to Abrogation Bates Treaty, December 16, 1903," Exhibit T in *Annual Reports of the War Department for the Fiscal Year Ended June 30, 1903*, vol. 5: *Report of the Philippine Commission*. Washington, DC: Government Printing Office, 1903.

Primary Works

Ade, G. *The Sultan of Sulu: An Original Satire in Two Acts*. New York: R. H. Russell, 1903.

Aptheker, H., ed. *The Correspondence of W. E. B. Du Bois*, vol. 1: *Selections 1877–1934*. Amherst: Massachusetts University Press, 1973.

Bullard, R. L. "The Calibre of the Revolver." *Journal of the Military Service Institution for the United States* 36 (1905): 300–304.

Bullard, R. L. *Personalities and Reminiscences of the War*. Garden City: Doubleday, Page, 1925.

Callwell, C. E. *Small Wars: Their Principles and Practice*, 3rd ed. London: HMSO, 1906.

Catalogue of Copyright Entries—Part 4: Engravings, Cuts, and Prints; Chromos and Lithographs; Photographs; Fine Arts. Washington, DC: Government Printing Office, 1907.

Churchill, W. S. *The Story of the Malakand Field Force: An Episode of Frontier War*. London: Longmans, Green, 1898.

Colby, E. "How to Fight Savage Tribes." *American Journal of International Law* 21, no. 2 (1927): 279–288.

Conrad, J. "Heart of Darkness." In *Youth: A Narrative, and Two Other Stories*, 49–182. Edinburgh: William Blackwood, 1902.

Davis, B. "Mount Dajo Expedition." *Infantry Journal* 25 (July–December 1924): 250–256.

Dolph, E. A. *"Sound Off": Soldier Songs from Yankee Doodle to Parley Voo*. New York: Cosmopolitan, 1929.

Du Bois, W. E. B. *Dusk of Dawn: An Essay Toward an Autobiography of a Race Concept*. New York: Oxford University Press, 2007 (1940).

Du Bois, W. E. B. "My Evolving Program for Negro Freedom" (originally published 1944), *Clinical Sociology Review* 8, no. 1 (1990).

Duncan, J. W. "The Fight at Bud Dajo." In *Year Book: Eighth Annual Reunion Army of the Philippines*. Kansas City: Camp Louis A. Craig, August 1907.

Dwight, H. O. "Our Mohammedan Wards." *Forum* 29 (March 1900): 15–31.

Ellett, F. G. *A Modern Hamilton*. Detroit: Frank H. West, 1912.

Foreman, J. *The Philippine Islands*. London: S. Low, Marston, 1899.

Freeman, E. "The Waco Horror." Supplement, *Crisis*, July 1916, 1–8.

Frothingham, R. *Around the World—Friendly Guide for the World Traveler*. Boston: Houghton Mifflin, 1925.

Givens, J. D. *Scenes Taken in the Philippines, Japan and on the Pacific—Relating to Soldiers*. N.p., 1910, 1912, and 1914.

Hicks, J. W. "Colonel John R. White: Keeper of Your National Playground, Says 'Any Man Can Succeed—If He Wants To!'" *Overland Monthly and Out West Magazine* 90, no. 3 (April 1932): 77–78, 82, 94.

Hobbs, H. P. *Kris and Krag: Adventures Among the Moros of the Southern Philippine Islands*. Self-published 1962, revised as *Kris and Krag: The Moro Campaigns*, 1964, https://emu.usahec.org/alma/multimedia/245537/20182903MN000263.pdf.

Hurley, V. *The Swish of the Kris: The Story of the Moros*. New York: E. P. Dutton, 1936.

Hurley, V. *Jungle Patrol: The Story of the Philippine Constabulary.* New York: E. P. Dutton, 1938.

Ingersoll, W. "Oral History Interview of W. E. B. Du Bois by William Ingersoll (1960)." W. E. B. Du Bois Papers (MS 312), Special Collections and University Archives, University of Massachusetts Amherst Libraries, https://credo.library.umass.edu/view/full/mums312-b237-i137.

Kann, R. *Journal d'un Correspondant de Guerre en Extrême-Orient: Japon, Mandchourie, Corée.* Paris: Calmann-Lévy, 1905.

Kann, R. "Voyages et Combat dans le Sud des Philippines." *Le Tour Du Monde* 13, n.s. no. 11 (March 16, 1907): 121–132, and no. 12 (March 23, 1907): 133–143.

Kipling, R. "The White Man's Burden." *McClure's* 12, no. 4 (February 1899): 290–291.

Landor, A. H. S. *The Gems of the East: Sixteen Thousand Miles of Research Travel Among Wild and Tame Tribes of Enchanting Islands.* New York: Harper & Brothers, 1904.

Lawton, E. P. *A Saga of the South.* Ft. Myers Beach, FL: Island, 1965.

Medal of Honor Recipients, 1863–1978. Washington, DC: US Government Printing Office, 1979.

Miles, P. L. *Fallen Leaves: Memories of an Old Soldier.* Berkeley, CA: Wuerth, 1961.

Montano, J. "Voyage aux Philippines." *Le Tour du Monde* 47 (1884).

Moorehead, W. K. "The Indian Messiah and the Ghost Dance." *American Antiquarian and Oriental Journal* 13 (January–November 1891): 161–167.

The Official Blue Book of the Jamestown Ter-centennial Exposition, A. D. 1907. Norfolk, VA: Colonial, 1909.

Orosa, S. Y. *The Sulu Archipelago and Its People.* Yonkers, NY: World Book, 1931.

Roosevelt, K. *The Long Trail.* New York: Review of Reviews, Metropolitan Magazine, 1921.

Roosevelt, T. *The Winning of the West,* 4 vols. New York: G. P. Putnam's Sons, 1889–1896.

Ross, J. D. *Sixty Years: Life and Adventure in the Far East,* 2 vols. New York: E. P. Dutton, 1911.

Runyon, D. *The Tents of Trouble.* New York: Desmond FitzGerald, 1911.

Russell, W. H. *My Diary in India, in the Year 1858–9,* 2 vols. London: Routledge, Warne, and Routledge, 1860.

Saleeby, N. *Studies in Moro History, Law, and Religion.* Manila: Bureau of Public Printing, 1905.

Saleeby, N. *The History of Sulu.* Manila: Bureau of Printing, 1908.

Saleeby, N. *The Moro Problem: An Academic Discussion of the History and Solution of the Problem of the Government of the Moros of the Philippine Islands.* Manila: E. C. McCullough, 1913.

Sanford, W. L. "Battle of Bud Dajo: 6 March 1906." *Indiana Military History Journal* 7, no. 1 (January 1982).

Scott, H. L. "The Skilled Packer." *Journal of the US Cavalry Association* 17 (July 1906–April 1907): 518–520.

Scott, H. L. *Some Memories of a Soldier.* New York: Century, 1928.

See! See! See! Guide to Jamestown Exposition, Historic Virginia and Washington. Washington, DC: Byron S. Adams, 1907.

Steevens, G. W. *With Kitchener to Khartoum.* Edinburgh: William Blackwood and Sons, 1898.

Stevenson, B. E., ed. *Poems of American History.* Boston: Houghton Mifflin, 1908.

Storey, M. *The Philippine Policy of Secretary Taft.* Boston: Anti-Imperialist League, 1904.

Storey, M. *The Moro Massacre.* Boston: Anti-Imperialist League, 1906.

Twain, M. "To the Person Sitting in Darkness." *North American Review* 172 (February 1901): 161–176.

Twain, M. *King Leopold's Soliloquy: A Defense of His Congo Rule.* Boston: P. R. Warren, 1905.

Twain, M. *Mark Twain's Autobiography, with an Introduction by Albert Bigelow Paine.* New York: Harper & Brothers, 1924.

"Untold Tales of the Navy by Ex-Marines in the US Navy." *International Socialist Review* 13, no. 5 (November 1912): 400–407.

The US Army/Marine Corps Counterinsurgency Field Manual. Chicago: University of Chicago Press, 2007.

Villard, O. G. *Fighting Years: Memoirs of a Liberal Editor.* New York: Harcourt, Brace, 1939.

Wells, I. B. *A Red Record: Tabulated Statistics and Alleged Causes of Lynchings in the United States, 1892–1893–1894.* Chicago: Donohue & Henneberry, 1895.

White, J. R. *Bullets and Bolos: Fifteen Years in the Philippine Islands.* New York: Century, 1928.

Wood, L., Jr. "A Woman of the Tropics." *Harvard Advocate* 96, no. 1 (September 26, 1913): 46–48.

Worcester, D. C. "The Malay Pirates of the Philippines." *Century* 56, no. 5 (1898): 690–702.

Wright, H. M. "The Awful Slaughter of 1,000 Moro Bandits—Men, Women, and Children." *Leslie's Weekly*, May 10, 1906.

Wright, H. M. *A Handbook of the Philippines.* Chicago: A. C. McClurg, 1907.

Secondary Works

Abbenhuis, M., B. Bogdan, and E. Wordsworth. "Humanitarian Bullets and Man-Killers: Revisiting the History of Arms Regulation in the Late Nineteenth Century." *International Review of the Red Cross* 920–921 (November 2022): 1684–1707.

Abinales, P. N. "The Good Imperialists? American Military Presence in the Southern Philippines in Historical Perspective." *Philippine Studies* 52, no. 2 (2004): 179–207.

Abinales, P. N. "The US Army as an Occupying Force in Muslim Mindanao, 1899–1913." In *Colonial Crucible: Empire in the Making of the Modern American State*, edited by A. W. McCoy and F. A. Scarano, 410–420. Madison: University of Wisconsin Press, 2009.

Abinales, P. N., and N. G. Quimpo, eds. *The US and the War on Terror in the Philippines.* Manila: Anvil, 2008.

Abraham, A. "Bai Bureh, the British, and the Hut Tax War." *International Journal of African Historical Studies* 7, no. 1 (1974): 99–106.

Adas, M. *Prophets of Rebellion: Millenarian Protest Movements Against the European Colonial Order.* Chapel Hill: University of North Carolina Press, 1979.

Adeleye, R. A. "Mahdist Triumph and British Revenge in Northern Nigeria: Satiru 1906." *Journal of the Historical Society of Nigeria* 6, no. 2 (1972): 193–214.

Adelman, J. "Don't Look Away: Photography and Humanitarianism." *Aeon*, September 12, 2017, https://aeon.co/essays/does-photography-make-us-act-or-inure-us-to-despair.

Afsaruddin, A. *Striving in the Path of God: Jihād and Martyrdom in Islamic Thought.* New York: Oxford University Press, 2013.

Allen, J., H. Als, J. Lewis, and L. F. Litwack. *Without Sanctuary: Lynching Photography in America.* Santa Fe: Twin Palms, 2000.

Amirell, S. E. "'An Extremely Mild Form of Slavery . . . of the Worst Sort': American Perceptions of Slavery in the Sulu Sultanate, 1899–1904." *Slavery & Abolition* 43, no. 3 (2022): 517–532.

Amirell, S. E. "Pirates and Pearls: Jikiri and the Challenge to Maritime Security and American Sovereignty in the Sulu Archipelago, 1907–1909." *International Journal of Maritime History* 29, no. 1 (2017): 44–67.

Amoroso, D. J. "Inheriting the 'Moro Problem': Muslim Authority and Colonial Rule in British Malaya and the Philippines." In *The American Colonial State in the Philippines: Global Perspectives*, edited by Julian Go and Anne L. Foster, 118–147. Durham, NC: Duke University Press, 2003.

Anderson, D. L., ed. *Facing My Lai: Moving Beyond the Massacre*. Kansas City: University Press of Kansas, 1998.

Angeles, V. "Moros in the Media and Beyond: Representations of Philippine Muslims." *Contemporary Islam* 4 (2010): 29–53.

Apel, D. "On Looking: Lynching Photographs and Legacies of Lynching After 9/11." *American Quarterly* 55, no. 3 (September 2003): 457–478.

Apel, D. "Torture Culture: Lynching Photographs and the Images of Abu Ghraib." *Art Journal* 64, no. 2 (2005): 88–100.

Arnold, J. R. *The Moro War: How America Battled a Muslim Insurgency in the Philippine Jungle, 1902–1913*. New York: Bloomsbury, 2011.

Asad, T. "Thinking About Terrorism and Just War." *Cambridge Review of International Affairs* 23, no. 1 (2010): 3–24.

Asain, C. A. "The Tausug Parang Sabil Kissa as Literary, Cultural, and Historical Materials." *Journal of History* 52, no. 1 (2006): 245–281.

Aune, S. *Indian Wars Everywhere: Colonial Violence and the Shadow Doctrines of Empire*. Berkeley: University of California Press, 2023.

Axtell, J., and W. C. Sturtevant. "The Unkindest Cut, or Who Invented Scalping." *William and Mary Quarterly* 37, no. 3 (July 1980): 451–472.

Axter, F. "'. . . Will Try to Send You the Best Views from Here': Postcards from the Colonial War in Namibia (1904–1908)." In *German Colonialism, Visual Culture, and Modern Memory*, edited by V. Langbehn, 67–82. New York: Routledge, 2010.

Azoulay, A. *The Civil Contract of Photography*. New York: Zone, 2008.

Azoulay, A. *Potential History: Unlearning Imperialism*. London: Verso, 2019.

Bacevich, A. J. *Diplomat in Khaki: Major General Frank Ross McCoy and American Foreign Policy, 1898–1949*. Lawrence: University Press of Kansas, 1989.

Bacevich, A. J. "Disagreeable Work: Pacifying the Moros, 1903–1906." *Military Review* 85, no. 3 (2005): 41–45.

Balce, N. S. "The Filipina's Breast: Savagery, Docility, and the Erotics of the American Empire." *Social Text* 24, no. 2 (June 2006): 89–110.

Balce, N. S. *Body Parts of Empire: Visual Abjection, Filipino Images, and the American Archive*. Ann Arbor: University of Michigan Press, 2016.

Barkawi, T. *Soldiers of Empire*. Cambridge: Cambridge University Press, 2017.

Barter, S., and I. Zatkin-Osburn. "Shrouded: Islam, War, and Holy War in Southeast Asia." *Journal for the Scientific Study of Religion* 53, no. 1 (2014): 187–201.

Barth, V., and R. Cvetkovski, eds. *Imperial Cooperation and Transfer, 1870–1930: Empires and Encounters*. London: Bloomsbury, 2015.

Batchen, G., and J. Prosser, eds. *Picturing Atrocity: Photography in Crisis*. London: Reaktion, 2012.

Bederman, G. *Manliness & Civilization: A Cultural History of Gender and Race in the United States, 1880–1917*. Chicago: University of Chicago Press, 1995.

Berardi, G., and I. Milazzo. *L'uomo delle Filippine*. Edizioni Cepim, 1980.

Berger, J. "Photographs of Agony." In *About Looking*, 3–40. New York: Pantheon, 1980.

Bijl, P. *Emerging Memory: Photographs of Colonial Atrocity in Dutch Cultural Remembrance.* Amsterdam: Amsterdam University Press, 2015.

Bijl, P. "Saving the Children? The Ethical Policy and Photographs of Colonial Atrocity During the Aceh War." In *Photography, Modernity and the Governed in Late-Colonial Indonesia*, edited by Susie Protschky, 103–130. Amsterdam: Amsterdam University Press, 2015.

Bilton, M., and K. Sim. *Four Hours in My Lai*. New York: Penguin, 1992.

Bjork, K. *Prairie Imperialists: The Indian Country Origins of American Empire*. Philadelphia: University of Pennsylvania Press, 2018.

Blackhawk, N. *Violence over the Land: Indians and Empires in the Early American West*. Cambridge, MA: Harvard University Press, 2008.

Boot, M. *The Savage Wars of Peace: Small Wars and the Rise of American Power*. New York: Basic Books, 2004.

Brantlinger, P. "Kipling's 'The White Man's Burden' and Its Afterlives." *English Literature in Transition, 1880–1920* 50, no. 2 (2007): 172–191.

Brewer, S. A. *Why America Fights: Patriotism and War Propaganda from the Philippines to Iraq*. New York: Oxford University Press, 2009.

Brody, D. *Visualizing American Empire: Orientalism and Imperialism in the Philippines*. Chicago: University of Chicago Press, 2010.

Brower, B. C. *A Desert Named Peace: The Violence of France's Empire in the Algerian Sahara, 1844–1902*. New York: Columbia University Press, 2009.

Brower, M. "Trophy Shots: Early North American Photographs of Nonhuman Animals and the Display of Masculine Prowess." *Society and Animals* 13, no. 1 (2005): 1–32.

Brown, D. *Bury My Heart at Wounded Knee: An Indian History of the American West*. New York: Holt, Rinehart & Winston, 1970.

Burns, K. "Being American Means Reckoning with Our Violent History." *Washington Post*, November 22, 2021.

Burrow, M. "The Imperial Souvenir: Things and Masculinities in H. Rider Haggard's *King Solomon's Mines* and *Allan Quatermain*." *Journal of Victorian Culture* 18, no. 1 (2013): 72–92.

Butler, J. *Frames of War: When Is Life Grievable?* London: Verso, 2009.

Byler, C. "Pacifying the Moros: American Military Government in the Southern Philippines, 1899–1913." *Military Review* (May–June 2005): 41–45.

Capeci, D. J., Jr., and J. C. Knight. "Reactions to Colonialism: The North American Ghost Dance and East African Maji-Maji Rebellions." *Historian* 52, no. 4 (1990): 584–601.

Capozzola, C. *Visualizing Cultures: Photography & Power in the Colonial Philippines*. Massachusetts Institute of Technology, 2017.

Carrington, Michael. "Officers, Gentlemen and Thieves: The Looting of Monasteries During the 1903/4 Younghusband Mission to Tibet." *Modern Asian Studies* 37, no. 1 (2003): 81–109.

Charbonneau, O. "'A New West in Mindanao': Settler Fantasies on the US Imperial Fringe." *Journal of the Gilded Age and Progressive Era* 18, no. 3 (2019): 304–323.

Charbonneau, O. *Civilizational Imperatives: Americans, Moros, and the Colonial World*. Ithaca, NY: Cornell University Press, 2020.

Charbonneau, O. "The Permeable South: Imperial Interactivities in the Islamic Philippines, 1899–1930s." In *Crossing Empires: Taking US History into Transimperial Terrain*, edited by K. L. Hoganson and J. Sexton, 183–202. Durham, NC: Duke University Press, 2020.

Charbonneau, O. "Visiting the Metropole: Muslim Colonial Subjects in the United States, 1904–1927." *Diplomatic History* 42, no. 2 (2018): 204–227.

Choi, S. "Silencing Survivors' Narratives: Why Are We Again Forgetting the No Gun Ri Story?" *Rhetoric & Public Affairs* 11, no. 3 (2008): 367–388.

Clancy-Smith, J. A. *Rebel and Saint: Muslim Notables, Populist Protest, Colonial Encounters.* Berkeley: University of California Press, 1994.

Cohen, P. A. *History in Three Keys: The Boxers as Event, Experience, and Myth.* New York: Columbia University Press, 1997.

Cole, T. "When the Camera Was a Weapon of Imperialism (And When It Still Is)." *New York Times Magazine*, February 6, 2019, www.nytimes.com/2019/02/06/magazine /when-the-camera-was-a-weapon-of-imperialism-and-when-it-still-is.html.

Condos, M. "Fanaticism and the Politics of Resistance Along the North-West Frontier of British India." *Comparative Studies in Society and History* 58, no. 3 (2016): 717–745.

Condos, M. "Licence to Kill: The Murderous Outrages Act and the Rule of Law in Colonial India, 1867–1925." *Modern Asian Studies* 50, no. 2 (2016): 479–517.

Cookman, C. "An American Atrocity: The My Lai Massacre Concretized in a Victim's Face." *Journal of American History* 1 (June 2007): 154–162.

Coppola, E. *Notes: On the Making of* Apocalypse Now. London: Faber and Faber, 1995.

Crane, S. A. "Choosing Not to Look: Representation, Repatriation, and Holocaust Atrocity Photography." *History and Theory* 47, no. 3 (2008): 309–330.

Cutlip, S. M. *The Unseen Power: Public Relations. A History.* Hillsdale, NJ: Lawrence Erlbaum, 1994.

Dale, S. F. "Religious Suicide in Islamic Asia: Anticolonial Terrorism in India, Indonesia, and the Philippines." *Journal of Conflict Resolution* 32, no. 1 (1988): 37–59.

Dawes, J. *Evil Men.* Cambridge, MA: Harvard University Press, 2013.

De Quesada, A., and S. Walsh. *The Spanish-American War and Philippine Insurrection 1898–1902.* London: Osprey, 2012.

Dean, C. J. "Atrocity Photographs, Dignity, and Human Vulnerability." *Humanity: An International Journal of Human Rights, Humanitarianism, and Development* 6, no. 2 (2015): 239–264.

Drinnon, R. *Facing West: The Metaphysics of Indian-Hating and Empire-Building.* Minneapolis: University of Minnesota Press, 1980.

Dwyer, P., and A. Nettelbeck, eds. *Violence, Colonialism, and Empire in the Modern World.* Basingstoke: Palgrave Macmillan, 2018.

Edgerton, R. K. *American Datu: John J. Pershing and Counterinsurgency Warfare in the Muslim Philippines, 1899–1913.* Lexington: University Press of Kentucky, 2020.

Edwards, E. *The Camera as Historian: Amateur Photographers and Historical Imagination, 1885–1918.* Durham, NC: Duke University Press, 2012.

Edwards, E. "Interpreting Photographs: Some Thoughts on Method." In *Framing the Interpreter*, edited by Anxo Fernández-Ocampo and Michaela Wolf, 19–26. New York: Routledge, 2014.

Edwards, E., and J. Hart. eds. *Photographs Objects Histories: On the Materiality of Images.* London: Routledge, 2004.

Einolf, C. J. *America in the Philippines, 1899–1902: The First Torture Scandal.* New York: Palgrave Macmillan, 2014.

Eisenhower, J. S. D. *Teddy Roosevelt & Leonard Wood: Partners in Command.* Columbia: University of Missouri Press, 2014.

Eyerman, R. "Perpetrator Trauma and Collective Guilt: The My Lai Massacre." In *Memory, Trauma, and Identity*, 167–194. New York: Palgrave Macmillan, 2019.

Fabian, A. *The Skull Collectors: Race, Science, and America's Unburied Dead*. Chicago: University of Chicago Press, 2010.

Federspiel, H. M. "Islam and Muslims in the Southern Territories of the Philippine Islands During the American Colonial Period." *Journal of Southeast Asian Studies* 29, no. 2 (September 1998): 340–356.

Field, R., and R. Hook. *Spanish-American War 1898*. London: Brassey's, 1998.

Foliard, D. *The Violence of Colonial Photography*. Manchester: Manchester University Press, 2022. Translated from *Combattre, punir, photographier: Empires coloniaux, 1890–1914*. Paris: La Découverte, 2020.

Fujii, L. A. "The Puzzle of Extra-lethal Violence." *Perspectives on Politics* 11, no. 2 (2013): 410–426.

Fujii, L. A. *Show Time: The Logic and Power of Violent Display*, edited by Martha Finnemore. Ithaca, NY: Cornell University Press, 2021.

Fulton, R. A. *Moroland: The History of Uncle Sam and the Moros, 1899–1920*. Bend, OR: Tumalo Creek, 2007.

Fulton, R. A. *Honor for the Flag: The Battle for Bud Dajo—1906 and the Moro Massacre*. Bend, OR: Tumalo Creek, 2011.

Fussell, P. *Wartime: Understanding and Behavior in the Second World War*. New York: Oxford University Press, 1989.

Galbraith, J. S. "Appeals to the Supernatural: African and New Zealand Comparisons with the Ghost Dance." *Pacific Historical Review* 51, no. 2 (1982): 115–133.

Gallois, W. "Dahra and the History of Violence in Early Colonial Algeria." In *The French Colonial Mind*, vol. 2: *Violence, Military Encounters, and Colonialism*, edited by Martin Thomas, 3–25. Lincoln: University of Nebraska Press, 2011.

Gedacht, J. "'Mohammedan Religion Made It Necessary to Fire': Massacres on the American Imperial Frontier from South Dakota to the Southern Philippines." In *Colonial Crucible: Empire in the Making of the Modern American State*, edited by A. W. McCoy and F. A. Scarano, 397–409. Madison: University of Wisconsin Press, 2009.

Gedacht, J. "Holy War, Progress, and 'Modern Mohammedans' in Colonial Southeast Asia." *Muslim World* 105, no. 4 (2015): 446–471.

Giblin, J., and J. Monson, eds. *Maji Maji: Lifting the Fog of War*. Leiden: Brill, 2010.

Gidley, M. "Visible and Invisible Scars of Wounded Knee." In *Picturing Atrocity: Photography in Crisis*, edited by G. Batchen and J. Prosser, 25–38. London: Reaktion, 2012.

Goldsworthy, P. "Images, Ideologies, and Commodities: The French Colonial Postcard Industry in Morocco." *Early Popular Visual Culture* 8, no. 2 (2010): 147–167.

Gordon, M. "Viewing Violence in the British Empire: Images of Atrocity from the Battle of Omdurman, 1898." *Journal of Perpetrator Research* 2, no. 2 (2019): 65–100.

Gordon, M. *Extreme Violence and the "British Way": Colonial Warfare in Perak, Sierra Leone and Sudan*. London: Bloomsbury Academic, 2020.

Gowing, P. G. *Mandate in Moroland: The American Government of Muslim Filipinos, 1899–1920*. Quezon City, Philippines: New Day, 1983.

Gray, T., and B. Martin. "My Lai: The Struggle over Outrage." *Peace & Change* 33, no. 1 (2008): 90–113.

Gregory, D. *The Colonial Present: Afghanistan. Palestine. Iraq*. Oxford: Blackwell, 2004.

Grenier, J. *The First Way of War: American War Making on the Frontier, 1607–1814*. Cambridge: Cambridge University Press, 2005.

Gross, J. T., and I. G. Gross. *Golden Harvest: Events at the Periphery of the Holocaust*. Oxford: Oxford University Press, 2016.

Grua, D. W. *Surviving Wounded Knee: The Lakotas and the Politics of Memory*. Oxford: Oxford University Press, 2016.

Guy, J. *Remembering the Rebellion: The Zulu Uprising of 1906*. Scottsville, South Africa: University of KwaZulu-Natal Press, 2006.

Hagedorn, H. *Leonard Wood, a Biography*. New York: Harper & Brothers, 1931.

Hagopan, P. "Vietnam War Photography as a Locus of Memory." In *Locating Memory: Photographic Acts*, edited by Annette Kuhn and Kirsten McAllister, 201–222. New York: Berghahn, 2006.

Harriman, R., and J. L. Lucaites. *No Caption Needed: Iconic Photographs, Public Culture and Liberal Democracy*. Chicago: University of Chicago Press, 2011.

Harris, S. K. *God's Arbiters: Americans and the Philippines, 1898–1902*. Oxford: Oxford University Press, 2011.

Harrison, S. "Skull Trophies of the Pacific War: Transgressive Objects of Remembrance." *Journal of the Royal Anthropological Institute* 12, no. 4 (2006): 817–836.

Harrison, S. *Dark Trophies: Hunting and the Enemy Body in Modern War*. Oxford: Berghahn, 2012.

Hartman, S. "Venus in Two Acts." *Small Axe* 12, no. 2 (2008): 1–14.

Hasian, M. A., Jr. *President Trump and General Pershing: Remembrances of the "Moro" Insurrection in the Age of Post-truths*. New York: Palgrave Pivot, 2018.

Hawkins, M. C. "Managing a Massacre: Savagery, Civility, and Gender in Moro Province in the Wake of Bud Dajo." *Philippine Studies* 59, no. 1 (2011): 83–105.

Hawkins, M. C. *Making Moros: Imperial Historicism and American Military Rule in the Philippines' Muslim South*. DeKalb: Northern Illinois University Press, 2013.

Hawkins, M. C. *Semi-civilized: The Moro Village at the Louisiana Purchase Exposition*. Ithaca, NY: Cornell University Press, 2020.

Hernández, M. J. "Kris vs. Krag." *Military History* 23 (2006): 58–65.

Hevia, J. "Looting Beijing: 1860, 1900." In *Tokens of Exchange: The Problem of Translation in Global Circulations*, edited by Lydia H. Liu, Stanley Fish, and Fredric Jameson, 192–213. Durham, NC: Duke University Press, 1999.

Hicks, D. *The Brutish Museums: The Benin Bronzes, Colonial Violence and Cultural Restitution*. London: Pluto, 2020.

Higonnet, M. R. "Souvenirs of Death." *Journal of War and Culture Studies* 1, no. 1 (2008): 65–78.

Hoganson, K. L. *Fighting for American Manhood: How Gender Politics Provoked the Spanish-American and Philippine-American Wars*. New Haven, CT: Yale University Press, 2000.

Hoganson, K. L., and J. Sexton, eds. *Crossing Empires: Taking US History into Transimperial Terrain*. Durham, NC: Duke University Press, 2020.

Holtschneider, K. H. "Victims, Perpetrators, Bystanders? Witnessing, Remembering and the Ethics of Representation in Museums of the Holocaust." *Holocaust Studies* 13, no. 1 (2007): 82–102.

Hopkins, A. G. *American Empire: A Global History*. Princeton, NJ: Princeton University Press, 2018.

Hoskins, J. "Postcards from the Edge of Empire: Images and Messages from French Indochina." *SPAFA Journal* 18, no. 1 (2008): 19–25.

Hull, I. V. *Absolute Destruction: Military Culture and the Practices of War in Imperial Germany*. Ithaca, NY: Cornell University Press, 2006.

Hynes, S. *The Soldier's Tale: Bearing Witness to Modern War*. London: Pimlico, 1998.

Hyslop, J. "The Invention of the Concentration Camp: Cuba, Southern Africa and the Philippines, 1896–1907." *South African Historical Journal* 63, no. 2 (2011): 251–276.

Ignacio, A., E. de la Cruz, J. Emmanuel, and H. Toribio. *The Forbidden Book: The Philippine-American War in Political Cartoons*. San Francisco: T'boli, 2004.

Immerwahr, D. *How to Hide an Empire: A History of the Greater United States*. New York: Farrar, Straus and Giroux, 2019.

Ingilan, S. S. "Tausug's Identity in Parang Sabil: A Critical Discourse Analysis." *CMU Journal of Science* 22, no. 1 (January–December 2018): 37–43.

Initiatives for International Dialogue. "Bud Dahu: Healing and Justice Is Sought for a 100-Year Old Injustice." March 29, 2006, https://iidnet.org/bud-dahu-healing -and-justice-is-sought-for-a-100-year-old-injustice.

Jacoby, K. "Of Memory and Massacre: A Soldier's Firsthand Account of the 'Affair on Wounded Knee.'" *Princeton University Library Chronicle* 64, no. 2 (2003): 333–362.

Jacoby, K. "'The Broad Platform of Extermination': Nature and Violence in the Nineteenth Century North American Borderlands." *Journal of Genocide Research* 10, no. 2 (2008): 249–267.

Jacoby, K. *Shadows at Dawn: An Apache Massacre and the Violence of History*. New York: Penguin, 2009.

Jacoby, K. "'The Bloody Ground': Nineteenth-Century Frontier Genocides in the United States." In *The Cambridge World History of Genocide*, edited by N. Blackhawk, B. Kiernan, B. Madley, and R. Taylor, 3:383–411. Cambridge: Cambridge University Press, 2023.

Jakob, J. B. "Beyond Abu Ghraib: War Trophy Photography and Commemorative Violence." *Media, War & Conflict* 10, no. 1 (2017): 87–104.

Jensen, R. E., R. E. Paul, and J. E. Carter. *Eyewitness at Wounded Knee*. Lincoln: University of Nebraska Press, 2011.

Jones, H. *My Lai: Vietnam, 1968, and the Descent into Darkness*. New York: Oxford University Press, 2017.

Juzda, E. "Skulls, Science, and the Spoils of War: Craniological Studies at the United States Army Medical Museum, 1868–1900." *Studies in History and Philosophy of Biological and Biomedical Sciences* 40, no. 3 (2009): 156–167.

Kalof, L., and A. Fitzgerald. "Reading the Trophy: Exploring the Display of Dead Animals in Hunting Magazines." *Visual Studies* 18, no. 2 (2003): 112–122.

Kamissek, C., and J. Kreienbaum. "An Imperial Cloud? Conceptualising Interimperial Connections and Transimperial Knowledge." *Journal of Modern European History* 14, no. 2 (2016): 164–182.

Kaplan, A., and D. E. Pease, eds. *Cultures of United States Imperialism*. Durham, NC: Duke University Press, 1993.

Kiefer, T. M. "Reciprocity and Revenge in the Philippines: Some Preliminary Remarks About the Tausug of Jolo." *Philippine Sociological Review* 16, nos. 3/4 (1968): 124–131.

Kiefer, T. M. "Modes of Social Action in Armed Combat: Affect, Tradition and Reason in Tausug Private Warfare." *Man* 5, no. 4 (1970): 586–596.

Kiefer, T. M. *The Tausug, Violence and Law in a Philippine Moslem Society*. New York: Holt, Rinehart and Winston, 1972.

Kiefer, T. M. "Parrang Sabbil: Ritual Suicide Among the Tausug of Jolo." *Bijdragen tot de Taal-, Land- en Volkenkunde*, 1ste Afl (1973): 108–123.

Kiernan, B. *Blood and Soil: A World History of Genocide and Extermination from Sparta to Darfur*. New Haven, CT: Yale University Press, 2007.

Kinsella, H. *The Image Before the Weapon: A Critical History of the Distinction Between Combatant and Civilian*. Ithaca, NY: Cornell University Press, 2011.

Kinsella, H. "Settler Empire and the United States: Francis Lieber on the Laws of War." *American Political Science Review* 117, no. 2 (2023): 629–642.

Kirschke, A. H. *Art in Crisis: W. E. B. Du Bois and the Struggle for African American Identity and Memory*. Bloomington: Indiana University Press, 2009.

Klein, C. "'Everything of Interest in the Late Pine Ridge War Are Held by Us for Sale': Popular Culture and Wounded Knee." *Western Historical Quarterly* 25, no. 1 (Spring 1994): 45–68.

Kloos, D. "A Crazy State: Violence, Psychiatry, and Colonialism in Aceh, Indonesia, ca. 1910–1942." *Bijdragen tot de Taal-, Land- en Volkenkunde/Journal of the Humanities and Social Sciences of Southeast Asia* 170, no. 1 (2014): 25–65.

Kohout, A. *Taking the Field: Soldiers, Nature, and Empire on American Frontiers*. Lincoln: University of Nebraska Press, 2023.

Kolsky, E. "The Colonial Rule of Law and the Legal Regime of Exception: Frontier 'Fanaticism' and State Violence in British India." *American Historical Review* 120, no. 4 (October 2015): 1218–1246.

Koole, S. "Photography as Event: Power, the Kodak Camera, and Territoriality in Early Twentieth-Century Tibet." *Comparative Studies in Society and History* 59, no. 2 (2017): 310–345.

Kozol, W. "Battlefield Souvenirs and the Affective Politics of Recoil." *Photography and Culture* 5, no. 1 (2012): 21–36.

Kramer, P. A. "Empires, Exceptions, and Anglo-Saxons: Race and Rule Between the British and United States Empires, 1880–1910." *Journal of American History* 88, no. 4 (2002): 1315–1353.

Kramer, P. A. *The Blood of Government: Race, Empire, the United States, and the Philippines* (Chapel Hill: University of North Carolina Press, 2006).

Kramer, P. A. "Race-Making and Colonial Violence in the US Empire: The Philippine-American War as Race War." *Diplomatic History* 30, no. 2 (2006): 169–210.

Kramer, P. A. "An Enemy You Can Depend On: Trump, Pershing's Bullets, and the Folklore of the War on Terror." *Asia-Pacific Journal* 15, no. 4 (2017): 3–9.

Krause, J. "Islam and Anti-colonial Rebellions in North and West Africa, 1914–1918." *Historical Journal* 64, no. 3 (2021): 674–695.

Kreienbaum, J. "Deadly Learning? Concentration Camps in Colonial Wars Around 1900." In *Imperial Cooperation and Transfer, 1870–1930: Empires and Encounters*, edited by Volker Barth and Roland Cvetkovski, 219–235. London: Bloomsbury, 2015.

Kreike, E. "Genocide in the Kampongs? Dutch Nineteenth Century Colonial Warfare in Aceh, Sumatra." *Journal of Genocide Research* 14, nos. 3–4 (2012): 297–315.

Kuß, S. *German Colonial Wars and the Context of Military Violence*. Cambridge, MA: Harvard University Press, 2017.

Lane, J. C. *Armed Progressive: General Leonard Wood*. Lincoln: University of Nebraska Press, 2009.

Langford, M. *Suspended Conversations: The Afterlife of Memory in Photographic Albums*. Montreal: McGill-Queen's University Press, 2001.

Lewinski, J. *The Camera at War: A History of War Photography from 1848 to the Present Day*. London: W. H. Allen, 1978.

Lindqvist, S. *Exterminate All the Brutes*. London: New Press, 1997.

Linn, B. M. *The Philippine War, 1898–1902*. Lawrence: University Press of Kansas, 2000.

Linstrum, E. *Age of Emergency: Living with Violence at the End of the British Empire*. Oxford: Oxford University Press, 2023.

Lower, W. *The Ravine: A Family, a Photograph, a Holocaust Massacre Revealed*. New York: Houghton Mifflin Harcourt, 2021.

Lydon, J. "'Behold the Tears': Photography as Colonial Witness." *History of Photography* 34, no. 3 (2010): 234–250.

Lydon, J. *The Flash of Recognition: Photography and the Emergence of Indigenous Rights*. Sydney: New South, 2012.

MacKenzie, M. "Why Do Soldiers Swap Illicit Pictures? How a Visual Discourse Analysis Illuminates Military Band of Brother Culture." *Security Dialogue* 51, no. 4 (2020): 340–357.

Madley, B. *An American Genocide: The United States and the California Indian Catastrophe, 1846–1873*. New Haven, CT: Yale University Press, 2016.

Mahone, S. "The Psychology of Rebellion: Colonial Medical Responses to Dissent in British East Africa." *Journal of African History* 47, no. 2 (2006): 241–258.

Mamdani, M. *Good Muslim, Bad Muslim*. New York: Pantheon, 2004.

Marks, S. *Reluctant Rebellion: The 1906–1908 Disturbances in Natal*. Oxford: Clarendon, 1970.

Matthews, J. J. *Reporting the Wars*. Minneapolis: University of Minnesota Press, 1957.

McCallum, J. *Leonard Wood: Rough Rider, Surgeon, Architect of American Imperialism*. New York: New York University Press, 2005.

McDougall, J. "Savage Wars? Codes of Violence in Algeria, 1830s–1990s." *Third World Quarterly* 26, no. 1 (2005): 117–131.

McKenna, T. *Muslim Rulers and Rebels: Everyday Politics and Armed Separatism in the Southern Philippines*. Berkeley: University of California Press, 1998.

McKittrick, K. "Mathematics Black Life." *Black Scholar* 44, no. 2 (2014): 16–28.

Medina, I. R. "A Historical Reconstruction of the Juramentado/Sabllallah Ritual." *Anuaryo/ Annales: Journal of History* 11, no. 1 (1993): 19–39.

Mégret, F. "From 'Savages' to 'Unlawful Combatants': A Postcolonial Look at International Humanitarian Law's 'Other.'" In *International Law and Its Others*, edited by A. Orford, 265–317. Cambridge: Cambridge University Press, 2006.

Menger, T. "Concealing Colonial Comparability: British Exceptionalism, Imperial Violence, and the Dynamiting of Cave Refuges in Southern Africa, 1879–1897." *Journal of Imperial and Commonwealth History* 50, no. 5 (2022): 860–889.

Menger, T. "'Press the Thumb onto the Eye': Moral Effect, Extreme Violence, and the Transimperial Notions of British, German, and Dutch Colonial Warfare, ca. 1890–1914." *Itinerario* 46, no. 1 (2022): 84–108.

Midtrød, T. A. "Calling for More Than Human Vengeance: Desecrating Native Graves in Early America." *Early American Studies* 17, no. 3 (2019): 281–314.

Miller, S. C. *"Benevolent Assimilation": The American Conquest of the Philippines, 1899–1903*. New Haven, CT: Yale University Press, 1982.

Montemayor, M. S. *Captain Herman Leopold Schuck: The Saga of a German Sea Captain in 19th-Century Sulu-Sulawesi Seas*. Honolulu: University of Hawaii Press, 2006.

Morris, E., and P. Gourevitch. *Standard Operating Procedure: A War Story*. New York: Penguin, 2008.

Munch-Jurisic, D. M. *Perpetrator Disgust: The Moral Limits of Gut Feelings*. Oxford: Oxford University Press, 2023.

Niedermeier, S. "Imperial Narratives: Reading US Soldiers' Photo Albums from the Philippine-American War." *Rethinking History: The Journal of Theory and Practice* 18, no. 1 (2014): 28–49.

Niedermeier, S. "'If I Were King'—Photographic Artifacts and the Construction of Imperial Masculinities in the Philippine-American War (1899–1902)." In *SpaceTime of the Imperial*, edited by Holt Meyer, Susanne Rau, and Katharina Waldner, 100–131. Berlin: Walter de Gruyter, 2016.

Niedermeier, S. "Intimacy and Annihilation: Approaching the Enforcement of US Colonial Rule in the Southern Philippines Through a Private Photograph Collection." *InVisible Culture: An Electronic Journal for Visual Culture* 25, "Security and Visibility" (2017), http://ivc.lib.rochester.edu/intimacy-and-annihilation-approaching-the-enforcement-of-u-s-colonial-rule-in-the-southern-philippines-through-a-private-photograph-collection.

Odumosu, T. "The Crying Child: On Colonial Archives, Digitization, and Ethics of Care in the Cultural Commons." *Current Anthropology* 61, no. 22 (2020): 289–302.

Oliver, K. *The My Lai Massacre in American History and Memory*. Manchester: Manchester University Press, 2006.

Oppenheimer, J. "Misunderstanding Images: *Standard Operating Procedure*, Errol Morris." In *Killer Images: Documentary Film, Memory and the Performance of Violence*, edited by Joram Ten Brink and Joshua Oppenheimer, 311–324. New York: Columbia University Press, 2012.

Oppenheimer, J., and M. Uwemedimo. "Show of Force: A Cinema-Séance of Power and Violence in Sumatra's Plantation Belt." In *Killer Images: Documentary Film, Memory and the Performance of Violence*, edited by Joram Ten Brink and Joshua Oppenheimer, 287–310. New York: Columbia University Press, 2012.

Ostler, J. *The Plains Sioux and US Colonialism from Lewis and Clark to Wounded Knee*. Cambridge: Cambridge University Press, 2004.

Ostler, J. *Surviving Genocide: Native Nations and the United States from the American Revolution to Bleeding Kansas*. New Haven, CT: Yale University Press, 2019.

Patterson, R. "'To Form a Correct Estimate of Their Nothingness When Compared with It': British Exhibitions of Military Technology in the Abyssinian and Ashanti Expeditions." *Journal of Imperial and Commonwealth History* 44, no. 4 (2016): 551–572.

Peffer, J. "Snap of the Whip/Crossroads of Shame: Flogging, Photography, and the Representation of Atrocity in the Congo Reform Campaign." *Visual Anthropology Review* 24, no. 1 (Spring 2008): 55–77.

Pinney, C. "Introduction: 'How the Other Half. . . .'" In *Photography's Other Histories*, edited by C. Pinney and N. Peterson, 1–14. Durham, NC: Duke University Press, 2003.

Protschky, S. "Soldiers as Humanitarians: Photographing War in Indonesia 1945–49." In *Visualising Human Rights*, edited by Jane Lydon, 39–62. Perth: UWA, 2018.

Protschky, S. *Photographic Subjects: Monarchy, Photography and the Making of Colonial Citizens*. Manchester: Manchester University Press, 2019.

Protschky, S. "Burdens of Proof: Photography and Evidence of Atrocity During the Dutch Military Actions in Indonesia (1945–50)." *Journal of the Humanities and Social Sciences of Southeast Asia/Bijdragen tot de Taal-, Land- en Volkenkunde* 176, nos. 2–3 (2020): 240–278.

Protschky, S. "Rethinking Histories of Military Atrocity, Ethnic Violence and Photography, from the Aceh War to the Indonesian National Revolution." In *Rethinking Histories of Indonesia: Experiencing, Resisting and Renegotiating Coloniality*, edited by Kate McGregor, Sadiah Boonstra, Ken Setiawan, and Adbul Wahid. Canberra: ANU Press, 2024, forthcoming.

Rafael, V. L. *White Love and Other Events in Filipino History*. Durham, NC: Duke University Press, 2000.

Redding, S. "A Blood-Stained Tax: Poll Tax and the Bambatha Rebellion in South Africa." *African Studies Review* 43, no. 2 (2000): 29–54.

Richardson, H. C. *Wounded Knee: Party Politics and the Road to an American Massacre*. New York: Basic Books, 2010.

Rixhon, G. "Levels of Discourse in the Tausug Parang Sabil Epic." In *Old Ties and New Solidarities: Studies on Filipino Communities*, edited by Charles J-H. Macdonald and Guillermo Mangubat Pesigan, 12–23. Quezon City: Ateneo de Manila University Press, 2000.

Rixhon, G. *Voices from Sulu: A Collection of Tausug Oral Traditions*. Quezon City: Ateneo de Manila University Press, 2010.

Rogers, M. "Twice Captured: The Work of Atrocity Photography." In *The Routledge Companion to Photography Theory*, edited by M. Durden and J. Tormey, 228–242. New York: Routledge, 2020.

Roque, R., and K. A. Wagner, eds. *Engaging Colonial Knowledge: Reading European Archives in World History*. Basingstoke: Palgrave Macmillan, 2012.

Roth, R. *Muddy Glory: America's "Indian Wars" in the Philippines, 1899–1935*. West Hanover, MA: Christopher, 1981.

Saito, N. T. "Colonial Presumptions: The War on Terror and the Roots of American Exceptionalism." *Georgetown Journal of Law and Modern Critical Race Perspectives* 1 (2009): 67–110.

Salman, M. *The Embarrassment of Slavery: Controversies over Bondage and Nationalism in the American Colonial Philippines*. Berkeley: University of California Press, 2001.

Schell, J. (unsigned). "Notes and Comments: Talk of the Town." *New Yorker*, December 20, 1969.

Schlesinger, A. M., Jr. *The Bitter Heritage: Vietnam and American Democracy, 1941–1966*. Boston: Houghton Mifflin, 1967.

Schroeder, E. J. "Interview with Michael Herr: 'We've All Been There.'" *Writing on the Edge* 1, no. 1 (1989): 39–54.

Sessions, J. E. *By Sword and Plow: France and the Conquest of Algeria*. Ithaca, NY: Cornell University Press, 2011.

Sharpe, C. *In the Wake: On Blackness and Being*. Durham, NC: Duke University Press, 2016.

Siegel, J. "Victory Without Surrender: The Jihad in Aceh." *Archipel* 87, no. 1 (2014): 29–62.

Silbey, D. J. *A War of Frontier and Empire: The Philippine-American War, 1899–1902*. New York: Hill & Wang, 2008.

Simon, R. S. *Spies and Holy Wars: The Middle East in 20th-Century Crime Fiction*. Austin: University of Texas Press, 2010.

Sjursen, D. "A Picture (of a War Crime) Is Worth a Thousand Words." AntiWar.com, October 1, 2019, https://original.antiwar.com/Danny_Sjursen/2019/09/30/a-picture-of-a-war-crime-is-worth-a-thousand-words.

Slotkin, R. *Regeneration Through Violence: The Mythology of the American Frontier, 1600–1860*. Middletown, CT: Wesleyan University Press, 1973.

Smiley, W. "Lawless Wars of Empire? The International Law of War in the Philippines, 1898–1903." *Law & History Review* 36, no. 3 (August 2018): 511–550.

Smith, G. A., D. Coffey, and K. Longley. *In Harm's Way: A History of the American Military Experience*. New York: Oxford University Press, 2020.

Smith, H. W. "The Logic of Colonial Violence: Germany in Southwest Africa (1904–1907) and the United States in the Philippines (1899–1902)." In *German and American Nationalism: A Comparative Perspective*, edited by Hartmut Lehmann and Hermann Wellenreuther, 205–231. New York: Berg, 1999.

Smith, S. M. *Photography on the Color Line: W.E.B. Du Bois, Race, and Visual Culture*. Durham, NC: Duke University Press, 2004.

Sontag, S. *Regarding the Pain of Others*. New York: Farrar, Straus and Giroux, 2003.

Sontag, S. "Regarding the Torture of Others." *New York Times Magazine*, May 23, 2004.

Stoler, L. A. "In Cold Blood: Hierarchies of Credibility and the Politics of Colonial Narratives." *Representations* 37 (1992): 151–189.

Stoler, L. A. *Duress: Imperial Durabilities in Our Times*. Durham, NC: Duke University Press, 2016.

Stout, W. "The Filipino Massacre." *Dark Horse Presents #23* (Dark Horse Comics, 1988): 1–5.

Stricklin, K. "With a Skull in Each Hand: Boneyard Photography in the American Empire After 1898." In *Imperial Islands: Art, Architecture, and Visual Experience in the US Insular Empire After 1898*, edited by Joseph R. Hartman, 62–81. Honolulu: University of Hawai'i Press, 2022.

Stur, H. M. *Beyond Combat: Women and Gender in the Vietnam War Era*. Cambridge: Cambridge University Press, 2011.

Sullivan, R. J. *Exemplar of Americanism: The Philippine Career of Dean C. Worcester*. Ann Arbor: University of Michigan Center for South and Southeast Asian Studies, 1991.

Suva, C. A-M. "In the Shadow of 1881: The Death of Sultan Jamalul Alam and Its Impact on Colonial Transition in Sulu, Philippines from 1881–1904." *TRaNS: Trans-Regional and -National Studies of Southeast Asia* 8, no. 2 (2020): 85–99.

Tan, S. K. *Sulu Under American Military Rule, 1899–1913*. Quezon City, Philippines: University of the Philippines, 1968.

Taussig, M. "Culture of Terror—Space of Death: Roger Casement's Putumayo Report and the Explanation of Torture." *Comparative Studies in Society and History* 26, no. 3 (July 1984): 467–497.

Thompson, J. M. *Great Power Rising: Theodore Roosevelt and the Politics of US Foreign Policy*. Oxford: Oxford University Press, 2019.

Trouillot, M-R. *Silencing the Past: Power and the Production of History*. Boston: Beacon, 1995.

Tuastad, D. "Neo-Orientalism and the New Barbarism Thesis: Aspects of Symbolic Violence in the Middle East Conflict(s)." *Third World Quarterly* 24, no. 4 (2003): 591–599.

Tuminez, A. S. "This Land Is Our Land: Moro Ancestral Domain and Its Implications for Peace and Development in the Southern Philippines." *SAIS Review of International Affairs* 27, no. 2 (Summer–Fall 2007): 77–91.

Turse, N. *Kill Anything That Moves: The Real American War in Vietnam*. New York: Metropolitan, 2013.

Twomey, C. L. "Framing Atrocity: Photography and Humanitarianism." In *Humanitarian Photography: A History*, edited by Heide Fehrenbach and Davide Rodogno, 47–63. Cambridge: Cambridge University Press, 2015.

Ugarte, E. F. "Muslims and Madness in the Southern Philippines." *Pilipinas* 19, nos. 1–2 (1992): 1–23.

Vann, M. G. "Of Pirates, Postcards, and Public Beheadings: The Pedagogic Execution in French Colonial Indochina." *Historical Reflections* 36, no. 2 (Summer 2010): 39–58.

Vann, M. G. "Fear and Loathing in French Hanoi: Colonial White Images and Imaginings of 'Native' Violence." In *The French Colonial Mind*, vol. 2: *Violence, Military Encounters, and Colonialism*, edited by M. Thomas, 52–76. Lincoln: University of Nebraska Press, 2011.

Vaughan, C. "'Demonstrating the Machine Guns': Rebellion, Violence and State Formation in Early Colonial Darfur." *Journal of Imperial and Commonwealth History* 42, no. 2 (2014): 286–307.

Vergara, B. M., Jr. *Displaying Filipinos: Photography and Colonialism in Early 20th Century Philippines*. Quezon City: University of the Philippines Press, 1995.

Wagner, K. A. *The Great Fear of 1857: Rumours, Conspiracies and the Making of the Indian Uprising*. Oxford: Peter Lang Oxford, 2010.

Wagner, K. A. "'Treading Upon Fires': The 'Mutiny'-Motif and Colonial Anxieties in British India." *Past & Present* 218, no. 1 (2013): 159–197.

Wagner, K. A. "Calculated to Strike Terror: The Amritsar Massacre and the Spectacle of Colonial Violence." *Past & Present* 233, no. 1 (2016): 185–225.

Wagner, K. A. "Savage Warfare: Violence and the Rule of Colonial Difference in Early British Counterinsurgency." *History Workshop Journal* 85 (Spring 2018): 217–237.

Wagner, K. A. *The Skull of Alum Bheg: The Life and Death of a Rebel of 1857*. London: Hurst, 2017/Oxford: Oxford University Press, 2018/Delhi: Penguin India, 2018.

Wagner, K. A. *Amritsar 1919: An Empire of Fear and the Making of a Massacre*. New Haven, CT: Yale University Press, 2019/South Asian edition, Delhi: Penguin India, 2019.

Wagner, K. A. "Rebellion, Resistance, and the Subaltern." In *The Oxford World History of Empire*, edited by Peter Fibiger Bang, Walter Scheidel, and C. A. Bayly, 416–436. Oxford: Oxford University Press, 2020.

Walsh, T. P. *Tin Pan Alley and the Philippines: American Songs of War and Love, 1898–1946, a Resource Guide*. Lanham, MD: Scarecrow, 2013.

Walther, K. V. "Islamophobia Is an American Tradition." *History News Network*, 2015.

Walther, K. V. *Sacred Interests: The United States and the Islamic World, 1821–1921*. Chapel Hill: University of North Carolina Press, 2015.

Warren, J. F. "The Structure of Slavery in the Sulu Zone in the Late Eighteenth and Nineteenth Centuries." *Slavery and Abolition* 24, no. 2 (2003): 111–128.

Warren, J. F. *The Sulu Zone: The Dynamics of External Trade, Slavery, and Ethnicity in the Transformation of a Southeast-Asian Maritime State*. Singapore: National University of Singapore Press, 2007.

Weigley, R. F. *The American Way of War: A History of United States Military Strategy and Policy*. Bloomington: Indiana University Press, 1977.

Welch, R. E., Jr. "'The Philippine Insurrection' and the American Press." *Historian* 36, no. 1 (November 1973): 34–51.

Welch, R. E., Jr. "American Atrocities in the Philippines: The Indictment and the Response." *Pacific Historical Review* 43, no. 2 (1974): 233–253.

Wheatley, J. "US Colonial Governance of Superstition and Fanaticism in the Philippines." *Method and Theory in the Study of Religion* 30 (2018): 21–36.

Wiener, M. J. *Visible and Invisible Realms: Power, Magic, and Colonial Conquest in Bali*. Chicago: University of Chicago Press, 1995.

Willcock, S. "Aesthetic Bodies: Posing on Sites of Violence in India, 1857–1900." *History of Photography* 39, no. 2 (2015): 142–159.

Wolters, W. G. "From Silver Currency to the Gold Standard in the Philippine Islands." *Philippine Studies* 51, no. 3 (2003): 375–404.

Wonders, K. "Hunting Narratives of the Age of Empire: A Gender Reading of Their Iconography." *Environment and History* 11, no. 3 (2005): 269–291.

Wood, A. L. *Lynching and Spectacle: Witnessing Racial Violence in America, 1890–1940*. Chapel Hill: University of North Carolina Press, 2009.

Wu, J. C. "Disciplining Native Masculinities: Colonial Violence in Malaya, 'Land of the Pirate and the Amok.'" In *Violence, Colonialism, and Empire in the Modern World*, edited by Philip Dwyer and Amanda Nettelbeck, 175–195. Basingstoke: Palgrave Macmillan, 2018.

Yee, J. "Recycling the 'Colonial Harem'? Women in Postcards from French Indochina." *French Cultural Studies* 15, no. 1 (2004): 5–19.

Zinoman, P., and G. Kulik. "Misrepresenting Atrocities: *Kill Anything That Moves* and the Continuing Distortions of the War in Vietnam." *Cross-Currents: East Asian History and Culture Review* 12 (2014): 162–198.

Zwick, J., ed. *Mark Twain's Weapons of Satire: Anti-Imperialist Writings on the Philippine-American War*. Syracuse, NY: Syracuse University Press, 1992.

Unpublished

Bryer, E. R. "Scramble for Photographs of Empire: Complicating Visions of the Philippine American War (1899–1913)." PhD thesis, University of Toronto, 2019.

Dphrepaulezz, O. "'The Right Sort of White Men': General Leonard Wood and the US Army in the Southern Philippines, 1898–1906." PhD thesis, University of Connecticut, 2013.

Garsha, J. "The Head of Chief Mkwawa and the Transnational History of Colonial Violence, 1898–2019." PhD thesis, University of Cambridge, 2020.

Jornacion, G. W. "The Times of the Eagles: United States Army Officers and the Pacification of the Philippine Moros, 1899–1913." PhD thesis, University of Maine, 1973.

Menger, T. "The Colonial Way of War: Extreme Violence in Knowledge and Practice of Colonial Warfare in the British, German and Dutch Colonial Empires, c. 1890–1914." PhD thesis, University of Cologne, 2021.

Oliveros, R. T. "Islam in the Moro-American War (1899–1913): Implications on Mindanao, the Philippines." PhD thesis, Temple University, 2005.

Suva, C. A-M. "Nativizing the Imperial: The Local Order and Articulations of Colonial Rule in Sulu, Philippines 1881–1920." PhD thesis, Australian National University, 2015.

Thompson, W. W. "Governors of the Moro Province: Wood, Bliss, and Pershing in the Southern Philippines, 1903–1913." PhD thesis, University of California, San Diego, 1975.

Ugarte, E. F. "'The Demoniacal Impulse': The Construction of Amok in the Philippines." PhD thesis, University of Western Sydney Nepean, 1999.

Films and Documentaries

The Act of Killing (documentary). Joshua Oppenheimer (dir.), Final Cut for Real, DK Film, 2012.

Apocalypse Now (film). Francis Ford Coppola (dir.), American Zoetrope, 1979.

Exterminate All the Brutes (documentary). Raoul Peck (dir.), HBO Documentary Films, Velvet Films, Sky Documentaries, ARTE France, 2020.

The Look of Silence (documentary). Joshua Oppenheimer (dir.), Final Cut for Real, Making Movies Oy, Piraya Film A/S, Spring Films, 2014.

The Real Glory (film). Henry Hathaway (dir.), Samuel Goldwyn Productions, 1939.

Index

Kim A. Wagner is professor of global and imperial history at Queen Mary, University of London. He is the author of several books, including *The Skull of Alum Bheg* and *Amritsar 1919*.

PublicAffairs is a publishing house founded in 1997. It is a tribute to the standards, values, and flair of three persons who have served as mentors to countless reporters, writers, editors, and book people of all kinds, including me.

I. F. STONE, proprietor of *I. F. Stone's Weekly*, combined a commitment to the First Amendment with entrepreneurial zeal and reporting skill and became one of the great independent journalists in American history. At the age of eighty, Izzy published *The Trial of Socrates*, which was a national bestseller. He wrote the book after he taught himself ancient Greek.

BENJAMIN C. BRADLEE was for nearly thirty years the charismatic editorial leader of *The Washington Post*. It was Ben who gave the *Post* the range and courage to pursue such historic issues as Watergate. He supported his reporters with a tenacity that made them fearless and it is no accident that so many became authors of influential, best-selling books.

ROBERT L. BERNSTEIN, the chief executive of Random House for more than a quarter century, guided one of the nation's premier publishing houses. Bob was personally responsible for many books of political dissent and argument that challenged tyranny around the globe. He is also the founder and longtime chair of Human Rights Watch, one of the most respected human rights organizations in the world.

•   •   •

For fifty years, the banner of Public Affairs Press was carried by its owner Morris B. Schnapper, who published Gandhi, Nasser, Toynbee, Truman, and about 1,500 other authors. In 1983, Schnapper was described by *The Washington Post* as "a redoubtable gadfly." His legacy will endure in the books to come.

Peter Osnos, *Founder*